REGNUM STUDIES IN MISSION

I0886413

Beyond Fragmentation

Series Preface

Regnum Studies in Mission are born from the lived experience of Christians and Christian communities in mission, especially but not solely in the fast growing churches among the poor of the world. These churches have more to tell than stories of growth. They are making significant impacts on their cultures in the cause of Christ. They are producing 'cultural products' which express the reality of Christian faith, hope and love in their societies.

Regnum Studies in Mission are the fruit often of rigorous research to the highest international standards and always of authentic Christian engagement in the transformation of people and societies. These are for the world. The formation of Christian theology, missiology and practice in the twenty-first century will depend to a great extent on the active participation of growing churches contributing biblical and culturally appropriate expressions of Christian practice to inform World Christianity.

REGNUM STUDIES IN MISSION

Beyond Fragmentation

A Critical Assessment of Some Recent Developments in Evangelical Theological Education

Bernhard Ott

First published 2001 by Regnum Books International
This edition 2019

Regnum is an imprint of the Oxford Centre for Mission Studies
St. Philip and St. James Church
Woodstock Road
Oxford OX2 6HR, UK
www.ocms.ac.uk/regnum

09 08 07 06 05 04 03 7 6 5 4 3 2 1

British Library Cataloguing in Publication Data
A catalogue record for this book is available from the British Library

ISBN: 9781506475004

Distributed by 1517 Media in the US and Canada

The majority of Christians now live outside the western world and they are very different from us. Mission can no longer be understood as the expansion of western Christianity. Mission studies have a future only *if they see the challenge of these different Christians as an opportunity for self-critical reflection (Hollenweger 1991:98).*

Contents

FOREWORD

The history of theological education is often a history of declension from noble goals. George Marsden's magisterial work on The Soul of the American University (New York, Oxford University Press, 1994) holds up the mirror of history to the dream of every bishop or house church group that wants set up their own training programme and in course of time seek public validation for its graduates. From Yale and Harvard onwards, such dreams seem inevitably to lead to the secularisation of theological education. Secularists take over and control the resources given by generations of Christian faith and generosity to build their temples of scepticism to disenchant the young at the height of their idealism. Whereon a new generation has to start the process again. Are theological educators condemned to a form of entropy, in which there will be a systematic departure from the Christian convictions of the founders?

It has been widely assumed that the academy and universities form the pinnacle of theological education for the church. But is their role always beneficial for Christian mission? David Bosch (Transforming Mission, Maryknoll, Orbis, 1992, pp 489–92) pointed out how the universities in the nineteenth and early twentieth centuries insisted that only topics that could be investigated by rational and objective study could form part of the curriculum. Therefore texts and history became the diet of theological education, rather than mission and spiritual life of the church. In recent years in many universities religious studies have taken the place of theology.

But there have always been alternative traditions in the church. In the United States the Bible School movement emerged to preserve the focus on mission and ministry in theological education. In the United Kingdom the theological colleges emerged as independent entities once university faculties ceased to provide the needed scope of training for pastoral ministry. In India while Alexander Duff followed the university model to bring Christian education to the children of Brahmins, mission societies focused on village schools to educate catechists for the church. (See Jonathan Ingelby, Education as a Missionary Tool: A Study in Christian Missionary Education by English Protestant Missionaries in India, Unpublished Ph.D Thesis at the Oxford Centre for Mission Studies for the Open University, 1998).

A network of thirty mission schools in Germany and Switzerland in the mid-twentieth century provided an alternative tradition to the university dominated sector of theological education. They are rooted in neo-pietistic renewal movements and many of them were founded in the wake of North American led concern to establish a lively evangelical Christian community amongst the state churches of Europe. The North American Bible College provided the model. These mission schools maintained a vision of preparing young people to serve the church in its mission throughout the world. They maintained high standards and succeeded in integrating mission and spirituality with academic excellence, yet outside the university system. To that extent they kept the faith. Ott is an appreciative historian of their work which has been overlooked for too long.

But now they are threatened from another side. By 1970 the percentage of Christians who lived outside Europe and North America was greater than those who lived inside. The call was increasingly to train Asian leaders for Asia in Asia and African leaders in Africa for Africa. What therefore was the role of these colleges to be? Could they adapt to the new global context of partnership in mission from everywhere to everywhere?

Bernard Ott answers this question from the inside. He is principal of one such college. Have the colleges of which his is a representative made a transition to the new reality of global mission? He argues that thus far they have been prevented from doing so by their own tradition of reading the Bible. This tradition suggests that there is one correct procedure for deriving orthodox theology from the Bible and then applying its results to all contexts. Ott's work suggests that this approach will actually spell the eventual demise of these colleges. Their students will find no place for the contribution or partnership of others save those who reproduce their approach as their juniors. They will always be teachers with decreasing numbers of learners as their approach has no echo in other parts of the world.

Their salvation lies where the salvation of the Jewish and Gentile Christians lay in the early church: in engaging with the insights and approaches of Christians from different cultural backgrounds with an equal commitment to the Lordship of Christ and authority of the Bible, but who reach and express this through a different intellectual and cultural path.

Bernard Ott offers a cold bath of realism to those whose passion is to contend for the faith once delivered to the saints and their funders. The question is whether his immediate audience can apply the courage and intellectual toughness which saw them through the acids of liberalism in the universities now to their own foundational assumptions, and place their faith in the Lord, the Spirit and their fellow Christians who wish them nothing but good as they embark on an important intellectual journey in a defence of the faith from positions which are initially strange to them.

Bernard Ott's work combines a history that has been overlooked, an educational approach to integrating mission and theological education which draws with appreciation from the approaches to mission in non-European parts of the world, and a discussion of the theory of knowledge that dominates in conservative evangelical circles.

Christopher Sugden
Oxford Centre for Mission Studies
Armistice Day
November 2000

PREFACE

Research and writing of this PhD thesis was conducted between 1994 and 1999 in connection with The Oxford Centre for Mission Studies (OCMS), Oxford, under the supervision of Dr Patricia Harrison, Australia, Prof Walter Hollenweger, Switzerland, and Dr Cristopher Sugden, Oxford. It was submitted to the Open University in the fall of 1999 and examined by Prof Werner Ustorf, Birmingham (external examiner) and Dr Bernard Farr, Oxford (internal examiner) 8th December 1999 in Oxford.

I have many people to thank for helping me bring this study to completion. On the academic level my thanks goes first of all to Dr Patricia Harrison. Her international experience and competence in the field of theological education opened many new avenues in my reflection on realities and visions of theological training. No less important was Prof. Walter Hollenweger's contribution. He challenged me to look carefully at the great controversy between ecumenicals and evangelicals and sharpened my critique of traditional western theological thinking and training. Finally, I am indebted to Dr Christopher Sugden, who was a patient and reliable guide as I moved into British academic research and writing and who has recommended this thesis for publication in the *Regnum Studies in Mission* Series.

On the institutional level, I had the privilege of doing research in the context of OCMS. Not only the advice of Dr Christopher Sugden and Dr Vinay Samuel, but also the administrative support of Hilary Guest and the other staff, as well the encouraging and thought-provoking fellowship of the community of international researchers at OCMS has contributed much to this study.

In my home context, I want to give thanks to the Theological Seminary Bienenberg in Switzerland, where I have been serving as Academic Dean for many years. Without the possibility of a sabbatical in 1994–1995 and the constant support by my colleagues since then, I cannot imagine having completed this research.

For several parts of this thesis I depended on the following institutions to get access to important data. The *Konferenz Bibeltreuer Ausbildungsstätten* allowed me to use its archive and all the data of its

1996 survey. *Bibelschule Adelshofen, Bibelschule Brake, Missionshaus Bibelschule Wiedenest* and *Missionsseminar Bad Liebenzell* have given me access to their archives. I want to thank all these institutions for their support.

Furthermore, in writing this thesis in a second language, I am grateful for my friend Mike Gray, who helped me with my English.

However, my deepest thanks go to my family, my wife, Margrit, and my children, Claudia, Eva, Thomas and Sarah. They have patiently endured a husband and father who for many years put almost all his time into research and writing. The fact that studying in Oxford every summer gave our family a chance to visit England several times during these years is a precious but only minimal payback. Special thanks goes to my parents who made it financially possible for me to be engaged in studies for so many years.

Abbreviations

ABH	*Albrecht Bengel Haus*
AEM	*Arbeitsgemeinschaft Evangelikaler Missionen*
AfbeT	*Arbeitsgemeinschaft für biblisch erneuerte Theologie*
AfeM	*Arbeitskreis für evangelikale Missiologie*
AfeT	*Arbeitsgemeinschaft für evangelikale Theologie*
AJTh	*Asia Journal of Theology*
AMN	*Allgemeine Missionsnachrichten* (later *Missions-Nachrichten*)
AMZ	*Allgemeine Missionszeitschrift*
ATS	Association of Theological Schools
B&G	*Bibel und Gemeinde*
BEMCT	*The Blackwell Encyclopedia of Modern Christian Thought*
BEnz	*Brockhaus Enzyklopädie*
BISAM	Biblical Study and Missiology Project of the IAMS
CETh	*Companion Encyclopedia of Theology*
CIU	Columbia International University
CRESR	Consultation on the Relationship between Evangelism and Social Responsibility
CWME	Committee on World Mission and Evangelization (of the WCC)
DEA	*Deutsche Evangelische Allianz*
DEMR	*Deutscher Evangelischer Missions-Rat*
DEMT	*Deutscher Evangelischer Missions-Tag*
EATWoT	Ecumenical Association of Third World Theologians
EEAA	European Evangelical Accrediting Association
EGL	*Evangelisches Gemeindelexikon*
ELThG	*Evangelisches Lexikon für Theologie und Gemeinde*
em	*Evangelikale Missiologie*
EMM	*Evangelisches Missionsmagazin*
EMQ	*Evangelical Mission Quarterly*
EMW	*Evangelisches Missionswerk*
EMZ	*Evangelische Missionszeitschrift*
EQ	*Evangelical Quarterly*
ER	*Ecumenical Review*
ERTh	*Evangelical Review of Theology*
ESMA	European Student Missionary Association
ETE	Ecumenical Theological Education (of the WCC)

ETh	*Evangelikale Theologie*
Eustat95	*Eurostat Jahrbuch '95*
FETA	*Freie Evangelische Theologische Akademie*
IAMS	International Association of Mission Studies
IBMR	*International Bulletin of Missionary Research*
ICAA	International Council of Accrediting Agencies
ICBI	International Council on Biblical Inerrancy
ICCC	International Council of Christian Churches
ICETE	International Council for Evangelical Theological Education
IDEA	*Informationsdienst der Evangelischen Allianz*
IMC	International Missionary Council
INFEMIT	International Fellowship of Evangelical Mission Theologians
IRM	*International Review of Mission*
JET	*Jahrbuch Evangelische Theologie*
JGPhS	*Journal for General Philosophy of Science/Zeitschrift für allgemeine Wissenschaftstheorie*
JM	*Jahrbuch Mission*
JPT	*Journal of Pentecostal Theology*
JTSA	*Journal of Theology for Southern Africa*
KBA	*Konferenz bibeltreuer Ausbildungsstätten*
KBG	*Konferenz Bekennender Gemeinschaften*
KEM	*Konferenz evangelikaler Missionen*
LCWE	Lausanne Committee on World Evangelization
LdM	*Lexikon der Mission*
LdPh	*Lexikon der Philosophie*
LMG	*Lexikon Missiontheologischer Grundbegriffe*
LWM	*Lexikon zur Weltmission*
MARC	Mission Advanced Research and Communication Centre
MForm	*Ministerial Formation*
Miss	*Missiology*
MJ	*Mennonitisches Jahrbuch*
Mstud	*Mission Studies*
NAMZ	*Neue Allgemeine Missionszeitschrift*
NDCT	*A New Dictionary of Christian Theology*
NDTh	*The New Dictionary of Theology*
NZM	*Neue Zeitschrift für Missionswissenschaft*
OJC	*Freundesbrief der ökumenischen Kommunität Offensive Junger Christen*
ÖR	*Ökumenische Rundschau*
PTE	Program on Theological Education (of the WCC)
RGG	*Religion in Geschichte und Gegenwart*
SEA	*Schweizerische Evangelische Allianz*
SPCK	Society for the Promotion of Christian Knowledge
STH	*Staatsunabhängige Theologische Hochschule*

StJSch	*Statistisches Jahrbuch der Schweiz 1998*
StudT	*Studia Theologica*
SVM	Student Volunteer Movement
Ted	*Theological Education*
TEE	Theological Education by Extension
TEF	Theological Education Fund (of the WCC)
ThBeitr	*Theologische Beiträge*
TPhTh	*Zeitschrift für Philosophie und Theologie*
TRE	*Theologische Realenzyklopädie*
VLM	*Verlag der Liebenzeller Mission*
WCC	World Council of Churches
WEC	World Evangelisation Crusade
WEF	World Evangelical Fellowship
WSCF	World Students' Christian Federation
WTJ	*Westminster Theological Journal*
YfC	Youth for Christ
YMCA	Young Men's Christian Association
ZaWT	*Zeitschrift für allgemeine Wissenschaftstheorie/Journal of General Philosophy of Science*
Zmiss	*Zeitschrift für Mission*
ZMR	*Zeitschrift für Missionswissenschaft und Religionswissenschaft*

For the abbreviations of the schools of the *Konferenz Bibeltreuer Ausbildungsstätten* see Appendix A.

PART ONE

INTRODUCTION

CHAPTER 1

Subject, Context and Objectives

1. General Introduction to the Subject

When in January 1997, in the context of the Mennonite World Conference's (MWC) Assembly in Calcutta, India, fifty educators from more than twenty countries gathered for a Consultation on 'Theological Education on Five Continents', Larry Miller, Executive Secretary MWC, called this consultation 'one of the most important events' of the Mennonite World Conference, pointing to its role in leadership training and identity formation. He concluded that 'international reflection on theological education and transnational pooling of educational resources are not only timely but vital' (Heisey and Schipani:iii). This focus on the critical role of theological education in the life of the church is by no means limited to churches in the Anabaptist-Mennonite tradition. Other recent international gatherings on theological education, such as 'The Consultation on Institutional Development for Theological Education in the Two Thirds World' at the Oxford Centre for Mission Studies in the summer of 1995,[1] and 'The Global Consultation on Ecumenical Theological Education' of the WCC in Oslo in August 1996,[2] have all pointed in the same direction: the renewal of theological education is imperative for the future of the Christian church.[3]

This is the focus of this thesis. It intends to contribute to this global and ecumenical search for the renewal of theological education for the church in its mission. This will be accomplished by focusing (1) at the *level of theory*: on theological education in general and on mission studies in particular. Recent paradigm shifts[4] in the theology of mission as well as in theological education will be traced and synthesised in such a way that criteria for the analysis of theological education can be deduced. (2) At the *level of praxis*: a selected group of schools will be analysed in the light of this theory.

In accordance with the Oxford Centre for Mission Studies' emphasis on Reflective Practitioner Leadership, which means 'resourcing those involved in ministry ... to engage continually in reflection on their experience in ministry' (OCMS), this thesis focuses on evangelical theological education in Germany and German-speaking Switzerland, the context in which the author himself is involved in theological training.[5]

2. Foreground and Background

a) Foreground: Evangelical Bible Schools and Seminaries in Germany and Switzerland

This study analyses evangelical theological education in Germany and German-speaking Switzerland with special reference to mission studies. The focus is on the examination of a selected number of evangelical Bible colleges and seminaries (hereafter *the Schools*). *The Schools* are closely related to the evangelical mission movement. Most of *the Schools* understand themselves as mission training centres. They have founded the *Konferenz Bibeltreuer Ausbildungsstätten (KBA)*, an association which incorporates thirtysix schools (see Appendix A). Many of *the Schools* are also members of the European Evangelical Accrediting Association (EEAA) which facilitates accreditation comparable to internationally recognised degrees.

These schools should be viewed as the educational wing of the evangelical mission movement in their respective countries. Evangelical missions in German-speaking Europe presently include at least eighty mission agencies supporting more then 2500 missionaries. In 1995 80 per cent of German Protestant missionaries working abroad were connected to the evangelical movement (Schrupp:146; *em* 4/1989:58, cf. Ustorf 1994:112; Reifler:66) most of whom were trained in *the Schools*. In the period considered in this study (1960 to 1995) more than 10,000 students have graduated from these institutions.[6]

The history of this significant tradition of theological and missionary training has never been investigated, nor has it been subject to critical analysis (Holthaus 1993:318). This study intends to contribute to a better understanding of this particular movement of mission training in the German-speaking world, to identify its significance in the context of the larger Christian community and to critically analyse its performance.

b) Background: Paradigm Shifts in Mission and in Theological Education

Walter Hollenweger raises the disturbing question which stands at the outset of this investigation: *What is the future of Christian mission and of mission studies in the western world in the light of the changing world situation?* It is in the face of this challenge that this study engages in self-critical reflection on western theological training. Consequently, *the Schools* will be examined in the light of the developments within the world Christian movement in the second half of the twentieth century. This global background scenery takes the following shape:

(1) PARADIGM SHIFT IN WORLD CHRISTIANITY

Hollenweger reminds us of the fact that 'the majority of Christians now live outside the western world and [that] they are very different from us.' Mission can therefore no longer be understood as it was in the colonial era. The community of missiologists would certainly agree with Hollenweger's assessment. Terms such as 'crisis,' 'change' and 'new directions' are frequently used when referring to developments in the western world and in mission in the post-war period. In recent studies the term 'paradigm shift' has often been used in reference to the tremendous changes which have shaped the world situation in the post-colonial era (Bosch 1991; Scherer and Bevans 1992:IX; Werner 1993:44–47; Wietzke:437–38). Scherer and Bevans have summarised this changed situation as follows:

> (1) We now live in a pluricentric, rather than a western-dominated world; (2) structures of oppression and exploitation are today being challenged as never before; (3) a profound feeling of ambiguity exists about the value of western technology and development and the older idea of 'progress'; (4) we inhabit a shrinking global village with finite resources, and this calls for growing mutual interdependence; (5) humans are for the first time aware of their capacity to destroy the earth and make it uninhabitable for future generations; (6) societies everywhere now seek their own local cultural identities and reject slavish imitation of western models; (7) freedom of religion and greater awareness of other faiths force Christianity to re-evaluate their own earlier attitudes toward other faiths (Scherer and Bevans 1992:IX).

But the world situation is not all that has changed: the face of the world Christian movement is experiencing equally dramatic shifts (Myers: 1993): (1) Over half of all Christians live in the Two Thirds World (Myers: 5); (2) traditional denominational churches are shrinking while Pentecostal/charismatic and non-white indigenous churches experience rapid growth (Myers: 4); (3) 'more cross-cultural Protestant missionaries will be sent from or within the Two Thirds World countries than from the West by the first decade of the twenty-first century' (Myers: 10); (4) 'the church in the West will increasingly look to the church elsewhere in the world for example and direction' (Myers: 34). All these changes call for a response from the church in the west.

(2) PARADIGM SHIFT IN THE THEOLOGY OF MISSION

The changed world situation raises questions about traditional western Christianity. The word 'crisis'[7] has become common currency as a description of the situation of the western church and its missionary endeavours. Christians in the west have been forced to face the changes and to respond in an appropriate manner. Hollenweger calls for self-critical reflection within the western church. Again, this has been confirmed by missiologists of all confessional traditions. Carl E. Braaten (:55) speaks for many others, saying, 'The church becomes a witness against itself when it refuses to criticise its own structures and functions in light of the changing missionary situations in the world'. There is broad agreement in the assessment of the state of affairs: the global situation of the world Christian movement has changed in such a way that we, as the western church, are called to a thorough reassessment of our western understanding of the gospel, the church and mission (cf. Ustorf 1994:135–38; Shenk 1993a). In 1991, the South African missiologist David Bosch presented a comprehensive view of 'an emerging ecumenical missionary paradigm' under the title *Transforming Mission: Paradigm Shifts in Theology of Mission*, reflecting the changes which have taken place and pointing towards the third millennium.[8] In the same manner, Dietrich Werner, referring to the development of ecumenical discussion on mission from 1961 to 1991, speaks of a 'dramatic process' of change in missionary thinking which has taken place in the last thirty to forty years (1993:23).

(3) PARADIGM SHIFT IN THEOLOGICAL EDUCATION

A third observation is on the level of theological education. Again, critical questions, crisis and the call for new directions can be observed. The traditional models of theological education employed in western university and seminary training have been severely criticised (Farley 1983; Duraisingh:37). Not only has it turned out to be a western model with minimal effectiveness in the Two Thirds World, but there is also an increasing awareness that this traditional model is not even adequate in the western world (Newbigin 1978b). The main limitations are (1) its heavy emphasis on detached academic reflection, (2) the one-sided deductive accumulation of knowledge, (3) the required residential presence for many years, (4) the professional orientation, (5) the limited access, (6) the institution-centredness (7) and the high costs (Kinsler 1981:3–24).

The early 1960s brought experimentation with new ways of leadership training in missionary situations. New models, commonly referred to by the broad term *Theological Education by Extension* (TEE), were created and developed over the years (Kinsler 1981, 1983; Youngblood; Padilla ed. 1988; Ferris 1990a). This has caused a thorough rethinking of theological education, both in ecumenical[9] as well as in evangelical circles.[10] In 1983, Andrew Kirk (:46) analysed the situation as follows:

> Third World Christians are not only challenging the theologically literate of the Western world to embark on a theological discussion more engaged with the changing realities of daily life, but they are

also questioning the assumptions which have dominated theological education for at least one hundred fifty years. The challenge to discover new models of theological thinking implies a change in current patterns of training.

3. Aim and Objectives of the Study

a) General Aim

In the light of the above considerations, the general aim of this inquiry can be stated as follows: *To synthesise the global and ecumenical paradigm shifts in mission theology, as well as theological education and apply these to evangelical theological colleges and seminaries in Germany and German-speaking Switzerland in order to contribute to theological education in general and mission studies in particular.*

b) Objectives

By the end of this investigation we should be able

1. to identify the contribution evangelical theological colleges and seminaries in German-speaking Europe are making to theological education in general and to mission studies in particular.
2. to identify the paradigm shifts in the theology of mission which have been taking place since World War II, as proposed by David Bosch in *Transforming Mission*, and to deduce from them criteria of general significance for mission studies in theological education.
3. to identify convergencies and divergencies between the established paradigm in theology of mission and the realities of *the Schools* and give the explanations and qualifications necessary to make the result significant for *the Schools* and beyond.
4. to review the theory, i.e., the proposed paradigm of mission theology in the light of the realities of *the Schools*.
5. to identify the paradigm shifts in theological education which have been taking place since 1960, in such a way that all significant strands of reflection and experiment are synthesised, and to deduce from them criteria of general significance for theological education.
6. to identify convergencies and divergencies between the established paradigm in theological education and the realities of *the Schools* and give the necessary explanations and qualifications to make the result significant for *the Schools* and beyond.
7. to review the theory, i.e., the proposed paradigm of theological education in the light of the realities of *the Schools*.
8. to identify the changed patterns of *the Schools* and to give reasonable explanations for their changes, as well as their resistance to changes.

Notes

1 For some of the contributions as well as a summary of the findings, see *Transformation* 12/4 (1995).

2 Reports and presentations in *MForm* 75 (1996) and in Pobee ed.

3 The author had the opportunity to participate in the first two of the conferences mentioned.

4 The concept of paradigm theory will be discussed later; see p. 31.

5 The author is Director of Studies of the *Theologisches Seminar Bienenberg*, Liestal/Basel, Switzerland, an institution rooted in the Anabaptist Mennonite tradition. In terms of social science research the author finds himself to some extent in the role of a practitioner researcher, and he is well aware of the possible problems this involves.

6 This is only a projected estimation by the author. Detailed statistics are lacking. A survey of 1985, covering 13 schools from 1975 to 1985 shows c. 3,500 graduates in that decade (Archive *KBA*). The 1996 survey counts 3,839 of 25 schools from 1987 to 1996 (*KBA* 1996:24). 10,000 graduates of some 30 member schools of the *Konferenz bibeltreuer Ausbildungsstätten (KBA)* over 35 years is a rather cautious estimate. Holthaus estimates 4000 graduates for all the Bible schools (1993:318). This figure, however, is much too low.

7 When the word 'crisis' became prominent in the post-war era, it was not for the first time. Already in the final decades of the 19th century, 'crisis' was a key term to describe the state of affairs in mission, which finally gave birth to the Student Volunteer Movement for Foreign Missions (Robert:31, n. 4).

8 Since the publication of *Transforming Mission*, several important contributions on mission studies have referred to Bosch's proposal, e.g., Scherer and Bevans 1992:IX; Werner 1993:44–47; Wietzke:436–38; Ustorf 1994:105; Saayman and Kritzinger. There is further discussion of Bosch's work in Part III.A. of this study.

9 See the work of the 'Program on Theological Education' (PTE) of the WCC and the journal *Ministerial Formation*.

10 See the work of the 'International Council of Accrediting Agencies for Evangelical Theological Education' and its publications (Kemp 1995).

CHAPTER 2

Issues of Focus and Scope

This study focuses on the following:

1. Focus on a Specific Group of Schools

The selection of schools which will be analysed has already been introduced (see p. 4).[1] *The Schools* are identified as a coherent group of institutions by the following common characteristics:

a) Common Language and Geographical Area

The Schools represent the German-speaking parts of Europe. They are all located in Germany or Switzerland. Austria, the third German-speaking region, did not have any evangelical training centre until recently.[2] These younger Austrian schools will not be part of this investigation.

b) Common Theological Tradition

The Schools have their roots in the pietistic-evangelical tradition. Helmut Egelkraut of the EEAA describes the origin of these schools as follows:[3]

> During the last two centuries private Bible schools and theological colleges developed: first at the beginning of the nineteenth century for the training of missionaries, later in the course of the neo-pietistic revival at the end of the nineteenth century for the preparation of evangelists, pastors of non-mainline congregations and youth ministers … . Quite a few of them came into existence after World War II as the fruit of U.S.-originated missionary endeavours (1990:33).

Needless to say, these schools have been highly committed to mission in the era of the modern missionary movement.[4] Over a period of more than 150 years,[5] hundreds of missionaries and church workers have received their training in *the Schools*.

c) Common Educational Tradition

Further, *the Schools* belong to a tradition of European training centres outside the theological faculties of state universities. This is due to several factors:

1. In Germany and Switzerland in the nineteenth century, the theological faculties of the state universities were (and still are) dominated by the Protestant and Catholic mainline churches and became the centres of liberal and critical theology.[6]

2. Groups and churches of neo-pietistic and free church origin were often highly suspicious of the 'liberal' and 'critical' universities. If they wanted to remain faithful to their evangelical convictions, they felt forced to establish their own training centres outside the university structures.[7]

3. In the nineteenth century (and to a certain extent still today) in Germany and Switzerland this meant remaining outside of the official educational system with no rights to grant recognised degrees.

This characterises the situation of *the Schools*. Nonetheless, this tradition of theological training has often produced quality training for missionaries and pastors. Many mission societies and churches have received their workers from these institutions. But quality standards have never been assured and *the Schools* have developed independently and in divers ways, without any comparable standard. Helmut Egelkraut writes,

> Academically vast differences exist. Till about twenty years ago hardly any library resources had been developed by the schools of neo-pietistic origin. The last two decades have seen a shift in this regard… . A number of these schools operate now on the M.Div. level. But in most cases their graduates are not allowed to enter the pastorate of main line churches. It is also very difficult for such schools to receive state recognition as institutions of tertiary education.
>
> One problem for graduates going overseas either for advanced studies or for missionary services is that no degree can be conferred… . Strong endeavours should be made to establish a clear evaluation system for the transfer of credits and the recognition of training received (1990:33).

This leads directly to a fourth common element of these schools.

d) Common Search for Recognition

In recent years the question of academic quality and internationally recognised degrees has become an issue of major significance for *the Schools*. In 1965, the German-speaking evangelical schools moved closer together by founding the *Konferenz Bibeltreuer Ausbildungsstätten (KBA)*. The main purpose of the co-operation was mutual sharing and the desire to strengthen evangelical convictions, especially regarding the authority of Scripture (in reference to the inerrancy question).

More than ten years later, in 1977, the European Evangelical Accrediting Association (EEAA) came into being. Its scope is broader than the German-speaking *KBA*, inviting all evangelical theological schools in Europe[8] to participate.

With this we have established the group of schools which are the subject of the analysis of this investigation. *The Schools* differ in their programs between short term Bible schools and seminaries offering Masters-level programs. We will consider only those institutions which today offer courses at the college (Bachelor) and/or seminary (Master) level.[9]

Beyond the investigation of the *KBA* schools in general, three schools are analysed in particular. The three schools represent three representative strands within the *KBA* movement: (1) The *Theologisches Seminar Bad Liebenzell* represents the strand of schools rooted in Lutheran Pietism. (2) The *Bibelschule Missionshaus Wiedenest* stands for the evangelical free church movement, closely related to the Evangelical Alliance. (3) Finally, *Bibelschule Brake* represents the schools rooted in the North American Bible school movement.

2. Focus on the Period from 1960 to 1995

The time frame of this study will be limited to the period from 1960 to 1995. Such a limitation has shown itself meaningful in regard to the recent development of the Bible colleges and seminaries as well as in the light of some significant turning points in mission and theological education.

1. The recent history of *the Schools* must be understood against the background of wider international developments in mission. The key event to be recognised is the integration of the International Missionary Council (IMC) with the World Council of Churches (WCC), which, after years of preparation, was finalised at the Third Assembly of the WCC in New Delhi in 1961. New Delhi stands for a significant shift in world-wide missionary thinking (cf. Werner 1993:20–22). It also caused the divergence of the missionary movement into an 'ecumenical' and an 'evangelical' wing. The paths of the two separated missionary movements after 1961 can be traced through the various 'ecumenical' and 'evangelical' conferences and documents. These developments provide the background to the development of *the Schools*.

2. As regards the WCC, the Theological Education Fund (TEF) was created in 1958. What began as a project to implement traditional western theological education in the Two Thirds World was completely

revolutionised in the 1960s as western educational models were increasingly called into question (Newbigin 1978b). Central to the revolution of theological education was the invention of Theological Education by Extension, first taken up in Guatemala in 1962–63 (Mulholland:9; Winter ed. 1969:3–6, especially the chart on p. 6).

3. Finally, with regard to *the Schools* we notice that the *KBA* was founded in 1963–64. This study will show that it was in the context of the new challenges in mission and in theological education that they joined in a newly founded association in the early 1960s.

All of this leads to the conclusion that the beginning of the 1960s is a meaningful point of departure for this study.

In the 1990s, the *KBA* schools experienced a severe crisis. A dramatic decrease in student enrolment in many of the traditional evangelical colleges and seminaries caused *the Schools* critically to analyse their performance. The 1995 annual assembly of the *KBA* commissioned a taskforce to provide a thorough analysis by means of a survey of the state of affairs. This author was involved in this evaluation and this study draws from some of the material of this analysis (cf. Faix, Faix, Müller and Schmidt). Therefore,1995 provides the end-point of this study.

Notes

1 For a list of all *KBA* schools, including the abbreviations used in this study, see Appendix A.

2 Attempts have been made to establish an evangelical Bible school in Austria since 1962 by the North American Missionaries of the Mennonite Brethren Church. However the attempts were not successful and the interdenominational evangelical Bible School at Ampfelwang (later Wels), founded 1983, was the first evangelical Bible school in Austria (Rathmair:87–94; Reimer:62–63). Due to low student numbers it was forced to close in 1999. On the expansion of evangelical churches in Austria in general see Börner.

3 At certain points Egelkraut also includes schools in other mainly Protestant countries of western Europe.

4 The term 'modern missionary movement' refers to the epoch whose beginning is normally seen in connection with William Carey's tract of 1792 'The enquiry into the obligations of Christians to the means for the conversion of heathens' and the founding of The Particular Baptist Society for the Propagation of the Gospel amongst the Heathen (see Shenk 1992:62).

5 The oldest, *Chrischona*, was founded in 1840.

6 On the present situation of theological faculties in state universities in Switzerland see Zumstein:82–100.

7 Often, the decision to establish a private school outside recognised state universities was long and difficult. It cannot be described fully at this point. For the influence of the neo-pietistic revival on theological education in Switzerland in the nineteenth century, see Pfister:351–76; Schlatter:28–37, 58–93, 149–58; Ramser:25.

[8] At that time limited to western Europe.

[9] Not included in this study are three major seminaries of free church orientation, namely the theological seminary of the German Baptists (earlier in Hamburg, now near Berlin), as well as that of the Methodist Church (Reutlingen). These two schools do not associate with the evangelical schools gathered in either of the two associations. The theological seminary of the Free Evangelical Churches (Ewersbach) holds membership in the EEAA, but not the *KBA*.

CHAPTER 3

Issues of Terminology

The following key concepts, which will be used throughout the book need preliminary clarification.

1. 'Theological Education'

The term *theological education* is problematic and has been criticised in recent years. Graham Cheesman suggests that

> the term Theological Education harbours radical mis-conceptions because both the words, theology and education, have unhappily narrowed down their field of meaning in the 20th century. Theology has become for us a group of scientific disciplines which can exist without the love and experience of God. Education is usually taken as synonymous with study and scholarship rather than a maturing of the person assisted by learning (1993:484–85).

In the reflections of the WCC, these deficiencies have led to the introduction of the term *ministerial formation*, 'which was interpreted in the broadest sense to include all the people of God.' With this definition it was clearly affirmed 'that theological education is not an end in itself, that it is not simply an academic or professional enterprise' (Kinsler 1982:137). Others have assigned the term *theological education* to the concept of a graduate school and the term *ministerial formation* to the concept of pastoral training (Schipani:34–35). In this study *theological education* will be maintained as a generic term referring to a wide range of models and conceptions of Bible-, theology- and ministry-oriented education. It is precisely one of the purposes of this investigation to contribute to a clearer understanding of the concept of theological education.

2. 'Mission Studies' and 'Theology of Mission'

The term *mission studies* in the title of this thesis is derived from Olav G. Myklebust's *The Study of Missions in Theological Education* (vol 1 1955/

vol 2 1957). Historically other terms have been used too, such as 'the theory of mission' (German: *Missionstheorie*), or 'the science of mission' (German: *Missionswissenschaft*). Today *missiology* is the most common and accepted term used to denote the field of mission studies (cf. Verkuyl:1–6; Kasdorf 1995:5–6; Jongeneel 1998:28). 'Missiology is the ordered study of the Christian church's mission' according to the *New Dictionary of Theology* (:434), and as such it has a broad, interdisciplinary scope, incorporating many different branches of academic research, basically in the fields of theology and social sciences, such as theology, history, religions, anthropology, ethnology, linguistics, cross-cultural communication, sociology, psychology, geography, economy and politics.[1] The subdivision of the field of missiology has been approached from various angles. (a) Following Warneck, some have suggested a material division of the subject matter: e.g., the history, the theology, the practice of mission (cf. Verkuyl; also Reifler). (b) Others have approached missiology methodologically, suggesting a formal or methodological division: e.g., the philosophy, the science and theology of mission.[2] It seems that the former is more concerned with the teaching of mission for the purpose of ministerial training, thus presenting the subject matter in a structured and ordered way (cf. Verkuyl; Reifler), whereas the latter is concerned with the study of missiology as an academic discipline in the context of the university, thus relating mission studies to the various fields of science.[3]

This study uses the terms *mission studies* and *missiology* interchangeably as referring to entire field of academic studies and theological education in relation to mission. *Theology of mission* is used for the biblical-theological reflection on mission.

3. 'Mission'

The term *mission* needs clarification at the beginning of this investigation. The term is often defined in relation to the Greek *apostello* and *apostolos*, as well as the Latin *missio*, as a key biblical concept describing the sending of individual Christians and the church (Kasdorf 1996:16). However, the word *mission* was introduced to the church as a technical term referring to church's sending only in the sixteenth century by Ignatius of Loyola. Subsequently it became a common term to describe the European (and later also North American) endeavour toward world evangelisation (Jongeneel 1998:27; Kasdorf 1996:17).

In this century, Christian mission has been challenged at its very foundation, including the suggestion of abandoning at least the term, if not the subject altogether (Werner 1993:1–7; Blaser 1987). This study will not defend Christian mission or engage in the discussion about its legitimacy. It is based on the presupposition that mission is part of the Christian church's nature, rooted in the Bible, which is the prescriptive text of the Christian faith. Despite all the discussions about the crisis of missions, all strands of Christianity have confirmed mission as an integral part of the church's identity. In a recent study, M. R. Spindler has convincingly shown that mission has been reaffirmed by churches around the world (1991b:161–258). This observation is taken for granted in this study.

Nonetheless, *the concept of mission deserves critical reflection* throughout this study. By way of preliminary definition, we refer to Bosch's 'Interim Definition' (1991:8–11) which serves as point of departure also for this study. In short this means:

1. We will use *mission* as referring to the *missio Dei* and *missions* as referring to the *missiones ecclesiae*.
2. We will understand mission/missions as God's or the churches' activities in all parts of the world.
3. We will use mission/missions in an inclusive sense, encompassing at least proclamation, fellowship and service.

4. 'Ecumenical' and 'Evangelical'

In the last three to four decades the terms *ecumenical* and *evangelical* have often been attached to the two opposing Protestant movements which are represented on the one hand by the WCC (ecumenical) and on the other by the World Evangelical Fellowship (WEF) and the Lausanne Movement (evangelical) – to mention only two major institutional expressions of the movement. But this usage of the two terms is neither uniform in the literature nor is it unproblematic. Both terms need clarification (cf. Hauzenberger 1985:XIV–XV).

a) Ecumenical

1. It is common to relate the terms e*cumenism* and e*cumenical* to the movement which traces its roots back to the Edinburgh World Mission Conference of 1910 and which led to the foundation of the World Council of Churches (WCC) in Amsterdam in 1948.[4] Today this refers to the WCC and its member churches and institutions, including the related continental and national bodies. This is the way the term will be used in many quotations in this study. In North America, instead of *ecumenical* the term *conciliar* is often used.

2. In recent years it has been pointed out that 'the claim to be 'ecumenical' – from *oikumene*, 'the whole inhabited earth' – can in no sense be the prerogative of any single church, denomination, or group of churches' (Scherer and Bevans 1992:X). It is therefore too restrictive to use the term only for those churches comprehended under the organisational structures of the WCC.[5] The search for the unity of the whole church can be

traced throughout history. The Roman Catholic Church and the evangelical movement are in the same sense *ecumenical* – i.e., encompassing the whole earth.[6] Beyond that, if ecumenists trace their roots back to the Edinburgh conference of 1910, to the Student Volunteer Movement for Foreign Missions (SVM), the Young Men's Christian Association (YMCA) and the World Student Christian Federation (WSCF), evangelicals would claim the same history. In this light, the term *ecumenical* cannot be limited to the WCC movement. It actually refers to the universality or catholicity of the church. This broader definition is used by Bosch when he spells out the 'elements of an emerging ecumenical paradigm' (Bosch 1991:368).

b) *Evangelical*

1. Historically, the roots of the term *evangelical* can be traced back to the revival movement in Britain in the 1730's (Bebbington:1–2). However, contemporary evangelicalism may be associated not only with the British revivals of the eighteenth century but with various Protestant movements which claim(ed) to give Protestant faith a vivid expression. As Scherer and Bevans summarise:

> Evangelicalism has roots in nineteenth-century evangelical movements, above all the Evangelical Alliance (established 1846). But those nineteenth-century movements, in turn, stand on the shoulders of earlier post Reformation evangelical movements, such as Pietism, Moravianism, Methodism, and similar awakening movements of the eighteenth and nineteenth centuries (1992:XII; cf. Allen:2–52).

2. In a narrower sense, the term *evangelical* often refers to the movement which is associated with two institutions, the World Evangelical Fellowship (WEF) and the Lausanne Movement. The former was founded 1951 at Woudschoten (NL), the latter goes back to the Lausanne Conference 1974 at Lausanne (Switzerland) (Howard:7, 29–30; 107–112).

3. In view of the evangelical movement in German-speaking Europe we should take note of the specific problem associated with the term in the German language since it is used in the Germanised form *evangelikal* as opposite to the term *evangelisch*. This will be discussed in relation to the historical background (see p. 27).

4. In connection with the evangelical movement we will also use the terms *fundamentalist/fundamentalism*.[7] These are ambiguous concepts carrying many meanings and connotations. The relationship between evangelicalism and fundamentalism has been the subject of much recent debate: (a) Many evangelicals attempt to dissociate from

fundamentalism. In most cases they affirm the need for foundational theological statements and concur with the doctrinal concerns of early fundamentalism, yet they reject the form of fundamentalist apologetics and separation (e.g., Schnabel 1995). In a similar way Barr (1988) has claimed that fundamentalist evangelicals can (and should) escape fundamentalism while still holding evangelical convictions. (b) Other evangelicals propose what they see as a valid form of fundamentalism and retain the term as a self-designation (e.g., Holthaus 1992).

5. In the use of the terms this study basically follows Holthaus's typology (1997). He distinguishes three types of evangelicals: (1) *separatist fundamentalists*, (2) *moderate fundamentalists/conservative evangelicals*, and (3) *open evangelicals*. By way of preliminary definition, it is safe to say that most of the schools under consideration belong to the group of *moderate fundamentalists/conservative evangelicals*.

c) Conclusion

The limitations of the evangelical-ecumenical terminology are evident: (1) Neither the notion of being faithful to the gospel nor the horizon of the entire *oikoumene* can be limited to a particular institutional structure, be it the WEF or the WCC. (2) Furthermore, the theological boundaries between the so-called ecumenical and evangelical ways of thinking neither follow institutional boundaries nor limit themselves to those given the labels ecumenical and evangelical (e.g., the Roman Catholic and the Orthodox Church). (3) In addition, one may also remark that the problem is mainly a western one and irrelevant to many churches in the Two Thirds World; and where it is an issue, it has probably been imported by western missionaries. (4) Finally, new movements are emerging which do not easily fit into the traditional schemes of the evangelical-ecumenical divide (e.g., the Pentecostal/charismatic movement and independent indigenous churches in the Two Thirds World); and there are likewise voices trying to overcome the polarisation by pointing to an integrative understanding of the gospel and mission (e.g., Newbigin 1978, Bosch 1991, International Fellowship of Evangelical Mission Theologians INFEMIT). Thus, there is good reason to reconsider the traditional use of the terms *ecumenical* (= WCC movement) and *evangelical* (= WEF/LCWE movement).

5. Theories, Models and Paradigms

Furthermore, this study frequently uses the terms *theory*, *model* and *paradigm*. This usage is not without difficulties and calls for clarification:

1. The definition of and distinction between *theory*, *model* and *paradigm* is itself debated. The following working definitions are assumed in

this study: (1) A *theory* is a more or less hypothetical construction of thoughts which explains reality or aspects of it in a rational way based on evidence (cf. LdPh:654). Differing theories are possible based on the same data, interpreting the data differently. (2) A *model* reduces differing theories to comparable key elements, i.e., it is a method to conduct comparative studies. (3) *Paradigms* are the larger frameworks of thinking, the (normally unquestioned) presuppositions of all theories in a given culture or community (Bayertz; Kramm:14–32; Stachowiak 1973).

Theories, models and paradigms offer 'ways of ordering experience' (Barbour:22, 45). They are the 'mental maps of reality' (Kraft quoted in Conn 1984:164) which affect our perception of data. They are not reality itself.[8] While they are in a certain correspondence with reality, they do not represent reality in an objective or comprehensive way. They select, reduce and structure reality. Stachowiak speaks of 'Originalverfremdung' (1980:53) and 'Verkürzungsmerkmale' [indications of foreshortening] (1973). There are obvious inherent limitations and even dangers with theories, models and paradigms. Harvie M. Conn speaks of the 'over extension of models' and he rightly says, 'Models are ways of viewing reality, and to promote a particular model is to impose limitations on one's perspective. Preconceptions become handicaps when the model is unable to handle new information' (1984:162). It is with the full awareness of these limitations that this study employs paradigm theory, compares educational models, and reflects upon theological and educational theories.

2. Special attention must be given to concept of *paradigm* as it appears in the theory of Thomas Kuhn (1970).[9] In recent years 'paradigm,' 'paradigm-shift' and 'paradigm-change' have become prominent and wide-spread words, employed in many contexts, sometimes without clear definition or even understanding of their meaning. David Bosch, introducing paradigm-terminology in *Transforming Mission*, writes, 'The term 'paradigm' is not without its problems. It is a slippery concept' (1991:185). The author is aware of the controversial discussion surrounding the Kuhnian theory.[10] Kuhn's thesis of paradigm changes has been criticised (MacIntyre 1977; 1988:349–69), as have the epistemological assumptions and the relativistic consequences of his theory (Hiebert 1999:38–46). Much attention has been given to the question of the applicability of the Kuhnian theory to other fields of studies (cf. Bayertz).

After careful consideration of possible pitfalls, this author has come to the conclusion that the Kuhnian theory has been applied carefully and convincingly to theology[11] and mission (cf. Bosch 1991) in such a way that it provides a meaningful tool for this investigation. Following Bosch (1991:183–85) we will employ Kuhnian vocabulary in defining paradigm as 'an entire constellation of beliefs, values, techniques, and so on shared by the members of a given community' (Kuhn 1970:175). Thus, a paradigm is an established and acknowledged pre-theory in a given field of science – a framework which affects the academic work in this field and renders possible mutual communication and understanding within the community of scholars. In this way we will refer to the underlying theoretical concepts which shape missiological thinking and theological education. Of special significance is Kuhn's theory of how paradigmatic changes take place. The concluding part the study will look at the changes in evangelical theological education from the perspective of the Kuhnian theory.

Notes

1 For a recent comprehensive introduction to missiology see Jongeneel 1995.

2 This approach is strongly advocated by Jongeneel, who traces it back to the Dutch missiologist François E. Daubanton (Jongeneel 1998:29).

3 See Jongeneel's definition, which implies the second approach: 'Missiology is the academic discipline which – from a philosophical, empirical, and theological point of view – reflects upon the history, theory and practice of (Christian) world mission as a means for both preaching the gospel, healing the sick and casting out 'evil spirits' (active in idolatry and immorality), for the glory of God and the well-being of all human beings' (1998:28).

4 On the history and present structure of the WCC see *What in the World is the World Council of Churches* (WCC 1978); also Ritschl:67–83; Linn; VanElderen; Moderow and Sens.

5 Cf. Ritschl (:8), 'It should not be overlooked that the WCC is by no means the only institution which operates in an ecumanical-theological scope.'

6 *The Blackwell Encyclopedia of Modern Christian Thought*, 'Ecumenism'; *New Dictionary of Theology*, 'Ecumenical Movement'; cf. Ritschl:13; Hauzenberger: XIV–XVIII.

7 See the following standard works on fundamentalism: Holthaus 1992; Barr 1977; and Harris.

8 'All processes of knowing are based on a process of modelling: the given original is modelled somehow' (Stachowiack 1980:53; cf. Kramm:14–32).

9 'The term "paradigm" ... was already used by Georg Christoph Lichtenberg (Professor of Natural Philosophy at Göttingen in the mid-eighteenth century). After the eclipse of German Idealism, Lichtenberg had a great influence on Ernst Mach and Wittgenstein, who picked up the term "paradigm" as a key to understanding how philosophical models or stereotypes act as "moulds" *(Gussform)* or "clamps" *(Klammern)*, shaping and directing our thought in predetermined and sometimes quite inappropriate directions. In this form the term entered general philosophical discussion and was first analysed in Britain by Wittgenstein's student W.H. Watson, by N.R. Hanson and by Toulmin himself. Finally, in the early 1950s, the term arrived in the United States' (Küng 1989a:8).

10 Significant reflections on the reception of Kuhn's theory are: (1) The question how much Kuhn was influenced by the philosophy of Wittgenstein is a question of debate and is discussed by Kindi. (2) General reviews of the Kuhnian

theory are found in Böhler and Bayertz. (3) For a Bibliography on the 'Kuhn-debate,' see Welter. (4) For the significance of the Kuhnian theory for theology see, Küng and Tracy; Murphy; and Hempelmann 1987b.

11 A major attempt to apply Kuhn's theory to the history of theology was undertaken at the ecumenical symposium at the University of Tübingen in May 23–26, 1993. The convenors were The Institute for Ecumenical Research of the University of Tübingen, the Institute for the Advanced Study of Religion of the University of Chicago and the international theological journal *Concilium*. Some 70 scholars from various parts of the world were convened by Hans Küng (Tübingen) and David Tracy (Chicago) to discuss the topic 'Paradigm Change in Theology' (Küng and Tracy 1984, 1989). More recently (1991) Konrad Raiser has used the Kuhnian theory to describe major shifts in the ecumenical movement (Raiser), an attempt which has not gone unchallenged (Ritschl:28–30, 37–39).

CHAPTER 4

Issues of Methodology and Data

We have decided to approach the subject in an interdisciplinary fashion, examining mission studies in theological education from the perspectives of various academic fields.

First, in Part II we approach the subject from a *historical* point of view, outlining the historical development of theological education and mission studies with special reference to evangelical theological education in German-speaking Europe.

Second, the subject will be analysed from a *missiological* point of view, analysing German evangelical theology of mission in the light of an emerging ecumenical paradigm of mission as propounded by Bosch. This is done in Part III of this study.

Third, Part IV will assess theological education (in general) and evangelical theological education in Germany and Switzerland (in particular) from an *educational* standpoint, analysing the schools under consideration in the light of the paradigmatic shift in theological education which has been taking place since the early 1960s.

Fourth, Part V will approach the subject from the point of view of *paradigm theory and epistemology*. In this concluding part the critical analysis will reach its climax, identifying the hermeneutical and epistemological undercurrents of *the Schools* under consideration.

This leads to the following outline of the study:

	II. History 5. The Historical Background of Evangelicalism, Theological Education and Mission Studies 6. The Developments of *the Schools* from 1960 to 1995 ↓	
III. Theology of Mission 8. Theory: Establishing a Paradigm of Mission Theology → 9. Analysis: *The Schools* in the Light of the Theory	***The Schools***	**IV. Theological Education** 10. Theory: Establishing a Paradigm of Theological Education ← 11. Analysis: *The Schools* in the Light of the Theory
	↑ **V. Change Theory** 12. The Results 13. Analysis in the Light of Paradigm Theory and Epistemology	

It is self-evident that such an approach involves background knowledge and research methodologies from various fields, especially from *church history, theology of mission, social sciences (education)* and *philosophy of science (paradigm theory and epistemology)*. Specific methodological issues are introduced at the beginning of the relevant chapters.

It follows that this study draws from a wide spectrum of data from the aforementioned fields. In order to make the thesis more readable, relevant secondary sources, as well as primary sources, are introduced at the beginning of each section.

Whilst this author is convinced that the chosen approach will lead to significant results, a possible limitation will not be hidden: this study focuses mainly on the input-side of the educational process, looking at history, structures, faculty, context, methods and content. We are aware of the fact that an output analysis, examining the long-term impact of graduates of *the Schools* would certainly add other important aspects to the subject-matter. For reasons of accessibility of data, time and lack of specialised competence in the field of social science research, this study deliberately focuses on the historical-theological dimension.

PART TWO

HISTORY

EVANGELICAL THEOLOGICAL EDUCATION IN GERMAN-SPEAKING EUROPE IN CONTEXT

In this first part we approach evangelical theological education in German-speaking Europe from a historical point of view. Chapter 5 will outline the historical background, chapter 6 concentrates on the period from 1960 to 1995, and chapter 7 provides some concluding reflections.

CHAPTER 5

The Historical Background

With the purpose of outlining the historical background of *the Schools* we concentrate on three intertwined strands of history:[1] (1) the historical background of German evangelicalism; (2) the general history of theological education and mission studies; and (3) the particular history of evangelical theological education and mission studies.

1. The Roots of German Evangelicalism[2]

The movement in German-speaking Europe explicitly called *evangelikal* is a relatively young phenomenon. Friedhelm Jung's thesis on German evangelicalism covers the period between 1965 and 1985, indicating that the German evangelical movement had its beginning in the 1960s (Jung:1).[3] However, the Christians in German-speaking Europe who Germanised the English 'evangelical' – and in so doing associated themselves with the international evangelical movement (cf. Laubach) – stand on the shoulders of much older movements which should be outlined briefly (Jung:9–34):[4]

a) The Heritage of Pietism

The revival movement later called *Pietism*[5] can be traced back to renewals in the context of the Lutheran church in Germany in the seventeenth century. The beginning of this movement has often been associated with Philipp Jakob Spener's (1635–1705) tract 'Pia desideria' (1675) (Wallmann 1990:37). Spener's call for spiritual renewal contains six points (Spener:55–79; cf. Lange:18): (1) Each church member must read the Bible personally and more intensively. (2) Priesthood applies to all believers; thus, the active participation of the laity in the church must be re-established. (3) True Christian faith must be realised in deeds. (4) Fighting over issues of faith should be avoided. (5) A reform of theological education is needed. (6) Preaching should promote spiritual renewal.

At its core, Spener's concern was the spiritual new birth of the individual (Lange:18). It follows that a personal faith-encounter with Jesus

Christ, conversion as a salvific turning point in the individual's life and the experience of new birth became the core of the pietistic legacy (Bockmühl 1985:11, 23–36; Beyreuther 1963:24–25).

In general, many contemporary evangelicals in German-speaking Europe see themselves as heirs of Pietism. However, the relationship of the evangelical movement to the pietistic tradition has been the subject of discussion (cf. Scheffbuch). Jung sees the theology of evangelicalism in basic agreement with the theological emphases of the pietistic tradition. He notes that many contemporary church leaders who understand themselves as Pietists are at the same time significant representatives of the evangelical movement. But the pietistic tradition composes only one part of the entire evangelical community (Jung:232 n. 26).

In the midst of the many – in some cases even conflicting – streams within the world-wide evangelical community, Klaus Bockmühl calls German evangelicals back to the centre (Bockmühl 1985:6–10). He sees this act of new orientation as a turning to God and a return to their own spiritual roots, which, according to Bockmühl most evangelicals in Germany may find in Pietism (1985:11). He spells out ten points which he claims still to be the valid heritage of Pietism which evangelicals should consider today (1985):

1. The ecclesiological model of the *ecclesiola in ecclesia*, i.e., the dialectic between the small groups of realised fellowship and the potential of the established church *(Grosskirche)*.
2. Commitment to the Bible as the Word of God, combined with the emphasis that a Bible belongs in every believer's hands.
3. The concentration on Jesus, with an emphasis on the personal relationship which every believer can have with their Saviour and Lord.
4. The emphasis on conversion and new birth as the personal experience of the individual.
5. The emphasis on sanctification as a growing love of God and other human beings manifested in deeds.
6. A vision for world mission.
7. Christian responsibility in the realm of education.
8. The renewal of theology and theological education.
9. The social responsibility of the church.
10. Contribution to social ethics, i.e., the readiness of the church to participate in the responsibilities of society.

At least to some extent, most of *the Schools* associate themselves with Pietism; however, none of them is directly rooted in early Pietism. This brings us to the next point.

b) British Evangelicalism and the Neo-Pietistic Erweckungsbewegung

In the eighteenth century the spark of revivalism moved from Germany to Britain. Inspired by German Pietism (Beyreuther 1977:4–5; Bebbington: 38–40), though in a different historical, cultural and religious setting, a movement emerged which has in retrospect been called the Evangelical Revival. In turn, it was Anglo-Saxon evangelicalism which in the nineteenth century was influential in the beginning of new revival movements on the continent. In this process, the seeds of British evangelicalism fell on the soil of the earlier German Pietism and gave birth to two movements commonly known as the *Erweckungsbewegung* (c.1820–1850; cf. Beyreuther 1977:1–4; Ruhbach 1992a:531–32) and the *Gemeinschaftsbewegung* (c.1875–1925; cf. Lange:10–45). Thus, beyond the pietistic heritage discussed above, the British influence on the continent formed a constitutive factor in German evangelicalism.

While the term 'evangelical' was formerly applied in Britain to those 'churches arising from the Reformation in the sixteenth and seventeenth centuries' and carried the simple meaning of 'the gospel,' it became the technical term for a movement within Protestant churches, which Bebbington (:1) describes as follows:

> Evangelical religion is a popular Protestant movement that has existed in Britain since the 1730's. It is not to be equated with any single Christian denomination, for it influenced the existing churches during the eighteenth century and generated many more in subsequent years. It has found expression in variety of institutional forms, a wine that has been poured into many bottles.

Despite differences within the evangelical movement, Bebbington (:3) identifies the following characteristics of Evangelicalism:

> There are the four qualities that have been the special marks of Evangelical religion: *conversionism*, the belief that lives need to be changed; *activism*, the expression of the gospel in effort; *biblicism*, a particular regard for the Bible; and what may be called *crucicentrism*, a stress on the sacrifice of Christ on the cross. Together they form a quadrilateral of priorities that is the basis of Evangelicalism.[6]

It was primarily through Bible and mission societies that British evangelicalism reached the continent in the nineteenth century. Ludwig Rott has convincingly shown how the *London Missionary Society*, the *Church Missionary Society*, the *British and Foreign Bible Society* and the *Church Mission to the Jews*, as well as the *Continental Society*, influenced the revival movements on the continent (:23–87; cf. Bebbington:76–78). In Germany and Switzerland these new British influences merged with the remnant of Pietism, which was especially alive in the Moravian Movement and the *Deutsche Christentumsgesellschaft* (founded 1779 – 80 in Basel, cf. ELTHG:367–68; Beyreuther 1977:16–9). Another strand of evangelicalism came through the Scottish free church movement and was first influential in the beginning of the *réveil* in Geneva (Beyreuther 1977:17). Given Bebbington's characterisation of British evangelicalism, it goes without saying that it renewed the ethos of early Pietism, with which it shares many characteristics. However, there are several features of British evangelicalism which have influenced the evangelical movement on the continent in a new and special way:

1. British evangelicalism introduced the concept of voluntary societies for the propagation of the gospel and for social work by means of institutions independent of official church structures (Beyreuther 1977:23–24).[7]

2. Furthermore, British evangelicalism of the nineteenth century held a critical attitude toward the established church, especially in the early phase preceding 1830 and – at least in the dissenting churches – beyond (Bebbington:94–104). It follows that British evangelical missionaries introduced a much more critical attitude toward the established Lutheran Church than was the case in Pietism.

3. To British missionaries and their German and Swiss collaborators, it seemed entirely natural to establish new independent congregations of free church orientation. This led to the foundation of several new denominations on the continent (Baptists, Methodists, Darbyists, Free Evangelical Church, cf. Geldbach 1989). With this, a new ecclesiological model was introduced[8] to a context dominated by established territorial churches.[9]

4. However, British influence also led to the foundation of neo-pietistic societies within the Lutheran and Reformed Churches, a development which finally led to the *Gemeinschaftsbewegung* toward the end of the nineteenth century (Lange).

5. British evangelicalism is also characterised by an anti-Enlightenment and anti-liberal attitude. Especially those evangelicals within the Anglican Church 'developed a sense of being a bastion under assault' and the 'hostile force' was identified as 'Liberalism' (Bebbington:99; cf. 50–60). This has also been influential on the continent.

6. Furthermore, continental evangelicalism owes to British evangelicalism the notion of the unity of the evangelical movement beyond denominational and confessional boundaries as represented by the *Evangelical Alliance* (Hauzenberger:26; Beyreuther 1977:8).

7. Finally, the early evangelical movement in Britain must also be seen, at least in part, as a movement outside the university system. While the clergy of the established Church of England were university-trained

men, many of the early evangelicals came from outside the more highly educated class. Persons with evangelical convictions had to face expulsion from the universities and were refused ordination in the Church of England. (Bebbington:17–18; 23–26). This means, in view of the topic of this thesis, that British evangelicalism introduced and supported a movement which functioned outside the established structure of theological education, which was based on an alliance between state church and state university. The revival movement of the nineteenth century established the means for missionary training – and later pastoral training as well – outside of university structures. *Chrischona*, the oldest of *the Schools* (founded in 1840), has its roots directly in the early phase of the revival movement.

In view of the subject of this study we notice that several of *the Schools* in consideration, or at least the denominations or movements to which they belong, have their roots in the revival movement of the nineteenth century. However, the British influence on the evangelical movement in German-speaking Europe – especially Germany – decreased in the twentieth century, not least under the influence of two wars in which England and Germany fought against each other. Here we may have one of the historical reasons for what we will observe later in this study: contemporary German evangelicalism finds itself to a considerable degree in isolation from the British world. On the other hand, contemporary German evangelicals have established flourishing relations with North American evangelicalism, a phenomenon which deserves further consideration.

c) The Impact of North American Evangelicalism

After World War I, and definitely after World War II, the dominant force of evangelical influence upon the continent shifted from Great Britain to North America (Wagner 1993:21–30).

For the purposes of this study we are mainly concerned with the shape of American evangelicalism at the time at which it reached continental Europe after World War II. The roots of American Evangelicalism can be sketched only briefly.[10]

1. The American Revival of the eighteenth century had two wings: on the one hand the Puritan Protestant wing, related to the person of Jonathan Edwards and on the other hand, the Wesleyan Methodist wing. Both contributed to the Great Awakenings of the eighteenth and nineteenth centuries.

2. The two movements merged in the nineteenth century in the revivalism of Charles G. Finney and D.L. Moody. These revivals shaped what can, in a general way, be called American Evangelicalism of the nineteenth century. Its contours have been identified in (a) an individual salvation experience, (b) emphasis on evangelism through crusades, (c)

interdenominationalism, (d) lay-oriented theology and (e) conservative, anti-liberal stances (Kraus ed. 1979:44–45).

3. Evangelical Revivals in America led to the foundation of new churches and denominations which resulted in an enormous denominational pluralism. American Christianity in general was used to denominational pluralism and religious freedom from its beginning. American denominationalism developed in a context lacking historically established territorial state churches. Denominations developed along the lines of immigrant communities, social structures[11] – and revivals.

4. By the end of the nineteenth century the holiness movement and thence Pentecostal evangelicalism developed as a new wing of evangelicalism with its own identity.

5. Around the turn of the century, parts of the evangelical movement developed in the direction of a strongly anti-liberal counter force, focusing on the battle against the rationalism of biblical criticism and Darwin's theory of evolution. The result was the movement called fundamentalism (cf. Harris:19–39; see introduction of this study p. 17).

6. American evangelicalism of the late nineteenth and early twentieth centuries was an educational movement. Virginia L. Brereton (:425–31) has shown that the more than 250 Bible schools which were founded between 1882 and 1940 made a tremendous impact on the evangelical-fundamentalist community. Her thesis is that the strength of the conservative evangelical movement as a grass-roots movement can only be explained by the significance of the Bible schools. If we add to this the impact of the Sunday school movement, we come to the conclusion that teaching the laity stands at the heart of American evangelicalism.

7. After World War II many evangelicals began to dissociate themselves from fundamentalism and established 'post-fundamentalist' evangelicalism. These 'new evangelicals' were associated with the National Association of Evangelicals (founded in 1942–43) which located itself between the ecumenically oriented Federal Council of Churches and the separatist-fundamentalist American Council of Christian Churches. Fuller Theological Seminary, *Christianity Today*, C.F. Henry, Bernard Ramm and Billy Graham, but also World Vision, Campus Crusade for Christ and the Church Growth Movement – to mention only a few – stand in the line of this new evangelical movements (Kraus ed. 1979:9–22). This evangelicalism is highly interdenominational and pragmatic as far as mission strategies and methods are concerned.

The impact of American Evangelicalism on the European continent since World War II has been tremendous:[12]

1. Between sixty and seventy North American mission agencies were already active on the European continent already in the first decade after World War II (1945 to 1954); about fifty per cent of them were denominational, the other fifty per cent interdenominational (Wagner 1993:24–26).

2. Wagner (:14–15) shows that most American Missions which were active in Europe represented the conservative and dispensational wing of American evangelicalism.

3. American evangelicalism has also challenged Christians in Europe through its missionary activism and pragmatism. Parachurch organisations such as Youth for Christ, Campus Crusade for Christ, The Gideons International, Youth With A Mission, World Vision and many others have been mobilising two generations of young European evangelicals since the 1950s. The Church Growth Movement has raised serious questions regarding the effectiveness of German and Swiss churches in evangelism and church growth. American evangelicals have significantly contributed to the awareness of the need for the re-evangelisation of post-Christian Europe. They have introduced the concept of church planting, which was virtually absent in the established state churches in Germany and Switzerland, because of their assumption that all members of the state are baptised members of the state church.

4. Furthermore, North American evangelical missions have confronted the established churches of continental Europe with a kind of denominationalism and para-church institution which has no understanding of the history and the concept of the state church. Part of the denominational culture of North America is a free market attitude in evangelism and church planting – an attitude which is hard for European churches to understand. North American evangelicals have questioned the nominal Christianity still promoted by the established churches (Rommen 1985; cf. Moltmann 1975b:252–58, 344–62). Time and again this has caused conflict between indigenous churches and American missions (cf. Wagner 1993:103–30; Ott 1995). Some of the missions have been directly involved in establishing or supporting Bible schools – especially Greater Europe Mission (Reimer:64) – and have transmitted this ecclesial philosophy to German and Swiss young people.

5. When North American missions engaged in theological education they came with the North American system of higher education and accreditation in their minds and they normally lacked an understanding of the European university system of theological education. North American Evangelicals have supported the existing Bible school system in Germany and Switzerland and have connected these schools with the North American accreditation system (see p. 84).

6. Finally, it is through contacts with North American evangelicalism that the various revivalist traditions in German-speaking Europe began to move in the direction of a common evangelical identity in the 1960s. They even introduced the Germanised form of evangelical – *evangelikal* – as a new label for this movement.

We summarise and conclude: In German-speaking Europe, evangelicalism – as a movement explicitly labelled *evangelikal* – is of recent origin.

The movement has taken its name from the English word 'evangelical'. At the same time, contemporary German evangelicalism has a long tradition. Historically, it is rooted in Lutheran Pietism and owes much to the British revival movement of the eighteenth and nineteenth century. However, the latest, and probably still predominate, influence comes from North American evangelicalism. As mentioned earlier, the shift from British to North American connections may be partially due to the differing roles the countries played in the two World Wars.

This raises the question of how these historical forces have actually shaped contemporary evangelical mission and theological education in the German-speaking context. However, before we can enter into a more detailed examination of the recent developments of German evangelical mission and theological education and draw necessary conclusions, we must add two other strands to the historical background.

2. A General Introduction to the History of Theological Education and Mission Studies

a) Theological Education in General

(1) EDWARD FARLEY'S HISTORICAL TYPOLOGY

In the field of *general studies of the history of theological education*, Edward Farley's *Theologia* is probably still one of the most comprehensive publications. He writes, 'There is no adequate history of "the study of theology" either as literature or as a movement, nor of the literature of theological encyclopaedia' (1983:66 n. 1). Other comprehensive works are dated in the early nineteenth century and before.[13] In view of the situation in Europe, Nicole (:33) affirms that 'no comprehensive historical study has been conducted in Europe on the origins and developments of theological education in the Christian churches since the three volume encyclopaedia of the Dutch scholar Abraham Kuyper ... in 1894'.

Whereas Farley concentrates mainly on 'North American Protestant institutions for the education of clergy' (1983:23 n. 1) he also deals with the European heritage of theological education and thus provides a meaningful point of departure for this historical overview.

Farley points to three major problem areas which deserve attention (1983:6–18): (1) the development of theological education from 'personal knowledge of God' ('an exercise of piety') to 'objective science' ('specialised scholarship'), and from there to 'professional training'; (2) the problem of institutions, i.e., the rise of the seminary as a distinct institution for the training of professional clegy; and (3) the *ratio studiorum*, i.e., the rationale for the unity, the content and divisions of theological education (unifying principle).

Farley's focus is on the third issue, and he posits three historical periods from this point of view, leading to four models of theological education (:29–48). The distinction between theology as personal knowledge of God (in Farley's terms, 'theology/knowledge') and theology as a discipline of studies ('theology/discipline') is the leading principle for Farley's historical survey. He states:

> First, theology is a term for an actual, individual cognition of God and things related to God, a cognition which in most treatments attends faith and has eternal happiness as its final goal. Second, theology is a term for a discipline, a self-conscious scholarly enterprise of understanding. In the former sense theology is a habit *(habitus)* of the human soul. In the latter it is a discipline, usually occurring in some sort of pedagogical setting (1983:31).

The four models proposed by Farley are:

1. The *monastic model* of the early Christian centuries, covering 'early patristic and early medieval Christendom prior to the rise of the medieval universities' (1983:32–34). In this period theology/knowledge was understood as 'mystical knowledge of the one God' and theology-discipline, in the setting of the monastery, was focused on 'reading, memorising, expounding, and meditating on scripture.' The unifying centre (*ratio studiorum*) has to be seen in the concept of *divinity*, the 'divine illumination of the mind' (Farley 1983:44). Theology/discipline and theology/knowledge were closely correlated, i.e., the study of scripture was to lead to an encounter with the Divine and the personal knowledge of God to illuminate the reading of scripture.

2. The *scholastic model* of the period 'from the origin of the universities in the twelfth century up to the so-called modern university' (Farley 1983:32, 34–39). Theology/knowledge, in Farley's view, was seen as a sapiential *habitus*. Knowledge (*scientia*) was understood as 'an enduring orientation and dexterity of the soul... . Theology is a *practical*, not theoretical, habit having the primary character of wisdom' (Farley 1983:35). On the other hand, theology/discipline, now located in the universities, became, along with law, medicine and arts-philosophy, an academic field of studies, a '*scientia* in the distinctive scholastic sense of a method of demonstrating conclusions' (Farley 1983:34). This indicated the 'transition of Christian learning and teaching based on Scripture *(sacra pagina)* into an Aristotelian science *(sacra doctrina)*' (Farley 1983:37). The unifying principle in this model is 'the classical patristic doctrinal scheme,' now reflected and expressed in the scholastic philosophical framework as *sacra doctrina* (Farley 1983:34, 38).

3. The third epoch, reaching from the rise of the modern university in the Enlightenment to the present time, gave birth to two models of

theological education which are now presented as models three and four (Farley 1983:32, 39–44). First is the *university model*, referring to theological faculties of the secular universities. According to Farley, theology/knowledge 'as a disposition of the soul towards God simply drops out of "the study of theology" ' (1983:43). Theology/discipline became part of the academic world of the modern university, with its revolutionary new emphasis on the 'emancipation of thought and inquiry from institutional and even cognitive authorities' (1983:41). This caused a major shift in theological education:

> In the pre-Enlightenment theologies, the *norms* for theology/discipline were the *articuli fidei* themselves. These doctrines of church tradition were not products, accomplishments of theology, but the *principia*, the givens. They were, accordingly, the norms for interpreting Scripture and determining Christian responsibility and Christian truth. With the Enlightenment and the modern university came the ideal of autonomous science, of scholarship, proceeding under no other canons than proper evidence (Farley 1983:41).

With the loss of the Christian faith as the normative and unifying centre of *all* university studies (scholastic university), theology/discipline lost its place as the integrative centre of all fields of studies in the university context and had to function according to the rules of the Enlightenment ideal of science. This, according to Farley, led to the introduction of all the new fields and methodologies of studies at the university to the discipline of theology causing the fragmentation of theology/discipline into many specialised areas – 'the pluralization of theology into independent disciplines' (Farley 1983:44; 73–124), which lead to the discipline's classical, encyclopaedic structure of a fourfold curricula pattern (Bible, systematic theology, history, practical theology). In view of the *ratio studiorum*, Farley concludes, 'The most serious and sobering aspect of this account of the career of theology is simply the disappearance of theology as wisdom and knowledge as discipline,' and with this the disappearance of the 'overall unity and rationale of theological study' (1983:44).

4. The fourth model can be called the *clerical, ministerial or professional model* (Farley 1983:85; cf. Schipani:34–35; Duraisingh:37). The focus now shifted to the professional training of the clergy. With this, a new unifying centre was introduced (Farley 1983:43). Farley traces the roots of this paradigm back to Pietism (1983:41) and especially to the influence of Schleiermacher (1983:84–98). It became the dominant model for the American seminary (Farley 1983:11–12, 44). Theology/knowledge, Farley says, shifted from sapiential *habitus* to practical know-how. Theological education 'as a disposition of the soul towards God has been transformed … into the know-hows required for the tasks of ministry'

(1983:43). Theology/discipline however, in the clerical-professional model leads to the development of practical theology, the fourth discipline of the fourfold pattern. Thus, the rationale of theological education

> lies in its power to prepare the student for designated tasks or activities which occur (or should occur) in the parish or in some specialized ministry. To the degree that this is the case, the theological student neither studies divinity nor obtains scholarly expertise in theological science, but trains for professional activities (Farley 1983:11).

Critical reflections: In many ways, Farley presents a valuable tool for the analysis of the history of theological education.[14] (1) First of all, he identifies the development of the concept of knowing as a crucial issue in theological education. The three steps from *existential knowledge (habitus)* to *academic knowledge (science)* and finally to *technical knowledge (know-how)* deserve further reflection as we look at theological education in this analysis. (2) He demonstrates the centrality of Schleiermacher in the development toward the classical fourfold pattern of the theological curriculum, a development which not only divided theory from practice but also narrowed down practical theology to the horizon of clerical practice – and this in the context of an established church which has lost its missionary vision. In this sense Farley provides the historical analysis for Bosch's critical assessment of theology and theological education in what he calls the Enlightenment paradigm (Bosch 1991:489–90).

However, Farley's stance (as of 1983) needs to be qualified and supplemented. The study reflects the discussion among the schools of the Association of Theological Schools in the 1970s and early 1980s. Farley addresses the agenda of highly pragmatic and professionalised pastoral training in North America. While Farley has presented a widely respected analysis of theological education, he has been criticised by Ferris for not proposing any helpful solutions capable of pointing beyond the crisis (Ferris 1990a:20) – a critique which we will challenge later in this study.[15] However, Farley looks at theological education from a western point of view and does not incorporate into his analysis those insights of Two Thirds World educators which have contributed considerably to the development of what we will call a new paradigm in theological education. From this perspective, Sidney Rooy's paper 'Historical Models of Theological Education' (Padilla ed. 1988:51–72) raises significant issues from a Two Thirds World perspective and points in some areas beyond Farley's analysis.[16] The significance of Rooy's contribution is not based on his fourfold typology (catechetical model of the early church, the monastic model, the scholastic model and the seminary model) for which he draws on Charles Davis,[17] but on the critique he advances: (1) 'The four models are dominated by those at the top and, therefore, serve to maintain and strengthen ecclesial society itself' (:69). (2) In all models theological training was 'attended almost exclusively by sons of the middle classes thereby guaranteeing this class's control of the lower classes' (:70). (3) Finally, historical models of theological education 'place so much emphasis on pure doctrine ... that we lose sight of the world' (:70).

As we look at the paradigm shift in theological education in Part IV of this study we will realise how significant Rooy's questions are.

(2) THEOLOGICAL EDUCATION IN CONTEXT OF THE MODERN UNIVERSITY

Farley's analysis focuses on what can be called the university model of theological education, albeit with an emphasis on recent developments in the context of North American pastoral training. In order to more properly understand theological education in the context of the university – especially in view of the European situation – we need to supplement Farley's contribution with some general reflections on the university.

The modern university is an institution of the Enlightenment.[18] Jaspers (:19) defines it as follows: 'The university is a community of scholars and students engaged in the task of seeking truth' (:19). This search for truth is based on a number of presuppositions which constitute the ethos of the modern university. At least four features can be identified (cf. Jaspers; Zumstein; RGG IV:1170):

1. *The 'academic ethos' of the university* (Zumstein:84–89; Jaspers:23–43). The fact that the modern university is an institution of the Enlightenment includes a threefold commitment: (1) *The commitment to truth,* in the sense of the free and rational search for an appropriate understanding and knowledge of reality, is the basic axiom of academic research, carried out in a disciplined, methodological and verifiable way. (2) *The commitment to the freedom of teaching and research,* as independence from any kind of affiliation with the state, economy, religion or any other power, includes the freedom to study without pragmatism. Only in this way can the university fulfil its task as the 'conscience of society.' (3) *The commitment is to human dignity.* Freedom of studies does not imply a lack of purpose and meaning. The university is committed to responsible research in the service of human dignity.

2. *The sociological role of the university.* Universities are training centres of the academic elite. The entrance requirements are purely academic: in Germany and Switzerland the *Abitur* or *Matura* (Zumstein:90). Only a selected minority of the population gain university training and they make up the academic elite of society.[19]

3. As the universities grew toward an increasing number of highly specialised academic disciplines, each one with its own set of methodologies, it encountered the problem of *dispersion and fragmentation.*[20]

Theology could not escape this development. As it sought its place as an academic discipline in the university it was forced to base theology upon scientific reasoning (cf. Hempelmann 1987; Murphy). Academic theological studies must be conducted according to the rules of science in other relevant fields: biblical studies according to the rules of historical and linguistic studies, church history according to the rules of historical investigation, systematic theology according to the rules of philosophical studies and practical theology according to the rules of the social sciences. One result of this is the *encyclopaedic pattern* of theological education, consisting of a broad variety of only loosely related disciplines and subjects. The traditional fourfold pattern (Bible, theology, history, pastoral praxis) has made room for an even greater fragmentation into different fields of specialist studies, each with its own methodology, history of research, problems and literature. This enormous fragmentation of theology (Farley 1983) is not without severe consequences for the study of theology, as Gerhard Ebeling states:

> The study of theology is beset by a crisis in orientation. Because our access to the unity and totality that constitutes the subject matter of theology is disrupted, the main domain of its subject matter and task has broken apart and crumbled into a bewildering conglomeration of individual items (1978:1).

4. *The dissociation of academic theological education from ministerial formation.* There is an integral tension between the church's desire to be in control of theological education and the ethos of the university (Zumstein:92–94, 98–100). Strictly speaking, the partner of the teachers and students of theology in the university context is the university and not the church (Nicole:34). The most consistent solution is to dissociate academic university training from pastoral education, as is done in some situations in Germany and Switzerland: 'After being awarded their theological degree, students are admitted into a three-year programme using mainly field-based education and case-study pedagogies' (Nicole:34; cf. Lange and Schmid:37–38). Other approaches to university-integrated pastoral education suffer from the foundational tension between the ethos of the university and the claims of the church (T. Hafner:11–13; Werner 1995:15–17).

It is not the objective of this study to discuss the university model of theological education at length. But we should take notice of some practical constraints theology has to face when it operates in the university system. Whenever theological education is undertaken in the realm of the university

- it has to function according to the rules and ethos of the university – with all its advantages and limitations.[21]

- it has to be aware of the fact that its training will be limited to the academic elite of society (at least in Germany and Switzerland).
- It will encounter the problem of fragmentation and lack of unity
- it must be aware that the university sets the agenda of theological education and not the church.[22]

Finally we need to point to some foundational critiques articulated from within the system. 'It is common place to say that churches, as future employers of theological students, have grown very dissatisfied with the achievements of university theological training,' says Nicole (:34). The study process of the WCC on 'Viability in Theological Education' has stirred discussions regarding the renewal of theological education in German universities (Engel and Werner; Werner 1995). Dietrich Werner complains:

> Until now it has looked as if the practical and theological questions of building up congregations and congregational renewal have been treated as themes predominantly outside or subsequent to the initial phase of theological training in the state faculties. The amount of time and energy devoted to critical study of the classical 'documents' of biblical ecclesiastical and doctrinal traditions is generally out of proportion in relation to the time and energy spent on a critical analysis of the present 'context,' the living conditions of human beings in our highly complex society (1992:78).

In a similar way in Switzerland, the possibility of a reformation of university theological education has been explored, at this stage with only minimal success (Bittner). Maybe Nicole (:34), pointing to the budgetary restrictions which are affecting European universities, is right in saying that

> it is perhaps these economic constraints rather than a pedagogical and theological reflection that will lead European theological educators to question what they have always considered as God-ordained, the so-called 'classical' model of theological education, sharing with colleagues from other parts of the oikoumene ways and means of developing a viable and credible ministerial formation for the whole people of God.

This serves merely to document that the classical model of theological education in the university context is in crisis. This becomes even more evident when we focus on the place of mission studies in theological education.

b) Mission Studies in Particular

In the field of *mission studies* in theological education, Olav G. Myklebust's two volume survey of 1955/1957 must still be considered the most comprehensive work on the history of mission studies as a discipline in theological education. But this leads only to the historical background information and does not cover the last 40 years.[23] Further, it is limited to western Protestant ministerial training. In a more recent article (1989) he gives further statistical data and covers all continents and schools of Protestant, Roman Catholic and Orthodox background.[24] But an eighteen page article cannot sufficiently cover the forty year period from his earlier study up to the present time. A comprehensive critical historical study has yet to be made. Myklebust himself writes:

> The place of mission studies in contemporary theological education has only in small measures been made the object of serious research. Among the subjects treated in the numerous doctoral dissertations bearing on the Christian mission that of Missiology as a theological discipline is conspicuous by its absence. Separate publications on the topic, and articles on it in journals, Festschriften, etc. have been few and far between (1989:88).

Myklebust's study is significant in view of the mission departments in traditional universities and theological seminaries up to 1957, however, his historical overview needs to be supplemented by other studies: [25]

1. Prior to the nineteenth century, Myklebust observes only minimal interest in explicit missiological thinking and teaching. Yet several theologians claim that theological reflection on the mission of the church was not absent in the period prior to the modern missionary movement, although it had a more implicit character.[26] Lutheran theologians claim a missionary dimension already in Luther's theology (cf. Gensichen 1969:5–6, with reference to K. Holl and W. Eller).

2. According to Myklebust, the first attempt to assign an official place to mission in the theological curriculum was made by Schleiermacher in his *Kurze Darstellung des theologischen Studiums zum Behuf einleitender Vorlesungen* (1850). He puts mission in the area of practical theology and refers to it in the field of ethics (cf. Verkuyl:6–7). But this allocation of a specific place in the curriculum had no significance for the study of missions as such. Missiology as an academic discipline of its own had yet to be established (Kasdorf 1988:225). The Protestant scholars Karl Graul (1814–1864) of Leipzig, Alexander Duff (1806–1878) of Edinburgh, Gustav Warneck (1834–1910) of Halle, as well as the Catholic Joseph Schmidlin (1876–1944) of Münster, are often referred to as the persons who shaped missiology as an academic discipline in the university curriculum (Myklebust 1955:67; Kasdorf 1988:225–28; cf. Verkuyl:12–13)

3. Kasdorf follows Myklebust in interpreting the first part of the twentieth century as a 'time of impressive flourishing' [imponierende Hochblüte] of mission studies in the university context. Warneck was the driving force up to the turn of the century. Mission agencies and their schools (e.g., Neuendettelsau, Basel, Barmen, Bad Liebenzell, Wiedenest), as well as university faculties (e.g., Amsterdam, Halle, Hamburg, Heidelberg, Münster) had taken up the Warneck heritage and established a profound missiological foundation (Kasdorf 1995:9). Missiologists such as Karl Hartenstein (1894–1952) and Walter Freytag (1988–1959) of Germany, as well as J. H. Bavinck (1895–1964) and Hendrik Kraemer (1888–1965) from the Netherlands shaped this epoch in Europe (Verkuyl:28–30, 35–51).

4. The assessment of the second half of the twentieth century is controversial. Bockmühl points to the 1950s as still belonging to the peak of mission studies, referring to European theologians like Hartenstein, Kraemer and Freytag (1974:9–24). At the same time, the post-war period has been critical for mission in the university context. The severe crisis of the missionary identity of the western church has questioned mission studies. Myklebust surveys the period since 1950 in his update study of 1989. Having considered more than 300 institutions,[27] both ecumenical and evangelical, Protestant and Catholic, western and non-western, Myklebust advances the following general conclusion:

> The development of mission studies since 1950 … has been characterised by two contrasting tendencies: the increasing recognition of the relevance of missiology for theological study, and the reluctance on the part of the majority of theological institutions to secure for it a separate and permanent place in their curricula (:98).

For Europe, Myklebust concludes that Germany and the Netherlands still lead the continent in promoting missiological teaching and research (:92) – yet Europe has also experienced the greatest decrease in professorships of Missiology since 1950 (:99).

Speaking of the general crisis of mission at the present time (1982), Bosch stated,

> The gradual disappearance of missions or missiology from the curriculum of one theological institution after another further emphasises the malaise. In some of the older European and American faculties of theology where in the early part of this century missiology appeared to be firmly entrenched, the chairs have been abolished or converted into others for world Christianity, ecumenical studies, Third World theologies, world religions and the like. This development has been linked with the rapid decrease in the

number of missionaries from the Roman Catholic Church and the World Council of Churches (1982:13–14).

5. In the post-war period, especially following the integration of the IMC into the WCC in 1961, there has been a growing awareness of mission as a subject of theology and theological education in German and Swiss university faculties (cf. Adamek); however, theology and mission have remained separate, and it is no secret, as Gensichen states, that 'the relationship between mission and academic theology has been for a long time and still is in many cases characterised by cool distance' (1971:42). Of course many proposals have been made toward the integration of mission studies into the field of academic theological studies.[28] Some theological educators have naturally pleaded that mission is not just an additional subject but rather the necessary dimension of all theology (Linz in Bohren 1964:34). Of course, inspired by the ecumenical discussion of the renewal of theological education, some theological educators have been developing models for the reorientation of theological education in state church faculties (see publications by Engel and Werner).

However, it seems that traditional higher theological education is successfully resisting changes in this regard. Despite the articulation at least since the 1960s of the need for a missionary orientation in theological education, only minimal change can be observed. The results of all initiatives towards renewal are meagre, as Werner observed already in his 1990 study (1990:65–68). Little has changed in the German university scene:

> Training continues to be unilaterally focused on the image of the full-time pastor ministering in the congregation ... ecumenical encouragements to reform theological training have so far made little headway where state theological faculties are concerned (Werner 1992:78).

In his more extensive report of 1995, Werner concludes regarding mission studies:

> The pressure of circumstances and the cut back of faculty posts hit the area of religious, mission and ecumenical studies [RMÖ Religion, Missionstheologie und Ökumenewissenschaft] much stronger than the so-called core courses. The freedom for intercultural encounter and the possibilities for travelling was cut back as a first priority. In the curriculum suggested by the commission for the reduction of the length of theological studies [Gemischte Kommission] which is presently at work, the RMÖ courses are in danger of being completely thrown out. Only in the examination

> regulation of some state churches are the RMÖ courses included. In a time of increased time pressure upon students, the majority concentrates on core courses and the offerings in the RMÖ area are used only to a insufficient measure (1995:12).

Result: A reform of theological education in the context of European universities which really implements the ecumenical vision of a missionary church is not in sight. It seems that traditional, western theological education, in its institutionalised affiliation with established churches, the university system and even the state, is almost incapable of change.

6. It is therefore no surprise that Bosch, Myklebust, Kasdorf and others observe that the centre of gravity of missiological interest moved from the ecumenical-oriented universities to the evangelically-oriented schools. In the words of Myklebust, 'Statistically speaking, "Lausanne" has taken a much more active interest in the Church's mission, and in the promotion of missiology as a theological discipline, than has "Geneva" ' (Myklebust 1989:89). Kasdorf sees an 'amazing revival' of missiology in the 1960s as due to the fact that the evangelical movement took the lead in the Christian missionary movement; and he observes that 'the revival of missiology in theological education at the university level in the evangelical sector took place parallel to the decrease of missiology in the schools of ecumenical orientation' (Kasdorf 1995:11–12).

This assessment of the evangelical role may be somewhat one-sided, but it does justice to the fact that the centre of missionary dynamism has moved from schools with an ecumenical orientation to the evangelical world. However, Kasdorf does definitely underestimate the significant ecumenical contribution to missiological reflection. Ecumenical missiology has changed and does not necessarily occur in the traditional form of *mission studies*. Often in the university context, missiological reflection has been integrated into other disciplines, in some instances into the classical disciplines of Bible, systematic theology, church history and practical theology (cf. Verkuyl:7–8), in other cases into new disciplines such as World Christianity, Ecumenical Studies, Third World Studies and World Religions (Bosch 1982:14; Jongeneel 1998; cf. Ebeling 1978). In the light of the paradigmatic shift in mission which is the subject of Part III of this study, this development can only be commended. However, the situation in Germany demonstrates that curricula restructuring does not automatically lead to a holistic integration of mission into theological education. Mission studies remain marginalised in the theological curriculum (Werner 1995:12).

We have demonstrated that much has been said and written in ecumenical, main-line university circles on the renewal of theological education and the place of mission studies in theological education. Nonetheless, we observe a great degree of disappointment and frustration in the realisation of this programme. On the other hand, we have realised that experts of the field have pointed to the evangelical movement as a carrier of fruitful developments in mission-oriented theological education. This we have to analyse more carefully.

3. The Heritage of Evangelical Theological Education and Mission Studies[29]

a) The Contribution of Pietism to Evangelical Theological Education and Mission Studies

Contemporary evangelical theological educators emphasise the abiding significance of Pietism's contribution to the renewal of theological education (cf. Riecker 1974:170–72; H. Hafner:37; Frische). This has its reasons. What Spener has outlined in *Pia desideria* is no less than an urgent call for the renewal of theological education. At the centre of the actual realisation of Spener's vision stands his suggestion to implement *Collegia pietatis*, i.e., community meetings where professors together with students and church members read the Bible, interpret it and apply it to practical life (Wallmann 1970:298–301).

Based on Spener's *Pia Desideria*, Reinhard Frische identifies five elements of the pietistic renewal of theological education:

1. 'Biblicism,' or the foundational and normative character of the Bible (:13–18; cf. Riecker 1974:112).
2. The focus of theology and theological education on God, his will, his intention, his kingdom (Frische:19–22).
3. Personal spirituality and the theologian's submission to God (Frische: 23–31).
4. The orientation of theology and theological education toward the practical life and the needs of the church and the world (Frische:32–39).
5. Theology and theological education as ministry (Frische:40–44).

Pietism also inspired specific mission training and academic mission studies. The *collegium orientale theologicum* instituted at the university of Halle in 1702 by Francke has been viewed as the particular contribution to mission studies of Pietism. The first Protestant missionary to India, Bartholomäus Ziegenbalg has been called the founder of the science of religions (Myklebust 1955:50; Wallmann 1990:74).

Following the general character of the pietistic renewal of the seventeenth century, the leaders of early pietism did not seek the establishment of alternative theological schools outside the Protestant state universities of that time. They rather promoted the presence of pietistic theologians within the established system. The focus was on the renewal of established theological institutions, at that time dominated by orthodoxy (Bockmühl 1985:38–41; Riecker 1974:111–12). This vision was most successfully achieved at Halle under the leadership of August Hermann Francke (Rüttgard:620; Wallmann 1990:72–75).

On the one hand, if we follow the development of theological education in German-speaking Europe from the eighteenth to the twentieth centuries, we recognise a tradition of pietistic theologians reaching from Johann Albrecht Bengel (1687–1752) to Adolf Schlatter (1852–1938) and Karl Heim (1874–1958) (Riecker 1974:112). Some universities have – or had – a tradition of a pietistic professorship or even a chair of pietistic theology. In other cases, study centres of a pietistic orientation have been established in order to support pietistic students during their studies at the university (H. Hafner:37–38).[30] On the other hand, it seems that the long-term impact of the pietistic renewal on theological education and mission studies as a whole was limited. As the theological faculties sought to re-establish their place in the modern university of the Enlightenment, there was little space for Spener's agenda of pietistic renewal (see discussion of the university p. 38) At the beginning of the twentieth century, Pietists within the Lutheran Church began to establish denominational seminaries (Kirchliche Hochschulen) which operated academically at a university level but maintained independence from the state universities (first at Bethel in 1905). This was done in reaction to 'modern theology' which dominated theological studies at the universities – and was done with minimal success, as G. Henning comments (ELThG:160).

Concluding reflections. We recognise that Pietism aimed at the renewal of theological education in general and at the introduction of specific mission studies in particular. We have shown that the schools under investigation identify with this pietistic tradition of theological education. However, they can be counted only partially as heirs of Spener, Francke and other Pietists. It is true that *the Schools* affirm the theological ethos of early pietism (see Frische); however, they have abandoned the idea of renewing theological education from within the state church and university structure and have established a tradition of theological education outside the established system of higher education. These values stem from the evangelical revivals and the Bible school movement of the nineteenth century, to which we now turn.

b) The Mission Movements of the Nineteenth Century and the Development of the Bible School Movement

(1) THE ROOTS OF THE BIBLE SCHOOL MOVEMENT

The so-called Bible School Movement must be seen in close relation to *the modern missionary movement*, especially the *faith mission movement* (Fiedler 1994:144–153).

The origins of the *modern missionary movement* are associated with the foundation of the Baptist Missionary Society by William Carey (1792). This also marked the beginning of the development of *classical missions*. A second wave of the modern mission movement, the so-called *faith mission movement*, begins with Hudson Taylor and the foundation of the China Inland Mission (1865) (Fiedler 1992:12–35; cf. Gensichen 1976:31–45) Both mission movements were concerned with the training of missionaries and contributed much to the history of evangelical mission training.

1. The *classical missions* of the early nineteenth century, such as the *Basler Mission* (f. 1815), the *Barmen Mission* (f. 1818) and the *Berliner Mission* (f. 1824) ran their own mission schools. The character of these schools is defined by Wilhelm Schlatter, historian of the *Basler Mission*, as follows:

> The Basler Mission began with a school of mission. This proved decisive as regards one important question. Whereas the old Franckshe Mission in Halle had only men with a university education, trained theologians who were sent to Trankebar – whereas the Moravians made do with simple craftsmen for their missionaries, the Basler Mission deliberately entered new terraine: a specific form of professional training, according to the procedure of Jänike's establishment in Berlin. This allowed them to occupy a middle ground between the two oldest German missions: they viewed neither a living and personal Christian faith as the missionary's complete equipment nor analytical training as an essential prerequisite; rather they emphasized the importance of a spiritual program of specialized training and accentuated the person's normal, inner relationship with his God. In other words, they emphasized a converted heart, which was fundamentally independent of the person's form of professional training (:30–31)

Even though these schools did not survive, they have contributed to the development of evangelical theological education as a model of mission-oriented training outside the university.

2. Many of the evangelical schools under consideration trace their roots back to the so-called *Bible school movement*, which is a child of the second wave of the missionary movement of the nineteenth century, the so-called *faith mission movement* (E. Schmid:38f; Fiedler 1994:144–48). One of *the Schools, Chrischona*, established 1840, has even been understood as the first Bible school of this movement world-wide (Fiedler 1994:145). Others have advanced the same claim for Spurgeon's Pastors' College, founded in 1856, or the East London Institute for Home and Foreign Mission, established in 1873 by Fanny and Grattan Guiness and initiated by Hudson Taylor (Fiedler 1994:145–46; Cheesman 1993:488). The

foundation of similar schools in North America followed soon: the New York Mission Training College (1883), Prairie Bible Institute (1888), Moody Bible Institute (1889) (Fiedler 1994:145–46).

The spirit of the missionary movement of the nineteenth century was the driving force in the early days of the Bible school movement. It is therefore beyond doubt that the early Bible schools were mission-oriented. As Witmer states it:

> *Go ye into all the world and preach the gospel to every creature.* This parting command of the risen Lord is the *raison d'être* for Bible institutes and colleges. It is the base of reference for the direction, the purpose, and the subject matter of Bible college education. The founders and their successors were dominated by the conviction that the church is under compelling obligation to make the gospel of salvation known to all mankind (1962:103).

It is evident that these schools were not academic centres, and it comes as no surprise that they did not contribute much to missiology as an academic discipline. For this reason investigations of the history of mission studies often neglect the Bible school movement (cf. Myklebust 1955; Verkuyl; Kasdorf 1988, 1995). However, the movement has contributed in a unique way to mission training – a fact which any study of the history of mission studies must take into account.

(2) THE ETHOS OF THE BIBLE SCHOOL MODEL

In order to estimate the contribution of the Bible school movement, we have to identify its specific ethos. Observing the North American Bible schools, Cheesman has summarised as follows (:488):[31]

1. 'To train Christian workers without the "corrupting" influence of universities or liberal denominational colleges.' The Bible school movement must be understood as 'a conservative response to the forfeiture of main-line seminaries to theological liberalism between 1890 and 1930,' say Ferris and Enlow in regard to the North American scene (:3).[32]

2. 'To prepare non-ordained missionaries.' Bible schools were mission schools by nature. According to Fiedler, 'they were to provide the new (faith) missions with trained missionaries… . Bible schools were uniquely intended for the training of missionaries/evangelists abroad *and* at home' (1994:144–45).

3. 'To train lay people for witness.' Bible schools expanded ministerial training beyond the limited circle of the academic elite studying in universities and seminaries. 'They were to provide missionary training for those who had no chance of receiving any theological training in the existing institutions, because they were not qualified and/or not wealthy enough to be accepted in them' (Fiedler 1994:144).

4. 'To emphasise spiritual development as key to equipping Christian workers'. A 'warm spiritual environment' as the context of theological education, 'created by scheduling numerous prayer meetings and worship services through the week,' was at the centre of the Bible school ethos (Cheesman:488).

While the Bible school movement had its origin in Europe (England and Switzerland, cf. Fiedler 1994:144–45), it came to its fullest flourishing in North America. Brereton speaks of more than 250 Bible schools founded in North America between 1882 and 1940. In 1960, Witmer counted 250 Bible institutes in North America with 25,000 students (1962:15, 34–38). Beaver estimates that in 1976 'probably the great majority of North American missionaries now serving overseas are graduates of these institutions' (Beavers 1976:85; cf. Conn 1983:3). Taking into consideration that in 1969 33,290 North American missionaries served overseas – more than 70 per cent of all missionaries world-wide – then, the impact of the (North American) Bible school/institute/college movement can hardly be overestimated (Pierard:157–60).

(3) FROM BIBLE SCHOOLS TO BIBLE COLLEGES AND SEMINARIES

However, the Bible school has experienced fundamental changes in the last 40 to 50 years. Most American 'Bible schools' became 'Bible institutes' and later 'Bible colleges'; some have even added a 'seminary.' This transition can be summarised as follows (Ferris and Enlow:3–4; Cheesman:488; Fiedler 1994:148; Egelkraut 1990:33–34):

1. By way of a general classification of the Bible schools, Cheesman, in his typology of theological education models, identifies the Bible schools with the monastic model (Cheesman:487–90). On the one hand, the positive potential of the monastic model was the emphasis on personality formation, somewhat removed from the world, focusing on spiritual formation and community life. This, according to Cheesman, can be very a powerful model of education. On the other hand, it creates an artificial atmosphere in which spirituality and community are scheduled by the institution in a way which has little correspondence with the world the students will later enter.

2. The Bible schools were established with the goal of training young, committed people for mission and Christian service. This intention was based on two presuppositions: (1) One, two or three years in the 'training camp' situation of the Bible school would be an adequate preparation for overseas mission work or full-time church service, and (2) young and single people would attend such schools. With this, Bible schools had the status of vocational schools. But these assumptions have changed: (1) Preparation for full-time service in the church and in mission work requires in most cases more education. Bachelor's and even Master's degrees are required. (2) At the same time the age of students has

increased and many married students with families now seek preparation for full-time ministry (Cheesman:489; Ferris and Englow).

3. In response to new needs, Bible schools started to gain accreditation – but this deeply affected their traditional character. The strength of the Bible school model (spirituality and community) suffered a continuing decrease as Bible schools developed in the direction of more academic colleges. The priority of the academic timetable and the pressure of academic work swamped community life and removed time for spiritual disciplines. Furthermore, it turned out to be difficult to fit community and spiritual formation in a measurable way into the accrediting structure. In most cases, the academics (lectures, study time, papers, books) set the pace (Cheesman: 489).

4. At the same time, the increasing number of older, married students, some even with families, has challenged the closed and structured community life of residential Bible schools. Marriage and family responsibilities, often combined with external living and even part time studies have made it impossible to fit everyone into the 'monastic' schedule of the Bible school.

5. Despite all the changes Ferris and Enlow claim that the Bible school heritage is still alive in many characteristics of contemporary evangelical Bible colleges (:3): (1) commitment to undergraduate preparation for vocational Christian service; (2) commitment to the priority of biblical formation – both mastery of the Bible and mastery by the Bible; (3) commitment to spiritual and ministerial development through the requirement to engage in practical ministry during training; (4) emphasis on Christian character development through setting and enforcing standards; (5) emphasis on indoctrination in orthodoxy as a safeguard to doctrinal purity; (6) emphasis on teaching practical ministry techniques; and (7) emphasis on a view of leadership which stresses the intrinsic authority which accompanies divine appointment and guidance.

6. Finally, as professional demands grew, evangelical pastoral education shifted to the denominational and interdenominational seminaries.[33] In many cases, evangelical Bible colleges have themselves added post-collegiate seminaries to provide adequate academic and professional preparation for pastors. The primary purpose of seminaries is professional pastoral training. As evangelical theological education entered the era of seminary-style pastoral education, many of the classical characteristics of the Bible school heritage were placed in jeopardy. The main focus was now on professional competencies. This changed students' interests, curriculum and the qualifications of faculty. In recent years, North American seminary training has been subjected to harsh critiques (Farley; Lynn; Stewart; Dearborn). Stewart identifies the following five problem areas:

- The tension between the academic competencies in research, reflection and writing and the practical demands of the pastoral task (:43–45).
- The tension between academic performance and the spiritual life of the students (:45–46).
- The increasing age of seminary students with new needs and demands (:46–47).
- The tension 'between those curricula and programmes which are mandated by the school mission and those curriculum and programmes which are driven by the market' (:47).
- Tension in the area of globalization: integrating cross-cultural courses, international students as well as faculty exchange (:48–49).

Concluding reflections: It is this North American Bible school/Bible college movement which has directly or indirectly shaped many of *the Schools*, especially in the post-war period when North American missions increased their activities in Germany. With the development of the North American Bible school ethos, a new force was introduced to the German scene of theological education. Of course, the aforementioned ethos of the Bible school movement had already been present in those older schools rooted in the neo-pietistic *Gemeinschaftsbewegung (Chrischona, Liebenzell, Tabor)*. These mission training schools were outside of the university system. They held a critical stance toward the liberal and critical developments in university theology, and they were closely related to the mission movement. Most of them carried the term 'mission' in their name *(Missionsseminar der Liebenzeller Mission, Prediger- und Missionsschule St. Chrischona)*. The arrival of the North American Bible school movement has certainly strengthened these schools in their identity over against the university establishment. However, the North American Bible school ethos has added some new dimensions not even mentioned by Cheesman since they are axiomatic to North American (conservative) evangelicalism: (1) The Bible school movement has introduced non-denominationalism to an extent formerly unknown in the German context.[34] The majority of the schools associated with the *KBA* have to be identified as non-denominational (see list Appendix A).[35] This fact has added to the tension between established, church- and state-recognised theological education and alternative theological education. While the schools of the neo-pietistic revivals operated in a certain tension with the establishment, they were still part of traditional denominations. Through the invention of North American non-denominationalism, evangelical theological education has moved into greater isolation. (2) However, one can also argue the other way around: as state-church dominated university faculties became more hostile toward conservative theological thinking (as we will demonstrate in chapter 7), the neo-pietistic schools were almost forced to ally themselves with the new evangelical movement from North America. In this way, the North American Bible school movement has strengthened evangelical identity in the German context (cf. Laubach). (3) Furthermore, the American Bible school movement is not only non-denominational but also lacks an understanding of the state-church concept which still dominates the European scene, especially established theological education in Germany and Switzerland. In a certain sense, from the perspective of the state-churches and the state university, American influence has led German evangelical theological education into a sectarian corner. Put the other way around, German evangelical theological education has, under the influence of North American evangelicalism, gained an identity and established its own educational structure, in general without interaction with state-church run university departments. (4) Finally, the North American Bible school movement is closely related to fundamentalism. This means that through North American influence, theological issues were imported to the German context which were not of major significance before, such as (a) the debate on biblical inerrancy, (b) issues related to Calvinism (eternal security), (c) dispensationalism and (d) creationism (anti-Darwinism).

As *the Schools* began to seek academic recognition in the 1970s (see further discussion p. 84) many of them looked again to North America. On the one hand, most of the American Bible schools which had served as their models thirty years earlier had now become theological colleges, offering accredited degrees at the Bachelor's level. On the other hand, denominational and interdenominational evangelical seminaries had developed, offering Master's degrees. Some American Missions have established seminary-level education in the German context (e.g., *FTA*). It goes without saying that Americans were teaching at some of these schools. Furthermore, more than a few of the national teachers at European Bible schools got their training at these North American schools. While some schools sought recognition through direct links with North American institutions, others have invented European accrediting structures modelled on North American accrediting standards and procedures (for the foundation of the EEAA in 1979 see p. 84).

All of this has led to the current situation of evangelical theological education in German-speaking Europe structured mainly according to North American nomenclature. With this *the Schools* have achieved higher academic standards, international recognition and a strengthened identity as a solid tradition of theological education. However, it goes without saying that evangelical theological education in German-speaking Europe has bought into a system which is foreign to their national contexts. The gap between *the Schools* and the educational system of the state and the university remains, or has even grown. Beyond this, by relying on the North American college and seminary model, many evangelical theological schools in Germany and Switzerland have adopted the curriculum and educational structure of North American theological education, a fact which will be critically analysed in Part Four.

With this we have established the general historical background of evangelical theological education and mission studies in German-speaking Europe. This puts us in a position to look in greater detail at the developments of *the Schools* in the time from 1960 to 1995.

Notes

1 We do not explicitly focus on general history and culture; however, whenever political and cultural issues appear to be of greater significance and to deserve attention, they will be included as appropriate.

2 German evangelicalism has been subject of several recent studies: Ludwig Rott's doctoral thesis *Die englischen Beziehungen der Erweckungsbewegung und die Anfänge des wesleyanischen Methodismus in Deutschland* (1968); Hans Hauzenberger's thesis on the history of the Evangelical Alliance (1985); Dieter Lange's dissertation *Eine Bewegung bricht sich Bahn. Die deutschen Gemeinschaften im Ausgehenden 19. und beginnenden 20. Jahrhunderts und ihre Stellung zu Kirche, Theologie und Pfingsbewegung* (1990); Friedhelm Jung's doctoral thesis *Die deutsche Evangelikale Bewegung – Grundlinien ihrer Geschichte und Theologie* (1992); Stephan Holthaus' thesis *Fundamentalismus in Deutschland: Der Kampf um die Bibel im Protestantismus des 19. und 20. Jahrhunderts* (1993); William L. Wagner's thesis *North American Protestant Missionaries in Western Europe: A Critical Appraisal* (1993)., A comprehensive investigation of the *German evangelical mission movement* is much needed. Partial studies have been presented by Dagmar Gleiss in her MA-thesis *Geschichte der Arbeitsgemeinschaft Evangelikaler Missionen, AEM* (1994). Klaus Fiedler's doctoral dissertation on the evangelical interdenominational 'Faith Missions' (1992) discusses German evangelical missions in the context of the wider movement of Faith Missions (:9–35). He also summarises the state of affairs of historical research on German evangelical missions (:35–51). See also his recent article 'It is time to write the History of German-Speaking Evangelical Missions' (1999).

3 According to Beyerhaus, the term *evangelikal* was for the first time used in the German context in 1966 in the context of the Conference on World Evangelisation at Berlin (Geldbach:52; Jung:7).

4 Geldbach writes: 'The movement in Germany called "evangelical" has two roots: (1) The German *Erweckungs- und Gemeinschaftsbewegung* [awakening and community movement] and (2) American influences' (Geldbach 1984: 54). We agree with this definition, adding that the German *Erweckungs- und Gemeinschaftsbewegung* has roots in German Pietism *and* British evangelicalism. Cf. Beyreuther: 'The origin of the entire protestant *Erweckungsbewegung* [awakening movement] is in England' (1977:4).

5 The earliest known occurrence of the label 'Pietism' has been dated in 1689 (Ruhbach 1992b:1571).

6 Bebbington provides a more detailed description of these four aspects on pp. 5–17.

7 'The new thing that England learned from Methodism, and what it then taught the entire world, was organisation of free associations which served

Christian purposes disconnected from the Church. This was the beginning of the age associations in the work for Gods kingdom (vgl. Deutsche Christentumsgesellschaft). With this the boundaries of the old confessional churches were opened. All differences between the clergy and the laity, between the classes, the sexes and the parties disappear. In most cases under the leadership of lay people the goal of this associations, which is the Christianisation of the world, is approached trough Christian principles of civilisation ' (Hauzenberger:28, quoting Hermelink).

8 Of course, the Anabaptists of the 16th century introduced the free church model much earlier. However, under the oppression of the dominating state churches, the Anabaptist-Mennonite movement was marginalised in such a way that it must be regarded as insignificant by the turn of the eighteenth to the nineteenth century (see summary and sources in Ott 1996:32–34.

9 The struggle of the free church movement on German territory and its difficult relationship to the established churches is analysed by Geldbach (1989:108–169).

10 This sketch is mainly based on Kraus ed. 1979; Beyreuther 1977:9–13; and Wagner.

11 To this see H. Richard Niebuhr's critical study *The Social Sources of Denominationalism* first published in 1929.

12 On behalf of the North American denominational mission agency, Mennonite Brethren Missions/Services, this author has conducted an evaluation of their mission work in Germany and Austria in the post-war period. Some of the insights presented in this section are based on this study (see Ott 1995).

13 Further bibliography in Farley 1983:45, 66.

14 In 1990 Robert F. Ferris writes, 'By far the most penetrating critique of theological education structures, and the most challenging call for renewal of ministry training to be heard in recent years, has come from the pen of Edward Farley' (1990:18). Stackhouse even claims that Farley 'is unsurpassed as a diagnostician' (:135).

15 For the further discussion of Farley see p. 234 of this study.

16 Rooy's twenty page article is certainly not comparable with Farley's two-hundred page history of theological education. However, he raises issues from a non-western point of view which have to be taken seriously.

17 Rooy gives the following reference: Charles Davis, *The Downside Review* (October 1963:307–16), cited in J.A.T. Robinson, *La nueva reforma* (Barcelona: Ariel, 1971), p. 109 This source was not accessible to the author.

18 We are at this point not concerned with the entire history of the university, which reaches back to the Middle Ages. In its modern appearance it is a child of the Enlightenment and was fully developed after the political restructuring of continental Europe in the context of the French Revolution in the early 19th century. In this process of development from the university of the Middle Ages to the modern university of the Enlightenment, theology lost its role as the integrative centre of all search for truth and knowledge. As independent reason became the leading force of university *academia*, theology had to struggle for its place in the university (RGG IV:1165–1172). For the modern university see also the critical study by Karl Jaspers: *The Idea of the University*. For the history of the university in Germany see also Friederich Paulsen's two volume work *Geschichte des Gelehrten Unterrichts auf den deutschen Schulen und*

Universitäten vom Ausgang des Mittelalters bis zur Gegenwart. For the North American context George M. Marsden's study *The Soul of the American University*, which gives a comprehensive account of the history of institutions of higher education.

19 In Germany about 30 per cent of all secondary school graduates went to university in 1993 (Lange and Schmid:36; Eurostat 1995:94). In Switzerland the figure is even lower. In 1996–97 about 22 per cent of all students at secondary level II (level 3 according to the UNESCO's International Standard Classification of Education ISCED) were seeking university entrance qualification (Matura) (StJS:423). In comparison, between 50 and 60 per cent (1990 to 1993 figures) of UK students at secondary level II are seeking university entrance qualification (Eurostat 1995:94).

20 'Ein blosses Aggregat disparater Fachinstitute' (RGG VI:1170).

21 They are powerfully summarised by Jaspers:24–43.

22 In a recent interview, two Professors of the Theology Department of Basel University, Ulrich Gaebler and Ekkehard Stegemann, have confirmed that the primary loyalties of theological studies are to the academic field and the university, while the church is only mentioned at a third level. In addition to that, Stegemann views the pastoral task as an academic task, not a practical one. From this he concludes that pastoral education needs to be academic (*Basellandschaftliche Zeitung* 3 April 1998:7).

23 For a more recent introduction to mission studies see Jongeneel 1995. However, Jongeneel does not cover the history of the discipline as extensively as Myklebust.

24 500 schools were surveyed, 65 per cent responded.

25 See Kasdorf 1988, 1994, 1995; Bosch 1991:489–98; the informative summary in Verkuyl:11–19 and most recently Becker's analysis of the German situation (:193–206).

26 Summaries in Verkuyl:11–12; 18–25; Kasdorf 1988:222–25.

27 Myklebust approached more than 500 institutions, 65 per cent responded (:87).

28 One of the most recent contributions in this regard has certainly been presented by Jongeneel (1995; 1998). He not only sums up the history of the debate, he also puts forward a fresh approach, dividing the field of mission studies according to the relevant disciplines of the university, in order to interact meaningfully in the context of the university (1998:29–30).

29 A comprehensive study of *evangelical theological education in German-speaking Europe in general or the Bible school movement in particular* is still a desideratum (Holthaus:318). Helmut Egelkraut's article 'Theological Education in Europe' (1990) summarises some aspects of evangelical theological education on one page. Beyond that, Otto Riecker's *Bildung und Heiliger Geist* needs to be consulted. Günther Wolke's MA thesis (1982) analyses some of the schools regarding curriculum development in the area of mission; however, his work remains very basic and lacks critical reflection.

30 See the discussion of the foundation of the *Albrecht Bengel Haus* at Tubingen, p. 79.

31 Cf. Brereton's *Protestant Fundamentalist Bible Schools 1882–1940* (1981).

32 Similar debates can be observed in the context of the foundation of the *Pilgermission St. Chrischona* in Basel, see Lindt; Burkhardt 1994.

33 Historically, 'the seminary' has to be considered a model of its own. It has its roots in the early 19th century when, in response to the secularisation of the universities (cf. Marsden 1994), alternative schools for pastoral training were founded. From this it follows that the term 'seminary' refers primarily to educational institutions committed to professional pastoral education (cf. Farley 1983; Lynn).

34 Even such schools as *Wiedenest*, which have always emphasised an openness at the level of the Evangelical Alliance, do not operate according to the North American notion of non-denominationalism, which functions as a parachurch structure quite separate from traditional denominational structures. In the case of Wiedenest, one would rather speak of an inter-denominational school which intens to serve various denominations.

35 Today most of them would prefer the term inter-denominational, because they seek to establish links with the existing denominations. However, historically they must be identified as non-denominational.

CHAPTER 6

The Development of Evangelical Theological Education in German-Speaking Europe between 1960 and 1995

We turn now to the period under investigation. The intention is to demonstrate how significant events, internal and external, national and international, have shaped the recent history of *the Schools*. We will cover the time span from the Third Assembly of the WCC at New Delhi in 1961 through the *KBA's* annual assembly in 1995. As we will see, both of them are turning points in the history of *the Schools*.

It is assumed that contemporary evangelical mission and theological education in Germany and Switzerland are shaped not only by the history outlined in the previous sections but by the recent interaction with the surrounding developments in church and society. We will argue that in a situation of identity crisis, German evangelicalism has over a period of several decades come to define itself less from within its own tradition and more in reaction to surrounding movements perceived as a source of danger.[1] There are two different but interdependent currents which have challenged the evangelical movement in the last thirty to forty years: (1) the integration of the IMC into the WCC in 1961 and the following development of an ecumenical theology of mission and (2) the liberal, modernist and critical theology of the established state universities in Germany and Switzerland. Furthermore, we will argue that in this phase of identity crisis, German evangelicals did gain significant strengthening through their relations to North American evangelicals (cf. Laubach).

We present the events of this period in a strictly chronological order, allowing us to follow the historical development, in some places at the cost of a synthetic overview which must be added in chapter 7.

1. Integration of the IMC with the WCC at New Delhi 1961

The integration of the International Missionary Council with the World Council of Churches at New Delhi 1961 has been viewed as a turning-point in the history of mission (Bosch 1991:371). With this event the three strands of the ecumenical movement which grew out of the Edinburgh conference of 1910 became structurally united. What had begun at Edinburgh finally came to its full unfolding. But New Delhi means more than just a structural merger of differing strands of the ecumenical movement. At least in theory, New Delhi stands for the integration of *church* and *mission*, a demand which had been put forward, based on theological insights, since the Willingen conference of 1952. There, the leading theme was 'The Missionary Obligation of the Church.'[2] Willingen stands for the 'shift from an emphasis on a church-centred mission (Tambaram) to a mission centred church' (Bosch 1991:370). This emphasis must be seen against the background of the following situation: on the one hand, churches – especially, at that time, the established churches of the west – were united by the newly founded World Council of Churches (in 1948). On the other hand, mission agencies of various types co-operated in the International Missionary Council.[3] This 'incongruence of a council of churches and a missionary council existing side by side was making itself felt,' and 'Willingen began to flesh out a new model' (Bosch 1991:370). Nine years later, at New Delhi, the vision was put into practice stucturally. The ideal of this integration was expressed with the following words:

> This spiritual heritage [of the mission movement] must not be dissipated; it must remain, ever renewed in the hidden life of prayer and adoration, at the heart of the World Council of Churches. Without it the ecumenical movement would petrify. Integration must mean that the World Council of Churches takes the missionary task to the very heart of its life (quoted in Bosch 1991:371).

However, it remained clear that this development toward integration of churches and missions brought out a fundamental tension between the representatives of established churches and mission agencies. The tension was not at that point of a theological issue, but it was a clash between the *bureaucrats* of the WCC and the *entrepreneurs* of the IMC. The integration of the IMC into the WCC simultaneously provided both the great chance for the churches to become truly missionary but also the danger of missions being paralysed by church bureaucracy. Lesslie Newbigin, who was instrumental in the integration process, was aware of both possibilities. With *One Body. One Gospel. One World* (1958) he presented a well balanced and firm foundation for an integration which would give the churches of the WCC more responsibility for world mission without dominating the mission agencies in a paralysing way. He introduced the now well-known terminology of *dimenion* and *intention*, by which he was able to set the missionary dimension of the whole life of the church in creative tension with the missionary intention carried out by mission societies (:21).[4]

However, when the integration was realised in 1961, the various mission agencies responded to it differently, according to their relation to the churches of the WCC. The following responses can be identified. (a) Mission societies run by churches of the WCC were most easily integrated. (b) The semi-independent missions which grew out of the revival movements within national churches which belong to the WCC tended toward closer relationships with their mother churches and with this toward integration into the new structure. This was the case with many of the pietistic and neo-pietistic missions in Germany which were associated with the Lutheran church.[5] (c) Mission agencies belonging to churches which were not members of the WCC could hardly find a place in the new structure. This applied to many evangelical churches of a free church orientation, especially for a large number of North American missions.[6] (d) Interdenominational missions were in a similar situation. This means that the integration of the IMC into the WCC contained a series of problems which were not automatically solved by Newbigin's proposal. However, the key issue which caused conflicts was at heart not of a theological nature – presumably most missions could have been integrated on the basis of Newbigin's theological conception – but was concerned rather with the issue of established church structures with regard to voluntary missionary movements.

Nonetheless, in order to understand the tensions which occurred soon after the integration at New Delhi, certain undercurrents of theological issues must be recognised. This author sees at least two: (a) the divergence between the more conservative, orthodox strand of Christianity on one side and the more liberal, critical strand on the other was an undercurrent throughout the development of the ecumenical movement in the twentieth century. Despite the fact that key leaders of the ecumenical movement – Hendrik Kraemer, Karl Freytag, Lesslie Newbigin, to name only a few – were able to play an integrative role, the issues of liberalism, historical criticism and secularism were on the (sometimes hidden) agenda of all the ecumenical meetings. (b) However, there is another theological issue which is also part of the picture. There has always been a tension between Lutherans and Calvinists. Those theologians of a more Lutheran orientation (mostly Germans and Scandinavians), with their emphasis on the sinfulness of humanity, the individual's justification by faith, pessimism regarding the transformation of society (the doctrine of the two kingdoms) and a strong eschatological orientation, were decisively sceptical about all attempts at world transformation, be it through world evangelisation or through the peace and justice movements. On the other hand, theologians of a more Calvinistic orientation, with their emphasis on the sovereignty of God, the kingdom of God and the transforming power of God, seem to be more enthusiastic about the great project of world transformation, be its emphasis on evangelisation or on humanisation. Much of what will be observed in this study can be seen as the emergence of these theological undercurrents.

With this we have established something like the point of departure for a great debate on missionary structures and mission theology – a debate which divided Protestant Christianity in the following years. At the centre of this debate, *the Schools* developed a new identity in the 1960s and 1970s.

2. The Foundation of the *Konferenz Bibeltreuer Ausbildungsstätten* (*KBA*) 1963–1964

We now turn to the foundation of the association of schools which are subject of this investigation. At the first meeting of the newly founded *Konferenz Bibeltreuer Ausbildungsstätten (KBA)* in 1964, the topic *'Einheit der Gemeinde Jesu – oder Ökumene?'* [The Unity of Jesus' Community – or Ecumenism?] was on the agenda. This shows that the *KBA* took to heart issues concerning the development of the ecumenical movement from the very beginning. However, this is only part of the picture. The *KBA* must primarily be seen as a child of the anti-modernist attempts of German fundamentalism.[7] In his thesis, Stephan Holthaus defines the key element of fundamentalism as defending the verbal inspiration and hence inerrancy of the Bible against the attacks of historical criticism. This leads directly to a second element, an 'anti-Darwinist,' i.e., 'creationist,' position and a third element, a 'pre-millenialist/ dispensationalist' view of eschatology (:63–68, cf. Geldbach 1993).[8]

Holthaus also established the thesis that German fundamentalism grows out of the German conservative movements of Pietism and revivalism and that it is significantly inspired by North American fundamentalism. In the 1960s, the fundamentalist voices were directed mainly against the historical-critical method and the demythologisation and existential interpretation of the Bible propounded by the Bultmannian school.

One of the leading figures of the fundamentalist movement was Heinrich Jochums, director of the *Evangelische Gesellschaft für Deutschland* and of the *Bibelseminar Wuppertal* (Holthaus 1993:244–46). Jochums took the initiative for the first meeting of representatives from the various Bible schools. On 6 January, 1964, he invited all schools to send delegates to a consultation held on 11 November, 1964, at Wuppertal (Archive *KBA*: Letter 6/1/64). Prior to this first larger gathering, a meeting between the faculties of the *Bibelseminar Wuppertal* and the *Bibelschule Brake* took place on 5 December, 1963, also initiated by Jochums. These events should be viewed as the beginning of what is today called the *Konferenz Bibeltreuer Ausbildungsstätten (KBA)*.

In his invitation of 6 January, 1964, Jochums explicitly defined which schools he wanted to be part of the new association:

> We agreed from the beginning that such a meeting would be meaningful only among those Bible schools that agreed with us that Jesus is the Son of God and our Lord and Saviour; that they would therefore reject any criticism of his Word, the Holy Scriptures; that they would freely and unconditionally allow themselves to be called into the service of the Lord Jesus and would strive to prepare others for such service (Archive *KBA*: Letter 6/1/64).

The following thirteen institutions followed this invitation: from Germany: *Bibelschule Adelshofen, Bibelschule Berlin, Bibelschule Brake, Bibelschule Hagen, Bibelschule Hamburg, Bibelschule Klostermühle, Bibelschule Neukirchen, Bibelschule Seeheim, Bibelschule Wiedenest, Bibelseminar Wuppertal* and *Soldatenmission Koblenz*. From Switzerland: *Bibelschule Aarau,* from the Netherlands: *Bibelschule t'Brandpunt* (Archive *KBA*: List of schools 11/11/64).

At this first consultation, a board was installed and decided to meet annually. The board met for the first time 9 December, 1964, and a second meeting took place 12 February, 1965. At these meetings the name *Konferenz bibelgläubiger Seminare und Lehrer* was given to the new association and the confession of faith of the *Evangeliums Rundfunk* was adopted as a binding foundation for member schools of the association (Archive *KBA*: minutes 12/2/64). The *Evangeliums Rundfunk* was founded in 1959 as the German branch of Trans-World-Radio. Its confession was clearly evangelical, very close to that of the Evangelical Alliance (Jung:45). It emphasises the inerrancy of the Bible, a fundamentalist characteristic which the founders of the *KBA* considered very important (Holthaus 1993:320–21; cf. Jochums in Archive *KBA*: Letter 6/1/63).

In the following years more schools joined the association and annual meetings have been held. In 1976 the name was altered to *Konferenz Bibeltreuer Ausbildungsstätten (KBA*). In 1977 twenty four schools were associated with the *KBA,* in 1997 the number was thirtysix (see Appendix A).

We conclude. From the very beginning of the *KBA,* two major issues were on the agenda of the association: (1) the developments of the ecumenical movement and the question how *the Schools* should relate to it; and (2) the key issue of fundamentalism – namely, the inerrancy of the Bible and the condemnation of historical-critical exegesis. Both are basically apologetic issues. In both cases, the *KBA* schools began to define themselves over against movements which they perceived as dangerous. With this we have already identified the backbone of conservative German evangelicalism as it developed in the 1960s and 1970s.

3. *Bibelbund* Reaffirmed 'Inerrancy Statement' 1966

Following a historical chronology, we now turn to an event which further contributed to the conservative evangelicalism of the *KBA*. 1966 is a noteworthy date in the history of the *Bibelbund* because a period of discussion concerning the inerrancy issue was at that time terminated with a strong reaffirmation of the inerrancy of the Bible (Holthaus 1993:216). What is the *Bibelbund*? Its history is much older and goes back to 1894. The *Bibelbund* represents an unbroken confession of the inspiration and inerrancy of the Bible. As such, Holthaus (:189–219) views it as one of the classical fundamentalist movements in Germany.

The 1966 decision for a strong reaffirmation of inerrancy was taken under the leadership of Samuel Külling, a name which should be kept in mind in the context of evangelical theological education in the German-speaking sphere. He presented one of the most powerful defences of the conservative evangelical movement *against* the historical-critical method and for *alternative* theological training in independent evangelical seminaries. In the same year, 1966, the theological journal of the *Bibelbund* published Külling's paper '*Das Übel an der Wurzel erfassen*,' a decisive summary of Külling's concerns and vision (Külling; cf. Holthaus 1993:217; 321–22). Külling maintained contacts with international fundamentalist circles, was one of the speakers at the International Council of Christian Churches' (ICCC) meeting at Worms in 1967, and served on the International Council for Biblical Inerrancy (ICBI) (Holthaus 1993:217).

The *Bibelbund* is of major significance for the Bible school movement under consideration. Not only has Samuel Külling, president of the *Bibelbund* from 1966 to 1979, become through the foundation in Basel of the *Freie Evangelisch-Theologische Akademie FETA* (Free Evangelical Theological Academy),[9] one of the most notable contemporary leaders in evangelical theological education in the German-speaking context, but many of the Bible school leaders and teachers associated with the *KBA* were—and still are – members of the *Bibelbund*. Holthaus concludes that 'the *Bibelbund* became the most visible sign of a fundamentalist position to the Bible in German' (1993:218), therefore the conclusion must be drawn that this fundamentalist position has been powerfully taught at the Bible schools of the *KBA*.[10] This connection of the Bible school movement with the fundamentalist inerrancy movement requires critical evaluation in the following parts of the thesis.

4. Wheaton and Berlin 1966

The chronology now returns us to developments in the mission movement and to the international scene. The conferences in Wheaton and Berlin mark the developments in the mission movement after the integration of the IMC with the WCC in 1961. We mentioned earlier that the North American evangelical missions interpreted the integration as a 'colossal loss' or even a 'mean betrayal' – to quote Winter again (Hedlund:155). Hedlund (:156) puts the view of American evangelicals as follows:

> Edinburgh had been both evangelical (dedicated to world evangelization) and ecumenical. It was generally inclusive. Hudson Taylor's China Inland Mission was as welcome as was the Basel Mission of Switzerland, the Church Missionary Society of England, or the American Baptist Foreign Mission Society. When organizational evolution and philosophical reorientation virtually excluded the evangelicals from world missionary structures, it is not surprising that they develop alternative means for cooperate expression. Nor is it unusual that these expressions concerned evangelism. Three events of evangelical significance took place at Wheaton and Berlin in 1966 and at Greenlake in 1971... . These three events indicate the rising evangelical leadership.

From a German point of view we are concerned above all with the Berlin Congress, but need to take a short look at Wheaton.

1. The Wheaton Congress took place over Easter 1966 and was devoted to the theme 'The Church's World-Wide Mission.' The congress brought together almost 1000 delegates from seventy one countries and more than 150 mission boards. In response to the integration of the IMC into the WCC and its implications for the evangelical mission movement, 'they set about to define their position, to express their needs for closer fellowship, and to reaffirm biblical principles of mission. The mandate to evangelise the world was to be affirmed in the light of the present world situation' (Hedlund:156). The 'Wheaton Declaration' (Hedlund:169–84) was issued, a mission statement which subsequently became one of the cornerstones to the understanding of mission for many evangelicals.[11]

2. In a certain way, the Berlin Congress stands on the shoulders of the Wheaton congress. While Wheaton focused on world mission, Berlin emphasised evangelisation under the heading 'One Race, One Gospel, One Task.' In his plenary address, Billy Graham linked the Berlin Congress to the Edinburgh Conference of 1910:

> Fifty six years ago a World Missionary Conference at Edinburgh, Scotland, met to consider the opportunities of evangelizing the world in their generation... . In many circles today the Church has an energetic passion for unity, but it has all but forgotten our Lord's commission to evangelize. One of the purposes of this World

> Congress on Evangelism is to make an urgent appeal to the world Church to return to the dynamic zeal for world evangelization that characterized Edinburgh 56 years ago (Hedlund:185).

From a German point of view, the congress must be seen in close relation to Billy Graham's ministry in Germany in the years following World War II (cf. Laubach:83–7; Jung:47; Schrupp 1995:145–46). He was also a key figure at the Berlin Congress of 1966. The International Congress on World Evangelization was sponsored by the North American journal *Christianty Today* and its editor, C. F. H. Henry, on the journal's tenth anniversary. Held at Berlin with Billy Graham as its honourary chairman, it can be seen as the culmination of Graham's ministry in Germany (Laubach:83–7; Hedlund:161). While there was no direct organisational link between the mass evangelisation by Graham just prior to the congress and the international congress itself, it definitely marks a turning point in the shaping of German evangelicalism (Jung:48–49). It was in the context of the Berlin Congress that German evangelicals – or Christians associated with the German Evangelical Alliance – began to use the Germanised word *evangelikal* for themselves and thus identified themselves with the international (or American) evangelical movement. This marks the breakthrough of a new identity in German evangelicalism (Jung:7)

What does this mean for the shaping of the German evangelical identity? (1) First of all it constitutes a selective association with one segment of the world-wide evangelical movement. With this German evangelicals laid the foundation of a strong relationship to North American evangelicals, which developed in subsequent years. (2) At the same time it seems that relationships to other strands of the global evangelical movement played only a marginal role. German evangelicals developed only minimal contacts with British evangelicals or to evangelicals of the Two Thirds World. (3) With their strong relations to American evangelicalism, German evangelicals have also exposed themselves to an evangelical strand which represents very different ecclesial traditions and structures, characterised by parachurch organisations, interdenominational missions and voluntarism. Those denominational ties which American missions have are certainly with younger denominations of free church orientation. As a result the synthesis of North American evangelical understanding of the church with the ecclesial traditions of continental Europe has become a key issue in the development of evangelicalism in German-speaking Europe.[12]

5. The Foundation of the *Arbeitsgemeinschaft Evangelikaler Missionen (AEM)* 1969[13]

We now turn to one of the most crucial issues after the merger of the IMC with the WCC in 1961 – namely, the consequences of this merger for mission agencies. Prior to the foundation of the *Arbeitsgemeinschaft Evangelikaler Missionen (AEM)* most of the Protestant missions in Germany associated with one another through the *Deutsche Evangelische Missions-Tag (DEMT)* (German Protestant Mission Day [=annual conference]) and its leading board, the *Deutsche Evangelische Missionsrat (DEMR)* (German Protestant Mission Council). These two institutions go back to the *Deutsche Evangelische Missionsbund* (German Protestant Mission Alliance) founded in 1922 and even to the *Deutsche Evangelische Missionsausschuss* which was founded by Gustav Warneck in 1885 (LWM:108; Gleiss 8–9). The *DEMT/DEMR* was a member of the IMC and the missions related to it were affected by the integration of the IMC in 1961. After 1961 most of the missions remained together in the *DEMT/DEMR* (Gleiss:9). As mentioned earlier, the significance of the merger of the IMC with the WCC for particular missions must be seen in connection to the agencies' relations to particular denominations. German missions' various responses to the new situation must be assessed from this point of view. (1) In 1963 the *Evangelische Kirche in Deutschland (EKD)* took the initiative in restructuring those missions related to the regional Lutheran churches. The goal was the restructuring of the *DEMT/DEMR* towards regional, church-based co-operatives (Rennstich:577; LWM:225–26; 455). Through this act the older missions were integrated into the WCC through their formal relationship to the Lutheran church (Gleiss:9–10; LWM:108–12; Fiedler:17). (2) More difficult was the situation for the neo-pietistic missions, which were closely related to the faith mission movement (e.g., the Liebenzeller Mission). Historically, these missions are associated with the *Gemeinschaftsbewegung*. They hold a much more critical position towards the official policy and theology of the Lutheran church. They were heavily involved in the internal struggle within the Lutheran church between its more conservative, neo-pietistic wing and the more liberal, critical movement of the Lutheran Church in general. For the further development of this thesis it is important to notice that it is within this group that Peter Beyerhaus found his place and the *Frankfurt Declaration* its context. (3) For the missions of the free churches which were not members of the WCC (such as the Wiedenester Mission) the situation was again different. On the one hand, a formal relationship to the WCC was not an option for them anyway. On the other hand they were not involved in pro- or contra-ecumenical struggles within their churches – as were the missions of the *Gemeinschaftsbewegung* – and this gave them the freedom to act more freely in relation to the *DEMT/DEMR*, as well as to the emerging evangelical association. Ernst Schrupp of *Wiedenest* is a good example of this position. Schrupp, at that time director of the *Missionshaus Bibelschule Wiedenest*, was at the same time the initiator of the *AEM* and active as an evangelical in the *DEMR* until 1973 (cf. Schrupp 1995:144–45). (4) Finally some interdenominational missions were basically in a similar situation. However, some of them were American international missions (WEC; Wycliff) and therefore more strongly influenced by the anti-ecumenical position of North American evangelicalism.

In the years after 1961 there was a great deal of insecurity about how the co-operation of missions would look in the future. Which missions would build relations to the WCC? Which would not? How would missions relate to churches – that is, how could one put into practice on a national level what had been performed on the global level at New Delhi? What role would the *DEMT/DEMR* play in these new circumstances?

By the middle of the 1960s, evangelical missions increasingly felt themselves excluded from the new ecumenical structures. For many missions this was, first of all, a structural issue, because they lacked church relations which could have connected them with the WCC. However, several other impulses finally led to the foundation of the *AEM*. (1) The aforementioned impact of the Berlin Congress on German evangelicals was a critical influence on the establishment of an association of evangelical missions. (2) An increasing dissatisfaction with the theological course taken by the ecumenical mission movement in the second half of the 1960s supported the idea of the foundation of an evangelical association. The ecumenical assembly at Uppsala in 1968 marks something of a turning point. Many leaders of those evangelical missions which had been integrated into the WCC after 1961 hoped to influence the WCC toward missionary thinking and acting consonant with evangelical missionary values. However, such hopes were shattered at Uppsala for many evangelicals perceive it as a definite turning away from an orthodox, biblical understanding of mission towards a purely secular humanisation (Gleiss:24–27; Beyerhaus 1970a). (3) Finally, the shaping of an evangelical missionary identity which finally led to the foundation of the *AEM* cannot be understood apart from the contributions of Peter Beyerhaus. The Lutheran theologian returned from a mission assignment in Southern Africa in 1966 and immediately involved himself in the great, contemporary debate about mission. As a Lutheran pastor with conservative, neo-pietistic convictions, he became Professor of Mission in the Protestant Theological Faculty of the University at Tübingen, and he decisively took sides with the growing evangelical cause (Beyerhaus 1987:IX). In 1969 he published his answer to Uppsala, *Humanisierung: Einzige Hoffnung der Welt*? It will be pointed out later how deeply

Beyerhaus has influenced large parts of the young evangelical movement in Germany. Especially after 1970, his strong anti-ecumenical position became basic for the *AEM* and with it for the *KBA* Bible school movement.

Based on this background information the concrete foundation of the *AEM* can now be summarised as follows: following Berlin 1966, Ernst Schrupp (*Wiedenest*) became the key leader in bringing together evangelical missions in Germany. Commissioned by the board of the German Evangelical Alliance, he invited in 1968 some thirty German evangelical mission agencies to a first meeting in Frankfurt in 1969.[14] The topic of this first gathering was 'Evangelical – What is it?' Subsequently the *Konferenz Evangelikaler Missionen (KEM)* (Conference of Evangelical Missions) became institutionalised and later renamed as the *Arbeitsgemeinschaft Evangelikaler Missionen (AEM)* (Schrupp 1995:146; Gleiss:28–30).

The new association did not intend to place itself in opposition to the ecumenical structures of the *DEMT* but understood itself as a complementary institution for fellowship and co-operation among evangelical missions. Out of the twenty six founding members, about half still co-operated with the *DEMT* (Gleiss:29–31). However, the tension between the *DEMT* and the *AEM* grew in the subsequent years, and the foundation of the *AEM* has in a certain way also contributed to the split in the German missionary movement.

The *AEM* grew into a significant force for the enhancement of the evangelical mission movement in Germany. Various additional mission related institutions were initiated by the *AEM* (Mann:113–14). In connection with our subject, the foundation of the *Freie Hochschule für Mission (FHM)* (Free Graduate School for Mission) in 1979 (see below), the *Arbeitskreis für evangelikale Missiologie (AfeM)* (Association for Evangelical Missiology) in 1985 (Troeger:115–16) and the publication of the missiological journal *Evangelikale Missiologie (em)* need to be kept in mind as significant contributions to evangelical mission studies in the German-speaking context.

The origin of the Swiss *AEM* must be seen in relation to the aforementioned developments in Germany. However, the split between ecumenical and evangelical mission agencies did not stand at the centre of the developments in Switzerland – only the desire of evangelical missions to engage each other in more close relationships. Consequently, the Swiss *AEM* functions in a less controversial and less anti-ecumenical climate than its German counterpart. While the German *AEM* holds the *Frankfurt Declaration* as one of its foundational documents, the Swiss *AEM* expects its members to subscribe to the less apologetic *Lausanne Covenant*. This also affects the evangelical theological schools related to the *AEM* (Reifler:66–67).[15]

In 1992 the German *AEM* assembled fiftytwo evangelical mission agencies with more than 1,800 missionaries on five continents (Mann:113). According to Schrupp, this constituted about 80 per cent of all the German Protestant missionaries working abroad at that time (1995:146).[16] The Swiss branch counted thirtytwo mission agencies in 1997, supporting 900 missionaries (Reifler:66). Most of these missionaries received their training in one of *the Schools*.

6. The *Konferenz Bekennender Gemeinschaften (KBG)* 1970[17]

Now we must shift to yet another stream within the German evangelical movement (Jung:31–34) which at first sight is not related either to the ecumenical-missionary, nor the inerrancy issue. However, the *Konferenz Bekennender Gemeinschaften (KBG)*, founded in 1970, became one of the most powerful instruments for the defence of the anti-ecumenical and anti-modernist position of German conservative evangelicals.

It is difficult to date precisely the beginning of the movement which finally led to the foundation of the *KBG* in 1970. A group of concerned theologians met as early as 1961 to discuss and refute Bultmann's programme of demythologisation and existential interpretation of scripture. The group became known as the 'Bethel-Circle,' after their meeting place (Jung:89–91). Jung speaks of the consolidation of the movement after 1966 as a broad based force in the struggle against neo-liberalism in theology and the church. It was also in that year that the Bethel-Circle was renamed *Bekenntnisbewegung 'Kein anderes Evangelium'* (Confessional Movement 'No Other Gospel') (Jung:94–106). In order to engage in a more serious theological controversy with 'Modern Theology,' a theological committee called *Theologischer Konvent* was added in 1969. Besides the *Bekenntnisbewegung 'Kein anderes Evangelium,'* other similar movements sprang up in the 1960s. There were mutual contacts but no unifying structure. At Peter Beyerhaus's initiative, the various confessional movements joined in 1970 to found the *Konferenz Bekennender Gemeinschaften (KBG)* (Jung:106). Critical reflection and apologetic declarations in many fields have been the products of the *KBG* and its *Theologische Konvent*. In view of the subject of this study, it is important to notice that mission and the ecumenical movement belonged to the main issues dealt with (Jung:100). The declarations issued by the *Theologische Konvent* have influenced both the evangelical mission movement in Germany and evangelical theological education, as will be shown later.

7. The *Frankfurt Declaration* 1970[18]

The *Frankfurt Declaration* must be discussed in close relation to Peter Beyerhaus and the *Theologische Konvent*. It became one of the key documents for German evangelical missions and *the Schools*. The *AEM* accepted it as one of its foundational statements in 1972 (Mann:113; Beyerhaus 1987:273). Gleiss (:39) concludes that 'it [the *Frankfurt Declaration*] unified the evangelical missions and strengthened them'. After 1972 subscription to the *Frankfurt Declaration* was one of the requirements for membership in the *AEM* (Gleiss:41).[19]

The *Frankfurt Declaration* was issued by the *Theologische Konvent* in March 1970. The seven statements were proposed by Peter Beyerhaus and Georg Vicedom (Berneburg 1992:622; Beyerhaus 1970:28). Still in response to developments in the ecumenical theology of mission at the Uppsala assembly, it articulates a strongly anti-ecumenical evangelical confession (Beyerhaus 1970:28–37).

The *Frankfurt Declaration* received a mixed reception. (1) Many evangelicals appreciated it as a clear statement in difficult times and adopted it as the foundation for an evangelical understanding of mission. (2) Others acknowledged the statement's intentions but did not subscribe to its aggressively apologetic tone (Beyerhaus 1987:18–25; Gleiss:41). (3) Finally, ecumenicals perceived it as the confrontation which ultimately caused the split within the mission movement (cf. Rennstich:577–78).

While Beyerhaus claims a world-wide impact for the *Declaration* (1987:21–22), others see its significance as limited to the European and North American context (Hedlund:250).

In the context of evangelical theological education in Germany, the *Frankfurt Declaration* became one of the key documents in the teaching of mission. It is positively integrated in such significant textbooks as Klaus Bockmühl's *Was heisst heute Mission* (1974:155–58). This will be further assessed in Part Three.

In 1973, after the WCC mission conference at Bangkok, and in 1976 after the WCC's assembly at Nairobi, the *Theologische Konvent* put out additional statements which sharply criticised further developments in the ecumenical understanding of mission (Beyerhaus 1973:233–35; 1976:338–42).[20]

If we review the years from 1963 (the foundation of the *KBA*) through 1970 (the issuing of the *Frankfurt Declaration*), we see that the German evangelical movement associated with *the Schools* strengthened its identity continually: new associations were established and identity-statements were issued. The general direction of all these identity-building steps is evident: the promotion of a clear anti-ecumenical and anti-modernist position. What we have described as an emerging backbone of conservative German evangelicalism has grown into a solid identity, which was, seemingly, strong enough to implement the next significant step.

8. The Foundation of Alternative, University-Level Evangelical Theological Training in 1970

The decision to establish an alternative evangelical school operating academically at the university level, implementing the theological identity developed in the 1960s, grew out of many evangelicals' deep dissatisfaction with the state of affairs at the Protestant faculties of the state universities. The issues were discussed in the 1960s in the realm of the *Bekenntnisbewegung*, the *Pfarrergebetsbruderschaft* (Prayer Fellowship of Pastors), as well as in the *Bibelbund* (Külling 1966; Beyerhaus 1996:13) and in evangelical Bible schools (e.g., *Bergstrasse*, cf. Stadelmann 1996:29). As mentioned earlier, Samuel Külling's paper *Das Übel an der Wurzel erfassen* ('Attacking the Evil at its Roots', 1966) was something of a ground breaker for the foundations of an alternative, evangelical theological seminary at university level (Holthaus:217, 321). Külling himself realised this vision by establishing the *Freie Evangelisch-Theologische Akademie (FETA)* in Basel, today named *Staatsunabhängige Theologische Hochschule (STH)*. But besides the *FETA/STH* project, other plans to realise alternative means of theological training were explored during the same period of time. At the *Bibelschule Bergstrasse*, an institution founded by the North American evangelical 'Greater Europe Mission' in 1955, the extension of the programme toward graduate studies at a university level was already discussed early in the 1960s; serious plans for the foundation of an alternative theological faculty were discussed in 1966–67 (Stadelmann:29). The *Freie Theologische Akademie (FTA)* started with eight students its first academic year in the fall of 1974 at Seeheim. In 1981 the school moved to Giessen (Stadelmann:30, 33–34). Through its connection to Greater Europe Mission, the founders of the *FTA* were inspired by North American evangelical seminaries (Stadelmann:31). Up to the present time, these two institutions represent alternative theological training at a university level (graduate studies), based on conservative evangelical convictions – especially, the inspiration and inerrancy of the Bible.[21]

Alongside of the foundation of alternative and independent new schools, attempts were made to establish evangelical theological study centres in university cities in order to support evangelical students during their studies at the state universities. Hence, it was also in 1970 that the *Albrecht-Bengel-Haus (ABH)* opened its doors at Tübingen. As the name of the centre suggests, the *ABH* is committed to a pietistic heritage. It was established by concerned theologians and pastors from the Lutheran church of Württemberg, from the pietistic fellowship of the *Ludwig-Hofacker-Vereinigung* and from the University of Tübingen. One of its initiators and its first academic dean was Peter Beyerhaus (Beyerhaus 1996b). Similar institutions have been established since then in other university cities – Heidelberg, Marburg, Mainz (Holland:34).

A third model of university-level evangelical theological training was realised by the *Geistliches Rüstzentrum Krelingen* (Cochlovius 1993; Cochlovius 1996) and the *J. J. Rambach Institut für Theologie und Kirche*, an institution of the *Freie Theologische Akademie* at Giessen (Stadelmann:33–34). These institutions offer preparatory courses for studies at state universities. They cover the biblical languages (Hebrew and Greek) and an introduction to the study of theology, with a focus on hermeneutics based on evangelical convictions (Cochlovius 1996:27–28)

All these attempts – as different as they are in confessional orientation and educational structure – understand themselves as a significant evangelical contribution to Protestant theological education. They grew, in their view, out of the concern for future church leadership trained in accordance with the orthodox, biblical tradition and out of disappointment with the theological faculties of the state universities, which, influenced by liberalism, historical criticism and modernist-Marxist thinking, eroded the foundations of biblical faith. By establishing new, alternative institutions for Protestant theological training, they are challenging the monopoly of state universities in higher theological training.

The foundation of these institutions must be interpreted as an answer to the developments within state church dominated universities. Under the axiom of open and free academic research, university theology developed toward the secularisation of theology, which found expression in the biblical criticism movement and led to theological exploration which was not rooted in believing faith. However, whilst the university claims to be objective and open to all points of view, it became clear that it was intolerant of conservative and evangelical points of view.

A closer look at the newly founded institutions introduced in this chapter shows that various evangelical groups responded differently to this situation: (1) The *Bengel-Haus* and the *Rüstzentrum Krelingen* are related to the neo-pietistic revival movement *(Gemeinschaftsbewegung)* within the Lutheran Church. These schools do not draw students from the universities but offer evangelical support while students are studying at the theological departments of state universities. These initiatives do not question the state-church system nor the theological faculties of state universities. They intend to work from within the system towards the recognition of orthodox, evangelical theology within the state-church system – and ultimately towards the restoration of orthodox faith. In this case 'alternative' does not imply that the existing system of state churches and university training needs to be replaced, rather that it needs to be reformed. (2) A different approach has been chosen by the *FTA* at Giessen. This seminary, founded by North American evangelicals and today run by Germans, is interdenominational and intends to offer a clear alternative to the theological training in state universities. The seminary promotes a strong free church ecclesiology even though some professors hold to a state-church view. The main goal is to train pastors capable of leading evangelical churches, be it in the context of free church denominations or within the Lutheran state-church. Here we have to speak of a clear alternative both to theological training in state universities and to the state church itself. (3) Finally, the *STH* at Basel combines the two aforementioned philosophies in a particular way. Founded by a pastor of the Reformed Church of Switzerland (S. Külling) it focuses on the training of pastors for the state church in order to renew the church from within. Beyond that, the school also trains pastors for various free church denominations. Professors come either from a state church or a free church background. However, in contrast to the founders of the *ABH*, Külling decisively holds the position that evangelical, Bible-based theological training is only possible in alternative seminaries where all professors are committed to the inerrancy of the Bible. In this sense the seminary does not seek any co-operation with theological departments of state universities. This seminary represents a clear alternative to theological training in state universities, yet it does not fundamentally question the state-church system.

From the viewpoint of the schools analysed in this study, two more aspects need to be mentioned: (1) All the institutions referred to in this section, except the *STH* at Basel, are members of the *KBA* and/or the European Evangelical Accrediting Association EEAA, and (2) many teachers at evangelical Bible schools were trained at these theological academies and seminaries. Thus, the impact of these seminaries on the Bible school movement must be recognised.

9. The *Frankfurt Statement* on Bangkok 1973

The chronology now brings us back to the international ecumenical scene, to examine the conference of the WCC's Commission on World Mission and Evangelism (CWME) in Bangkok in 1973. We are especially interested in how conservative German evangelicals responded to the development of the WCC's missionary thinking and how this contributed to the shape of the identity of German evangelicalism and theological education.

The Bangkok Conference of the CWME stands between the General Assemblies of Uppsala 1968 and Nairobi 1974 (see list of ecumenical conferences Appendix B, p. 320) and was devoted to the topic 'Salvation Today'.[22] What are some of the achievements of Bangkok?

1. Bangkok was a distinctive conference first of all because of its methods and its style. Bangkok put more emphasis on community, worship, witness and celebration than any of the earlier ecumenical conferences. At its centre was the process of an open encounter between people from all continents (Potter:7–8; Beyerhaus 1973:43–80).

2. One of the main achievements of Bangkok was the formulation of a so-called 'comprehensive' definition of mission including the social, economic and political as well as the personal and eschatological dimensions of salvation (Potter:196; cf. Werner 1993:119–24; 201).

3. Bangkok moved also beyond the western-centred concept of humanisation – the leading notion of Uppsala – to the concept of liberation in the various contexts of oppression in the world (Potter:9; Werner 1993:200–06). With this a further significant step was taken away from a western-dominated understanding of mission.

4. Along these lines the significance of the context in the articulation of salvation gained significance. Potter (:9) writes, with special reference to the German churches:

> We must fully realise how strongly our theological and ecclesiological convictions – which dictate both form and content – are determined by the cultural conditions of our respective standpoints and by our times. This task is particularly urgent in a land like Germany, which boasts such a rich theological tradition and, what is more, has gone through such far-reaching changes over the last sixty years. But it is, fundamentally, a task which poses itself to every people in every land.

5. A significant place was given to the theme of partnership within the global church (Potter:214–17; Beyerhaus 1973:228–31). In order to leave room for the development of real partnership between the western churches and the young churches of the Two Thirds World, western churches were urged to withdraw all dominating missionary activities. In this context a limited 'moratorium' on western missionary activities was suggested (Potter: 216; Beyerhaus 228–31).

6. In retrospect Bangkok has been interpreted as the 'hour of the Third World' (cf. Werner 1993:119–24; 200–15), the end of the missionary era of the western church and the beginning of world mission (Emilio Castro, quoted in Beyerhaus 1973:31).

In general evangelicals have assessed Bangkok negatively. The most severe critiques were articulated by American evangelicals (cf. Winter ed. 1973; Hedlund:257–89; Johnston:267–82), as well as by conservative German and Scandinavian Lutherans. We concentrate on the German response put forward by Beyerhaus and the *Theologische Konvent*. Beyerhaus formulates his critique by means of seven questions (Beyerhaus 1973:13–135):

1. 'With what sort of salvation was the theme of Bangkok concerned?' For Beyerhaus, despite the promising theme of 'Salvation Today,' Bangkok maintained a one-sided horizontal understanding of salvation as humanisation and liberation. He expressed deep disappointment that

all the concerns articulated by conservative evangelicals since Uppsala had been ruled out by 'those from Geneva.' Beyerhaus identifies the lack of authority attributed to the Bible as the key problem. In his assessment, the leaders of the ecumenical movement defined salvation solely on what the world expresses as need. With this, the transcendent and eschatological dimension of salvation was abandoned.

2. 'Where do we locate the task and meaning of Bangkok?' Beyerhaus views Bangkok as a further step on the way to the integration of the IMC into the WCC, intentionally and strategically planned by WCC staff. After the *organisational* integration at New Delhi, Bangkok accomplished the *ideological* integration. Given the fact that WCC leadership had opted for a humanistic, secular understanding of the church's mission at the expense of a biblical view, this means that the positive IMC heritage had definitively been given up at Bangkok.

3. 'How would those in Bangkok have answered the question of salvation?' The methodology and style of the Bangkok conference – as described in the previous section – was perceived by Beyerhaus as an experiment in group dynamics intentionally and carefully staged by WCC staff. In almost forty pages he tries to unmask the psychological manipulation which he felt had taken place at Bangkok (Beyerhaus 1993:43–80). He interprets the outcome of the conference from this perspective. The agreement on a new understanding of salvation was, according to Beyerhaus, not achieved through theological reflection 'but through a clever strategy of group dynamics, which in psychological terminology is called "engineering consent" ' (:75–76).

4. 'What has Bangkok said about the question of salvation?' Due to the participation of some evangelical theologians, the official documents and statements contain many biblical and orthodox expressions on mission, states Beyerhaus. However this is, in his view, not the view shared by WCC staff. He accuses WCC officials of having put nice pietistic formulations into certain texts in order to satisfy conservative evangelicals and mission leaders in the churches at home. But when it comes down to the real substance of the WCC's understanding of mission, it is purely social and political.

5. 'What is the moratorium's background?' The call for the withdrawal of western money and personnel from traditional mission-fields shocked western evangelical missions. Beyerhaus goes so far as to agree that there is a certain value in the officially formulated motivation for this step, namely to give the churches of the Third World room to develop their own identities without the domination of the west. However, he points to what he understands to be the real motive, namely to use western money to subsidise the re-education of the western church toward the WCC's understanding of mission and to support political liberation movements in the Two Thirds World.

6. 'How did Bangkok deal with the foundational crisis in Mission?' With this question Beyerhaus refers to the attempt to bring the agenda of the *Frankfurt Declaration* to the table (Beyerhaus's motion in Beyerhaus 1973:177–80). Participants from various backgrounds formulated their unwillingness to make the agenda of conservative German Lutherans into the agenda of an international gathering.[23] Philip A. Potter has decisively rejected Beyerhaus's motion (in German translation published in Beyerhaus 1973:180–82). This was interpreted by Beyerhaus as a clear signal that the conference – or at least its leadership – was not willing to address the real crisis of mission, which he identifies as the loss of the biblical foundation.

7. 'How should mission-conscious Christians react to Bangkok?' The most natural response should be, says Beyerhaus, to urge the WCC to rebuild the biblical foundation of mission. However, in his judgement, this no longer seems possible. Hence, what needs to be done is to continue mission work in the biblical, evangelical sense in co-operation with those missions which have a clear commitment to world evangelisation.

This position put forward by Beyerhaus is expressed in the *Frankfurt Statement* of 1973. It calls on all the delegates of the *DEMT*, which participated as representatives of the German Protestant mission with full voting rights at the Bangkok Conference, officially to denounce the recommendation of a moratorium. Furthermore, all missions associated with the *DEMT* – church missions as well as interdenominational missions – are urged to dissociate publicly from the WCC's CWME. Finally, all churches and all Christians are advised to stop giving money to any mission agency which engages in what Bangkok has defined as mission (Beyerhaus 1973:233–35).

What are the consequences of the *Frankfurt Statement* for German missions and for evangelicals in Germany? It provoked the definitive separation of the conservative evangelical missions – coalescing around Beyerhaus, the *Frankfurt Declaration* and the *AEM* – from the ecumenical missions. In this process, even George F. Vicedom, Professor of Mission at the university of Erlangen, member of the *Deutsche Evangelische Missionsrat (DEMR)* and at the same time one of the early subscribers of the *Frankfurt Declaration*, criticised Beyerhaus's statements after Bangkok (Beyerhaus 1973:235–38) and withdrew from the *Theologische Konvent* and the *Frankfurt Declaration* (Beyerhaus 1973:239). In an open letter he – together with Martin Pörksen, vice-president of the *DEMR* – accused Beyerhaus of having instrumentalised the *Theologische Konvent* to pronounce his opinion on behalf of all German missions. In a ten point statement, Vicedom and Pörksen articulated that they too were disappointed with the results of Bangkok. However, they felt that the message of salvation in Jesus Christ was the foundation at Bangkok. To expect that an international conference only confirms one's own view is unrealistic. The reality of diverse experiences in mission and diverse approaches in different contexts is a reality. It is presumptuous, they say, to deny someone's good faith in such an inquisitorial and arrogant manner as the *Frankfurt Statement* adopts. (The letter is published in Beyerhaus 1973: 235–38). While Vicedom supported the prophetic call of the *Frankfurt Declaration* of 1970, he could not agree that the *Frankfurt Statement* of 1973 by Beyerhaus and the *Theologische Konvent* claimed confessional status.

Vicedom has been called the last German missiologist to represent ecumenical as well as evangelical theology and to have been accepted by both camps (ELThG:2099). With this schism between the *DEMR* and the conservative evangelical movement centred around Beyerhaus and the *Theologische Konvent*, the polarisation of the German mission movement reached a critical point. In that schism, the *AEM* and *the Schools* were on the side of Beyerhaus and the conservative evangelicals.

Before formulating an evaluative summary of these developments (see p. 78) we have to consider the following conference:

10. The *Berlin Declaration* on Ecumenism 1974

The next event of significance in the shaping of German evangelicalism is the Berlin Conference of the confessing evangelicals of the Protestant church in Germany in 1974, which issued the *Berlin Declaration* on Ecumenism.[24] Only one year after Bangkok, in 1974, the German *Konferenz bekennender Gemeinschaften* convened a European Congress of Confession at Berlin. In view of the preparations for the WCC's Nairobi Assembly of 1975, the fellowship of German and European confessing Christians intended to state their concerns about the WCC's theology one more time. The so-called 'Berlin Declaration on Ecumenism,' a shattering critique of the development of ecumenical theology, was issued, containing the following twelve statements:[25]

1. The new humanism promoted by the WCC is an anti-Christian temptation.
2. The new polarisation within the WCC leads to an unavoidable schism in the church.
3. The new watchman's call of the conservative evangelicals is a commandment of responsibility.
4. True liberation is revealed in scripture alone.
5. True liberation has been accomplished by Jesus Christ alone.
6. True liberation is transmitted through the gospel alone.
7. The idea of a one world church is false.
8. The idea of a one world religion is false.
9. The idea of a one world community (of all races, religions and ideologies) is false.

10. Ecumenism is a false spirit.
11. Ecumenism is a strategy for world conquest.
12. What we need is discernment of the spirits, resistance, gathering of the true church and sending.

The *Berlin Declaration* should be commented on as follows: (1) This document must be read in the context of the Lutheran Church in Germany. It mirrors Beyerhaus's own struggle as a conservative evangelical Lutheran within his own church. (2) Furthermore it mirrors the deep gap between secularised theology and the revivalist tradition within the Lutheran state church in Germany. (3) It also marks a tremendous step from an attitude of hope through participation for changes from within the church to separation; the schism is declared unavoidable. (4) The document is set up in a style which must be described as 'apocalyptic apologetics'. (5) Finally we have to notice that this document does not represent the entire evangelical movement either world-wide or in Germany.

The *Berlin Declaration* goes beyond the *Frankfurt Declaration* and *the Frankfurt Statement* in scope and style. Rather than presenting a statement restricted to the concerns of mission, as is the case with the other two documents, it confronts the ecumenical movement in its total manifestation. And it does this in an 'apocalyptic apologetic' style (cf. Hummel) which includes the ultimate condemnation of the WCC and calls for radical separation.

Needless to say, ecumenicals were disqualified by the Declaration in such a way that no constructive response was possible (cf. Gliess:45). But how did the evangelical world receive the Declaration? Again, some American evangelicals have articulated positive comments on the *Berlin Declaration* (cf. Hedlund:341). However, our focus is again on the German situation. In Germany the Declaration has stirred mixed reactions. (1) The *AEM* indicated agreement with the Declaration, although it did not formally accept it as one of the foundational statements of the association because it was not an explicit mission document (cf. Gleiss:52). (2) Klaus Bockmühl in his *Was heisst heute Mission* (1974) valued the *Berlin Declaration* not so much as solid theological foundation but as an 'emergency brake.' He agrees in many ways with the Declarations's analysis; however, he states that this refers not to the ecumenical movement as a whole but rather to some 'radical tendencies' within the WCC. Bockmühl (1974:162) suggests moving beyond the antithetical formulations of Frankfurt and Berlin toward positive evangelical reflections on mission. This position is shared by many other evangelicals in Germany. While they respect the Declarations of Frankfurt and Berlin in their function as an 'emergency brake' they dissociate themselves from the separatist and aggressive character of the two statements.

For many, the *Lausanne Covenant* finally brought the desired positive document (cf. Bockmühl 1974:162–79).

Some intermediate evaluative reflections are in order: Within the six years between Uppsala 1968 and Berlin 1974 we observe a growing twofold schism. It runs on the one hand between the ecumenical movement centred around the WCC and the evangelical movement, especially its conservative wing. On the other hand, this conservative evangelical position, centred in Germany around Peter Beyerhaus and the *Bekenntnisbewegung*, also provoked a split within the evangelical movement itself, basically because of conflicting views about how a critical evangelical view should be articulated over against the WCC. There are several forces and rationales behind this development. (1) The theology articulated by the official voices of the WCC has definitely changed between 1961 and 1974. In retrospect, ecumenical theologians speak of a dramatic process towards contextualisation. This included, in the first phase, a turning to the world under the *Leitmotiv* 'the world sets the agenda,'[26] and, in a second phase, a turning to the churches of the Two Thirds World. The result was nothing less than a foundational questioning of the universal claims of traditional, orthodox western theology, including the missionary practice of at least two hundred years (cf. Werner 1993:18–47). (2) In this process there was a growing movement – inside as well as outside the churches related to the WCC – which articulated serious concerns regarding this development, claiming that the turning towards the world and towards the Two Thirds World was carried out at the expense of the evangelistic dimension of the church's mission. (3) However, there was no consensus within the so-called evangelical movement about how one should respond to the developments of the WCC and how one should relate to the WCC's structures.

The position articulated by the documents of Frankfurt and Berlin must be interpreted in context. (1) The response by Beyerhaus and the *Bekenntnisbewegung* ought to be read in the context of the Lutheran confessional tradition. Based on the formulation of the *Confessio Augustana* (1530), the Lutheran tradition admits to the possibility of a *status confessionis*, or the situation in which a person is forced to decide between a position of truth – expressed in word and deed – and the denial of Christ himself. Such situations are 'yes or no situations' with no room for *adiaphora*. The *status confessionis* always contains an implicit or explicit condemnation of the other position because it leaves no room for other positions. According to Thielicke, the *status confessionis* is demanded when the denial of Christ or blasphemy is at stake (cf. ELThG:1901–02). In this century the position of the *Bekennende Kirche* in the Third Reich is one of the prominent examples of the church pronouncing such an ultimate confession. The *Bekenntinsbewegung* chose Ascension Day 1974 for the Berlin Conference – the fortieth anniversary of the Barmen Declaration –

in order to associate deliberately with the tradition of the *status confessionis* (cf. Künneth and Beyerhaus 1974:8). From this point of view the development from the *Frankfurt Declaration* of 1970 to the *Berlin Declaration* of 1974 gains significance. The *Frankfurt Declaration* of 1974 was a call for repentance. It was addressed to the WCC as an urgent call for change. The *Frankfurt Statement* of 1973 was already a call for separation. It was not addressed to the WCC but rather to the evangelical missions and churches. Finally, the *Berlin Declaration* of 1974 goes even farther. Walter Künneth and Peter Beyerhaus express the conviction that only an 'exorcising renunciation' of such 'demonic humanism' could save the WCC (Künnerth and Beyerhaus:9). The *Declaration* goes beyond the earlier statements in that it includes explicit statements of condemnation. With this, the process reaches a point where dialogue seems neither desirable nor possible – the point of the *status confessionis*.

Regarding the subject of this study we should note that Beyerhaus and the declarations of the *Theologische Konvent* have significantly influenced evangelical theological education and mission training in German-speaking Europe. Many of the publications by Beyerhaus and the *Bekenntnisbewegung* were published by the publishing house of the *Liebenzeller Mission*, one of the most prominent evangelical mission agencies in Germany, which runs its own seminary for the training of missionaries and holds membership in the *AEM* as well as in the *KBA*. The aforementioned books have to be considered as primary textbooks in conservative evangelical Bible schools – a fact which will be subjected to closer examination in Part Three.

11. The Congress on World Evangelization at Lausanne 1974[27]

In retrospect, the evangelical Congress on World Evangelization, held at Lausanne in French speaking Switzerland in 1974, has been interpreted as a milestone in the development of the international evangelical movement (Dayton and Wilson 1984). Lausanne builds on the earlier evangelical conferences at Wheaton and Berlin in 1966. After several conferences which represented only certain ecclesial groups, geographical areas or particular interests, Lausanne was the first international congress bringing together a wide spectrum of evangelically-minded individuals and missions representatives (cf. Hedlund:292). The Congress must be seen in close relation to two persons: Billy Graham, who initiated the conference, and John Stott, who designed the *Lausanne Covenant*, which was issued by the assembly.[28] The intended goal of Lausanne 'was to focus attention on the evangelization of the non-Christian world.' Against the 'moratorium' suggested by the ecumenical conference at Bangkok, Lausanne was planned to 'call attention to the two-billion "unreached" non-Christians, and would contradict the naive opinion that the geographical spread of Christianity nullifies the need for cross-cultural evangelists' (Hedlund:291). With this it 'put world evangelization decisively on the agenda of world Christianity and even set the tone of much that was said about world evangelisation in the last half of the century' (Steuernagel 1990:12). Valdir R. Steuernagel (1990:12) has put Lausanne in context and summed up the relevance of Lausanne with the following statement:

> The reasons why Lausanne and the Covenant it produced provided a fresh look at the understanding of the church's mission are several:[29] [1] the strong presence and participation of the Third World; [2] the openness that characterized the preparation period of the congress; [3] Billy Graham's ability to perceive the importance to many participants of the social issue; [4] the posture of John Stott, who patiently incorporated suggestions and criticism but at the same time firmly maintained his own position; [5] the preceding regional congresses that had followed Berlin '66 and which dealt with the issue of social responsibility; [6] the pressure of, and the opposition to the ecumenical movement and its process of articulating a contemporary theology of mission; and [7] the evangelical development within the USA, as well as the turmoil of Watergate.

The significance of the Lausanne Congress is unquestioned by evangelicals as well as ecumenicals (cf. Bockmühl 1974:162–79; Wietzke:1–3; Hollenweger 1995). The *Lausanne Covenant* has even be called the *Magna Carta* of the evangelical movement (Adomeit in Wietzke:1). Steuernagel concludes, 'Lausanne was a congress that became a movement, an event that became a symbol' (1990:12).

What is the significance of Lausanne for German evangelicals? How did they participate in the congress and receive its outcome? First of all, while the congress took place on the soil of continental Europe, it was neither initiated nor organised by continental evangelicals. However, a considerable number of German and Swiss evangelicals participated in the congress. Some of them were on the list of speakers, such Peter Beyerhaus, Bruno Herm and Günter Wieske. The German delegation appointed a committee of seven who actively participated in the process of theological reflection toward the formulation of the *Lausanne Covenant*. Kurt Heimbucher represented the German position in the committee which edited the *Covenant* (Beyerhaus 1975:296).

It is evident that the scope of evangelicalism represented at Lausanne was much broader than that of the German evangelicalism as we have outlined it in the previous chapters. There is an obvious discrepancy between the *Frankfurt Declaration* – not to speak of the *Berlin Declaration* –

and the *Lausanne Covenant*, in content and in tone. This alone indicates that Lausanne was a challenge to German evangelicals.

1. We first consider Beyerhaus's assessment (Künneth and Beyerhaus:294–313; Beyerhaus 1987:232–49). The title of his article 'Lausanne zwischen Berlin und Genf' (Künneth and Beyerhaus:294–313) already indicated his overall assessment. He locates Lausanne between the ecumenical position of the WCC (Geneva) and (his) *Frankfurt Declaration*. In retrospect he suggests the following as Lausanne's main achievements (1987:234–37): (1) Lausanne served as a place of gathering. The majority of missions organisations came together with a new readiness to co-operate in the common task of world evangelisation. Beyerhaus sees Lausanne as the point where many small rivers merged into a broad, deep and powerful stream.[30] (2) Lausanne gave a vision for the global dimension of evangelisation. It opened eyes for the 2.7 billion unreached people and stimulated 2,000 participants to 'enter in a solemn covenant with God and with one another, to pray, to plan and to work together for the evangelization of the whole world' (formulation of the *Lausanne Covenant*). (3) Lausanne emphasised the significance of strategies and methods as a central aspect of the modern mission movement. To the call 'it has to be done,' the confirmation 'it can be done' was added. (4) The *Lausanne Covenant* is a solid biblical foundation for mission which indicates continuity with the classical mission movement. Beyerhaus especially emphasises: (a) the affirmation of the authority of scripture, (b) the biblical understanding of salvation (the vertical dimension) and the priority of evangelisation over against social action, as well as (c) the eschatological horizon.

However, Beyerhaus's assessment of Lausanne was also critical. He criticises the fact that the Lausanne conference did not take as clear a position against the WCC as the *Frankfurt Declaration*. He calls this 'a fatal aspect of Lausanne' (1975:302). Beyerhaus explicitly mentions five reasons for this 'mild' attitude toward the WCC (1975:307–09): (1) Billy Graham was too pragmatic and tried to incorporate as many evangelicals as possible from as many churches as possible. (2) In this wide spectrum of so-called evangelicals, the *radical evangelicals* and the *ecumenical evangelicals* particularly tended toward a more open relationship with the WCC. (3) In addition to this, there was a tendency toward an 'eschatological optimism' which hindered many from seeing the dangers of the WCC's strategy. (5) This finally led to a 'deficient ability to discern the spirits.'

Beyerhaus has time and again criticised the evangelical development towards the integration of social responsibility and evangelisation. In his assessment, terminology such as *holistic gospel, kingdom theology* or *contextualisation* is dangerous, because it already implies a tendency towards the ecumenical understanding of mission. On several occasions he has criticised the open and conciliatory attitude of the Lausanne Committee on Word Evangelism (LCWE), especially that of the *radical evangelical* wing of the movement, toward the WCC (1987:245; 1996:13; 1981:212–23; 1996:11–12,13, cf. also Schnabel 1993:28–82).

It is evident that Beyerhaus perceived the scope of evangelicalism represented at Lausanne, and in the subsequent Lausanne movement, as a threat to what he understands to be an orthodox, biblical understanding of mission – as it is expressed by the *Frankfurt Declaration*. In order to overview the spectrum of evangelicals at Lausanne and to locate himself in this spectrum, he suggested the following classification: (1975:307–08).

1. *New Evangelicals*[31] associated with Billy Graham and the network of the World Evangelical Fellowship (WEF).
2. *Separatist fundamentalists* associated with C. McIntire and the International Council of Christian Churches (ICCC). Their representation at the Lausanne Conference was minimal.
3. *Confessional Evangelicals* rooted in the mainline confessional churches (e.g., Lutherans); these can be associated with the declarations of Frankfurt (1970) and Berlin (1974).
4. Evangelicals of *Pentecostal* and *charismatic* orientation.
5. *Radical evangelicals* characterised by their engagement in the socio-political dimension of discipleship and mission.
6. *Ecumenical evangelicals* who also participate in the WCC and try to build bridges between the two movements.

Beyerhaus's classification requires several comments: (1) It is evident that Beyerhaus and German evangelicals around the *Bekenntnisbewegung* and the *Frankfurt Declaration* associate themselves with group three (*confessional evangelicals*). (2) Through his classifications, Beyerhaus dissociates himself from the *separatist fundamentalism* of McIntire. However, as shown earlier, the German *Bekenntnisbewegung* maintains relations to the ICCC and should probably be classified very close to the separatist evangelicals.[32] (3) By using the term *confessional evangelical* for himself, Beyerhaus occupies a classification which other evangelicals who belong to confessional churches (e.g., Lutherans and Reformed) might also claim, although they would not associate themselves with the *Bekenntnisbewegung* and its declarations. In the German context this would include theologians of the pietistic wing in the Lutheran Church, e.g., people around Albrecht Hauser in the church of Württemberg. Many of this group would rather associate with what Beyerhaus calls *ecumenical evangelicals*. (4) Beyerhaus has also explicitly stated that Samuel Escobar and the *radical evangelicals* marked the 'left wing' at Lausanne and that it is because of this group that a more radical anti-ecumenical position was not welcomed in the *Covenant* (Beyerhaus 1975:296). The group associated with Beyerhaus is in clear opposition to the *radical evangelicals*.

2. Klaus Bockmühl, another influential German evangelical, assessed Lausanne more favourably than Beyerhaus. In *Was heisst heute Mission* (1974) he appreciates Lausanne (congress and covenant) because of its positive theological contribution to an evangelical theology of mission, something that was missing in the apologetic declarations of Frankfurt and Berlin (Bockmühl 1975:162; 175–79). He especially commends the foundational theological presentations by John Stott, Michael Green, Gottfried Osei-Mensah and Peter Beyerhaus. However, Bockmühl's primary interest was Lausanne's contribution to social ethics (1975:168–179). He discusses Padilla's, as well as Escobar's, contributions to the Congress (1975:168–173). While he supports Padilla's call for a comprehensive approach which sees human beings in their wholeness, he criticises his theological argument which bases the necessity for social ethics on the biblical understanding of the 'world.' Similarly, Bockmühl follows Escobar in his argumentation for an integral understanding of salvation which includes social ethics. However, he points to the weaknesses of Escobar's argument in its lack of a clear distinction between the order of preservation and the order of salvation. For the Lutheran Bockmühl, all attempts to base Christian social ethics on other grounds than the Lutheran doctrine of the two kingdoms fail. Bockmühl has articulated this concern time and again in the discussions after Lausanne (cf. Bockmühl 1975; 1982; 1983). With this observation we touch again on one of the critical issues in the debate on social ethics between German Lutheran evangelicals and the so-called radical evangelicals. Put in other words, the contribution of Padilla and Escobar at Lausanne introduced a foundational challenge to the established western and Lutheran view of God's work in the world. This issue has been on the table through all the years from Lausanne until the present time. It still marks the line of demarcation between German Lutheran evangelicals and those called radical evangelicals. This needs to be further developed in Part Three.[33]

3. Furthermore, in view of *the Schools* it is important to notice that Lausanne has encouraged mission studies in evangelical theological education. Bruce J. Nicholls's presentation on 'Theological Education and Evangelism' was well received by German evangelicals and was one of the impulses toward the foundation of the European Evangelical Accrediting Association (see next section). New efforts were taken to develop qualified evangelical theological scholarship and education after Lausanne. Bruce Nicholls was instrumental in that process among German evangelicals (Egelkraut 1990:33).

4. In the end, the *Lausanne Covenant* proved to be a key document for an evangelical identity in Germany and Switzerland – for missions as well as theological schools. The German *AEM* adopted it as a second

foundational statement besides the *Frankfurt Declaration* (Mann:113). For the Swiss *AEM* it became the main confessional statement besides the statement of the Evangelical Alliance.

12. The Foundation of the European Evangelical Accrediting Association (EEAA) 1979

As mentioned above, Lausanne has further strengthened the identity of German and Swiss evangelicalism. We have also noticed that it gave the impetus to undertake concrete steps toward the academic accreditation of missionary Bible schools and colleges. This was put into practice in the second half of the 1970s.

It was in *AEM* circles where the concern for accreditation was expressed and solutions were demanded. Since most of the Bible schools and seminaries operate outside of the government-recognised educational system, they cannot confer internationally recognised degrees. In the 1970s, the international situation regarding qualifications for overseas personnel put pressure on German-speaking schools. They became aware that, if they could not gain international academic recognition in reasonable time, their graduates would no longer be qualified to enter Two Thirds World countries. This caused the *AEM* to push for the accreditation of Bible schools and seminaries (Gleiss:81; Egelkraut 1990:33). Some already had connections to North American evangelical colleges and seminaries and sent their graduates there to complete degrees. At the initiative of the mission agencies (*AEM*) and Bruce Nicholls[34] of the WEF, the European Evangelical Accrediting Association (EEAA) was founded by the delegates of twenty three Bible schools and seminaries in 1979 (Gleiss:81,130; Egelkraut 1990:33; Born:554). The EEAA was established as an European association inviting schools from all (at that time western) European countries. Fifteen of the twenty three founding members were from German-speaking Europe and at least fourteen of them were associated with the *AEM* (cf. Gleiss:130). The objective was to establish accreditation procedures in close co-operation with the International Council of Accrediting Agencies (ICAA), which was founded in 1980 (Kemp 1995:314; Born:554). However, 'the idea of accreditation was difficult to introduce in a continent where the whole educational system has always operated under government supervision' (Egelkraut 1990:33–34).

We notice at this point that national state accreditation was hardly considered by *the Schools* at this time. The developments of the 1960s and 1970s, outlined in the previous chapters, had already led the conservative evangelical movement into such an isolation from the established churches and their theological faculties that negotiations with the state, the established churches and the universities were unrealistic. In this situation, to co-operate with the international – or American – accreditation system seemed to be the most promising avenue.

The 1980s became the decade of accreditation for evangelical theological schools in German-speaking Europe. Schools from Germany, France, Switzerland and Scandinavia took the lead and most of the institutions in view applied for accreditation in the 1980s. Yet the negotiation of accreditation standards which would meet international requirements and simultaneously fit European categories took time. It soon became clear that the various schools – often with long histories – could not easily fit into the clearly defined categories of an accreditation structure. Several schools were far from meeting the required standards. In the last decade of the century, the accreditation process continued. Yet several schools could not be convinced to associate with the EEAA. They were seeking other forms of accreditation, be it through state recognition or through direct relations to North American colleges and seminaries. This has certainly weakened the position and validity of the EEAA. In addition, new schools, offering new forms of education, have entered the scene. Several models of Theological Education by Extension are attracting more students than the traditional residential schools. Up to the present time the EEAA has not proved capable of providing means for the accreditation of such new models. Some of these developments will be evaluated in Part Four.

13. The Foundation of the *Freie Hochschule für Mission* 1984

Another major step in evangelical mission training in the German-speaking context was taken when the *AEM* founded the *Freie Hochschule für Mission (FHM)* (Graduate School of Missiology). It is not easy to determine the date of its foundation. The year 1984 indicates the school's move to its current location in Korntal near Stuttgart and, at that same time, the implementation of a graduate programme leading to an academic degree (Gleiss:140–42). But this event was only the result of what had been started much earlier.

Traditionally, Protestant missionaries in Germany have received their basic training at the Bible schools or colleges and seminaries, the mission schools of certain mission agencies or at the faculties of state universities. Beyond this, specific missionary preparation as well as continuing education of missionaries was needed. For that purpose the *Missionsakademie Hamburg* (Mission Academy Hamburg) was founded by the *Deutsche Evangelische Missionstag* (*DEMT*) in 1954. Walter Freytag was its first academic director (LWM:354; Gleiss:12). The *Missionsakademie Hamburg* was affiliated with Hamburg University and mainly served the mission agencies of mainline Protestant churches. In the mid 1960s missions of free church or interdenominational background began to offer courses for missionaries at *Wiedenest*, Ewersbach and *Liebenzell*. After 1967 such seminars were co-ordinated by the *Arbeitsgemeinschaft für freikirchliche Missionskurse*, later called *Arbeitsgemeinschaft evangelikaler Missionskurse*. (Gleiss:11, 67). In 1975 *Liebenzell* intensified its training offerings for missionaries on furlough by offering five-week courses leading to a diploma. As, due to all the reasons mentioned above, the *AEM* withdrew more and more from the *DEMT* and hence from the *Missionsakademie*, an increased desire for an evangelical missiological study centre in German-speaking Europe became evident. Several projects already were discussed in the 1970s. Peter Beyerhaus, academic director of the *Albrecht-Bengel-Haus* at Tübingen, initiated the installation of a missiological branch of the *ABH* alongside the pastoral studies department, which was already in existence. But the project did not succeed. Others suggested the foundation of an academy for mission studies in Basel. While some focused on preparation for missionaries and continuing education, others wanted an evangelical research centre (Gleiss:77–80). In 1978, the *AEM* took over responsibility for the project and soon thereafter started the *Seminar für missionarische Fortbildung* in Monbachtal/Bad Liebenzell, close to the mission and seminary of Bad Liebenzell yet as an independent and new educational institution (CIU Catalogue 1997/98:3; Gleiss:80). The North American evangelical missiologist, Georg W. Peters, was appointed to establish this new graduate school and research centre. Earlier, Peters served as academic dean at the Mennonite Brethren Biblical Seminary at Fresno (USA), and was head of the mission department of Dallas Theological Seminary.[35] Under his leadership from 1978 to 1987, the *Seminar für missionarische Fortbildung* grew to become a widely respected evangelical graduate school of missiology. After an interim period Peter Beyerhaus became director of the school until 1994 (Gleiss:147, 181).

As mentioned earlier, the school moved to Korntal/Stuttgart in 1984 and changed its name to the *Freie Hochschule für Mission* (Graduate School of Missiology) in 1985 (Gleiss:140–43). The short history of the *FMH* also shows a constant struggle for academic recognition. An attempt to obtain accreditation from the state of Baden-Württemberg as a *Hochschule* (graduate school) failed (Gleiss:141–42). The European Evangelical Accrediting Association did not at that time offer accreditation for this type of school (post graduate studies, leading to an MA). Through its North American connections, the *AEM* maintained relationships to Grace Theological Seminary, Biola University and Columbia Biblical Seminary (all in the USA). Accreditation through one of these schools was finally the way sought towards the end of the 1980s. In 1988, four students graduated through Grace Theological Seminary, but Grace could not maintain the accreditation of an extension centre in Europe because of ATS regulations. After 1988 the *FHM* concentrated on a co-operation with Columbia Biblical Seminary (Gleiss:145). Since 1992 it has been offering courses accredited by Columbia Biblical Seminary and in 1994 it received full accreditation as an extension centre of the Columbia University's Columbia Biblical Seminary & Graduate School of Missions division, offering MA degrees in missiology and Biblical studies (catalogue 1997/98:3; Gleiss:181).

This rather extensive summary of the origin of the *FHM* is crucial for an understanding of evangelical mission studies in German-speaking Europe – and this for the following reasons. (1) The *FHM* is the first and so far the only fully accredited evangelical graduate school for missiological studies in this language area. (2) It is run in close relations with the *AEM* and carries the same missiological profile. (3) Such prominent evangelical missiologists as G. W. Peters and Peter Beyerhaus have influenced the school and its theology. (4) In its early days, it was established by a North American evangelical missiologist and is today the extension centre of a North American evangelical school. (5) Many of the graduates of *the Schools* have sought further training at the *FHM*. (6) Finally, several mission teachers of *the Schools* are graduates of the *FHM*.

All this only underlines the significance of the *FHM* for evangelical mission studies in Germany and Switzerland and suggests that the impact of this missiological study centre upon the Bible colleges and seminaries deserves further analysis in Part Three and Four.

14. The Lausanne II Congress on World Evangelization at Manila in 1989

The *Lausanne II Congress on World Evangelization*, held at Manila in July 1989, sought to be understood as the affirmation, clarification and actualisation of *Lausanne I* and the process of the Lausanne Movement between 1974 and 1989[36] (cf. Marquardt and Parzany:329 and the introduction to the *Manila Manifesto*). The Congress and the *Manifesto* were shaped around two declarations: 'Proclaim Christ Until he Comes' and 'Calling the Whole Church to Take the Whole Gospel to the Whole World' (see introduction to the *Manifesto* in Hedlund:419). Participants and commentators have identified the significance of *Lausanne II* not so much in its theological contribution but in its consolidation of the evangelical mission movement associated with Lausanne (Hedlund:412–18; *em* 3/1990:34; Beyerhaus 1996:9). The key terms 'urgency,' 'unity' and 'sacrifice' reflect the strength of the Manila Congress. It was a call for world evangelisation (Berneburg 1997:200; Reifler:63–64). However, the following weaknesses of the Congress have been identified: (1) It was 'long on celebration but short on content' (Hedlund:414); (2) it did not deal adequately with the charismatic question; (3) the paralysing effect of modernity on evangelism was articulated by Os Guiness but not articulated in a concrete fashion by the Congress (Teschner in Marquardt and Parzany:30); and finally (4) the divergent views on the issue of evangelism and social concern could not be overcome – indeed, the split between the 'pure evangelism wing' and the 'integrative mission wing' seemed greater than before.[37]

How have German evangelicals received *Lausanne II*?

1. First of all, the Manila Congress has been widely recognised by evangelicals in the German-speaking context. *Lausanne II* was visited by a broad spectrum of evangelical representatives from German-speaking Europe as reflected in the report volume *Evangelisation mit Leidenschaft* (Marquardt and Parzany). This also implies that the response is not univocal. As a particularly controversial point, German evangelicals noted the role of charismatic evangelicals at the congress (:30–32; 311–13; *em* 3/1990:36). They definitely appreciated all the clear statements on the uniqueness of Christ as the only way to salvation.

2. It is interesting to observe the responses to developments in the area of holistic mission and social responsibility. (a) The German report volume devotes a major part to the topic *Good News to the Poor*. Six major contributions from Manila are included and German commentators responded favourably to the presentations by Tom Houston, Michael Cassidy, Valdir Steuernagel, Vinay Samuel and others (Marquardt and Parzany:100–53). However, the two German commentators do not represent the *conservative-fundamentalist* wing of German evangelicalism. (b) German evangelicals more closely associated with Beyerhaus and the *Frankfurt Declaration* assess the outcome of Manila more critically (*em* 1990/3:35–36; Schnabel 1993:28–82, especially 57–62, 66–82; Berneburg 1997:200–34). Berneburg severely criticises Samuel's, Sugden's and Steuernagel's presentations and sees the success of the Social Concern Movement as shaped by a holistic understanding of salvation, a political orientation, a non-eschatological view of God's kingdom, contextual hermeneutics and the option for the poor – concepts which in Berneburg's view need to be refuted (1997:222–34).

Looking back on the responses of conservative German evangelicals to the developments of the Lausanne Movement from 1974 to 1989 we can draw the conclusion that they identify with the Lausanne Movement insofar as it corresponds to the *Frankfurt Declaration*. This can be observed from the early interpretations by Peter Beyerhaus (1975) through Berneburg's thesis of 1997. In practice, this means that German conservative evangelicals use documents such as the *Lausanne Covenant* and the *Manila Manifesto* eclectically to support the emphasis of the theology of the *Frankfurt Declaration*. At the same time they not only distance themselves from the WCC but also from the evangelical Social Concern Movement. Granted that after Manila the evangelical movement is more than ever in danger of breaking apart into a wing which gives priority to the evangelistic proclamation and a wing which seeks the practice of integral evangelism, German conservative evangelicals clearly identifying with the former (Berneburg 1997:373).

However, on the international scene, evangelical and ecumenical, the focus of attention had been shifting in the late 1980s from the issues touching on social responsibility and integral mission[38] towards theology of religions and dialogue with people of other faiths. Of course the issue had been on the table for a long time, but received only marginal attention in the 1980s. It was the new interest in pneumatology, stirred by the Eastern Orthodox Churches and the growing charismatic movement, which opened new avenues of reflection on the relationship of the Christian faith to other religions (Werner 1993:419–81). The clear emphasis on the uniqueness of Christ, which was pronounced at Manila (Marquardt and Parzany:79–99), as well as the interaction with the Pentecostal/charismatic movement (Marquardt and Parzany:176–99, 311–13), have to be read in this context. However, Manila did not look at the theology of religion from a pneumatological point of view; this was to be developed further at the next ecumenical conference at Canberra.

15. The WCC Assembly at Canberra 1991 and the Evangelical Response

This historical survey now enters the 1990s with the discussion of the evangelical response to the Seventh General Assembly of the WCC held 7–20 February, 1991. The main theme of Canberra was *pneumatology*. According to Werner, the 1991 conference indicates a *caesura*, as did the New Delhi conference thirty years earlier (1993:20, 22). He summarises the shift from New Delhi to Canberra in the following way:

> Between New Dehli and Canberra, between the historical connection and the cosmological connection, between the christological confession *to* the world and the pneumatological confession *with* the world, between the first, cautious questioning of western theological domination and the great controversies about the legitimacy and boundaries of a non-western inculturation of the Gospel, the *dramatic process of the discovery and theological elaboration of the 'contextuality' of mission* stretches out of thirty years (1993:23).

It is this shift from a Christological witness *to* the world to a pneumatological community *with* the world which dominates the agenda of the WCC's reflection at and around Canberra. Based on a redefinition of the Nicene Creed (*filioque-formula*),[39] which drops the subordination of the Spirit under the Son, new horizons have been opened for the Spirit's work beyond and outside of Christ; and with this, new possibilities for an inter-religious dialogue have been prepared (Werner 1993:419–81).

The developments at Canberra have been severely criticised by evangelicals world-wide (Ro and Nicholls; Padilla 1991). In an open 'Letter to Churches and Christians Worldwide from Participants Who Share Evangelical Concerns,' they addressed Christians around the world. Bruce J. Nicholls and Bong Rin Ro summarise this in an *Evangelical Response* to Canberra:

> The emphasis on worship, rich in ecclesiastical traditions, powerful and symbolic acts and colourful art forms was no doubt the highlight of the assembly. However, the absence of any discussion of evangelism and the work of the Holy Spirit in conversion and renewal of the churches and the radical approach to many of our contemporary issues concerned all of us... Many felt that the justice activists, feminists and environmentalists, who dominated the Seoul Consultation on Justice, Peace and Integrity of Creation in 1990, hijacked the agenda and the centre stage at the Canberra Assembly (Rin Ro and Nicholls:7–8).

The German evangelical theologian Rolf Hille, Director of Studies at the *Bengel Haus* (introduced earlier in this chapter) decisively rejected the controversial contribution of the Korean theologian Chung Hyun-Kyung as 'Spirit and Soil Theology', which, in Hille's view, has nothing to do with biblical-Protestant faith but a great deal to do with syncretism (Hille 1993:64–68). He concludes:

> In this ecumenism, justification of the sinner through faith in Jesus Christ alone can be bent and reinterpreted as the self-saving efforts of the politically active person. And not a single church leader out of the great churches of the Reformation – not even anyone of the 54 members of the German delegation which included Protestant bishops from a number of established regional churches – rose up to contradict seriously this presentation of works-righteousness. Are there no more Protestants within ecumenism (:67)?

Many of the contributions to the *Evangelical Responses* to Canberra show an equally sharp critique of some of the contents of the Canberra Assembly (cf. Padilla 1991). This clearly indicates that the open agenda between ecumenicals and evangelicals is still far from being cleared.

Yet, the evangelical response *Beyond Canberra* also stands for a new tone in the evangelical-ecumenical dialogue which developed in the 1980s. The editors of the booklet write:

> The intention of this book is wholly positive. The writers believe that evangelicals should be stimulated by the theological vitality of many ecumenists, and share many of their concerns – with the environment, for example, with justice issues, with right relationships between women and men ... But they also believe that current ecumenical thinking needs to be exposed to constructive criticism from a biblical point of view (Rin Ro/Nicholls: back cover).

Can this be interpreted as a positive step forward toward a fruitful dialogue between evangelicals and ecumenicals beyond the condemnatory style of the *Frankfurt Declaration* and the *Berlin Statement on Ecumenism* – or are evangelicals going astray, as Peter Beyerhaus worried already in his response to the evangelicals' role at Melbourne in 1980 (Beyerhaus 1981:212–23, 1996:11f.). In view of the schools to be analysed in this study, we find that German conservative evangelicals are deeply sceptical towards all attempts at harmonising evangelical and ecumenical understandings of mission on the assumption that both movements emphasise certain truths which could be brought together to a more holistic view of mission. Again in the words of Beyerhaus: 'it is a question of take it or leave it' – which leaves no space for negotiation or compromise (1981:200).

Looking at the agendas of the *KBA* assemblies in the 1990s we realise that these missiological issues are not taken up. This does not mean that evangelical mission theologians did not deal with these issues or that they were absent from teaching at *the Schools*, as we will see in Part Three. However *the Schools* were preoccupied with other questions in the 1990s to which we will now turn.

16. The *KBA*-Schools in the 1990s: Affirmation and Crisis

We close the review of the period under consideration by referring to the two *KBA* assemblies of 1993 and 1995. Both are strong indicators of the current situation:

1. The 1993 assembly was devoted to the thirtieth anniversary of the association. The concern of the early days, the legacy of the 'Battle for the Bible' against modernism and biblical criticism was at the centre of the conference. The three key papers presented at the conference univocally focused on the evangelical community's struggle to remain faithful to the Bible as the word of God against the forces of biblical criticism. *KBA* 1993 was an impressive affirmation of its heritage from the 1960s.

2. At the same time *the Schools* suffered a considerable drop in student numbers. Between 1990 and 1994 enrolment dropped more than 30 per cent, from 565 to 395 (counting twenty five schools). The number of

graduates decreased between 1990 and 1996 from 467 to 222, which is less than 50 per cent (Faix and Faix and Müller and Schmidt). This certainly caused serious concern and reflection among *the Schools*. The issue was brought to the table at the 1995 assembly and the decision was taken to engage in serious analysis and implement such changes as the situation should demand. A research team was mandated to conduct a thorough investigation by means of a survey, assisted by the research centre of the *FHM*. First results were presented at the 1996 assembly followed by a deeper analysis one year later. Six analytical papers were presented at the assembly approaching the date from different angles:[40]

1. The KBA-Schools in the light of globel changes in theological education (Bernhard Ott).
2. The influence of youth-cultures and their impact on students (Tobias Faix)
3. Evangelical theological education confronted with (post-)modernism: concrete alternatives for the future (Stephan Holthaus).
4. The pedagogical qualification of the teachers and the challenge of the biographies of young people (Wilhelm Faix).
5. The challenge of personality formation: the task of mentoring (Klaus W. Müller)
6. How can the concern for Bible-committed education be presented more effectively in the public (Klaus Schmidt).

This must be viewed as a significant step in the *KBA's* history, since it was the first time that schools in a common project engaged in self-critical analysis.

Notes

1 There are exceptions, such as Bockmühl who calls German evangelicals to recover their pietistic heritage in order to regain an identity which is not only based on reaction (1985:6–10).

2 Documentation of Willingen in International Missionary Council 1952 and in Freytag, ed. 1952.

3 At Willingen the following four types of missions were identified: (1) mission agencies 'as boards of churches' (mainly in North America); (2) 'missionary societies which resulted from an evangelical awakening in the setting of national churches' (mainly in Europe); (3) 'inter-denominational societies ... which regard themselves as providing a special witness to the universality of the mission of the church'; (4) 'functional societies which address themselves to specific needs' (IMC:13).

4 Some 25 years later, Ralph D. Winter tried to show that throughout history, Christian mission has been accomplished by churches (local and denominational) as well as mission agencies. He calls the former *modalities* and the

latter *sodalities* (Winter 1981). While Winter may be accused of reading contemporary conceptions into history, his theory picks up Newbigin's thesis and deserves attention.

5 In Germany, the potential for the split between so-called ecumenical and evangelical missions which developed in the second half of the 1960s applied to this group of missions, too. See further discussion in connection with the conferences at Wheaton and Berlin (p. 62) and the foundation of the *Arbeitsgemeinschaft Evangelikaler Missionen* (p. 65)

6 For that reason, the integration was seen very critically by many North American evangelicals. Hedlund says: 'Leadership control passed from evangelicals committed to mission into the hands of ecclesiastical officials having many interests' (Hedlund:155). Winter comments that this integration indicates the shift 'from councils of para-church mission structures to councils of churches' and perceives this as a 'colossal loss' or even a 'mean betrayal' (Winter quoted in Hedlund:155).

7 According to the definition of Holthaus we actually speak of *moderate fundamentalism/conservative evangelicalism* (1997:17–18).

8 A somewhat different characterisation of fundamentalism from a British point of view is Harris:1–18. Harris' thesis is that fundamentalism is primarily characterised by its epistemology and hermeneutics, a position which is shared by this author and will be picked up again at the end of the study.

9 Today *Staatsunabhängige Theologische Hochschule STH* (State-Independent Theological Graduate School)

10 See the presentations at the 30th anniversary of the *KBA* 1993: Stephan Holthaus, 'Streiflichter aus der Auseinandersetzung um die Bibelfrage im 19. und 20. Jahrhundert,' Helge Stadelmann, 'Biblisch-theologische Grundlagen der Bibeltreue," Helmuth Pehlke, 'Umgang mit den Schwierigkeiten der Bibel' (unpublished manuscripts).

11 German evangelicals value the Wheaton Declaration. Klaus Bockmühl takes it as the evangelical answer and alternative to the developments of the ecumenical understanding of mission (1974:153).

12 Ecclesiological reflections have been avoided among German evangelicals for many years. To the traditionally conflicting views of the state churches, free churches and pietistic communities, new concepts of interdenominationalism, parachurch structures and independent churches were added over the past three decades. It was only in 1998 that the Association of Evangelical Theologians approached the topic of ecclesiology at its annual conference (Stadelmann ed. 1998).

13 The history of the German *AEM* has been investigated in an MA Thesis by Dagmar Gleiss, *Geschichte der Arbeitsgemeinschaft evangelikaler Missionen, AEM – 25 Jahre AEM: 1969–1994*. Korntal: Freie Hochschule für Mission (1994). For the somewhat different developments around the origin of the Swiss wing of the *AEM* see Reifler:66–67

14 According to Gleiss, the German Evangelical Alliance was inspired to create an association of evangelical missions in Germany by the contacts at the World Evangelical Fellowship's meeting in June 1968 (:28 n. 15).

15 The reasons for these differences are hard to point out. A systematic study is not available. This author suggests the following possible reasons: (a) the tensions between liberalism and historical criticism of the state church

universities and the conservative movements was at one time less confrontational in Switzerland; (b) there is no strong fundamentalist movement in Switzerland, i.e., the *Bekenntnisbewegung* (see next chapter) has only a minimal following; (c) in Switzerland, the *Gemeinschaftsbewegung* as a neo-pietistic movement within the state church plays only a marginal role, whereas in Germany it is at the heart of the controversies between 'liberals' and 'conservatives,' between 'ecumenicals' and 'evangelicals'; (d) the anti-Pentecostal Berlin Declaration of 1909, issued by people of the *Gemeinschaftsbewegung* has had only a minimal impact on Switzerland, and this has allowed a much more open attitude towards Pentecostal and charismatic churches; (e) consequently, the Evangelical Alliance has a much broader scope, including large numbers of state church pastors with a pietistic orientation but also Pentecostal and charismatic Christians; (f) finally, Swiss people are used to a completely different understanding of democracy, emphasising consensus and not opposition.

16 Ecumenical missiologists would argue that this is due to the fact that the evangelical understanding of mission supports an uncritical continuation of traditional, colonial western mission work, while ecumenicals, after careful considerations, reduced their classical missionary engagement in the Two-Thirds World (Hollenweger in personal conversation with the author).

17 For an overview over the history of the *Bekenntnisbewegung*, see Jung:88–155.

18 See Appendix D. The German text in Beyerhaus 1970a; 1987:3–9, the English translation in Hedlund:250–55. The English version has been published in *Christianity Today* June 19, 1970 (see Hedlund:234 n. 54 for an English bibliography on the *Frankfurt Declaration*).

19 It is important to notice that the adoption of the *Frankfurt Declaration* as the foundational statement of the *AfeM* was debated in the initial stages. George Peters advocated a more open course of the *AfeM* committed to the confession of the Evangelical Alliance. But the *AEM* leadership, especially Peter Beyerhaus and Thomas Schirrmacher, brought forward the motion to include the *Frankfurt Declaration* in the statutes of the *AfeM*, which was followed by the assembly (Müller 1995:16–17). This already indicates the varying positions within the evangelical movement in German-speaking Europe.

20 The statement to Nairobi 1975 was issued together with the *AEM*.

21 According to Holthaus these two schools represent fundamentalist theological education and scholarship in Germany (1993:321–24).

22 For documentation of the Bangkok Conference, see the official German edition by Potter, as well as Beyerhaus 1993, which also includes the response by the *Theologische Konvent*. In English some of the documents in Hedlund:269–89.

23 Several statements – some of them by evangelicals from the Two Thirds World – are mentioned by Hollenweger in his essay 'Professor Unrat geht nach Bangkok' (in Potter:248–49).

24 Conference documentation in Künneth and Beyerhaus:16–41.

25 This is not a literal translation of the original statements but a summary of their intention.

26 The concept that 'the world sets the agenda' was introduced to the discussion by Walter Hollenweger in 1966 ('The World is the Agenda', in *Concept* XI September 1966, Geneva: WCC). The *Leitmotiv* was further developed in *The*

Church for Others (Geneva: WCC, 1967:23–27). It became a current term around the Uppsala 1968 Conference (cf. Werner 1993:21).

27 For German documentation see Beyerhaus ed: *Alle Welt soll sein Wort hören*. The full text of the *Lausanne Covenant* is in Appendix E of this thesis.

28 According to Beyerhaus (1975:296) a first draft was drafted before the conference by the Scottish Presbyterian James Douglas and discussed in a preparatory committee led by Leighton Ford. At the conference the editorial committee was led by John Stott who shaped the document in style and theology in its final from.

29 Numbers added by this author.

30 'Das, was Lausanne '74 zu einem so einmaligen Ereignis machte, war die Tatsache, dass hier viele kleine Flüsse – von denen einige zuvor kaum beachtet worden waren – ineinander mündeten und auf diese Weise einen mächtigen Strom bildeten, der tief und breit genug war, eine ganze Flotte evangelistischer Fischerboote zu tragen, und der Wasser genug mit sich führte, um den ausgedörrten Boden der Christenheit des ausgehenden 20. Jahrhunderts geistlich zu tränken' (Beyerhaus 1987:233).

31 The term 'new evangelicals' was introduced earlier: 'In 1947 Harold J. Ockenga coined the term "the new evangelicalism" to identify this movement away from the negative connotations which had come to characterize fundamentalism' (Howard:4).

32 Beyerhaus's position is very close to what the North American evangelical Arthur P. Johnston articulated in *The Battle for World Evangelism*.

33 We need only to compare two doctoral dissertations on the same topic by the Latin American, Valdir R. Steuernagel, *The Theology of Mission in its Relevance to Social Responsibility within the Lausanne Movement* (1988) and by the German Lutheran, Erhard Berneburg, *Das Verhältnis von Verkündigung und sozialer Aktion in der evangelikalen Missionstheologie* (1997).

34 The *AEM* invited evangelical schools to an initial meeting at Ewersbach on 4 November, 1977 (Letter of 12 September 1977). Bruce Nicholls, at that time General Secretary of the Theological Commission of the World Evangelical Fellowship and well acquainted with the accrediting agencies in Asia and Africa, was at that meeting. His main arguments for accreditation were put forward in his paper of August 1976 which he presented at Ewersbach (Archive *Bienenberg*).

35 Biographical and bibliographical data on G.W. Peters is in Kasdorf and Müller:20–50.

36 See the list of the 18 consultations in Appendix C.

37 The two wings were represented by the 'Social Concern Track' led by Vinay Samuel on the one hand (see *Transformation* 1990/1) and the 'AD 2000" movement supported by the presentation by Luis Palau and North American evangelicals on the other hand (cf. Berneburg 1997:200–34). These diverging trends within the evangelical movement in and after Manila have been analysed by Samuel Escobar in 'A Movement Divided" (1991). Padilla proposes three strands: (a) post-imperial missiology around John Stott, (b) managerial missiology around the North American church growth movement, and (c) critical missiology from the periphery articulated by evangelicals from the Two Thirds World.

38 The debate on the integration of social responsibility and evangelism has

reached a certain climax at the CWME Consultation on Evangelism at Stuttgart in 1987. This consultation brought together ecumenicals as well as evangelicals. The result was *The Stuttgart Statement*, a declaration on integral mission which demonstrates a considerable overlap between ecumenicals and evangelicals (cf. Wietzke:353–66; Samuel and Hauser). In view of German conservative evangelicalism we notice that the 1987 consultation, though it took place in Germany, remained almost unrecognised; where it was recognised it was rejected (cf. Berneburg 1997:350–51).

39 See the summary of the discussion by Werner under the title 'Zur missionstheologischen Bedeutung des Verzichts auf das westliche filioque' (The Significance of the drop of the filioque of the western church for a theology of mission) (1993:451–6). For a critical discussion see Helfenstein 1998:269–78.

40 The findings of the survey as well as the analytical papers presented at the 1997 assembly are published in Faix, Faix, Müller and Schmidt. The author was himself a member of the analysing team. He presented an analysis under the title 'Die KBA-Schulen im Lichte globaler Veränderungen in theologischer Ausbildung' (Faix, Faix, Müller and Schmidt:38–76). The material of this broad assessment of *the Schools* provides substantial data for the analysis in Part Four of this study.

CHAPTER 7

Concluding Reflections

It is time to bring together the findings of Part Two. (1) In chapter 5 we have looked at the general background of evangelicalism and have shown how the German neo-pietistic movement gained new momentum in the post-war period through interaction with North American evangelicalism, and this to such a measure that it even introduced the label *evangelikal*, the Germanised version of *evangelical*, to the German-speaking world. We have also demonstrated how the place of mission studies in theological education has been the subject of constant debate in the twentieth century, though with hardly any progress as far as the established universities are concerned. On the other hand, we have highlighted the contribution of the pietistic-evangelical mission movement, arguing that considerable initiative, in terms of mission-oriented theological education, is derived from this tradition of Bible schools, Bible colleges and evangelical seminaries. (3) Finally, in chapter 6 we have surveyed the recent history (1960–1995) of *the Schools'* context, demonstrating that in a time of identity crisis, anti-ecumenism and anti-modernism (defence of the inerrancy of the Bible) became the backbone of the evangelical movement around the *KBA* schools. It appeared that Peter Beyerhaus and the *Frankfurt Declaration* played a major role in this identity-building process.

For the further development of this study, the following points should be taken into consideration:

1. In the light of the international evangelical movement, the evangelicals connected with *the Schools* must be defined as *conservative/moderate fundamentalist*, to re-use Holthaus' terminology. Even within the German-Swiss scene this conservative evangelical movement does not represent all evangelicals. At least three groups ought to be added: (1) the pietistic wing of the Lutheran and Reformed churches around the *Pfarrer-Gebets Bruderschaft* and its journal *Theologische Beiträge*; (2) the classical free churches (Mennonites, Baptists, Methodists), despite the fact that some of them hesitate to associate too freely with evangelicalism, especially in the form of American evangelicalism or the German *Bekenntnisbewegung* (cf. Marquardt; Kraus; Holthaus 1997:18); and (3) a

network of institutions such as the *Offensive junger Christen* (which holds relationships to the *Kairos-Centre* of René Padilla in Buenos Aires) or the journal *Unterwegs* (the German counterpart of the American journal *Sojourners*, associated with Jim Wallis).[1] This means that as we proceed to an analysis of the mission theology and theological education represented by *the Schools*, we are not giving a comprehensive picture of German-Swiss evangelicalism but only of its conservative/fundamentalist wing.

2. We have realised that *the Schools* under consideration are the heirs of the pietistic/neo-pietistic tradition, which, historically, has made a significant contribution not only to mission but also to mission training and theological education. This is a significant heritage. Further research must show to what extent *the Schools* have developed their potential – that is, how much they have gained their identity from within their own rich tradition.

3. The preliminary reading of the historical background suggests that the conservative German evangelical movement under consideration has defined its identity since the 1960s primarily in contrast to the state-church universities and the WCC. We have demonstrated that this is partially due to an historical situation in which the dominant alliance between the established churches and the state leaves only minimal space for alternative movements. Since the days of early Anabaptism, such movements have often been forced to move into sectarian separation.

4. We have argued that this historic situation becomes extremely evident in the realm of higher theological education, where the field is completely dominated by the state-church run departments of state universities. The university system in Germany and Switzerland simply does not provide a means for the recognition of theological schools outside the state churches.

5. We have demonstrated that conservative German evangelicals have, by their strong defensive and apologetic stance toward the WCC and the established theology of the state universities, moved themselves into a critical stage of separation and isolation. Particularly, the escalation of the late 1960s and early 1970s (*Frankfurt Declaration* and *Berlin Declaration*) has made dialogue virtually impossible. Further research will show how this has affected the development of mission theology (Part Three) and theological education (Part Four).

6. It became evident that throughout the process of finding a new identity, conservative German evangelicals were significantly strengthened by relating themselves to North American evangelicals. On the other hand, we have observed only minimal relations to the wider international evangelical scene. We have argued that the role of Germany in the two world wars has isolated Germany internationally and that this is

at least one reason for the isolation of German evangelicalism. Here again we have to ask how this has affected mission theology and theological education.

7. In the historical overview it became quite evident that American influence and support is most visible in the development of a new missiological interest among German evangelicals (e.g., the role of the *Freie Hochschule für Mission*) and in the establishing of the European Evangelical Accrediting Association. Through the latter, evangelicals in the German context were able to escape their isolation from university access. Advantages and disadvantages of this step need further analysis in the following parts of this study.

With this we have established the framework in which evangelical theological education in general and mission studies in particular takes place in German-speaking Europe. In two analytical steps we now look in greater detail at the *theology of mission* represented by *the Schools* (Part Three), and at the way they do *theological education and mission studies* (Part Four).

Note

[1] For the division between conservative and radical evangelicals in Germany, see Wolfgang Vorländer, 'Zwei Lausanne-Bewegungen unter einem Dach?'

PART THREE

THEOLOGY OF MISSION

GERMAN EVANGELICAL THEOLOGY OF MISSION IN THE LIGHT OF PARADIGM SHIFTS IN MISSION

The aim of *Part Three* is to examine evangelical mission studies in German-speaking Europe in terms of its *content*. This means that the *theology of mission* taught at *the Schools* will be analysed as it has developed between 1960 and 1995. This objective will be reached in two major steps. (1) First, a *theoretical foundation* needs to be laid – that is, *criteria* for the analysis of the content of mission studies must be established (chapter 8). (2) Then, based on these criteria, the actual analysis can be conducted (chapter 9).

CHAPTER 8

Theory: Towards a Holistic Paradigm in the Theology of Mission

This chapter culminates in the identification of the key elements of a *theology of mission* capable of serving at the turn from the twentieth to the twenty first century as criteria for the evaluation of mission studies in theological education. The main source is David Bosch's proposal of an *emerging ecumenical missionary paradigm* (1991).[1] We will not simply present a summary of Bosch's *Transforming Mission,* but generate an in-depth analysis of Bosch's work, drawing from many of his writings and putting his theology in context, all with the purpose of establishing valid criteria for the analysis of contemporary theology of mission. Thus, the argument of this section is as follows:

1. The *validity* of Bosch's proposal
2. The *context* of Bosch's proposal
3. The *content* of Bosch's proposal
4. The *consequences* of Bosch's proposal

1. The *Validity* of Bosch's Proposal

First, Bosch must be validated as a valuable standard for the evaluation of mission theology as taught at *the Schools.* It goes without saying that this can be done only on a preliminary level at this stage. The analysis of *the Schools* may shed additional light on the validity of his theory. This preliminary validation of the theory will be carried out in two steps. (1) The first argument is based on an examination of how Bosch has applied paradigm theory to mission. (2) The second argument is based on the reception of Bosch's proposal.

a) Applying Paradigm Theory to Mission

When Bosch applies paradigm theory to mission,[2] he relies heavily on Hans Küng – to wit, the proposal to apply paradigm theory to theology put forward by the Tübingen Symposium of 1983 (Küng and Tracy 1984; 1989).[3] Shortly after this symposium, Bosch began to apply paradigm theory to the theology of mission.[4] When, seven years later, *Transforming Mission* was published, it appeared to be a comprehensive and well-reflected application of this theory. It is Bosch's conviction that the idea of paradigm changes is of relevance to the study of theology generally and, in the context of his book, to the study and understanding of mission in particular; but he qualifies this by saying, 'This is not to suggest that we should uncritically apply Kuhn's ideas to the area of theology' (Bosch 1991:185). In this sense he basically follows Küng's application of the theory. He deliberately emphasises Küng's key phrase that in theology 'any paradigm shift can only be carried out on the basis of the gospel and because of the gospel, never, however, against the gospel' (Bosch 1991:187; cf. Küng and Tracy 1984:65).

Having introduced the concept of paradigm and paradigm shift according to Kuhn and Küng, Bosch applies Küng's theory in three basic ways:

1. He employs Küng's subdivision of history as one possibly helpful tool in understanding and interpreting developments in the history of mission (Bosch 1991:181–345).
2. He spells out the crisis of the Enlightenment paradigm with regard to Christian mission (1991:363–67).
3. And he outlines an emerging, new paradigm of mission comprising thirteen elements (1991:368–510)

On the basis of this internal data and of a preliminary reading of *Transforming Mission* (informed by an awareness of many of Bosch's earlier publications), we conclude that *Transforming Mission* is a valuable study which applies paradigm theory carefully and critically and presents a broad picture of contemporary missiological reflections.

b) The Reception of Bosch's Proposal

Bosch's proposal has been widely accepted, though it has not remained unchallenged.[5] The following issues have been raised:

1. Several scholars agree with Bosch in the analysis that mission has been undergoing tremendous changes and that these changes have to be seen within the context of larger global shifts, yet they hesitate to use the term paradigm. Wietzke rejects the term as referring to epochal shifts which can only be identified from a certain distance. For him it is too early to employ such terminology.[6] Werner uses the term in reference to Kuhn and Bosch but does not want to over-estimate it. How the change to a new paradigm will take place and what shape such a new paradigm of mission will take is – according to Werner – still in process. He understands his study as a contribution to the definition of this process (1993:44–47).

2. Secondly, there are some doubts regarding the reality of the paradigm Bosch describes (Wietzke:437–38; Werner 1993:44–47). The following questions are raised: Is it really emerging? To what extent are the contours already visible? Is it already an established paradigm? Bosch himself states,

> Today there is a growing sense of disaffection with the Enlightenment and a quest for a new approach to and understanding of reality. There is, on the one hand, a search under way for a new paradigm; on the other hand, such a new paradigm is already presenting itself (1991:185).

The question remains: is the new paradigm in mission presented by Bosch really emerging, or is it merely Bosch's personal view, at best his vision for the future of the Christian mission? Bosch's presentation calls for a threefold response. (a) Describing the elements of the new paradigm, he draws from a variety of theological and confessional traditions (ecumenical, evangelical, Catholic, Orthodox, western world and Two Thirds World), and with this he demonstrates that the features of the new paradigm do not come from his imagination but from what is already present in various currents within the Christian church. (b) It can also be said that others have also observed an *emerging* ecumenical paradigm long before Bosch's writing. Already in 1952, after the mission conference of Willingen, Karl Hartenstein wrote, 'We find ourselves at the dawning of a truly ecumenical theology, which, throughout every confession and denomination, has found its grounds in the testimony of the New Testament' (Freytag ed:52). With his significant contribution to the IMC conference of Ghana in 1958, Lesslie Newbigin spelled out in greater detail what one may call a new missionary paradigm (Newbigin 1958). The optimistic outlook of Hartenstein, Newbigin, Freytag and others was certainly shattered as the polarisation between the ecumenical and evangelical movements diminished hopes for the unity of the church in the sixties and seventies. But in 1978 Lesslie Newbigin observed new signs of hope that a truly ecumenical and holistic understanding of mission would emerge (Newbigin 1978:11). Others have indicated the same emerging development (Scherer/Bevans 1992:lx-lxi; Wietzke:425–440). (c) Bosch takes the risk of spelling out in greater detail how such an emerging ecumenical paradigm of mission will be shaped. He intends to present an accurate picture of an emerging paradigm with all its 'centrifugal and centripetal forces' (1991:367). Yet Bosch goes beyond what is already emerging to create a more comprehensive *vision* of the new paradigm, pushing further ahead towards a holistic understanding of mission. In this sense it is a very optimistic outlook. The notion of *creative tension* is Bosch's key element in keeping even the polarised elements together

(1991:367). Such an optimistic view is not shared by all his colleagues. Joachim Wietzke's proposal may therefore be more realistic, pointing to areas of convergence as well as areas of divergence. For Wietzke, the changes are still taking place and what could prove to form a new paradigm is still taking shape.

Bosch himself seems to be aware of these limitations. He qualifies his proposal by saying, 'Throughout, my reflections will remain tentative, suggesting rather than defining the contours of a new model' (1991:367). It is the task of this study to evaluate how German evangelicalism fits into the picture.

3. From this flows another issue which has been the subject of debate. Is Bosch's proposal really ecumenical? According to Küng, '*the transition from particularist to universal thinking*, and from *"controversial" theology to "ecumenical" theology* is an imperative requirement' in the new paradigm.[7] Bosch's phrase, 'an emerging ecumenical missionary paradigm,' indicates that it is certainly one of Bosch's intentions to move in that direction. The critical question to be raised is how far he went on this road. He has definitely pushed beyond the *liberal-conservative (ecumenical-evangelical)* polarisation. Yet various reviewers have pointed out that Bosch's ecumenical horizons need to be expanded. (a) In general, it can be observed that Bosch depends heavily on western contributions. The sources show that 'his dialogue was primarily with scholars in Europe and North America.' In his companion to *Transforming Mission*, Thomas has deliberately included texts from Africa, Asia, Latin America and Oceania to complement the ecumenical scope of Bosch (Thomas 1995:XV). (b) In addition to that, Bosch's discussion of Two Thirds World theologies is heavily weighted towards the ecumenical and liberation theology movements. He does not pay much attention to the contribution of the evangelical theologians of the Two Thirds World, represented by theologians around the International Fellowship of Evangelical Mission Theologians (INFEMIT) (Sugden 1996 :148–49). (c) Bosch also fails to give a voice to the *oral traditions* of the growing movement of independent churches in the Two Thirds World, which Walter Hollenweger has articulated in the ecumenical movement (Hollenweger 1991:98–99). (d) It has also been pointed out that Bosch does not take into account the growing awareness of women's roles in mission, nor does he refer to women theologians.[8] Looking at the history of mission and the larger horizon of the paradigm shift taking place in society, a new definition of the role and the relationship of the sexes can hardly be overlooked. Küng has pointed to the fact that the '*oikoumene between the sexes*' is one of the crucial aspects of a new paradigm in theology (Küng and Tracy 1989:450). (e) One of the central elements of the post-Enlightenment paradigm is a new awareness on the supernatural. A new missionary paradigm in intercultural partnership with those cultures of the world which have not

gone through the Enlightenment era ought to pay attention to the recovery of the supernatural. In this context the experience of the Pentecostal-charismatic movement, which must be seen as the fastest growing segment of world Christianity (Hollenweger 1997:13–15), can make a vital contribution. Bosch pays almost no attention to the Pentecostal-charismatic tradition (Sugden 1996:140).

A new *ecumenical* paradigm of mission will therefore definitely need expansion beyond the scope of David Bosch's proposal.

4. Furthermore, the question must be put as follows: Can Bosch's proposal be called a paradigm? A paradigm is, again according to the definition of Thomas Kuhn, 'an entire constellation of beliefs, values, techniques, and so on shared by the members of a given community.' A paradigm change definitely embraces more than some marginal changes in certain areas. In considering Bosch's contribution, the following question has to be answered: Is Bosch simply pulling together a variety of critical but independent issues touching on the current situation in mission; or does he adequately show the inter-relatedness of all the elements in such a way that they form the 'entire constellation of beliefs, values, techniques, and so on shared by the members' of the Christian community? Bosch himself gives an answer already in the introduction to the chapter on the elements of the new paradigm:

> The elements discussed below should by no means be seen as so many distinct and isolated components of a model; they are all intimately interrelated. This means that in discussing a specific element each other element is always somewhere in the background. The emphasis throughout should therefore be on the wholeness and indivisibility of the paradigm, rather than on separated ingredients (1991:368).

Bosch constantly connects the developments in mission with the larger picture of theology and society in general. Thus, what happens in Christian mission is part of the larger paradigm change taking place in western society, from an Enlightenment to a post-Enlightenment way of looking at reality. Time and again Bosch struggles with the fact that the division of the thirteen themes is somewhat artificial and by no means satisfactory because the various themes are interrelated in such a way that it is almost impossible to deal with them separately. We may therefore conclude that Bosch definitely presents a quite comprehensive and integrated picture.

5. Some have critically asked whether Bosch actually gives 'criteria for evaluating the components of the current paradigm.' From the point of view of a Christian theology, the issue at stake is whether the proposed and emerging paradigm is 'the result of Christian reflection or of the

impact of the culture on the church' (Sugden 1996:140, referring to Baillie).[9] As crucial as it is to raise such a question from the standpoint of theology, Bosch can certainly not be blamed for dismissing this issue. The biblical foundation plays a crucial role in his thoughts, as will be discussed later. Nevertheless, the question regarding the *norma normans* remains critical and should be reformulated in the following way: Does Bosch provide a normative biblical-theological foundation for mission? The answer has been given by Bosch himself:[10]

> Far from leading us into a morass of subjectivism and relativism, the approach I am advocating actually fosters a creative tension between my ultimate faith commitment and my own theological perception of faith. Instead of viewing my own interpretation as absolutely correct and all others by definition as wrong, I recognise that different theological interpretations, including my own, reflect different contexts, perspectives, and biases. This is not to say, however, that I regard all theological positions as equally valid or that it does not matter what people believe; rather, I shall do my uttermost to share my understanding of the faith with others while granting them the right to do the same. I realise that my theological approach is a 'map', and that a map is never the actual 'territory.' Although I believe that my map is the best, I accept that there are other types of maps and also that, at least in theory, one of those may be better than mine since I can only know in part (cf. 1 Cor 13:12) (1991:187).

One objection, put forward by Du Plessis, certainly deserves to be noticed: despite the fact that Bosch criticises the one-sided results of historical-critical exegesis (as will be discussed later on), he exclusively uses exegetical material from the historical-critical tradition or related disciplines. The vast mass of material produced in recent years in New Testament studies making use of the literary or textual communication approaches (especially in the United States) is not taken into account at all (Du Plessis:79–80). This is certainly a limitation to Bosch's work.

6. Finally, this author would like to add that Bosch's application of paradigm theory does not focus on the heart of the Kuhnian theory, namely the actual change process. While Bosch points to various paradigms in history, to the crisis of the enlightenment paradigm and also to the contours of an emerging new paradigm of mission, he never discusses the actual process of change in the light of Kuhn's theory. This observation does not diminish Bosch's contribution but it points beyond Bosch to even greater potential of the Kuhnian theory. This thesis will make use of this potential in its final part.

c) Conclusions

Based on these observations we come to the following conclusions regarding the validity and normativity of Bosch's proposal:

1. Bosch's proposed new missionary paradigm has validity in the sense that it provides a broad picture of the current situation as well as the direction in which the global Christian movement is going. It is also deeply rooted in his knowledge of the Bible. His proposal is a valuable standard by which any church or Christian institution may measure its present position within the larger world-wide Christian movement. Bosch's paradigm of mission can serve as a valid point of reference to measure mission studies in theological education in western Europe.

2. Bosch's paradigm shows deficiencies, gaps and one-sided tendencies. We must take into consideration the supplements and revisions spelled out above. Bosch cannot be the only point of reference.[11]

3. Bosch's proposal is not the *norma normans* of mission theology. He does not even pretend to provide a normative theology of mission, but he is actively involved in what is called the 'international hermeneutic community.' His contribution certainly does reflect a wide ecumenical exchange and has to be taken seriously by anyone who wants to engage in an ecumenical search for a biblical foundation for mission.

Based on this preliminary validation, Bosch's proposal will be used as the theory for the analysis of *the Schools*. After the analysis, in the concluding Part Five of this study, Bosch's paradigm will be reviewed in the light of the findings of this study.

2. The *Context* of Bosch's Proposal

Bosch's theory has to be seen in context.[12] This context is shaped (1) by the tremendous changes mission has been experiencing in the post-war period and the crisis this has caused the established tradition of the western church and (2) by the tensions which arose between the ecumenical and the evangelical ways of responding to the crisis. Bosch's contribution in this context is significant and needs to be reviewed in this chapter.

a) The Context of Crisis and Change

In the years after World War II, the western missionary movement was haunted by the observation that an era in mission had come to an end. The epoch of de-colonialisation had caused a severe crisis in the western understanding of mission. In the 1950s and 1960s western mission activities had been radically questioned. One of the most quoted texts in recent publications on mission is Walter Freytag's famous statement at the World Mission Conference at Achimota of 1958: 'Then, mission had problems, today it is a problem' (Freytag:111; cf. Werner 1993:3; Beyerhaus 1970:3). There is obviously a wide agreement in the diagnosis: mission is in crisis!

Consequently, the fact that mission is in crisis is the starting point for Bosch in his earlier book *Witness to the World* (1980:2–10), as well as in *Transforming Mission* (1991:1–11). 'Crisis' – says Bosch, referring to the Japanese characters for 'crisis' – 'is the point where danger and opportunity meet, where the future is in the balance and where events can go either way' (1991:3). His key thesis is that there is 'no possibility of ignoring the present crisis in mission, nor any point in trying to circumvent it, the only valid way open to us is to deal with the crisis in utmost sincerity yet *without allowing ourselves to succumb to it*' (1991:7).

It seems that Bosch is making a distinction between the *external crisis* caused by the circumstances of the post-colonial era and the *internal crisis* this has caused within the western church.

(1) THE EXTERNAL CRISIS

Bosch sees the external crisis – what he calls 'the wider crisis' – on three levels (1980:1–11, 188–89; 1991:264–73, 302–13):

1. The modern missionary movement is closely connected to the era of western colonialism, and this epoch definitively belongs to the past. Bosch summarises the consequences of this historical change for the church as follows (1980:3–4; 188–89):

- The west has lost its dominant position in the world. Western theology and church practice are no longer the universal norm.
- Secularisation has made God redundant. The western world has been de-christianised.
- The world can no longer be divided into 'Christian' and 'non-Christian' territories.
- There is a profound feeling of ambiguity about western technology and development and about the idea of progress.
- Unjust structures of oppression and exploitation are being challenged as never before. There is a sense of guilt among western Christians because of their complicity in the exploitation of the Two Thirds World.
- The world is, apparently irreversibly, divided between the rich and the poor.
- We know that we live on a shrinking globe with finite resources. We are able to kill God's earth and wipe out humankind.
- Freedom of religion is regarded as a basic human right.
- The church has lost its privilege and its powerful position alongside the state, which dominated not only the west but also missions of the colonial era.

- Missionaries are no longer the ambassadors of the powerful west. 'They now go to countries frequently hostile to Christian missions.'

With this crisis assessment, Bosch finds himself in good company, as the studies of Werner, Collet, Newbigin and others demonstrate. Referring to the colonial model of mission, Newbigin concludes:

> The one thing that can certainly be said about this chapter of human history is that it is over. For more than two centuries it has provided the framework in which the Western churches have understood their world missionary task. To continue to think in the familiar terms is now folly. We are forced to do something that the Western churches have never had to do since the day of their own birth – to discover the form and substance of a missionary church in terms which are valid in a world which has rejected the power and the influence of the Western nations. Mission will no longer work along the streams of expanding Western power. They have to learn to go against the stream (1978:6).

2. But it is not only the fact of a changed world situation that puts pressure on the church. Because of its alliance with the western colonial powers, the mission movement of the western churches itself has been severely criticised. Churches of the Two Thirds World have experienced western mission work not always as a help but often as an embarrassment. 'Many of the grand institutions erected by mission agencies, often at great cost and with tremendous dedication ... have turned out to be impediments rather than assets to the life and growth of the younger churches' (1991:365). The image of the missionary has changed. They are no longer the 'rugged heroes of the faith of an earlier era, who "brought" the "gospel" to the uttermost ends of the earth.' Rather, they are 'feeble folk,' not always very wise and holy – just ordinary Christians (1991:363–66).

3 David Bosch interprets these elements of the challenge to the Christian church within the larger framework of the paradigm shift from the Enlightenment to the post-Enlightenment era, as summarised in the chart below (1991:264–73, 352–62; cf. Newbigin 1983).

Bosch concludes:

> Never before in the history of humankind have scholars in all disciplines (including theology) been so preoccupied as they are today, not with the study of their disciplines themselves, but with the metaquestions concerning these disciplines. This state of affairs in itself is indicative of the presence of a crisis of major proportions or, to put it in Kuhnian terms, of the advent of a significant 'paradigm

	Features of the Enlightenment paradigm	**Impact upon theology**	**Challenges to the Enlightenment paradigm**
1.	The Age of Reason	Theology as a science → secularisation of theology	Expansion of reality – recovery of transcendence and religion
2.	Subject-object separation	The 'ugly ditch' (Lessing) between the Bible and life today	New epistemology – holistic, symbiotic
3.	From purpose to causality	Dependence on planning and methods (cause-effect)	Rediscovery of the teleological dimension
4.	Belief in progress	Optimistic and triumphalistic view of the Christianisation of the world	Challenge to progress thinking and western 'developmentalism'
5.	Separation of knowledge and value	Withdrawal of theology to religious matters	From a 'objectivist framework' to a 'fiduciary framework'
6.	All problems are in principle solvable	Dependence less on God, more on technology – optimism	New pessimism – new awareness human limitations and the evil in the world
7.	Emancipated, autonomous individualism	Religious individualism – theological relativism	New call for commitment and interdependence

> shift' in *all* branches of science ... It was unthinkable that the Christian church, theology and mission would remain unscathed (1991:363).

Such are the external data which have caused, and continue to cause, the crisis in mission.

(2) THE INTERNAL CRISIS

This leads to the current crisis of mission, which has to be seen as something inside the church. The challenges described above challenge the western church in its very being. The real problem is 'not "outside," on the mission field, but in the heart of the western church itself,' says Bosch (1991:5; cf. Beyerhaus 1970:11–12). He suggests that the crisis of mission – which is actually the crisis of the church – must be seen on several levels (1991:4; referring to Gensichen 1971:27–29).

1. The Crisis of the *Foundation of Mission*. Alongside the biblical foundation, Warneck emphasised the following 'natural' grounds for mission:

> (a) the absoluteness and superiority of the Christian religion when compared with others; (b) the acceptability and adaptability of Christianity to all peoples and conditions; (c) the superior achievements of the Christian mission on the 'mission fields'; and (d) the fact that Christianity has, in past and present, shown itself to be stronger than all other religions (Bosch 1991:5).

It is obvious that such foundations were shaken by the changes in the world situation. Today there is certainly a wide agreement that only scripture can provide the foundation for Christian mission. A biblical theology of mission stands at the outset of virtually every serious book on mission. All the diverging streams of the world mission movement agree on this point.[13] Yet such a basic confession of scripture as the foundation for mission does not automatically provide for a serious foundation, as Bosch points out (1991:4–6). (a) Sometimes the 'success' of missions has served as a strong foundation for the Christian mission. In an oversimplified identification of missionary 'accomplishments' with some of the biblical stories, 'the success of the Christian Mission became the foundation for mission.' (b) Often in the past, a biblical basis for mission has been established by pulling 'a series of proof-texts out of the Old and New Testament' (cf. Verkuyl:90). Such methods obviously do not lead to a serious foundation. There is, therefore, an 'increased urgent need for a biblical foundation' for mission, based on a responsible interpretation of Scripture (cf. Bosch 1978; 1986; 1993b).[14]

2. The crisis in the *motives and aims of mission*. As a result of the sometimes ambiguous foundation, the 'motives and the aim of mission were often equally ambiguous' (Bosch 1991:5). (a) Many traditional motives and goals were biased by the notion of western superiority. But the changed world situation has called into question any missionary enterprise which aims at the Europeanisation or Americanisation of Two-Thirds World peoples and cultures. (b) The diversification of theological options in the past fifty years has even added to the crisis of motives and goals. While ecumenicals tend to call for mission as humanisation and liberation in this world, evangelicals have emphasised eternal salvation.

3. The crisis in the *nature and practice of missions*. Finally, the combination of ambiguous foundations, motives and goals led to questionable practices. 'The young churches "planted" on the "mission fields" were replicas of the churches on the mission agency's "home front," "blessed" with all the paraphernalia of those churches, "everything from

harmonium to archdeacons" ' (Bosch 1991:5; referring to Newbigin 1969:107). This again, has been severely criticised (cf. Collet:26ff.).

Conclusion: Bosch's analysis is in broad agreement with the crisis awareness in the wider ecumenical scene. From Walter Freytag's comment at the Achimota Conference of 1958 up to present day evaluations, the colonial era of the western mission movement has been critically analysed and new directions have been called for (cf. Scherer and Bevans 1992; 1994). The Catholic scholar Giancarlo Collet has summarised all the elements which constitute this crisis into a fundamental critique of western mission (Collet; cf. Werner 1993:56–61). Lesslie Newbigin (1987a; 1984) has pointed convincingly to the crisis of the Enlightenment paradigm and calls for a revision of traditional western thinking and action. Shenk, and with him a range of Mennonite missiologists, points to the failure of the Christendom model of mission and proposes a 'transfiguration of mission' (Shenk ed. 1993). Walter Hollenweger, addressing the Pentecostal community, pleads for a 'non-colonial model' of mission and evangelism (1995a; cf. 1973). Using Kraemer's words, Bosch claims that 'strictly speaking, one ought to say that the Church is always in a state of crisis and that its greatest shortcoming is that it is only occasionally aware of it' (1991:2). However, it is precisely this awareness of its critical circumstances which would help the church to discover its true nature and mission. To all those who try to push aside the crisis, Bosch says:

> If the atmosphere of crisislessness still lingers on in many parts of the West, this is simply the result of a dangerous delusion. Let us also know that to encounter crisis is to encounter the possibility of truly being the *church* (1991:2–3).

However, Bosch does not rest with a critical analysis of the shortcomings of the modern missionary movement. He makes the helpful distinction between the wider crisis of a changed world situation and the inner crisis, which is ultimately the crisis of the church's identity. The former, according to Bosch, must be seen in the larger context of the paradigm shift from modernity to post modernity, the latter draws the church back to its biblical roots.

b) The Context of the Ecumenical-Evangelical Polarisation

There is apparently a search for answers, for meaningful, probably new paradigms of mission at the turn of the millennium. The collection of texts published in the *New Directions in Mission and Evangelization* series is an indicator of that search for new perspectives 'for the church's mission and the post-modern world.' Scherer and Bevans have been including contributions from Roman Catholics, Orthodox, conciliar Protestants, evangelicals and Pentecostals in their collections (1992; 1994). The contributions to these two volumes also show evidence that in the search for new answers, the world Christian movement does experience convergencies but also divergencies, conflicts and even polarisations.[15]

Bosch has identified several patterns of response to the crisis:

1. One part of the Christian missionary movement has 'drawn the conclusion that the Christian mission and everything it stood for now belong to a bygone era. It should be eulogised and then buried; it was an episode, not more, in the history of Christianity and may now be safely banished to the archives' (Bosch 1991:365). The result is 'an almost complete paralysis and total withdrawal from any activity traditionally associated with mission, in whatever form' (Bosch 1991:7; cf. Werner 1993:3–7).

2. Some have reshaped mission in completely new directions, interpreting it as 'action for humanisation in the secular life of the world' (Newbigin 1978:10). Bosch accuses these circles of having 'a diluted gospel' (1980:212).

3. For others mission goes on as 'business as usual.' They continue in a fully uncritical way with mission in the traditional fashion. But the solution cannot be 'in a simple return to an earlier missionary consciousness and practice' (Bosch 1991:7).

4. Others have emphasised the church's abiding mission but call for repentance and change (Bosch 1991:365–66).[16] They search for a model of mission which is faithful to the biblical foundation, moves beyond the polarisation within the Christian missionary movement in the present time, and is holistic in its understanding and practice of mission (Bosch 1980:221; 1991:7; cf. Newbigin 1978:10–12). This is the avenue Bosch proposes.

Thus, we recognise that the search for the transfiguration of mission has not necessarily united the Christian church for the sake of a great common task; rather, it shakes it and tears it apart into diverging, even opposing strands. In view of the Protestant mission movement one cannot escape the fact that the division between the ecumenical and evangelical view of mission has dominated the last thirty five years. Bosch's work must be seen in the context of a polarisation in which he attempted to play an mediating role.

(1) THE ECUMENICAL-EVANGELICAL POLARISATION

Bosch wrote in *Witness to the World*:

> The evangelical and ecumenical approaches to mission have to a large extent dominated the theory and practice of mission in recent decades. The polarisation appears to be complete: Proclamation

> stands over against 'Christian presence,' Jesus as Redeemer over against Jesus the Man for others, redemption over against humanisation, the salvation of the soul over against liberation and revolution (1980:39–40).

This theology of mission, published in 1980, begins with 'contrasting missionary models' (1980:28–35) and concludes with the 'shortcomings in the evangelical theology of mission' under the heading 'An emaciated gospel' (1980:202–) and the ecumenical view of mission under the title 'A diluted gospel' (1980:212–) He characterises the two streams as follows:

The Ecumenical View of Mission = 'A Diluted Gospel'	**The Evangelical View of Mission = 'An Emaciated Gospel'**
– The Bible is interpreted from within a socio-political context – the concrete world sets the agenda and shapes theology. – Mission focuses on the development of the total human world towards *shalom* – Social action is an integral part of mission. – The concern is not so much the eternal lostness of humanity but its this-worldly struggle for liberation and justice. – Redemption is the universal process towards *shalom.* – The church should not separate from the secular world; rather, it needs to become secularised to serve the world. – The Christian faith should 'create theological space' to include other religions.	– Universally valid theological statements can be derived directly from the Bible. – Mission is primarily (or even solely) evangelism. – Social action may be an aid to or the result of evangelism. – 'The people who have not heard the gospel will perish eternally.' – 'The forgiveness of personal sin is equated with redemption.' – The world in which we live is essentially evil. – God's work and Lordship is seen as mainly limited to the realm of the church. – Evangelicals hold to a strong futurist eschatology. – It is not the church's task to get involved in structural changes in society. – Other religions are viewed as the religious quest of a fallen humanity deceived by Satan.

Bosch's comparison may not do justice to all who identify themselves with either movement. Identifying the main issues in the ecumenical-evangelical controversy is a rather delicate venture. It turns too easily into an oversimplified presentation of a polarisation which does not do justice to complex realities. With Saayman we state: 'We therefore have to guard against caricatures. Nevertheless, it *is* possible to differentiate between the two schools of thought' (1990:100).

Nevertheless, Bosch has certainly identified the key areas of the 'great debate in mission' (Hedlund), as is confirmed by many other studies.[17] A comparison-of-models-study,[18] focusing on the German context of this thesis, can isolate the following critical issues:

1. Crisis and response (continuity and discontinuity in a time of changes)
2. Bible, context and hermeneutics (normativity of the Bible and contextualisation)
3. Salvation and mission (words and deeds, evangelisation and social action)
4. Salvation history and eschatology (the work of God inside and outside the church, today and in the future)
5. The church (the church as instrument, witness and result of mission)
6. Theology of religions (mission and dialogue in relation to other living faiths)

It goes beyond the scope of this study to engage in an extensive discussion of the two opposed positions. At this point we are only establishing the background for Bosch's proposal. Taking into account the literature introduced above, we propose the following comparative chart:

Theme	Ecumenical focus[19]	Evangelical focus
Crisis and Response	Crisis *because* of a changing world situation Critique of the traditional western mission movement Focus on discontinuity: the world sets the agenda and this calls for a radical rethinking of mission and changes; not only forms but also content (theology of mission)	Crisis *because* of a deviation from the Biblical view of mission Critique of the developments of the WCC's understanding of mission[20] Focus on continuity: Mission in continuity with the classical (= biblical) mission movement – changes in forms may be necessary[21]
Bible, context and hermeneutics	The context determines theology 'A once for all fixed "depositum fidei" does no longer exist'	The Bible determines theology The universal authority of the Bible remains unquestionable[22]

Theme	Ecumenical focus[19]	Evangelical focus
Salvation and mission	Salvation as integral to human liberation (*shalom*) Mission as holistic action towards *shalom*	Salvation focuses on reconciliation with God through Jesus Christ appropriated by faith Mission primarily as evangelisation
Salvation history and eschatology	God's action in history, beyond the church – 'Christus extra muros ecclesiae' God-world-church-order Kingdom of God in this world, beyond the church, wherever God moves history toward *shalom* Emphasis on the 'here and now' and the future of *this* world	God's salvific action primarily in and through Jesus Christ and the church God-church-world-order Kingdom of God primarily in the future – in a limited way already today in the church Emphasis on the eternal and the eschatological *new* world[23]
The church	The church as participating in God's mission Focus on society 'Open' ecclesiology – the hidden church – the church of the poor	The church as agent and instrument of mission Focus on individuals 'Closed' ecclesiology – church of believers[24]
Theology of religions	Inclusivism and Pluralism Pneumatological reinterpretation of the trinity – openness for God's revelation beyond Christ and the Bible[25] Focus on Dialogue	Exclusivism Christological understanding of the trinity – concentration on God's revelation in Christ and the Bible Focus on Evangelisation[26]

Following this agenda we will consider Bosch's 'emerging paradigm of mission' and later the theology of mission taught at *the Schools*. As Saayman suggests (1995), Bosch's work has to be interpreted against this background. We also notice that Bosch sees the differences not as slightly different emphases but as a deep split. He writes, 'If we now … switch from evangelicalism to the ecumenical position, it is as if we are moving from one planet to another – planets that are often apparently light-years apart!' (1980:35). A deep awareness of this sad separation has shaped Bosch's entire work, not only in 1980 when he was writing *Witness to the World* but also in the last years of his life, when *Transforming Mission* took shape.

(2) 'CREATIVE TENSION' AND 'BEYOND'

On the other hand Bosch asks, 'Are these two reconcilable positions?' and his answer is, 'Hopefully yes!' (1980:39). He belongs to those theologians who search for a new paradigm of mission theology which moves beyond the status quo of the separation between ecumenicals and evangelicals.[27] Others have been pointing in the same direction and suggest ways to overcome the controversy, which Jürgen Moltmann has called 'a wrong alternative, a suicidal polarisation' (quoted in Bosch 1980:32). Despite all the divergencies, there have always been convergencies. Four recent collections of mission statements from different backgrounds demonstrate growing convergencies – though there is no need to point out the remaining differences: (1) 'Mission Reaffirmed: Recent Authoritative Statements of Churches Around the World (1982–1991)' (Spindler 1991b); (2) *New Directions in Mission and Evangelization 1: Basic Statements 1974–1991* (Scherer and Bevans); (3) *Roots of the Great Debate in Mission* (Hedlund); and (4) *Mission erklärt. Ökumenische Dokumente von 1972 bis 1992* (Wietzke).

Bosch is certainly one of the most pronounced advocates of a position 'beyond' the paralysing controversy. In his *Witness to the World* (1980) he follows the ecumenical-evangelical dichotomy. According to Willem Saayman, the book is even 'structured around this polarisation' (1990:99). Saayman, who has analysed Bosch's approach to the ecumenical-evangelical polarisation (1990) states, 'Bosch does not consider bridging the gulf by forming some kind of synthesis or compromise of ecumenical and evangelical views. Rather, he advocates a transcending of the division' (1990:105). He proposes a new missionary paradigm which 'moves beyond' in many ways.[28] It is part of the newness of the paradigm that it points beyond the *status quo* of the current situation. Bosch suggests a 'move beyond' in the following areas:

1. The new paradigm moves beyond *colonialism* as well as *anti-colonialism*, beyond *dependence* and *independence* toward a paradigm of truly mutual global *interdependence* (cf. Hiebert 1991).

2. The new paradigm moves beyond the *liberal* versus *conservative*, or *ecumenical* versus *evangelical*, toward a truly *ecumenical* paradigm of mission.

3. The new paradigm moves beyond the emphasis on *spiritual* versus *socio-political*, or *evangelism* versus *social action* toward a truly *holistic paradigm* of salvation and missions.

Bosch suggests that the differing positions be seen not as irreconcilable but rather as creative tensions (1980:39–40, 221ff; 1991:367). The notion of *creative tension* is present in all of Bosch's thought to such an extent that *Missionalia* gave its issue on the dialogue with David Bosch the title 'Mission in Creative Tension' (issue January 18, 1990). In Bosch's perception, all the divergencies and polarisations mentioned above do not appear to be a tragedy; they carry rather the potential of creative tensions (cf. 1991:367). Whether this potential can be exploited is still open – even in Bosch's view (1991:367).

With this we have reviewed the context in which we ought to read Bosch's proposal outlined in *Transforming Mission*. (1) It is a context which is characterised by the *crises and changes* which have shaped the recent decades of the Christian missionary movement. Bosch analyses this crisis in the light of the larger shift from modernity to post-modernity and points to the internal as well as the external dimensions of the crisis. (2) It is also the context of a growing polarisation within the Christian church concerning the proper response to the crisis. Bosch identifies key issues in the ecumenical-evangelical debate and becomes one of the main forces pointing beyond a seemingly fruitless dichotomy. It is in this light that the content of Bosch's ecumenical paradigm of mission now can be introduced

3. The *Content* of Bosch's Proposal

It is not the objective of this chapter to present a mere summary of the thirteen elements of what Bosch calls 'an emerging ecumenical missionary paradigm.' In order to test whether Bosch succeeds in moving beyond the status quo of the ecumenical-evangelical polarisation, the agenda established in the previous chapter will be addressed.

The first item, Bosch's perception of the crisis and his response to that crisis, has just been discussed in the previous section. Now we turn to the five theological issues:

a) Bible, Context and Hermeneutics: Creative Tension between the Universal Claim of the Bible and Contextual Interpretation

As we approach the controversial issues, we will first tackle the tension between the emphasis on the context and the emphasis on the authority of Bible. This leads to the question of hermeneutics, as well as to the questions surrounding the concept of contextualisation.

(1) DAVID BOSCH AND HERMENEUTICS

Bosch, a trained New Testament scholar (DTheol Basel, 1959), has devoted large sections of his books and many articles to the question of hermeneutics in the theology of mission.[29] Bosch's reflection on hermeneutics from 1978 to 1993 can be summarised as follows:

1. The Bible is the ultimate source, the *norma normans*, for the theology of mission. This foundation leads to the conviction that in times of crisis the church has to turn to the Bible to get its perspective right.

2. The traditional use of the Bible as 'a mine from which "missionary texts" could be extracted' has been criticised by Bosch for at least two reasons (1978:439; 1986:73; 1993b:175–92): (a) It depends too heavily on a few single commands such as the classical text in Matthew 28:18–20. (b) It pre-supposes a knowledge of what mission is and uses selected biblical texts as proof-texts.

3. Bosch also criticises any attempt to narrow down a biblical theology of mission to one term. In the context of the BISAM project of the IAMS, he rejected the idea of concentrating on the concept of 'witness,' since 'choosing *one* biblical concept as the focus for a study on something like "biblical foundations for mission," is bound to lead to distortions' (1986:67).

4. Historical-critical scholarship has been equally criticised by Bosch. He complains of the direction biblical scholarship has taken in the Enlightenment paradigm. The idea of finding the original meaning of the text by detached academic research has turned out to be a dead-end street (1986:70–73). The results – for example, the emphasis on 'the diversity of the biblical message and the historical conditioning of each text' (1985:532) – leave the missiologist, and finally the church in its mission, without a solid ground for its task.[30]

5. Bosch is also reluctant about missiological publications which begin with 'biblical foundations of mission' without having discussed their hermeneutical presuppositions. 'We usually assume far too easily that we can employ the Bible as a kind of objective arbitrator in the case of theological differences, not realizing that every one of us approaches the Bible with his own set of preconceived ideas about what it says.' He commends Verkuyl's approach of first discussing the discipline of mission studies and the history of missiological thinking, before developing the biblical foundations of mission (Bosch 1978:437–38).

6. Bosch points beyond the proof-text and single-term method to biblical themes of the Old and the New Testament which demonstrate the mission of God and therefore the missionary dimension of the church.[31]

Finally, with the publication of *Transforming Mission*, Bosch has put forward a proposal for a biblical theology of mission which gives witness to his hermeneutic (1991:56–178):

1. It is based on the presupposition that the Bible is the point of orientation, the foundational document on which any theology of mission must be based. Referring to changes and paradigm shifts, he states, 'For Christians this means that any paradigm shift can only be carried out on

the basis of the gospel and because of the gospel, never, however, against the gospel' (1991:187; referring to Küng).

2. Bosch approaches the New Testament with the general understanding that the New Testament texts must be read as 'a missionary document' born in the context of the early church in mission (1991:15–16; referring to Kähler's phrase 'mission is the mother of theology').

3. He begins his study with 'a brief overview of the missionary character of the ministry of Jesus and the early church' (1991:15; cf. 25–55), and then develops three models of mission – according to Matthew, to Luke-Acts and to Paul (1991:54–178).

4. In terms of hermeneutics, our key interest must be on the rationale he gives for such a procedure and the way he relates the biblical texts to the present time. Bosch depicts the early church's missiological paradigm as possessing a homogenous core:

> Some firm and enduring elements of mission appear, however, to have emerged in the course of our investigation. The mission of the church is rooted in God's revelation in the man from Nazareth who lived and laboured in Palestine, was crucified on Golgotha, and, so the church believes, was raised from the dead. For the New Testament mission is determined by the knowledge that the eschatological hour has dawned, bringing salvation within reach of all and leading to its final completion... The New Testament witnesses assume the possibility of a community of people who, in the face of the tribulations they encounter, keep their eyes steadfastly on the reign of God by praying for its coming, by being its disciples, by proclaiming its presence, by working for peace and justice in the midst of hatred and oppression, and by looking and working toward God's liberating future (1991:54).

With this he establishes, within the biblical text, a 'firm and enduring' core of what mission is, as well as the process of contextualisation of this core by Matthew, Luke and Paul, each in the situation of his community. 'Each represents a subparadigm of the early Christian missionary movement' (1991:54).

5. Furthermore, the process of contextualisation Bosch observes in the New Testament provides our interpretative key. We have to 'discover how they interpreted mission for their communities, and emulate the imaginative way in which they did this as a model for our missionary involvement today' (1991:54). Thus, Bosch sustains both a core of missiological concepts with a higher degree of normativity for us and also models of contextual interpretations *already* in the biblical texts, which encourages us to contextualise the core understanding of the New Testament mission in our own time.[32]

6. Here, Bosch moves beyond the polarised positions both of those who posit a biblical, unchangeable understanding of mission and of those who understand the biblical text to be entirely contextual. For Bosch, both the unchangeable core and the principle of contextualisation are found in the New Testament.

Du Plessis (1990) has claimed that Bosch's hermeneutical approach has not succeeded in escaping from the tension between a literal quoting of missiological proof-texts and the destructive fragmentation and relativism of critical scholarship, though the present writer, having reviewed Bosch's use of scripture, does not share such criticisms.

(2) CONTEXTUALISATION AND INCULTURATION

Moving on to the issue of contextualisation, two points must be affirmed at the outset: (1) for Bosch, there is a core of biblical truth which makes up the 'firm and enduring elements of mission'; (2) at the same time, there is a considerable degree of contextualisation taking place already in the biblical writings (such as the models of Matthew, Luke and Paul).

It is with this understanding in mind that one should approach Bosch's chapters on 'Mission as Contextualisation' (1991:420–32) and 'Mission as Inculturation' (1991:447–57). In Bosch's view, 'there can be no doubt that the contextualisation project is essentially legitimate, given the situation in which many theologians find themselves.' But Bosch wants to qualify that because there are some remaining ambiguities, 'particularly insofar as there is a tendency in contextual theology to overreact,' stressing only the break with the past and denying continuity (1991:425). A new missionary paradigm should therefore incorporate a revised and balanced model of contextualisation, with the following main features (1991:427–28):

1. The construction of 'local theologies' without falling into the traps of relativism and absolutism.

2. The affirmation of 'the universal and context transcending dimension of theology,' without falling into the trap of understanding one theology as the final form of eternal revelation.

Therefore, 'the best contextual theologies indeed hold on to this dialectic relationship' between a *theologia localis* and the *theologia oecumenica.*

The *concept of inculturation,* used in missiology since the early 1960s, points to the fact that 'the Christian faith never exists except as "translated" into a culture.' Inculturation is one of several steps needed to break western domination and the assumption that the western form of Christianity has eternal value. The concept of inculturation leads beyond the earlier concepts of 'adaptation,' 'accommodation' and 'indigenisation' to a truly new paradigm:

1. While 'adaptation,' 'accommodation' and 'indigenisation' have focused mainly on methods and forms, 'inculturation' also includes

content. To the traditional 'three self' (self-government, self-support and self-propagation), a 'fourth self' is added: *self theologising*. This leads to so-called *local theologies*.

2. While 'adaptation,' 'accommodation' and 'indigenisation' have been mainly implemented and supervised by western missionaries, 'inculturation' is fully in the hands of the local community (and the Holy Spirit).

3. Inculturation is based on the biblical model of *incarnation*.

At the same time, inculturation must, in Bosch's view, be aware of some possible one-sided tendencies:

1. Inculturation has to be a double movement: inculturation of Christianity *and* Christianisation (not westernisation!) of culture.

2. The emphasis on local theology must be complemented by an emphasis on global theological interaction. The new paradigm promotes not only inculturation but also *inter*culturation.

Bosch calls for a move beyond local-universal polarities to an 'intercultural' theology (1991:455–57; cf. Hollenweger 1979; 1982; 1988).[33]

b) Salvation and Mission: Creative Tension between the Spiritual and Social Dimensions

(1) TOWARDS AN INTEGRATIVE UNDERSTANDING OF SALVATION

Bosch describes the debate over the meaning of salvation historically, pointing to three succeeding models (1991:393–7): (1) The model of the Greek Patristic period, in which salvation was understood in terms of being lifted up in Christ to a divine status; (2) the concept of the west, stressing sin, the substitutionary death of Christ and the redemption of individual souls; and (3) the modern understanding of salvation, resulting from the Enlightenment and secularism, focusing on *shalom* as this-worldly salvation (cf. Hoekendijk). In addition, Bosch observes that the Greek model focuses on the beginning of Jesus' life (incarnation) and the western model on the end of Jesus' life (death, cross), whereas the modern model draws from Jesus' life itself (model, teacher).

As pointed out earlier, the debate between ecumenicals, advocating the *horizontal- external* dimension of salvation, and evangelicals, claiming the primacy of a *vertical-spiritual* understanding of salvation, has determined to a large extent the missiological discussion in the last decades.

Once more, Bosch suggests a *new paradigm* which leads to a synthesis beyond the polarisation, 'toward comprehensive salvation' (1991:399–400). What Bosch attempts is to integrate his observations concerning the three historical models of salvation into a holistic understanding of Christ *and* of salvation. Therefore, a comprehensive understanding of salvation includes: (1) an emphasis on the incarnation and the transformational character of salvation; (2) an emphasis on the life of Jesus and the socio-political dimension of salvation, and (3) an emphasis on Jesus' death on the cross and the 'soul-saving' dimension of salvation. Bosch emphasises the 'need of an interpretation of salvation which operates within a *comprehensive* Christological framework, which makes the *totus Christus* – his incarnation, earthly life, death, resurrection and parousia – indispensable for church and theology' (1991:399). He stresses – against McGavran and some evangelicals[34] – the fact that 'redemption is never salvation *out of* this world *(salus e mundo)* but always salvation *of* this world *(salus mundi)*. Salvation in Christ is salvation in the context of human society en route to the whole and healed world' (1991:399, with reference to Aagaard). At the same time he argues – addressing ecumenicals – that

> final salvation will not be wrought by human hands, not even by *Christian* hands. The Christian's eschatological vision of salvation will not be realized in history... We therefore hold on to the transcendent character of salvation also, and to the need of calling people to faith in God through Christ. Salvation does not come but along the route of repentance and personal faith-commitment (1991:400).

Bosch proposes an *indicative* dimension of salvation (salvation is already a reality), a *subjunctive* dimension of salvation (comprehensive salvation is yet to come), and an *imperative* dimension of salvation (get involved in the ministry of salvation) (1991:400).

(2) TOWARDS AN INTEGRATIVE PRACTICE OF MISSION

An integral understanding of salvation ought to lead to an integral practice of mission. In the words of Bosch, 'The integral character of salvation demands that the scope of the church's mission be more comprehensive than has traditionally been the case' (1991:400). In a new paradigm of mission, the dichotomy between *evangelism* and *social action* must be overcome. For Bosch 'the relationship between the evangelistic and the societal dimension of the Christian mission constitutes one of the thorniest areas in theology and practice of mission' (1991:401). In the modern missionary period, the major discussions centred in the distinction between the two mandates (spiritual and social) and the question of the right relationship between the two – and this again has been on the agenda of the ecumenical-evangelical debate for years.

Bosch challenges the two-mandate concept, calling for a 'full-orbed' gospel which incorporates the spiritual as well as the social dimension. He already sees the convergence of the two aspects in the ecumenical, the evangelical, the Catholic, as well as in the Orthodox movement. The emerging new paradigm of mission is shaped by an increasing conviction 'to overcome the old dichotomies between evangelism and social action. The "spiritual Gospel" and "material Gospel" were in Jesus one Gospel' (1991:408, quoting 'Missions and Evangelism – An Ecumenical Affirmation,' WCC 1982). Nonetheless, Bosch moves on to describe evangelism and social action as two dimensions of mission:

1. The *evangelistic dimension* of mission: In this century, a 'plethora of definitions' have been used to define evangelism and have obviously created much confusion, especially in the dialogue between evangelicals and ecumenicals. The former have tended to use evangelism as the key term to describe the Church's mission, because they did not agree with the way they think ecumenicals have 'reconceptualized' mission. The latter seem to understand evangelism in a broader way, including the entire mission of the church.

Bosch again attempts to move beyond the present stage of discussion by outlining the meaning of evangelism in the emerging paradigm of mission. In order to understand the direction in which Bosch is pointing, his eighteen statements on evangelism must be spelled out here (1991:411–20):

1. Mission is wider than evangelism. Mission embraces the totality of the church's sending into the world. Evangelism is one aspect of the mission.
2. 'Evangelism should therefore not be equated with mission.'
3. 'Evangelism may be viewed as an essential "dimension of the total activity of the Church." '
4. 'Evangelism involves witnessing to what God has done, is doing and will do. Evangelism thus involves the "gospel events." '
5. 'Even so, evangelism does aim at a response,' it is the call to *metanoia*.
6. 'Evangelism is always invitation.'
7. 'The one who evangelises is a witness not a judge.'
8. 'Even though we ought to be modest about the character and effectiveness of our witness, evangelism remains an indispensable ministry.'
9. 'Evangelism is only possible when the community that evangelises – the church – is a radiant Manifestation of the Christian faith and exhibits an attractive lifestyle.'
10. 'Evangelism offers people salvation as a present gift and with it assurance of eternal bliss.'
11. 'Evangelism is not proselytism.'
12. 'Evangelism is not the same as church extension.'
13. 'To distinguish between evangelism and membership recruitment is not to suggest, though, that they are disconnected.'

14. 'In Evangelism, "only people can be addressed and only people can respond." '
15. 'Authentic evangelism is always contextual.'
16. 'Because of this, evangelism cannot be from divorced from the preaching and practising of justice.'
17. 'Evangelism is not a mechanism to hasten the return of Christ.'
18. 'Evangelism is not only verbal proclamation.'

Spelling out this view, Bosch draws from ecumenical, evangelical, as well as Catholic sources, indicating that this is definitely an *emerging ecumenical* model of evangelism.[35]

In David Bosch's summary then, evangelism is

> that dimension and activity of the church's mission which, by word and deed and in the light of particular conditions and a particular context, offers every person and community, everywhere, a valid opportunity to be directly challenged to a radical reorientation of their lives, a reorientation which involves such things as deliverance from slavery to the world and its powers; embracing Christ as Saviour and Lord; becoming a living member of his community, the church; being enlisted into his service of reconciliation, peace, and justice; and being committed to God's purpose of placing all things under the rule of Christ (1991:420).

2. The *social and political dimension* of mission: Bosch deals with the social and political dimension of mission under the headings 'Mission as the Quest for Justice' (1991:400–08) and 'Mission as Liberation' (1991:432–47). He sees liberation theology 'as one of the most dramatic illustrations of the fundamental paradigm shift that is currently taking place in mission thinking and practice,' which has drawn our attention to the social and political dimension of mission. Liberation theology does not call for the addition of a social and political dimension to the church's mission; it rather claims that that mission always has and always will have a social and political dimension, be it for bad or good.

Of course, liberation theology has sometimes been one-sided, being influenced by Marxism and tending to overreact against colonialism – even approving of violent revolution. Bosch sees a healthy development in liberation theology: 'The second phase of Latin American liberation theology thus appears to be more modest, more sober, than the first.' Liberation theologies contribute at several levels to a new missionary paradigm (1991:432–47):

1. Liberation theologies push beyond the western concentration on modernity and secularism, beyond its focus on 'whether it still makes

sense to talk about God in a secular age' to an 'almost naively religious, sometimes even biblicistic' understanding of the life and the cross of Jesus. Their question is not whether God exists but whose side he is on – 'and this is a *post*-modern question.' Liberation theology helps the church to recover its faith in a God who is actively involved in history.

2. Another mark of the new paradigm of mission is an integral understanding of sin and liberation: (a) 'from social situations of oppression and marginalisation', (b) 'from every kind of personal servitude', and (c) 'from sin, which is the breaking of friendship with God and with other human beings.'

3. Finally, in an integral missionary paradigm, orthodoxy and orthopraxis belong together.

(3) CRITICAL COMMENTS

Bosch's proposal is open to critical comments at several levels:[36]

1. If Bosch's proposal wants to measure up to the claim of *moving beyond* towards a new paradigm, it must show evidence that the whole is greater than the sum of the parts, as Wilbert Shenk suggests in his article 'The Whole is Greater than the Sum of the Parts: Moving beyond Word and Deed' (1993). There is certainly a creative element in keeping the two opposite dimensions together (spiritual-material, personal-social, immanent-transcendent) and Bosch should be commended for doing that. His suggestion that we root an integrative understanding of salvation and mission in an integrative christology is another important contribution. But beyond that, his approach sometimes gives the impression of collecting many elements and pieces without shaping them into a fresh and holistic approach. Shenk (1993) intends to point beyond the mere addition of word and deed to the true holism which he sees in the ministry of Jesus in the call to the 'new order,' to the kingdom of God, to God's *shalom*, which definitely contains more than the addition of word and deeds can express.

2. When it comes to the realisation of what Bosch calls integral mission, it is certainly a pity that he gives only minimal reference to the witness of the movements constituted by evangelical Christians and theologians from the Two Thirds World, who have not only contributed fresh theological reflection on the subject but have actually lived out an integrated understanding of the gospel and mission, such as Samuel's theological reflections in the context of Indian experience add substantially to Bosch's proposal. He identifies the limitations of many western theological concepts, which, despite trying to surmount the dichotomy between evangelism and social action by knitting them together in various ways, still remain captives to their departmental thinking. Rooting holistic mission in the biblical concepts of the incarnation, the Lordship of Christ over the whole of life, and the wholeness of the gospel,

Samuel achieves a step beyond the dichotomy which seems to be inherent in western thinking (Sugden 1997:338–53).[37]

3. Finally, Bosch does not adequately discuss the question of the relationship between evangelisation and social responsibility. On the one hand, he rejects the 'two mandate' distinction (1991:403–8), but at the same time he himself upholds that dualism, as Saayman rightly demonstrates (1990:105). He discusses at length the developments in evangelical circles from Wheaton 1966[38] through Wheaton 1983[39] with the conclusion that evangelicals have finally overcome any priority thinking (Bosch 1991:406–08).[40]

There are at least two problematic issues in this presentation: (a) There is no corresponding assessment of ecumenical developments. Have ecumenicals always held to a holistic understanding of salvation such that it would not be necessary to discuss the matter? Bosch's analysis of 1980 would certainly suggest that the ecumenical view desperately needs growth toward an integrated understanding of the gospel (1980: 35–39, 212–20). (b) Bosch does not review the evangelical position adequately. The Wheaton '83 statement maintains the evangelical conviction that 'only by spreading the Gospel can the most basic need of human beings be met: to have fellowship with God' (Samuel and Sugden 1987:254). Ecumenical and evangelical positions have not yet been harmonised on this point, and not even Bosch's proposal leads beyond the still unresolved debate regarding the ultimate priority of the 'eternal destiny' of human beings, as claimed by evangelicals.[41]

These critical comments do not undermine Bosch's call for an integrated understanding of salvation and mission as a decisive element of a new missionary paradigm. But we must be aware that there is still an open agenda as to how this holistic understanding of the gospel is spelled out in detail. As pointed out, others have developed this understanding further, and we will take their contribution into consideration as well.

c) Salvation History and Eschatology: Creative Tension between God's Action in the Church and God's Action beyond the Church

Under the title 'salvation history and eschatology' we synthesise several related themes in Bosch's proposal:

(1) TOWARDS AN UNDERSTANDING OF MISSION AS MISSIO DEI[42]

The *missio Dei* concept (Bosch 1991:389–93) has developed since the Willingen Conference of the IMC (1952) and should be seen as influenced by Karl Barth's emphasis on mission as an act of God himself.[43] It initiated a shift of focus from the church to God as the agent of mission. The church is hence seen as participating in God's mission (cf. Freytag 1952:54–55). The result was the distinction between *mission* as *missio Dei* and *missions* as *missiones ecclesiae*. After Willingen, the concept of *missio Dei* gradually developed in the ecumenical movement to mean God's activity in the world – even beyond the church, 'even to the point of suggesting that it *excluded* the church's involvement' (Bosch 1991:392). This finally indicated the end of mission in the traditional sense, since God is at work in the world without and beyond the church (cf. Yates 1994:196–97). Such a view has been rejected by evangelicals, who have therefore employed the terminology only with great hesitation.

Bosch sees a modified concept of *missio Dei* as an integral element of the new paradigm today 'embraced by virtually all Christian persuasions.' In his view, it helps

> to articulate the conviction that neither the church nor any human agent can ever be considered the author or bearer of mission. Mission is, primarily and ultimately, the work of the Triune God, Creator, Redeemer, and Sanctifier, for the sake of the world, a ministry in which the church is privileged to participate... The recognition that mission is God's mission represents a crucial breakthrough in respect of the preceding centuries. It is inconceivable that we could again revert to a narrow, ecclesiocentric view of mission (Bosch 1991:392–93).

Thus, mission as *missio Dei* leads beyond all denominationalism and ecclesiocentrism to a theocentric view of mission.

(2) TOWARDS MISSION IN ESCHATOLOGICAL TENSION[44]

Secondly we turn to the eschatological dimension of salvation history. After discussing various historical models of eschatology, Bosch turns to Oscar Cullmann's understanding of salvation history, which, in Bosch's opinion, has influenced recent missiological thinking, both ecumenical and evangelical.[45] He then points to two extreme eschatological developments which he rejects:

1. The 'extreme eschatologization of mission' (1991:507) of evangelical millennialism, which tends to devalue history and to overemphasise 'heaven.' In view of mission this means:

> The overriding purpose of mission is the preparation of people for the hereafter, ensuring for each a safe passage to heaven. At best, history is a prologue, a preparation, a provisional stage. At worst, it is the believer's enemy, an abiding threat, and a possible source of contagion, since the continuation of history only increases the 'distance' between the dreary present and the glorious future (Bosch 1991:505).

2. The second extreme to be rejected is the 'extreme historization of mission' (1991:507) with its equation of salvation and history, as is the case in ecumenical theology. Here, salvation history becomes secularised and thus, by implication, world history sacralised (1991:506). Bosch points to the Uppsala meeting of the WCC (1968) and comments:

> The 'divine' is to be experienced *only* in historical risk and engagement, since God is a *only* God insofar as he is acting in the world. Thus Christians can recognize their mission *only* in the midst of worldly processes. Where liberation to true humanity has taken place, we may conclude that the *missio Dei* has reached its goal. All people already belong to the new humanity, constituted in Christ, whether they are aware of it or not (1991:507, with reference to Rütti and Hoekendijk).

Again, Bosch sees a creative tension between these two positions, capable of helping formulate the eschatological dimension of mission in the new paradigm (1991:507–10):

> We need a way beyond both. We need an eschatology for mission which is both future-directed and oriented to the here and now. It must be an eschatology that holds in creative and redemptive tension the already and the not yet (1991:508).

He suggests solving the tension between world history and salvation history by saying that 'there are not two histories, but there are two ways of understanding history' (1991:508). Evangelicals are called to concentrate not only on God's plan for the future but to ask 'about the Christian's involvement in the world.' They are invited to see the world no longer as a hindrance but rather as a challenge (1991:509). Social activists are warned of Pelagianism with its romantic confidence that 'we have the will and the power to usher in a new world' (1991:509). It would be an unrealistic dream to believe that we will realise the kingdom of God. 'The ultimate triumph remains uniquely God's gift. It is *God* who makes all things new (Rev 21:5)' (1991:509).

Bosch summarises his view of 'eschatology and mission in creative tension' with the following words:

> The transcendent message of God's sure triumph gives us the necessary distance and sobriety in respect to this world as well as the motivation to involve ourselves in the transformation of the status quo...
> We do distinguish between hope for the ultimate and perfect on the one hand, and hope for the penultimate and approximate, on the other hand... We know that our mission – like the church itself –

belongs only to this age, not to the next. We perform this mission in hope (1991:510).

(3) CRITICAL COMMENTS

Again, Bosch develops his thought along the same lines: describing the tension, understanding it as 'creative tension' and moving beyond one-sidedness. This can be commented on as follows:

1. Bosch has clearly brought to our attention the issues at stake. (a) Is God's mission (*missio Dei*) to be seen as carried out primarily in and through the church, or can it be seen as his work in secular history even beyond and without the church? (b) This leads to the following question: Should salvation history and world history be seen as two distinct strands of history – namely, the church and the world – or do salvation history and secular history finally fuse into the one history which is subject to God's action? (c) And furthermore there is the issue of whether the coming of the kingdom of God is an immanent development of history towards *shalom* or whether we are waiting for God's ultimate act in the future. (d) Finally, what consequences will this have for an understanding of the church? Again, Bosch has pointed to the two poles which create the tension and helpfully encourages us to leave the two in creative tension. However, we doubt that he has convincingly shown how we could move 'beyond.' Here again, Samuel's reflections on the world of God inside and outside the church provide a valuable expansion of Bosch (Sugden 1997:210–32). His critique of an individualistic approach to redemption and the concept of providence, both determining categories in western theology, opens new ways for an understanding of God's action outside the church, without losing sight of the significance of God's work in the church.

2. Regarding eschatology, Bosch has certainly pointed toward an emerging paradigm. The two positions are no longer held by most ecumenicals or evangelicals in such an exclusive way. There is definitely a movement toward a creative eschatological tension, including the 'already' and the 'not yet' of the kingdom of God. Many theologians of a more ecumenical orientation know that the kingdom of God is not to be mixed up with our human projects of liberation and humanisation. There is a new search for the spiritual dimension which points beyond our human possibilities (cf. Werner 1993:414–16). On the other hand, there is definitely a strand within the evangelical movement which does not hold to a view of mission engaged only in 'soul saving,' without a view to its responsibility for change in this world.[46] Yet there is at least one eschatological issue which needs to be addressed and which is not satisfactorily solved in Bosch's proposal: the issue of universalism.[47] This points to some reflections which will be presented later on concerning the relationship of Christianity to other religions (see p. 143).

d) The Church: Creative Tension between 'Participation in God's Mission' and 'Carrying out God's Mission'

Based upon Bosch's publications prior to 1989, Livingston sees 'the missionary nature of the church as the theological horizon for Bosch's missiology' (1990:3). Bosch himself confesses that the discovery of the church as an *alternative community* and the significance of this for mission was one of his key discoveries in the 1970s (Bosch 1982b).[48] It is therefore no surprise that one finds a strong emphasis on the church in *Transforming Mission* (1991:368–89, 467–74). He develops the ecclesiology of a new missionary paradigm in connection with four themes:

(1) TOWARDS A MISSIONARY CHURCH

'In the emerging ecclesiology, *the church is seen as essentially missionary*' (Bosch 1991:372). According to Bosch, this conviction is rooted in the important shift which took place at the Willingen conference (1952) and thereafter in the 1950s. (1991:370).[49] Despite all the later developments and qualifications of the church-mission relationship (Werner 1993:68–69, 156–58, 262–64), a new missionary paradigm cannot return to the thinking which preceded the 'Copernican Shift' which took place at Willingen (Werner 1993:66).

The pre-history of Willingen is characterised by two elements. (1) Traditionally 'missions were enterprises which belonged to the exterior of church life. They were carried on somewhere else – in Asia, Africa, or the South Pacific' (Newbigin 1978:1–2). Mission has operated on the basis of mission societies which have been only loosely related to the church – denominational or interdenominational. Mission societies have disconnected mission from the church (Fiedler 1994:11–34). They have fostered the understanding that mission is 'primarily the business of full-time specialists.' The church does 'not regard itself as the missionary agency ... it is not the *raison d'être* of the whole body' (Newbigin 1958:16, cf. 25). (2) On the other hand – and this almost sounds like a contradiction – mission has tended to be ecclesiocentric. Even though the western churches have not really understood themselves to be the mission, mission work, as it was carried out in the Two-Thirds World, was seen as 'church planting' (*plantatio ecclesiae*) in the sense of the expansion of western churches (on the ecclesiocentric understanding of *plantatio ecclesiae*, see Verkuyl:181–84).

The radical shift at Willingen must be read against this background: the missionary dimension of the church was seen in the light of the *missio Dei*. 'The "Missio ecclesiae" derives from the "Missio Dei" alone' (Freytag ed:62). This *missio ecclesiae* 'is not simply entrusted to the Church as a human corporation' but to 'the community of the Holy Spirit,' the 'one body of Christ,' the 'fellowship created by the Holy Spirit,' which is 'both local and universal.' In this sense, 'the Church's mission is none other than the carrying on of the mission of Christ Himself' (Newbigin 1958:17–24).

The key insights of Willingen must therefore be kept in mind:

1. Mission was seen as the major task of the church, or even as the only task of the church. As Karl Hartenstein put it in his report, 'God's Magna Carta for his church has only one sort of content: mission' (Freytag ed:55).

2. The conference report of section I ('A statement on the missionary calling of the church') says,

> There is no participation in Christ without participation in His mission to the world. That by which the Church receives its existence is that by which it is also given its world-mission. 'As the Father has sent me, even so send I you' (IMC:3).

In a similar way, Karl Barth has emphasised that mission is not secondary to the church's being, but 'the church exists in being sent' (cf. Bosch 1991:372, referring to Barth 1956:725).

3. At the same time Willingen indicates the shift from the earlier *church-centred* understanding of mission to *mission-centred* understanding of the church (Bosch 1993:370).

4. The conclusion was therefore, 'One can no longer talk about church *and* mission, only about the mission *of* the church' (Bosch 1993:372, referring to Glazik 1984:52). The church must be seen as essentially missionary and mission as essentially ecclesial (Bosch 1993:372). 'Because church and mission belong together from the beginning, a church without mission or mission without a church are both contradictions. Such things exist, but only as pseudostructures' (Braaten:55)

Therefore, in a new missionary paradigm, the church has to be understood as 'missionary by its very nature' (Bosch 1991:372).

(2) TOWARDS A CHURCH 'IN THE WORLD' WITHOUT BEING 'OF THE WORLD'

As mentioned earlier, the interpretation of the relationship between the *missio Dei* and *missiones ecclesiae* has moved in two directions in the 1960s and later, corresponding to the divergence between the ecumenical and evangelical movements.

1. In ecumenical circles under the influence of J.C. Hoekendijk, *missio Dei* came to be understood as God at work in history even beyond and without the church. The direct God-world movement was put over the God-church-world movement. The world has to set the agenda for mission, not the church. Mission has to be world-, not church-centred (Bosch 1991:376–8; Yates:196–97).

2. Such an emphasis went definitely beyond the understanding of *missio Dei* in the fifties. For Vicedom (1958:43–48), God carries out his

mission (*missio Dei specialis*) through his Son. There is no mission outside of Jesus Christ. And the continuation of this mission was entrusted to the apostles and the church. It was this church-centred view of God's mission which was later advocated by evangelicals in the 1960s and 1970s.

Bosch sees the tension between these two foci in the interpretation of the *missio Dei* concept as an integral part of a new paradigm of mission. He concludes:

> The new paradigm led to an abiding tension between two views of the church which appear to be fundamentally irreconcilable. At one end of the spectrum, the church perceives itself to be the sole bearer of a message of salvation on which it has a monopoly; at the other end, the church views itself, at most, as an illustration – in word and deed – of God's involvement with the world (1991:382).

Bosch calls for new reflection on these seemingly mutually exclusive poles and suggests a move from a destructive to a more creative tension, challenging and supplementing each other. He suggests that one 'perceive the church as an ellipse with two foci' (1991:385), one as the church apart from the world, engaged in prayer and worship as the source of life, the other as the church in the world, engaged in service and mission. His thesis is that the church can be missionary only by 'being-in-the world' and at the same time by 'being-different-from-the-world' (1991:386).[50]

(3) TOWARD THE COMMUNITY AS AN AGENT OF MISSION

Another legacy of the old paradigm is the 'evolution of the ordained ministry ... For almost nineteen centuries and in virtually all ecclesiastical traditions, ministry has been understood almost exclusively in terms of the service of ordained ministers' (Bosch 1991:467). In the new paradigm this is changing. The emerging 'movement away from ministry as the monopoly of ordained men to ministry as the responsibility of the whole people of God, ordained as well as non-ordained, is one of the most dramatic shifts taking place in the church today' (1991:467). This statement by Bosch points to the three major obstacles in the way to the ministry of the whole church: (a) the concept of ordination, (b) the domination of men and (c) the understanding of ministry.

1. Bosch develops the history of the concept of ordination in greater detail. He points to the 'clericalizing of the church' and the 'sacerdotalizing of the clergy,' which led to the distinction between clergy and laity already in the early centuries of Christianity (1991:468–69). He raises the question 'whether *Protestants* have really done any better,' even if Luther did rediscover the priesthood of all believers. Only the Anabaptists, Bosch says, have broken with the idea of the ordained ministry (1991:469).

2. Secondly, Bosch points to the important role of women in the history of mission, where 'they did all things men used to do, including preaching' and administering the sacraments. This development was only possible outside the domination of the established churches with their strong emphasis on ordination and church hierarchy. The 'voluntary movement,' the 'faith missions,' as well as some leaders of free-church background (such as Frederik Franson), have fostered the women's movement (Tucker 1993:284–87). When the women's missionary movement was integrated into the denominational missions, 'the "home front" slowly began to catch up,' as Bosch puts it (1991:470–71).

3. The third related critical issue is the definition of ministry. Instead of limiting the ministry to the task of the ordained minister, as it has been done in most ecclesiastical traditions (Bosch 1991:467), Bosch refers to Moltmann and calls for a new understanding of ministry which 'will be directed not only toward divine service in the church, but also toward divine service in the everyday life of the world' (1991:473).

4. Thus, the new paradigm of mission is based on a 'theology of the laity' (1991:472). (a) It breaks with the distinction of clergy and laity and 'ordains' each member of Christ's body to be a 'missionary.' (b) It breaks with the male domination and gives women equal opportunities, recognition and empowerment for Christian ministry. (c) Finally, it breaks with a definition in which ministry equals 'pastoral functions' and understands every-day life in the world, as well as the so-called pastoral functions, as divine service. 'For the community is the primary bearer of mission' (1991:472).

(4) TOWARDS A COMMON WITNESS OF THE CHURCH

The emphasis on the church contains yet another element: the unity of the entire body of Christ or, in other words, the ecumenical dimension of the church. Historically, Bosch says, the notion of a united body of Christ, witnessing to the world, is rooted in the interdenominational student missionary movement and the entire foreign missionary movement of the late nineteenth and early twentieth century, which reached its peak with the mission conference of Edinburgh in 1910 (1991:457–59; cf. Yates:7–33; Hedlund:7–12). Increased nationalism and denominationalism, as well as two World Wars, caused the ecumenical movement to lose momentum. It was only in the post-war period that the vision was recaptured and steps taken toward the unity of Christ's body: the WCC was founded in 1948; in the circles of the IMC there was increased reflection on ecclesiology; and finally, the IMC was integrated into the WCC. Of course, Christianity was still far from reaching the vision of 'One Body, One Gospel, One World' (Newbigin 1958). Neither the Roman Catholic nor the Orthodox Church have been incorporated into the movement, and the evangelical missionary movement has split off from the ecumenical movement as it was represented in the WCC (cf. Yates:133; Hedlund:117–30). The past thirty years have been a time of struggle for the ecumenical idea. The polarisation between the evangelical and ecumenical movements in the sixties and seventies left little hope for a quick fusion of the two streams of the Protestant mission movement. It was only in the eighties and nineties that some leaders began to move toward increased dialogue and mutual recognition. Beyond what has been reached (or not reached) thus far, Bosch draws the following contours of the new paradigm (1991:464–67).[51]

1. 'Mutual co-ordination of mission and unity is *non-negotiable.*' This is deeply rooted in the biblical understanding of the church.

2. This *'presupposes tension'*! 'The aim is not a levelling out of differences, a shallow reductionism, a kind of ecumenical broth. Our differences are genuine and have to be treated as such.'

3. To speak of the unity of the world-wide church means 'an end to *the distinction between "sending" and "receiving" churches.*' This certainly leads beyond any western domination but also beyond the anti-colonial mentality to 'new relationships, mutual responsibility, accountability and interdependence (not independence!)'

4. Consequently, the *proliferation of new churches* has to be resisted.

5. Only a united church will be 'a prophetic sign and foretaste of the unity and renewal of the human family.'

6. Finally, the church has to be aware of the fact, 'that the *loss of ecclesial unity is not just a vexation but a sin.* Unity is not an optional extra.' It is already given in Christ and it is at the same time a command (Bosch 1991:467).

(5) CRITICAL COMMENTS

1. Regarding the church, Bosch has advanced several key aspects of a new paradigm, which are (a) the emphasis on the missionary nature of the church; (b) the creative tension of the church as being called out of the world and yet sent into the world; (c) the shift from a professionalised and inward-oriented understanding of ministry to an outward-oriented ministry of the whole people of God; (d) and the emphasis on the visible unity of the body of Christ.

2. But there are also some problematic areas which need further reflection. (a) It has to be questioned whether Bosch, with his theory of the two foci of the church, really does solve the real issue of the ecumenical-evangelical debate. None would doubt that there is a – hopefully creative – tension between the church's separation from the world and its mission into the world. In this regard, Bosch's view of the church as 'alternative community' is certainly a helpful contribution.[52] But in the ecumenical-evangelical discussion, the crucial question is 'who belongs to the church?' (Beyerhaus 1981). Are the boundaries of the church

defined by faith and a personal relationship to Christ, as evangelicals claim, or is 'church' an open concept, as ecumenicals emphasise? Bosch does not address this issue and his suggestions to move beyond the ecumenical evangelical polarisation do not solve this problem at all (Bosch 1991:381–9). (b) Bosch's emphasis on the unity of the church can only be underscored. Yet his conception of the realisation of ecumenical unity seems to depend heavily on established institutions. There is a certain fixation with the unifying process within the WCC, with its focus on institutional churches. The ecumenical understanding, as it is represented in evangelicalism and in the so-called faith missions, with its emphasis on the relationship of the individual to the entire body of Christ finding its realisation in some sort of cross-denominational ecclesiology, is hardly taken into account by Bosch.[53] Furthermore, given the fact that, in the post-modern era, global institutions – and not only in economy and politics but also in the church – will lose their significance; and given that networking among grass-roots communities will increase, an ecumenical outlook cannot be limited to the traditional global institutions, be they ecumenical or evangelical (Myers 1992).

e) *Theology of Religions: Creative Tension between Dialogue and Mission*

Finally Bosch's proposal of a new paradigm in the area of 'witness to people of other living faiths' will be discussed (Bosch 1991:474–89).

(1) CRITIQUE OF THE TRADITIONAL THEORIES

After the introduction of the history of the problem, Bosch introduces three models in the current debate (Bosch 1991:478–83; with reference to Küng; cf. Newbigin 1978:191–97).

1. *Exclusivism*, which sees 'no point of contact between religion and God's revelation' (Bosch 1991:479; referring to Karl Barth).

2. *Fulfilment*, prominent since the Edinburgh conference (1910), sees Christianity as the fulfilment of all other religions. This leaves room for a certain revelation of God in other religions but maintains the claim of the uniqueness and superiority of the Christian faith. The fulfilment model can even be divided into two sub-models: (a) the *ecclesiocentric*, claiming that Christianity is the supreme revelation of God and (b) the *Christocentric*, which sees in Christ the ultimate revelation of God. Of course, the past forty years of mission history have caused a shift from ecclesiocentrism to christocentrism (Bosch 1991:480; cf. Newbigin 1977).

3. *Relativism*, which, in Bosch's assessment, is rooted in Enlightenment thought, emphasising 'more the complementary than the contradictory' dimension of the various religions, including Christianity (Bosch 1991:481; referring to Lessing). This leads to the conclusion that 'all

religions are equally valid and other revealers and saviours may be as important as Jesus Christ.' This model finds its post-modern expression in the theories of Hick and Knitter (Bosch 1991:482).

Bosch claims that the three models represent pre-modern, modern and post-modern answers and are not able to present a convincing theology of religions which takes into consideration the complexity of the issue. He criticises all three theories of being 'all too neat. They all work out too well. In the end everything – and everyone! – is accounted for. There are no loose ends' (1991:483).

(2) AN ALTERNATIVE PARADIGM?

Again, Bosch calls for a 'theology of religions characterized by creative tension, which reaches beyond the sterile alternatives between a comfortable claim of absoluteness and arbitrary pluralism' (1991:483). Referring to Stackhouse, he then calls for a theology of religions which needs 'the aid of *poiesis* rather than of *theoria*,' open for the mystery, for a 'meeting of hearts rather than of minds.' Based on this general understanding of the dialogic of experience he points to several features of a possible new way of dealing with other religions (1991:483–89):

1. A willing acceptance of the fact of the coexistence of different faiths, not as a threat to Christian faith, but even as a formative factor in Christian theology.[54]

2. At the same time, true dialogue presupposes commitment to the gospel. 'Dialogue means witnessing to our convictions.'

3. 'Dialogue is only possible if we proceed from the belief that we are not moving into a void, that we go expecting to meet the God who has preceded us and has been preparing people within the context of their own cultures and convictions.'

4. True mission and dialogue can only be done 'in an attitude of humanity.' This calls for vulnerability in the inter-religious encounter.

5. In dialogue with people of other faiths, one has to recognise that 'religions are worlds in themselves' and have therefore to be taken seriously in their totality.

6. 'Dialogue is neither a substitute nor a subterfuge for mission.' The commitment to dialogue and the commitment to evangelism have to be kept together.

7. Conversion to the Christian faith, cannot only be seen in the light of the 'question whether other religions also "save." ' Conversion is 'a change in allegiance in which Christ is accepted as Lord and centre of one's life,' in order to 'accept the responsibility to serve God in this life and promote God's reign in all its forms.'

8. Finally, the encounter with people of other faith leaves us with the tension of being 'both missionary and dialogical.' We can only say 'We cannot point to another way of salvation than Jesus Christ; at the same

time we cannot set limits to the saving power of God' (quoting WCC 1990:33).

(3) CRITICAL COMMENTS

Bosch's critique of the traditional theories follows the suggestions of many recent publications.[55] There seems to be a common understanding that many of the traditional models no longer provide satisfactory answers to the burning questions of religious pluralism. Yet whether Bosch's proposal does move *beyond*, towards a new paradigm, must be raised again:

1. The eight criteria for dialogical mission outlined by Bosch demonstrate a high degree of sensitivity. They touch upon crucial areas and can only be commended as guiding principles in the practice of dialogue. This is a key element of the new paradigm. It turns around the methodology of the theology of religion. The first step in the process of dialogue with other religions is not a predefined theory, an *a priori* defined conclusion about the Christian faith and the possible validity of the other religion: the first step is practice, the real encounter with people of other living faiths (cf. Samuel and Sugden 1983; Sugden 1997:399–407).

2. However, on the level of the second step of theological reflection, Bosch leaves many questions open. Such significant issues as revelation, truth, epistemology, salvation in relation to the Bible, the Christian faith and other faiths are not dealt with, let alone answered. To be sure, one finds a valuable definition of the boundaries in the phrase of the WCC San Antonio conference 'We cannot point to another way of salvation than Jesus Christ; at the same time we cannot set limits to the saving power of God' (quoted in Bosch 1991:489). Bosch's advice to keep the two statements of this expression together is central. But between the two points marking the boundaries is a gap full of theological questions which demand further reflection.

3. This leads to a final comment: the discussion has gone beyond Bosch in recent years. The development of the WCC's Programme on Interreligious Dialogue has been analysed by Helfenstein in a comprehensive and critical way (1998), and he has shown how the reinterpretation of the trinity in favour of a stronger emphasis on the independent ministry of the Spirit has entered the debate since the consultation of the WCC commission in Baar, Switzerland, in 1990 (Helfenstein 1998:263–68). This has opened new avenues beyond the christocentric and the theocentric approaches.[56]

f) Comparative Summary

With this we have completed the survey of Bosch's proposal,[57] and are now in a position to add a third model to the comparative chart:

Theme	Ecumenical focus	Evangelical focus	New paradigm focus (Bosch)
Crisis and Response	Crisis *because* of a changing world situation Critique of the traditional western mission movement Focus on discontinuity: the world sets the agenda, which calls for a radical rethinking of mission and for changes; not only to the forms but also to content (theology of mission)	Crisis *because* of deviation from the biblical view of mission Critique of the development of the WCC's understanding of mission Focus on continuity: Mission in continuity with the classical (= biblical) mission movement – changes in forms may be necessary	Crisis *external* and *internal*. Enlightenment paradigm needs critical evaluation. Neither 'business as usual' no 'paralysis.' Focus on *transformation/ trans-figuration*: mission in creative tension between continuity and discontinuity
Bible, context and hermeneutics	The context determines theology 'A once and for all, fixed "depositum fidei" no longer exists'	The Bible determines theology The universal authority of the Bible remains unquestionable	Bible is *norma normans* Bibel gives 'firm and enduring elements of mission,' but also models of contextualisation
Salvation and mission	Salvation as integral human liberation (*shalom*) Mission as holistic action towards *shalom*	Salvation central as reconciliation with God through Jesus Christ appropriated by faith Mission primarily as evangelisation	Salvation based on the *totus Christus*, comprising transformation, liberation and reconciliation Mission as ministry towards transformation, liberation and reconciliation

Theme	Ecumenical focus	Evangelical focus	New paradigm focus (Bosch)
Salvation history and eschatology	God's action in history, beyond the church – 'Christus extra muros eccleisiae' God-world-church-order Kingdom of God in this world, beyond the church, wherever God moves history toward *shalom* Emphasis on the 'here and now' and the future of *this* world	God's salvific action primarily in and through Jesus Christ and the church God-church-world-order Kingdom of God primarily in the future – in a limited way already today in the church Emphasis on the eternal and the eschatological *new* world	The church in the tension between God's action in its midst and God's action in the world Kingdom of God which transforms humanity-in-community in the church and beyond Emphasis on the tension between 'already' and 'not yet'.
The church	The church as participating in God's mission Focus on society 'Open' ecclesiology – the hidden church – the church of the poor	The church as agent and instrument of mission Focus on individuals 'Closed' ecclesiology – church of believers – 'boundaries-oriented'	The church as incarnation of the gospel, as sacrament, sign and instrument Focus on people-in-community Covenant communities and discipleship 'centre-oriented'
Theology of religions	Inclusivism and Pluralism Pneumatological reinterpretation of the trinity – openness for God's revelation beyond Christ and the Bible Focus on Dialogue	Exclusivism Christological understanding of the trinity – concentration on God's revelation in Christ and the Bible Focus on Evangelisation	Beyond neat theological theories toward vulnerability in an open dialogue based on the premise 'We cannot point to another way of salvation than Jesus Christ; at the same time we cannot set limits to the saving power of God'

4. The *Consequences* of Bosch's Proposal

As we now move towards the analysis of *the Schools*, we draw conclusions in such a way that we put forward criteria which are meaningful for the examination of mission studies in theological education. Bosch's proposal shows the potential of providing criteria on several levels. He challenges us to do mission studies

- in the context of crisis and change
- in dialogue with the wider ecumenical community
- within the context of an integral paradigm of mission.

a) Doing Mission Studies in the Context of Crisis and Change

The fact that Bosch synthesises and even creates an understanding of mission in response to the contemporary crisis in mission proposes a criterion in and of itself. His distinction between the external and the internal crises, as well as his understanding of crisis as danger and opportunity must be considered. This leads to the following questions regarding mission studies in theological education:

1. Are the developments from the colonial to the post-colonial era reviewed?
2. Are the features of the colonial and the post-colonial era of mission outlined?
3. Is mission taught with the awareness that the paradigms of mission have changed throughout history and that the paradigm of the modern missionary movement is not *the* ultimate paradigm but a child of its time?
4. Are students exposed to the crisis in mission?
5. How is this crisis perceived and evaluated?
6. Is there a fair critical analysis of the colonial model of mission or is there a tendency either to condemn everything that was done in the past or else to glorify the modern mission movement?
7. Are the features of the Enlightenment paradigm critically reviewed?
8. Is the traditional biblical foundation for mission critically reviewed?
9. Are the traditional motives and aims of mission critically reviewed?
10. Are traditional mission practices critically reviewed?
11. How is this entire crisis interpreted? What conclusions are drawn? Is there a tendency either towards 'business as usual' or towards 'paralysis'?
12. Is there an openness for changes? Has the view of mission been changing in the last decades?
13. Is there a tendency either toward hasty changes without serious reflection or toward change resistance?

b) Doing Mission Studies in Dialogue with the Wider Ecumenical Community

On a second level, we recognise that Bosch deliberately reflects on mission in the context of great diversities in the theology of mission. Despite having pointed to certain limitations in the scope of his work, we find that he challenges us to conduct mission studies in an open dialogue with the various strands of the world Christian movement. It is especially in the context of divergence between the ecumenical and the evangelical views of mission that he points beyond polarisation towards integration. This leads to the following questions:

1. Are students exposed to various, differing views of mission?
2. Are primary texts from divergent theological positions on the reading lists?
3. Is the split between the evangelical and ecumenical mission movements reviewed as it developed in the 1960s and 1970s?
4. Are the different strands represented fairly?
5. Are there signs of integration and moving beyond the polarisation or rather of ideologising it?
6. Are different views within the evangelical strand discussed?
7. Are different views within the ecumenical strand discussed?
8. Are Catholic and Orthodox texts considered?
9. Are voices from the Two Thirds World considered?
10. Does the school promote a climate of ecumenical openness or does it tend toward separation?

c) Doing Mission Studies in the Context of an Integral Paradigm of Mission

Finally, the content of Bosch's paradigm provides criteria for mission studies in terms of content. Bosch's proposal is firmly rooted in scripture, thoroughly aware of history, deeply dedicated to integration and decisively oriented towards the future. Many questions flow from this:

1. Are Bosch's publications known and used in teaching mission?
2. How is his contribution received and reviewed?
3. To what extent are the elements of an emerging new missionary paradigm taken up in mission training?
4. How is the Bible used in establishing the theological foundation for mission?
5. Are students introduced to the concept of contextualisation? How is contextualisation defined and applied? Which views of contextualisation are adopted, which rejected?
6. Are students introduced to the concept of holistic mission?

7. How is evangelisation and social action viewed as part of the church's mission?
8. Is the concept of the 'missionary' church taught?
9. How is the church's role in the world defined?
10. Is the concept of the laity as bearer of mission introduced?
11. Is the missionary potential of the unity of the church taught, i.e., the ecumenical dimension of mission?
12. Are the students introduced to the concept of *missio Dei* as a key concept in contemporary mission theology?
13. Are the students introduced to the concept of *transformation* as a key concept in contemporary mission theology?
14. Are the students introduced to the concept of *dialogue* in recent mission theology, its various aspects, problems, definitions and consequences?
15. How are the questions of the theology of religions approached? Are different theologies reviewed?

With this the theoretical background is established and the investigation will proceed to the analysis of *the Schools*.

Notes

1 Bosch' s broader work, beyond *Transforming Mission*, will also be taken into consideration. A (almost!) comprehensive bibliography of Bosch's writings is to be found in Saayman and Kritzinger:167–70. Unfortunately Bosch's doctoral thesis *Die Heidenmission in der Zukunftsschau Jesu. Eine Untersuchung zur Eschatologie der synoptischen Evangelien* (1959) is missing from that list.

2 The major chapter in which he defines his use of paradigm theory is 1991:181–89.

3 At this point this study does not reflect on the contribution of Küng and the Tübingen consultation, yet in the final chapter of the thesis, Kuhn's application of paradigm change theory will be applied to *the Schools*.

4 The German edition of Küng and Tracy was published 1984, the English edition only in 1989. As early as October 1985 Bosch introduced the Kuhn and Küng theory to the realm of mission theology in an article published in *IRM* (Bosch 1985). However, the term 'paradigm' had already been used in missiological studies prior to 1980 (cf. Schenk 1980b).

5 Besides the many book reviews the following contributions are of special significance: Livingston 1989; *Missionalia* 18/1 (1990); Baillie 1993; Thomas 1995, Saayman and Kritzinger 1996.

6 'We hesitate to speak of a new "paradigm". The facts mentioned by D. J. Bosch, and following him J. A. Scherer and S. B. Bevans, in order to show a "post-modern ecumenical paradigm", are nor convincing., because they point to realities which already for a long time have been identified as problems of modernity. At a point in time where we are still so close to the events we do not want to use such a significant term, because we do not want to call any change a paradigm change' (Wietzke 1993:438).

7 Küng and Tracy 1989:450; cf. Hollenweger: 'If mission and mission studies are to have a future, they must be rigorously *ecumenical*' (1991:95).

8 Cf. Thomas 1995:XV; Sugden 1993:1. Bosch's only references to the role of women 1991:470–71, 472.

9 Usdorf's critique also points in the same direction. His phrase 'The ruling paradigm was always the paradigm of the rulers' (:137–38) reveals the limitations of a paradigmatic approach which accepts an emerging paradigm uncritically.

10 Cf. Bosch's various exegetical contributions (Bosch 1978; 1986; 1993b)

11 The thoughts and praxis of Vinay Samuel, outlined and critically analysed by Chris Sugden in *Seeing the Asian Face of Jesus*, will be one of the significant supplements to Bosch.

12 We do not speak of Bosch's socio-political context as an individual and theologian, an issue tackled by Sugden (1996:143–7), but of the larger context of the changes in mission which gave birth to his proposal.

13 See the documents of the various Christian traditions in Scherer and Bevans 1992.

14 See also Lesslie Newbigin's chapter 'The unchanging basis' (1958:17); as well as Newbigin 1978:12 'I believe, however, that our first need is for the theological understanding and that the reordering of structures must follow this.' Furthermore Verkuyl (:89): 'The increased urgent need for a biblical foundation.' This is also Peter Beyerhaus's concern in all of his writings.

15 See also Wietzke (1993:426–36) who has identified some of the convergencies and divergencies which became apparent in the last decades, based on significant mission documents from 1972 to 1992.

16 See also Newbigin (1958:14–17), 'Repentance of both sides', referring to the churches and the missions agencies.

17 See the following contributions in English: Roger C. Bassham, *Mission Theology: 1948–1975. Years of Worldwide Creative Tension: Ecumenical, Evangelical and Roman Catholic* (1979); James A. Scherer, *Gospel, Church and Kingdom: Comparative Studies in World Mission Theology* (1983); and Arthur Glasser and Donald McGavran, *Contemporary Theologies of Mission* (1983). Glasser and McGavran suggest a fourfold typology including (1) the evangelical, (2) the ecumenical (conciliar), (3) the Roman Catholic, and (4) liberation theology's understanding. Glasser and McGavran see the polarisation between the evangelical and the Roman Catholic position on one side and the ecumenical and the liberation theology's understanding on the other side. The former two are, according to Glasser and McGavran, in line with the traditional missionary movement, the latter two indicate a radical break with the tradition. In the German context the following studies were conducted: (1) The two comparative studies by the catholic scholars Kramm (1979) and Hering (1980); (2) the presentation of the developments of the ecumenical understanding of mission from 1961 to 1991 by Werner (1993); (3) the analysis of the ecumenical approach to other religions in this century by Helfenstein (1998); (4) the evangelical responses to the ecumenical developments by Beyerhaus (all of his publications), Sautter (1985), Hamel (1993); and Berneburg (1997).

18 See p. 18 for the definition of comparison-of-models methodology.

19 This model is mainly based on Werner 1993.

20 This is manly based on Beyerhaus's publications.

21 Beyond Beyerhaus see also Bockmühl 1974.

22 Beyond Beyerhaus see Hamel.
23 Beyond Beyerhaus see Kramm and Sautter.
24 Beyond Beyerhaus see Berneburg 1997.
25 Beyond Werner 1993 see Helfenstein 1998.
26 Beyond Beyerhaus see the sections on evangelicals in Helfenstein 1998.
27 See his Bosch's article ' "Ecumenicals" and "Evangelicals": A Growing Relationship?'
28 Though Bosch does not expand explicitly on this topic, it is certainly one of the implicit themes throughout the book.
29 Bosch 1980:42–49; 1991:15–55, 186–87; see also the following articles by David Bosch, 'The Structure of Mission: An Exposition of Matthew 28:16–20' (1983); 'Mission in Biblical Perspective' (1985); 'Towards a Hermeneutic for "Biblical Studies and Mission" ' (1986); 'Reflections on Biblical Models of Mission' (1993); 'Hermeneutical Principles in the Biblical Foundation for Mission' (1993).
30 Cf. Beyerhaus 1996:176–96; concluding with G. Vicedom (1975:9), 'Our theology of biblical criticism has deprived mission of its theological foundation.'
31 E.g., Bosch 'compassion', 'history', 'suffering' and 'conduct' (1978:442–51), or 'compassion', 'martyria', 'God's mission' and 'history' (1993b:180–92).
32 At this point we do not agree with Du Plessis' critique of 'Bosch's use of Scripture' (1990), pointing out that Bosch uses the term 'paradigm' referring to something which is changing, and the term 'model' for that which is firm (82). On the contrary, Bosch uses the term 'paradigm' already with reference to the 'firm and enduring elements of mission' and the term 'model' refers to the contextualisation of Matthew, Luke and Paul; he also refers to models as 'subparadigms' (Bosch 1991, 54).
33 At this point Vinay Samuel makes a valuable contribution (Sugden 1997:369–382). He not only affirms theoretically much of what Bosch is suggesting – he also demonstrates it in practice.
34 For more recent evangelical contributions to an integral understanding of the gospel and mission see *ERTh* 20/3 (1996), with the issue theme 'Towards Integral Mission Theology.'
35 Cf. the 'Statement of The Stuttgart Consultation on Evangelism', a joint statement of Ecumenicals and evangelicals which points in the same direction as Bosch's proposal (Samuel and Hauser:212–24). Bosch himself participated in this CMWE consultation of 1987.
36 The major critical study on Bosch's understanding of mission and evangelism by Kevin Livingston, *A Missiology of the Road: The Theology of Mission and Evangelism in the Writings of David J. Bosch* (Unpublished PhD thesis, University of Aberdeen, 1989), was written before the publication of *Transforming Mission* and hence does not adequately analyse Bosch's most recent ideas. See summary in Livingston 1990.
37 To the development of a more holistic model of mission see also Escobar and Driver; Padilla 1985, 1986; Samuel and Sugden 1982, 1987, 1991; Samuel and Hauser; Costas 1982, 1989. Ron Sider's collection of examples of holistic ministry around the world says much, not only about theory but also about practice (Sider 1994).
38 The Congress on The Church's World-Wide Mission and The Wheaton Declaration see Hedlund 1993:169ff.

39 Wheaton '83 Consultation on the Church in Response to Human Need, see Sine.

40 German evangelicals apparently have a different reading of the developments among evangelicals outlined by Berneburg 1997:177–99. This will be considered later in the analysis of German evangelical theology of mission.

41 See John Stott's recent article 'Die ganzheitliche Mission. Im Spannungsfeld von Evangelisation und sozialem Handeln' (1993). A biblical study which convincingly shows the holistic understanding of salvation and the kingdom of God has been put forward by Vinay Samuel and Chris Sugden (1985). On the whole issue, also Berneburg 1997, who claims that the 'holistic-evangelism' position is held only by a minority group within the evangelical movement.

42 Bosch's chapter, 'Mission as *Missio Dei*' (1991:389–93).

43 It presumably was first used by Karl Hartenstein (Bosch 1991:392)

44 Bosch's chapter 'Mission as action in hope' (1991:498ff.).

45 Bosch, who did his doctoral studies at the University of Basel under Oscar Cullmann, favours Cullmann's approach, despite some critiques (1991:504).

46 E.g., the discussion on mission and eschatology at the CRESR, Grand Rapids 1982 (Bockmühl 1983) and the Articles by Stephen Williams and Miroslav Volf in *Transformation* 1990/3:24–31).

47 In his study on the interpretation of salvation history in ecumenical and evangelical theology of mission, Sautter mentions universalism as one of the critical issues of divergence between ecumenicals and evangelicals (1985:253–56).

48 He also admits – which is no surprise – that he came to these insights through his encounter with the Mennonite tradition (1982b; 1979).

49 The theme of Willingen was 'The Missionary Obligation of the Church' (IMC 1952).

50 Referring to the following statement of the Lund meeting of the WCC's Faith and Order Commission (1952), 'The Church is always and at the same time called out of the world and sent into the world' (see also Livingston 1990:12).

51 This is only a summary of some of the elements of Bosch's proposal.

52 Livingston (1990:11–16) has put forward the thesis that Bosch's ecclesiology centres in the concept of an 'alternative community'.

53 Regarding the ecclesiological concept of 'individual unity' in the evangelical faith missions see Fiedler 1994:169–97.

54 Bosch (1991:483) refers to R. Pape who has suggested other religions to be an additional formative factor of Christian theology beyond the six factors suggested by Macquarrie (experience, revelation, scripture, tradition, culture, and reason). Other religions may be formative for Christian theology insofar as they provide the context in which theology is shaped, as it was in the pre-Constantinian early church.

55 Cf. Knitter's critique of the 'conservative evangelical model', the 'mainline Protestant model', the 'Catholic model', and the 'theocentric model' (1985). Gavin D'Costa discusses the 'pluralist paradigm,' the 'exclusivist paradigm' and the 'inclusivist paradigm', favouring an elaborated version of the latter (1986). Ken Gananakan surveys 'exclusivism,' 'relativism,' 'inclusivism' and 'pluralism,' and suggests a model which turns out to be a moderate form of exclusivism (1992). See also Newbigin 1989; Kirk 1992; Helfenstein 1998.

[56] According to Helfenstein the WCC has not continued to develop the trinitarian approach to theology of religion rigorously. Due to several factors, other items have dominated the agenda of WCC Program on Dialogue (1998:278, 288–93, 296–300). Helfenstein himself develops the trinitarian approach further and proposes it as a real paradigmatic breakthrough in theology of religion (1998:377–410). See also the last chapter of Dietrich Werner's thesis (1993:54, 386ff.).

[57] His chapter on 'Mission as Theology' has not been reviewed. It will be introduced in Part Four which deals explicitly with tasks of theologising and theological education.

CHAPTER 9

Analysis: Theology of Mission in Evangelical Theological Education in German-Speaking Europe

The analysis of the theology of mission taught at *the Schools* will be conducted in two steps, diachronically and synchronically. (1) First, the period from 1960 to 1995 will be analysed in a *diachronic* way, showing the developments of a German evangelical theology of mission. (2) In a second step, the findings will be presented *synchronically* and reviewed critically in the light of the paradigm shift in mission.

1. Developments in German Evangelical Theology of Mission 1960 to 1995

The focus of this chronological presentation is on mission teaching at Bible colleges and seminaries. In view of this concentration, the following three levels will be examined:

1. On a more general level the development of a German evangelical theology of mission will be observed under the title: *Theology of Mission: Research and Publications*. This provides the background to the teaching at the Bible colleges and introduces the textbooks available in the libraries of *the Schools*.
2. Secondly, the evangelical conferences which have impacted theology of mission will be considered. Beyond some of the major national, continental and international congresses, the assemblies of the *KBA* and the EEAA will be assessed – that is, those gatherings of *the Schools* which indicate common concerns. Mission played a significant role in the history of these conferences.
3. Finally, the curricula of *the Schools* are taken up with a particular view to determining the contents of mission teaching.

a) The 1960s: Theology of Mission between the Legacy of German Missiology and a New Evangelical Identity

The 1960s mark the beginning of the German evangelical movement in the modern sense (see historical introduction Part Two). It is a time 'between.' The 'old generation' of German missiologists who had shaped the previous decades, Karl Hartenstein (1894–1952) and Walter Freytag (1899–1959), were dead. A new generation of evangelical theologians, who would give shape to an evangelical mission theology in the light of the developments since New Delhi 1961, had yet to emerge. This situation also had an impact on evangelical mission studies.

(1) DEVELOPING THEOLOGY OF MISSION: RESEARCH AND PUBLICATIONS

1. The period from 1960 to 1969 is a time of relative silence regarding evangelical missiological contributions of German origin. In the 1960s it was especially Georg Vicedom who represented an evangelical position. He stood in the tradition of Hartenstein and Freytag. He affirmed this *classical* understanding of mission over against the new missiological ideas which emerged in the context of the WCC in *Die Mission am Scheideweg* (1967). Klaus Bockmühl's *Die neuere Missionstheologie* (1964) stands in the same tradition. Based on the writings of Hartenstein, Freytag and Kraemer, Bockmühl develops what he calls a *more recent theology of mission.*

2. In terms of textbooks available at the Bible colleges and seminaries, two observations need to be made: First, evangelical textbooks at a scholarly level were rare in all fields of studies at that time. This is also true of mission. Hardly any German evangelical books on mission theology beyond those mentioned above were available. Second, library work, including the reading of academic theology, was then absent in many Bible schools. Several Bible schools maintained only small libraries, containing mostly Bible commentaries, devotional literature and biographies (e.g., *Brake, Beatenberg*) (cf. Egelkraut 1990:33). The situation was somewhat different in the older mission seminaries like *Chrischona* and *Liebenzell*, which already had larger library holdings.

This means that the main input in the theology of mission came from the teachers themselves; and they drew from two sources. (a) The German and Dutch theologians mentioned above – such as the Hartenstein-Freytag-Kraemer-tradition. In retrospect, the period of these missiologists – from 1940 to 1960 – was viewed as the *great epoch* of German and Dutch missiology (cf. Bockmühl 1964; 1974: 9–62). (b) Many of the Bible school teachers came from a North American evangelical background or were missionaries. They were acquainted with the evangelical literature of the English-speaking world.

3. In view of the 1960s it must be noticed that hardly any evangelical theological academic literature from the English-speaking world had been translated into German. When Laubach introduced some significant contemporary North American theologians in 1972, adding a short bibliography of each, he could not refer to a single German title (Laubach:122–23).[1] It was only in the 1970s that translations of evangelical literature of an academic or semi-academic character appeared in German-speaking Europe.

Nonetheless, translations of English literature did make a significant contribution to mission teaching in the 1960s. It was not the academic type of literature but the spiritual and motivational publications which in most cases came through the interdenominational evangelical missions to Europe. The book *Glühende Retterliebe* (*The Passion for Souls*) by Oswald J. Smith can be mentioned as a *prototype* of such literature. It was introduced to the German language area through *Youth for Christ* (YfC), which had already been active in German-speaking countries since 1947 (Reimer:264). Its first German edition was published in 1952. Eight additional editions followed until the end of the 1960s. The book was promoted by Billy Graham, who was vice-president of YfC for many years, and gained wide influence among German evangelicals as a passionate call to preach the gospel to those who never had a chance to hear it. Such publications did not reflect critically on the changing world situation with all its problematic implications for world mission, nor did they engage in a dialogue with the controversial missiological debate of that time. They were basically concerned with the fact that millions of individuals had still not heard the Good News, and they issued an urgent call to the young generation of western Christians not to forsake these unreached people.

4. Also of great significance for students were the publications of mission agencies. Almost each mission had some kind of information bulletin reporting from its various mission fields. Many schools were associated with a particular mission, and consequently the concern for world mission was omnipresent at *the Schools*. In some of these publications, the missiological issues of the 1960s were reflected as well. For example; the developments of the 1960s were discussed with all the resulting questions in *Offene Türen*, published by *Wiedenest*. Ernst Schrupp, in particular, but also Daniel Herm, commented on the developments following the integration of the IMC into the WCC and all the subsequent struggles in missiological thinking.[2] The publications of such schools as *Liebenzell*, *Beatenberg* and *Chrischona* made a similar contribution.

5. After the middle of the 1960s a new epoch began which can be called *the Beyerhaus era*. In 1966, Peter Beyerhaus returned from missionary service in South Africa and immediately involved himself with a 'passionate engagement' in the struggle for an evangelical view of mission against the direction the ecumenical movement was taking (Beyerhaus 1987:IX). *Humanisierung. Einzige Hoffnung der Welt* was published in 1969 as an answer to the WCC's assembly at Uppsala 1968. It is a significant document for several reasons:

(a) It is a witness to the early period of the ecumenical-evangelical polarisation and does not have the strongly apologetic, even polemical, sound of later publications by Beyerhaus and the *Theologische Konvent*. In the preface to the second edition (1970) Beyerhaus explicitly claims to be a 'friend of the ecumenical movement' (1970a:4).

(b) Beyerhaus diagnoses a shift from the traditional understanding of mission, with its focus on redemption and eternal life, to a new interpretation of mission restricted to immanent humanisation. He had at that time already identified what he believed to be the key issue. It was in Beyerhaus's view not simply a matter of balance, not only an over-correction of a one-sided vertical understanding of salvation, which now tended to become one-sidedly horizontal. It was at the deepest level a 'crisis of faith.' Western Christianity had lost confidence in a God who exists and acts in history. Missing is the acknowledgement of a supernatural reality and an existential encounter with this God in Jesus Christ (1970a:51).

(c) Furthermore, in view of Bosch's call for a new understanding of mission beyond the polarisation of the last two decades, it is illuminating to consider Beyerhaus's assessment of a possible synthesis of the two diverging positions. He devotes an entire chapter to the topic in *Die Notwendigkeit einer wechselseitigen Korrektur* (The Necessity of Mutual Correction) (1970a:33–48). In the period between Uppsala 1968 and Bangkok 1972 Beyerhaus asks, 'Is there a theoretical possibility and a qualified hope that an "evangelical" and an "ecumenical" understanding of mission can move closer again by accepting mutual correction' (1970a:46)? His answer is, *yes*, there is a *theoretical* possibility, if evangelicals would transcend their *quietism* in social ethics and integrate a concern for the present and concrete historical situation and if ecumenicals would overcome their *activism* and eschatologically prolong their historical perspective. Beyerhaus called such an understanding of mission 'integral' – already in 1969! (1970a:46). But Beyerhaus is rather sceptical regarding the *real* possibility of such a development. He did not want to make a final judgement but was very concerned with the direction in which the WCC was moving at that time (1970a:49–68).

In the following twenty years Beyerhaus has published more than twenty monographs, not counting edited books and articles.[3] Almost all his contributions centre around a single theme: the apologetic defence of what he views as a biblical understanding of mission over against developments in the context of the WCC. Beyerhaus became very influential in German evangelical missiology, and his publications became textbooks in every evangelical Bible school in the 1970s and 1980s.

(2) DEBATING THEOLOGY OF MISSION: EVANGELICAL CONFERENCES

Furthermore, a German evangelical theology of mission gained contours through various conferences.

1. First of all, we turn to the Berlin Congress of 1966. It is related to the Bible schools and seminaries in a more indirect way. Evangelists and leaders of mission agencies of the Evangelical Alliance attended the

congress. Many of them were related to the Bible schools, and some even taught in them (e.g., Schrupp, *Wiedenest*). The theological impact of Berlin can be demonstrated in Billy Graham's plenary address (Hedlund:185–96) in two ways:

(a) The one key word in Graham's speech was *urgency*. It was a plea to realise that 'the fields are white unto harvest' (referring to John 4:35), that 'harvest time is always the ever-present now' and that therefore 'the evangelistic harvest is always urgent.' Graham claimed,

> There seems to be periods of special urgency in history when it can be said with peculiar relevance, 'The fields are white unto harvest.' I believe that we are now in such a period of history. We stand at the heart of a world revolution. The next 25 years will be the most decisive years since Christ walked on the roads of Galilee (Hedlund:186).

Graham was convinced of the unique moment in history and urged evangelicals to respond to this call:

> Almost every newspaper and every book screams from its pages: 'The harvest is ripe.' Never has the soil of the human heart and mind been better prepared. Never has the grain been thicker. Never have we had more efficient instruments in our hands to help us gather the harvest. Yet at a time when the harvest is the ripest in history, the church is floundering in tragic confusion (Hedlund:187).

(b) A second significant contribution of Graham's presentation was the definition of evangelism. Against the confusion which he felt dominated missiological discussions at that time (referring to the developments of the WCC) he claimed, 'Evangelism has social implications, but its primary thrust is the winning of men to a personal relationship to Christ' (Hedlund:187). And later he added:

> Thus evangelism has a social responsibility. The social, psychological, moral and spiritual needs of men become a burning motivation for evangelism. However, I am convinced if the Church went back to its main task of proclaiming the Gospel and getting people converted to Christ, it would have a far greater impact on the social, moral and psychological needs of men than any other thing it could possibly do (Hedlund:191).

We conclude that Graham, and following him the entire conference at Berlin 1966, has impacted evangelicals at least on the level of *motivation* and *urgency*, and in a clear statement on the *primacy of the proclamation* of the Gospel in evangelism over against the social responsibility – although not without referring to the social implications of the Gospel. This message has also reached German evangelicals (Jung:48–49) and has shaped the ethos of mission teaching at the Bible schools.[4]

2. Secondly, the assemblies of the *Konferenz Bibeltreuer Ausbildungsstätten (KBA)* will be considered. The *KBA* is not an explicitly missiological association and its annual gatherings are not necessarily devoted to mission themes. Nonetheless, the close relationship between the schools of the *KBA* and the mission movement is evident and can be documented through the mission themes of the annual conferences:

1965 'The work of Trans World Radio and its missionary significance for the world' (Horst Marquardt, ERF)
'The consequences of Karl Barth's theology today' (Heinrich Jochums, Wuppertal)
1967 'The significance of missionary activity for the existence and service of Christians and their integration into the life of training facilities' (Otto Riecker, *Adelshofen*)
1968 'Our mobilisation for world mission today' (Ernst Schrupp, *Wiedenest*)
1969 'Our missionary activity within the training period (Ernst Klassen, *Brake*)

We notice that in the early years of the *KBA*, almost every meeting had a mission theme on its agenda. This only underlines the high commitment to mission training at the Bible schools and seminaries. The themes of the 1960s mirror four concerns: (a) information about and motivation for world mission; (b) the missionary *dimension* of Bible school training; (c) the defence of an evangelical view of mission against 'liberal dilution' (i.e., Barth's universalism as a dilution of missionary urgency); and (d) new challenges to mission in a changing world situation.[5] All topics are pragmatic. They grew out of needs on the mission field and at the Bible schools. Foundational reflection on a biblical theology of mission and critical encounter with the missiological discussions of that time were rare.

(3) TEACHING THEOLOGY OF MISSION: CURRICULA

In the light of the facts (a) that the strength of the evangelical Bible school movement was in the area of spirituality and motivation and not in academic excellence, (b) that 'til about twenty years ago hardly any library resources had been developed by the schools of neo-pietistic origin' (Egelkraut 1990:33), and (c) that there was a severe lack of serious theological reflection in evangelical circles (cf. Bockmühl 1982:5–6), it is not surprising that in the 1960s the theology of mission was taught at evangelical Bible schools in very simple ways. The great missiological discussions which dominated the agenda of the IMC and the WCC since the 1950s were hardly the subject of the courses on the theology of mission at that time, as can be demonstrated by two examples: as regards *Brake*,[6] the catalogue of the academic year 1960–61 offers courses in mission each semester from the second to the sixth semester. No specific content of the mission courses is indicated – just *mission*.[7] For the academic year 1962–63, *Theology of Mission* was scheduled for the second semester, followed by *History of Mission* in the third and fourth semester and *Methods of Mission* in the final year (semester five and six). The same curriculum was still in use in 1970. A closer examination of the content of the courses shows[8] that information about the world mission movement was given high priority. It included an introduction to each continent, even each country. Theology of mission was based on *The Biblical Basis of Mission*, written by the missionary Robert Glover in 1945. Other schools of the same tradition, such as *Bergstrasse* and *Beatenberg*, follow the same pattern. *Liebenzell*[9] offered only one mission course with the title *Missionskunde* in the academic year 1963–64. By the end of the decade, *Evangelium und Religionen* and *Missionsgeschichte* were added to the curriculum.[10]

b) *The 1970s: Theology of Mission in the Wake of* Frankfurt *and* Lausanne

At the centre of the decade between 1970 and 1979 stand the two mission declarations which are claimed by many German evangelicals as their theological foundation: the *Frankfurt Declaration* and the *Lausanne Covenant*. Much of what was said and written by German evangelicals in these years centres around these two statements. Beyond this, the 1970s are also the decade of the beginning of a tidal wave of translations from the English-speaking – especially the North American – world. As mission theology was developed more extensively and debated more broadly, the curricula of the Bible institutes were affected as well.

(1) DEVELOPING THEOLOGY OF MISSION: RESEARCH AND PUBLICATION

Publications concerning the ecumenical and evangelical mission conferences of the 1970s make up the largest contribution to mission publications in the German language.

1. Most of these books were written, edited or co-edited by Peter Beyerhaus and published by the publishing house of the *Liebenzeller Mission* (Verlag der Liebenzeller Mission). In several cases they were edited in the name of the *Theologische Konvent* of the *Konferenz Bekennender Gemeinschaften*. A list of Beyerhaus's major publications in the 1970s shows his domination in German evangelical missiology:[11]

1970 *Die Wheaton-Erklärung: Grundfragen der Mission*
1970 *Die Grundlagenkrise der Mission*
1970 *Die Versuchungsstunde des ÖRK*
1971 *Mission und Rassismus*
1972 *Allen Völkern zum Zeugnis*
1973 *Bangkok '73: Anfang oder Ende der Weltmission*
1973 *Jesus Christus und die Weltreligionen*
1974 *Alle Welt soll sein Wort hören. Lausanner Kongress für Weltevangelisation*
1975 *Mission in urchristlicher und endgeschichtlicher Zeit*
1975 *Reich Gottes oder Weltgemeinschaft*
1976 *Ökumene im Spiegel von Nairobi*
1977 *Die Wahrheit in der Auseinandersetzung mit Religionen und Ideologien*
1979 *Ideologien – Herausforderungen an den Glauben*
1979 *Zwischen Anarchie und Tyrannei*

The tone of all these publications was set by the *Frankfurt Declaration* (1970), with its sharp condemnation of the theology of the WCC in and after Uppsala. We note that all these books not only advocate a certain theology but also convey a decisively anti-ecumenical attitude. It is not without significance for the evangelical Bible school movement that Beyerhaus's publications belong to the core of the missiological literature available at the libraries of these schools.[12]

2. If we consider missiological textbooks in evangelical Bible colleges and seminaries beyond Beyerhaus' work published in the 1970s, we must turn first of all to Klaus Bockmühl's *Was heisst heute Mission*? (1974). Bockmühl reviews the period from Hartenstein, Freytag and Kraemer up to the Lausanne Congress in 1974.[13] His argument is clear: the legacy of Hartenstein, Freytag and Kraemer stands for the biblical, pietistic, positive tradition of mission (1974:9–62). After 1961 a 'new understanding of mission' emerged in the context of the WCC, an understanding which deviates considerably from the traditional view of mission and must be rejected (1974:63–152). The only answer is an alternative theology of mission – and such an alternative was given by the evangelical movement at Wheaton (1966), Frankfurt (1970), Berlin (1974) and Lausanne (1974) (1974:153–79).

Bockmühl's assessment pushes in the same direction as the *Frankfurt Declaration* and some of Beyerhaus's statements, but intends to point beyond the antithesis of *Frankfurt* and *Berlin* – which he understands as an 'emergency brake' – to a positive biblical conception of mission (1974:162). On the one hand, he criticises some of the developments in the WCC's view of mission, especially the anthropological orientation of its theology in general and the secularisation of its understanding of mission, in which everything is reduced to the human and the immanent

(1974:184). On the other hand, Bockmühl points to the *Lausanne Covenant* as a significant step toward a positive and biblical conception of mission (1974:162–79). He was especially pleased with John Stott's foundational definition of the key terms of mission. An expanded version of Stott's contribution was published afterwards (*Christian Mission in the Modern World*, 1975) and translated in German (*Gesandt wie Christus*, 1976). Bockmühl, not actually a missiologist but rather a specialist in systematic theology and social ethics, was especially alert to the social dimension of Lausanne (1974:168–75). Only one year after Lausanne he wrote a thorough analysis of Lausanne's contribution to social ethics, especially the famous article five of the *Covenant* (1975). While he affirms the general thrust of the article, he calls for more precise theological reflection and definitions. He critically analyses each of the nine 'action-concepts' of article five of the *Lausanne Covenant* and qualifies them in the light of their biblical foundation (1974:20–46).

3. The 1970s were also the period in which translations of publications from the English-speaking world gained prominence on the German evangelical book market.

(a) On a semi-academic level, the following translations gained influence in the 1970s:

John Stott's *Einheit der Evangelikalen. Gegen die falsche Polarisierung (Balanced Christianity)* was translated in 1975; *Gesandt wie Christus (Christian Mission in the Modern World)* followed only one year later. It is especially the latter which became one of the key textbooks in the theology of mission courses at the Bible schools and seminaries.

Also in the footsteps of *Lausanne* is *The New Face of Evangelicalism* edited by René Padilla and published in German *Zukunftsperspektiven. Evangelikale nehmen Stellung* in 1977.

In the same year, another significant text was made available in German. G.W. Peters' *Missionarisches Handeln und biblischer Auftrag (A Biblical Theology of Mission)* is still considered to be the only comprehensive evangelical theology of mission available in the German language.[14] Peters chooses not to engage in critical dialogue with all the statements of mission conferences, be they ecumenical or evangelical, he only wants to present a biblical view of God's missionary intention (1977a:10). Peters's definition of mission proved important for many evangelicals. He distinguishes between *mission* (in the German translation, *Sendung*) and *missions* (in the German translation, *Mission*), in that he defines *mission* as referring to the entire *sending* of the church as 'pilgrim, stranger, witness, prophet, servant, as salt, as light, etc.', and *missions* as a specialised term referring to the proclamation of 'the gospel of Jesus Christ in gospel-destitute areas, to win converts from other faiths or non-faiths to Jesus Christ, and to establish functioning, multiplying local congregations' (1972:11). Along the same lines, Peters distinguishes between the *cultural mandate* which calls all human beings to work under God toward a healthy social order, and the *mission mandate* which focuses on the church and its primary task to evangelise, to make disciples, to plant churches and to educate the church. He decisively rejects every mixing up of the two mandates, especially the tendency to include aspects of the *cultural mandate* into to the *mission mandate* (1977a:166–71).

A second book by Peters translated into German, *Evangelisation. Total – durchdringend – umfassend (Saturation Evangelism)*, was also published in 1977. It contains a theology of evangelisation and an analysis of the two internationally applied strategies, *Evangelism-In-Depth* and *New Life for All*. Both of Peter's books became standard textbooks in *the Schools*.

It was also in that decade that the first books of the so-called *Church Growth Movement* were published in Germany. Hans Kadorf's *Gemeindewachstum als missionarisches Ziel* [*Church Growth as the Missionary Goal*] (1976) was something like an introduction to the church growth philosophy. *Wachsen oder Welken (=How to Grow a Church*) by Donald A. McGavran and Win Arn (1978) and *Handbuch für Evangelisation und Gemeindeaufbau (=God's Way to Keep a Church Going & Growing*) by Vergil Gerber (1979) followed in the same decade.

(b) In the context of the evangelical Bible schools, publications of a more popular character were probably at least as important as the academic and semi-academic literature. We mention just a few examples translated and published in 1970, which have influenced the German evangelical mission movement:

1971 Bill Bright, *Handbuch für persönliche Evangelisation* [*Handbook for Personal Evangelisation*]
1972 Michael Griffith, *Es gibt Grösseres (Give Up Your Small Ambitions)*
1973 Paul Little, *Weitersagen. Zeugnis geben, wie macht man das (How To Give Away Your Faith)*
1979 Robert E. Coleman, *Des Meisters Plan der Evangelisation (The Masters Plan of Evangelism)*

4. One final comment is needed regarding academic research by German evangelical theologians. Although academic studies by German evangelical missiologists were still minimal in the 1970, there was be one exception: Klaus Fiedler, a Baptist missionary, who completed his doctoral thesis in 1978 for the University at Daressalam, Tanzania.[15] Klaus Müller has called Fiedler 'the first evangelical missionary of the post-war period who completed doctoral studies' (Müller 1995:16). Fiedler is something of a forerunner to the new generation of German evangelical missiologists who began to emerge only in the 1980s.

(2) DEBATING THEOLOGY OF MISSION: EVANGELICAL CONFERENCES

1. The trajectory of German evangelical theology of mission in the 1970s was also influenced by the conference of the *Theologische Konvent* in 1970 at Frankfurt and the *International Congress on World Evangelisation* in 1974 at Lausanne, with their respective documents, the *Frankfurt Declaration* and the *Lausanne Covenant*. The significance of these two consultations for the identity of the German evangelical mission movement has been introduced in Part II, and the impact of the two documents upon the theology of mission taught at *the Schools* will be further analysed in the next section.

2. On the programme of the annual meetings of the *Konferenz bibeltreuer Ausbildungsstätten* we observe a missiological theme on two occasions:

1974 'Education for Church Ministries: The Mission Field' (Ernst Vatter, *Liebenzell*)
1978 'The Current Situation in Missions and how it Effects the Training of Missionaries' (Ernst Vatter, *Liebenzell*)
'Church and Missions Today – A Survey' (Ernst Vatter, *Liebenzell*)

On both occasions the speaker was Ernst Vatter, director for foreign missions of the *Liebenzeller Mission*, president of the *AEM* and one of the key figures of the German evangelical mission movement at that time.

(3) TEACHING THEOLOGY OF MISSION: CURRICULA

In the 1970s the curricula of the Bible colleges began to be developed beyond the simple biblical foundation and spiritual motivation of the earlier decades toward a more complex and differentiated presentation of a broader missiological field. In all the cases examined, this was not so much the result of a deliberate decision of the academic leadership of the schools but rather the result of changes in faculty. A new generation of mission teachers introduced more complex missiological curricula (cf. Wolke). A survey among the Bible colleges of the *KBA* conducted in 1980 confirms this development toward a more complex and comprehensive curriculum in mission (Archive *Bienenberg*).

c) The 1980s and Beyond: Theology of Mission between North American Impact and Home-Grown Scholarship

The years after 1980 can be characterised by two foci: (1) an increasing number of translations of English books were made accessible to the German public; and (2) a German based evangelical academic missiological tradition emerged. This has influenced theological reflection in the context of evangelical conferences, as well as mission studies at Bible schools and seminaries.

(1) DEVELOPING THEOLOGY OF MISSION: RESEARCH AND PUBLICATION

1. The *Beyerhaus era* of the 1970s continued into the next decade, though at a somewhat reduced intensity. He published additional books commenting on the ecumenical conference at Melbourne 1980 (Beyerhaus 1981) and the development of the ecumenical Third World theologies (expressed in the *Ecumenical Association of Third World Theologians* founded in 1976) (Beyerhaus 1986). In 1987, a one-volume collection of his major works since 1970 was edited (Beyerhaus 1987). This became a handy textbook for Bible school use, summarising the main theses of Beyerhaus's struggle against the WCC's understanding of mission.

2. Yet one of the main features of the 1980s is certainly the flood of North American missiological literature which reached the German-speaking world. The whole range of missiological topics introduced by the Church Growth Movement established a footing in Germany and Switzerland. North American evangelical theology of mission and its contribution to the German-speaking context was even the subject of a doctoral thesis presented by Edward Rommen at the University of Munich in 1986. Rommen (1987) analysed the works of Peters, Tippet, Kraft, McGavran, Wagner, Hesselgrave and Winter and their contribution to German missiology. One of the results of this North American influence is that German evangelicals widened their perspectives in missiological thinking beyond pure biblical-theological reflections and historical investigations, toward the inclusion of anthropology, social sciences, communication and strategy (Rommen 1987). Müller refers to three streams which together make up missiology: 'biblical theology of mission,' 'history of mission' and 'anthropology.' The last, he claims, we owe to G. W. Peters (that is, North American missiology) (Müller 1995:13–14).

But there is an additional segment of English language literature which was translated in the 1980s and deserves attention. *Salz der Erde. Fragen an die Kirche heute (The Other Side of 1984-Questions for the Church)* by Lesslie Newbigin (1985), *Anstiftung. Evangelium für die armen Reichen* [*Incitement: Good News for the Poor Rich*] by René Padilla (1986)[16] and *Der ganze Christus für eine geteilte Welt. Evangelikale Christologie der Zwei-Drittel-Welt (Sharing Jesus in the Two Thirds World)* by Vinay Samuel and Chris Sugden (1987). All these publications represent the wider international evangelical world, including voices from the Two Thirds World. To use Holthaus' typology again, these authors represent rather the 'open evangelicals' than the 'conservative evangelicals' (Holthaus 1997:17–18). In view of the schools under consideration, it is important to notice that literature from this segment of evangelicalism is less represented in their libraries and rarely present on syllabi and reading lists.

3. A second main feature of the 1980s is the rise of German evangelical missiological scholarship.

(a) On the one hand, this is indicated by a number of individuals who completed doctoral studies in the 1980s and early 1990s. These theses cover two main areas. Several studies were historical, dealing with the biographies of individuals or with the histories of missions (e.g., N. Schmidt; Fiedler; Franz; Brandl). Other research projects approached theological topics, in most cases aspects of the ecumenical-evangelical controversy (Sautter; Hammel; Berneburg).

(b) On the other hand, the foundation of the *Arbeitskreis für evangelikale Missiologie (AfeM)* (Association of Evangelical Missiology) in 1985 with its journal *Evangelikale Missiologie (em)* was a significant catalyst and promoter in the emergence of a home-grown German evangelical missiology. In his editorial to the first issue of *em*, Peter Mayer indicates how indebted German evangelicals are to the North American missiologist, G.W. Peters, for the promotion of an evangelical missiology in German-speaking Europe (*em* 1985/1:2). Yet in the same issue, Peters himself warns German evangelicals against simply becoming 'an American Satellite' (*em* 1985/1:8).

4. More recent publications, such as *Werkbuch Mission* (Herm and Herm) and *Mission unter Beschuss* (Holzhaus) shows evangelicals dealing in a somewhat more critical way with the sensitive issues of world mission. Serious reflection in the areas of culture, anthropology and ethnology, as well as a good sense for partnership, can be observed.

Ernst Vatter, in his address to the annual assembly of the *AEM* in 1987, states, 'The global context for the mission of the Church of Jesus Christ has completely changed since World War II' (Vatter:3). He identifies six major changes which demand fresh missiological reflection and, in some areas, a new missionary conduct (Vatter:3–9). This includes (a) the issue of mission and social responsibility, (b) the issue of the indigenisation of the gospel in other cultures, (c) the training of indigenous church leaders, (d) the relationship of mission and church, and (e) the issue of Christian mission and pluralism. Vatter's call for responsible reflection and transformation in a rapidly changing time allows the conclusion that key leaders of the German evangelical mission movement did take seriously the contemporary critical issues in mission.

Most recently, Hans Ulrich Reifler, a former missionary in Latin America (1976–1991) and today missiology teacher at *Chrischona*, has published what can be called the first evangelical German textbook on missiology, comprising introductions to the theology of mission, anthropology, cross-cultural communication, mission strategy and mission praxis. Its theological section sums up the discussion among conservative evangelicals in German-speaking Europe of the last three decades. The results will be considered in the next section.

(2) DEBATING THEOLOGY OF MISSION: EVANGELICAL CONFERENCES

Looking again at the conferences of the *KBA*, we find the following missiological subject-matter discussed at the annual assemblies:

1981 'Who is an Evangelist' (Anton Schulte, *Neues Leben*)
'The Character of Evangelistic Preaching' (Anton Schulte, *Neues Leben*)
'Evangelisation in the Concept of Bible School Training' (Doyle Klaassen, *Brake*)

1982 'The Theology of Paul in the Context of his Missionary Mandate' (George W. Peters, *FHM*)
'The Demands of Missions in our Schools ' (George W. Peters, *FHM*)
'The World of Mission' (George W. Peters, *FHM*)

1990 'Recent Developments of the Kingdom-of-God-Concept in Evangelical Theology' (Eckhard Schnabel, *Giessen*).

This leads to the following observations, questions and conclusions: (a) After 1982, explicitly missiological topics disappear from the agenda of the *KBA*. It seems that the evangelistic urgency which characterised the 1960s and 1970s had ceased in the 1980s and early 1990s. (b) The topics dealt with in 1981 and 1982 emphasise the evangelistic dimension of mission.[17] (c) At the same time, those issues in the international discussion of mission which focused on a more integrated and holistic understanding of mission were not picked up in the *KBA* conferences until 1990, when Schnabel discussed various interpretations of the Kingdom of God among evangelicals. (d) In view of the main topics of the other conferences between 1980 and 1995, it appears that other issues have caught the attention of the German Bible school movement, especially the educational challenges to theological education posed by the ideological forces of modern western culture (1980, 1983, 1985, 1989, 1992), the question of spiritual formation in theological education (1984, 1988) and the integration of social sciences into the curriculum of Bible colleges and seminaries (1991).

(3) TEACHING THEOLOGY OF MISSION: CURRICULA

1. Under the leadership of the *AEM*'s *Seminar für Missionarische Fortbildung* and with G. W. Peters as a resource person, additional steps were taken toward a reflected and intentionally designed missiological curriculum at the beginning of the 1980s. In March 1980, the mission teachers of the Bible colleges and seminaries met at Holzhausen in order to develop a 'first common conception' for the teaching of mission.[18] The meeting issued a 'Recommendation of certain normative standards for the teaching of mission in evangelical Bible colleges.' [19] It contains the

following statements: (a) The reason for the recommendation is the demands on the mission field, the deficiencies recognised in continuing education and the need for an improved and unified standard. (b) Defined standards are necessary in view of the accreditation of *the Schools*. (c) At least three courses in mission should be required: *History of Missions, Theology of Mission and Religions.* Beyond this, elective courses in *Mission Anthropology, Mission Methods, Indigenous Churches and Theologies* and *The Missionary* should be offered. This ought to become the common nomenclature for mission studies in evangelical schools. (d) Each course should contain at least twenty four to thirty six teaching hours.[20] (e) The *Seminar für missionarische Weiterbildung* offers a course for mission teachers at the Bible colleges. As regards the theology of mission, the list of textbooks recommended by the consultation is remarkable. G.W. Peters' *Missionarisches Handeln und biblischer Auftrag* is suggested as the main textbook for students. It can be complemented by Catholic and ecumenical texts. Beyond this and if time allows, the mission statements of Wheaton, Frankfurt, Lausanne and Seoul should be discussed. For additional reading the following books are recommended: Vicedom, *Missio Dei*, Blauw, *Gottes Volk in dieser Welt*, Beyerhaus, *Allen Völkern zum Zeugnis*, Bockmühl, *Was heisst heute Mission*? and Stott, *Gesandt wie Christus*.

2. A survey conducted in 1996[21] allows an analysis of the developments between 1980 and 1996. Some of the developments can be summarised as follows: (a) Most of *the Schools* have introduced new courses in mission and increased the number of teaching hours in mission considerably. The average number hours is 130. (b) The curricula developed into a more diversified and comprehensive discussion of the various fields of missiology. The subject areas suggested in 1980 were introduced by most schools. (c) It was not possible to introduce a common nomenclature in mission studies. At least twenty names of courses are used with a considerable overlap in content (Böker Survey:3). (d) It was also not possible to establish a common number of teaching hours for each subject. The range of hours varies between twelve and eighty one for one course (Böker Survey:3). (e) In addition, it was not possible to establish accrediting standards for mission studies. The EEAA gives only a very vague description of what is expected in mission studies, without any clear specifications of the sort formulated by the *KBA* consultation in 1980 (EEAA:13–14).[22] In terms of the content of mission theology, the survey does not give additional information.

3. A more detailed study of the contemporary situation in teaching mission theology in particular schools shows the following picture: (a) an increasing number of mission teachers are graduates from the *FHM*. (b) This indicates that what could be called the Peters-Beyerhaus-school gained broad influence in the Bible colleges and seminaries. (c) This fact

is supported by the observation that in required readings and bibliographies Beyerhaus, Bockmühl and Peters are the most commonly mentioned authors.[23]

We have now reviewed the developments from 1960 to 1995 and can turn to a systematic analysis of the mission theology represented by *the Schools*.

2. Analysis of German Evangelical Theology of Mission

This analysis will be carried out in comparison to the missiological models outlined in chapter 8 and will follow the same agenda. Research has shown that the theology of mission of evangelicals in German-speaking Europe can be defined within the boundaries of the *Frankfurt Declaration* and the *Lausanne Covenant*.[24] All *the Schools* would accept these as proper boundaries for an evangelical theology of mission. Thus, our analysis will take the *Frankfurt Declaration* and the *Lausanne Covenant* as its starting point. Then it will focus on Hans Ulrich Reifler's recently published *Missionarisches Handeln am Ende des 20. Jahrhunderts*, which is one of the most representative recent textbooks in *the Schools*. It shows how the missiological influences and debates of the last three to four decades are being transmitted to students towards the end of the century.[25]

a) General Remarks to the Reception of Bosch's Proposal

First of all we recognise a great lack of familiarity with Bosch's literature among German evangelicals. Hardly any of Bosch's publications are available in German. The fact that his doctoral thesis in New Testament studies at the University of Basel (1959) is written in German does not contribute much to an acquaintance with Bosch in the German (evangelical) context because this academic publication of the 1950s is rarely available in the libraries of evangelical schools and does not address contemporary issues in the theology of mission. Neither *Witness to the World* (1980) nor *Transforming Mission* (1991)[26] have been translated into German. His recent booklet *Believing in the Future* (1995) was published in the German language [*An die Zukunft glauben* (1996)] – but by the *Evangelische Missionswerk* at Hamburg, not by an evangelical publisher. The libraries of evangelical Bible colleges and seminaries consulted for this study do not contain any of Bosch's books. This leads to the conclusion that Bosch's writings are not accessible to students at the respective schools and that his work is considered to be of no relevance for mission studies by these schools. On the other hand, it is surprising to notice how positively Bosch's work was greeted after the publication of *Transforming Mission* and definitely after his sudden death in 1992. Not only journals of a more ecumenical orientation reviewed Bosch's work,[27] but evangelicals acknowledged Bosch's contribution as well. This is to a certain extent due to Hans Kasdorf, who has taught frequently in Germany and Switzerland. He pursued doctoral studies under Bosch at the University of South Africa. In his memorial essay on Bosch in *Evangelikale Missiologie* (Kasdorf 1992) he speaks very favourably of Bosch. He refers to *Transforming Mission* as a *magnum opus*, as *the* theology of mission of the twentieth century, a book which belongs on the required reading list of any missiologist. It is somewhat surprising that Kasdorf does not mention Bosch's concern for a new ecumenical missionary paradigm which views the contemporary polarisation as 'creative tensions' and intends to move 'beyond' them. Of course, at the level of academic research, theologians read English and are aware of Bosch's literature (e.g., Berneburg 1997).

Thus, we are not merely looking for explicit references to David Bosch in the teaching of mission, but for indicators which may reveal how evangelical theology of mission in Germany and Switzerland relates to Bosch's proposal.

b) Crisis and Response: Focus on Continuity

1. The *Frankfurt Declaration*, with the full name of *Frankfurt Declaration on the Fundamental Crisis in Christian Missions*,[28] presupposes a crisis in mission. Beyerhaus addresses this crisis in mission from the very beginning of his publications in the context of the controversies of the 1960s. The first chapter of *Humanisierung. Einzige Hoffnung der Welt?* begins with the phrase, 'For an analysis of the current crisis of world mission regarding its foundation and purpose …' (1970a:7). And his second publication on the subject was entitled *Die Grundlagenkrise der Mission* (*The Crisis at the Foundations of Mission*) (1970b). Yet these phrases already indicate a remarkable emphasis. Beyerhaus identifies the crisis of mission as a crisis of its biblical foundation. He primarily diagnoses a theological crisis. In *Die Grundlagenkrise der Mission*, he distinguishes between an external (*äussere*) *and* an internal (*innere*) crisis (1970b:5–7).

(a) The external crisis is on the level of an increasing resistance to the gospel in all parts of the world, which represents a real challenge to the world missionary movement. This is a given fact, and the church must take it seriously. Beyerhaus speaks of 'discouragements,' but they do not represent the foundational crisis of mission.[29] In another context Beyerhaus identifies four external factors which have caused the crisis (1970a:8–11): (i) the association of mission with colonialism and subsequently an anti-missionary attitude as a result of the general anti-colonial context; (ii) anti-western nationalism of Afro-Asian people, including the recovery of old religious practices; (iii) the tendency toward a syncretistic coexistence of different religions as promoted mainly by Asians; and (iv) the undermining of a biblical theology of mission in the footsteps of a critical, secularised western theology. All of this is not actually the crisis, but only the causes of the crisis.

(b) For Beyerhaus, the real crisis is interior; that is, in the way the ecumenical movement is responding to the external crisis. In its response he sees mission reduced to revolution, development and dialogue (1970b:12–15). The 'perversion of mission to a this-worldly attempt to change the world, in contradiction with the traditional understanding of mission, leads to a conflict within the missionary movement.' This, in Beyerhaus's view, is the real crisis. It is a crisis inside the church. It is a theological crisis; christology and, finally, the authority of scripture are at stake (1970b:11, 17–27). The *Frankfurt Declaration* was understood as the direct response to *this* foundational crisis in mission (1970b:28–37; cf. Vicedom 1967).

We also notice that neither Beyerhaus nor the *Frankfurt Declaration* engage in critical reflection on the western mission movement of the colonial epoch. The most self-critical statement by Beyerhaus can probably be found in his early publication *Humanisierung. Die einzige Hoffnung der Welt*, where he discusses some of the deficiencies of the traditional mission movement and acknowledges that the evangelical understanding of mission needs correction (1970a:33–48). Later he questions the radically critical, anti-colonial assessment of the traditional western missionary movement (cf. Beyerhaus 1987:146). The *Frankfurt Declaration* does not refer to any deficiencies of the traditional missionary movement of the colonial age nor does it call for any changes in world mission in the light of a changing world situation.

For Beyerhaus, the true answer to this critical situation can only be given in faithfulness to the traditional understanding of mission. Time and again he refers to the 'traditional' or 'classical' understanding of mission, which in his view is basically the biblical understanding and which stands in sharp contrast to the developments of the ecumenical view (Beyerhaus 1969; 1970:12; 1987:58; 1996:101–61, 282). With regard to tradition and the Bible, he therefore calls for continuity, although not without an openness for minor corrective changes in the traditional understanding (1970b:15–17; 1996:15). But Beyerhaus perceives the developments in ecumenical circles not as slight corrections of the traditional understanding of mission, but as a totally new approach to mission. To such developments he can only say: NO (1970:17). This decisive NO is pronounced in the *Frankfurt Declaration* and confirmed in the *Berlin Declaration*.

2. The *Lausanne Covenant* implies discontinuity as well as continuity. Basically, it presupposes 'that a new missionary era has dawned,' in which 'the dominant role of western missions is fast disappearing' (# 8). While the *Covenant* confirms the ultimate biblical mandate of world evangelisation and the urgency of that task in the light of the 2,700

million people who have not heard the gospel (Introduction; # 4 and # 9), it also indicates a more self-critical attitude and comments in a more moderate way on the WCC's view of mission. Several statements of the *Covenant* express penitence for the neglect of the past and confession of failures, and they contain commitments to change (# 5 regarding social action, # 7 regarding the unity of the church, # 10 regarding the export of western cultures, # 11 regarding training of indigenous leadership, # 12 regarding manipulation in evangelism).

The *Lausanne Covenant* also indicates an openness to take up some of the crucial issues discussed in the ecumenical context, such as the socio-political dimension of the churches' responsibility (# 5), the withdrawal of western missionaries (moratorium) in certain situations (# 9), the cultural domination of the western church (# 10) and the independence of indigenous churches (# 11) (cf. Bockmühl 1974:177). In his foundational theological presentation at beginning of the congress, John Stott addressed the critical topics of mission, evangelisation, dialogue, salvation and conversion. He did this on the basis of evangelical foundations and in an open dialogue with ecumenical positions (Beyerhaus 1974 vol. 1:60–84).[30] Stott received mixed responses from evangelicals. Bockmühl commended Stott's address as a clarifying biblical perspective which indicates a significant step forward in the ecumenical-evangelical controversy and should be made available to German readers (1974:165–66), while Hedlund criticised Stott for not having clearly stated an evangelical view of evangelisation as 'discipling the nations.' Referring to Stott's presentation, he concludes, 'The failure to grasp the heart of the Great Commission set the Congress on an inadequate and erroneous theological foundation' (Hedlund:294).

3. How do the themes of crisis and change appear in Reifer's *Missionarisches Handeln*? Reifler pays only minimal attention to the changes in the world and in world mission in the post-war period. In his review of the heritage of German missiology, he uses two sentences to explain the background to the tensions between the ecumenical and evangelical understandings of mission (Reifler:36). In the discourse on anthropology and culture, he admits that western missionaries have made mistakes in the past, but that today most mission agencies are avoiding these mistakes (Reifler:138–39). The chapter on missionary praxis begins with a short (two page) introduction to some changes which have taken place in the last decades and which make it impossible to do mission work in the same way as it was done in the last century (Reifler:204–05). Overall, the readers of this textbook (most likely the students of *the Schools*) do not get the impression that world mission has been undergoing dramatic changes in the last forty to fifty years, nor are they confronted with a critical assessment of the colonial epoch. They do not get the sense of a crisis, and they will not put this book back on the

shelf with the impression that anything should change. The entire book is highly affirmative in the way it claims continuity with the pietistic and neo-pietistic tradition of mission, in the way it establishes a biblical foundation of mission and in the way it outlines missionary practice.

4. Conclusion: It is evident that the theology of mission taught at *the Schools* basically follows the Beyerhaus-Bockmühl-Peters tradition. There is a strong sense of continuity with the earlier Hartenstein-Freytag-Vicedom line. There is hardly any serious discussion of the paradigmatic shifts in world mission with their critical assessment of the colonial epoch. Crisis awareness is absent, and consequently there is no need for changes. Given the parameters of the *Frankfurt Declaration* and the *Lausanne Covenant*, there seems to be a much stronger impact of the former. Or put differently, the *Lausanne Covenant* is often interpreted in the light of the *Frankfurt Declaration*, emphasising its affirmative statements.[31] Consequently, *the Schools* must be deemed to belong to that category which Bosch characterises as doing mission with a 'business as usual' attitude. According to Bosch, they can hardly be excused for such a lack of awareness (1991:7).

c) Bible, Context and Hermeneutics: Focus on the Normativity of the Bible

1. In its first paragraph, the *Frankfurt Declaration* says, 'The surrender of the Bible as our primary frame of reference leads to the shapelessness of mission and a confusion of the task of mission with a general idea of responsibility for the world.' The conviction that the Bible, as the authoritative word of God, is the unquestionable foundation not only of mission but of any Christian theology makes up the heart of evangelical theology. From this point of view, evangelicals identify the crisis in mission in 'the surrender of the Bible as the primary frame of reference' by the theologians of the WCC. In this regard, the prominent phrase, 'the world sets the agenda,' used in ecumenical circles since 1966 has been perceived by evangelicals as a turning away from the Bible as the sole source for the definition of the foundation, the goals, the tasks and the content of mission (*Frankfurt Declaration* #1; cf. Bockmühl 1974:156; Hedlund: 223–26).

In his affirmation and call to faithfulness, Beyerhaus points to three major challenges to the evangelical movement. First of all, he calls evangelicals to be faithful to the normative authority of scripture in the light of the challenge posed by *contextual hermeneutics*, which tends to weaken the universal authority of the biblical text (Beyerhaus 1987:245–46). It is therefore no surprise to find that Beyerhaus devotes almost 100 pages of the first volume of his recent theology of mission to the problem of contextualisation. The title of the chapter indicates the thrust of his argument: 'The contextual relativism of biblical authority' (Beyerhaus

1996a:197–282). It is a critical analysis of the developments of an 'ecumenical hermeneutic.'[32] Beyerhaus's verdict is twofold: on the one hand he values the contributions of a contextual hermeneutic in raising necessary and important questions regarding traditional western theology (1996a:235–49). On the other hand, he clearly points to the limits of contextual hermeneutic (1996a:249–64): (a) the mixture of 'general revelation' and 'special revelation', (b) the opening up of the canonical boundaries, (c) the loss of a normative foundation for Christian doctrine, and (d) the anthropocentric appropriation of biblical revelation. What is at stake, in Beyerhaus's view, is the authority of scripture, and he therefore warns of the consequences for the Christian mission: when the church in mission does not stand on the solid ground of the authority of the Bible, then its spiritual authority will soon be paralysed (1993:281). The task of an evangelical theology of mission can only be – according to Beyerhaus – to regain the pneumatological and salvation-historical tradition of biblical interpretation of the earlier German theology of mission (1993:282).

2. The *Lausanne Covenant* affirms this Bible-centredness already in its second paragraph (cf. Uda; Bockmühl 1974:176). Yet several of its voices identify more closely with the ecumenical concern of contextualisation. Michael Green's biblical study of the early church's methods and strategies of evangelisation concludes that the early Christians did take the *agenda of the world* seriously and that we are called to do the same (1975:224). Article 10 of the *Covenant* has opened a discussion among evangelicals regarding *gospel and culture*, which was continued beyond the congress at Lausanne and reached its culmination in the Willowbank Consultation in 1978 (Stott/Coote). While the *Willowbank Report* confirms 'the normative nature of Scripture,' it also acknowledges a certain 'cultural conditioning of Scripture' and calls for a 'contextual approach' in hermeneutics which goes beyond the 'traditional approaches' (Stott and Scoote:315–17). The issues have been further developed at the consultation of the International Council of Accrediting Agencies (ICAA) in 1991 (Kemp 1994). This indicated that in the years since *Lausanne*, evangelicals have been engaged in serious reflection on cultural and anthropological issues, with a strong emphasis on cross-cultural communication (Rommen 1987:95–115; Hesselgrave). The contribution of this wing of the evangelical movement to the issues of inculturation and contextualisation has been acknowledged by ecumenical leaders as a sign of growing convergencies between the two opposed movements (Werner 1993:332–335).

3. Looking at Reifler's *Missionarisches Handeln* we again observe that an emphasis on biblical authority is characteristic for evangelicals. The Beyerhaus-Bockmühl-Peters position, as well as the conference statements from Wheaton, Frankfurt, Berlin, Lausanne and Manila are

repeated and affirmed (Reifler:48–64). There is no discussion of the issues connected with contextualisation as a hermeneutical and epistemological problem. The only section dealing with contextualisation is in the chapter on cross-cultural communication, and it focuses exclusively on the question of how the gospel can be communicated in another culture. The whole concept of contextualisation is reduced to the question of communication. The student who reads this book is not exposed to the discussion concerning a subject which has dominated missiological reflection for two decades.[33]

4. Conclusion: At the centre of an evangelical attitude towards the issues of gospel and culture stands a commitment to the Bible as the God-given and unchangeable *pre-text*. The concept of contextualisation is applied only on the level of cross-cultural communication. The deeper hermeneutical issues are seldom discussed at the classroom level, and when scholars assess them, they tend to reject any hermeneutical implications (Beyerhaus 1996a; Sautter; Hamel; Berneburg 1997). Again, the position held by *the Schools* is closer to the *Frankfurt Declaration* than to the *Lausanne Covenant*. This becomes evident in Berneburg's critique of the contextual hermeneutics of Two Thirds World evangelicals (1997:239–47). In Sundermeier's words (:260):

> According to this notion of mission theology the *What* of faith is beyond contention. Its essence is agreed by consensus, and the rest is simply a matter of finding the most effective method of adapting the available means, and of applying these economically towards achieving the goal of mission, which is to 'convert the heathen.' The discussion of methods is therefore central... Mission *is* communication. The party at the receiving end is seen merely as the object of mission'.

This indicates a tragic ignorance or a deliberate avoidance of one of the central issues of the paradigm shift – namely, the awareness that context shapes theology, which means that our western theology is conditioned by our context and that the emergence of culturally shaped theologies must be on the agenda of relevant mission studies. German evangelical missiologists can and should keep their high view of scripture, yet they have to engage on a much deeper level with the issues of contextual theology and hermeneutics.[34]

d) Salvation and Mission: Focus on Conversion and Evangelism

1. When Peter Beyerhaus addressed evangelicals in 1984, he called them to hold faithfully to a biblical soteriology in the light of the challenge posed by a *holistic gospel* which tends to weaken the priority of the

spiritual dimension of salvation (Beyerhaus 1987:245). In the same manner, the *Frankfurt Declaration* defines mission as '*the witness and presentation of eternal salvation* performed in the name of Jesus Christ by his church and fully authorized messengers by means of preaching, the sacraments, and service' (# 4), and 'the appropriation of this salvation to individuals,' says the *Declaration*, 'takes place first however, through proclamation, which calls for decision, and through baptism, which places the believer in the service of love.' This personal appropriation of salvation has far-reaching consequences: 'Just as belief leads through repentance and baptism to eternal life, so unbelief leads through its rejection of the offer of salvation to damnation' (# 4). Therefore, 'the primary visible task of mission is to *call out the messianic, saved community* from among all people' (# 5). From this point of view, the *Frankfurt Declaration* states that '*Humanization* is not the primary goal of mission' (# 2) and strongly opposes any 'one-sided emphasis on salvation which stresses only this world, according to which the Church and the world together share in a future, purely social, reconciliation of all mankind' (# 5). All these statements define the priority of the spiritual and eternal dimension of salvation, the personal faith-decision of the individual. This leads subsequently to a 'closed ecclesiology,' or an understanding of the church as a body whose members have appropriated salvation through 'repentance and baptism.' This is decisively spelled out by the *Frankfurt Declaration* in direct opposition to the WCC's understanding of salvation and the church as developed since 1961 (cf. Beyerhaus's responses to Bangkok and Melbourne 1973; 1981)

2. The *Lausanne Covenant* advocates with equal clarity the primacy of the spiritual, transcendent dimension of salvation and subsequently the priority of evangelisation.

> To evangelize is to spread the good news that Jesus Christ died for our sins and was raised from the dead according to the Scriptures, and that as the reigning Lord he offers the forgiveness of sins and the liberating gift of the Spirit to all who repent and believe... But evangelism itself is the proclamation of the historical biblical Christ as Saviour and Lord, with a view to persuading people to come to him personally and so to be reconciled with God (# 4, see also # 9).

At the same time, the *Covenant* pushed the issue of social responsibility further than any of the previous evangelical statements.[35] Bockmühl, referring to C.F.H. Henry, claims that 'no other topic was so much at the forefront at Lausanne as was the relationship of the Gospel to the public life' (1974:168). This was to a large extent due to the contributions of the Latin Americans Samuel Escobar and René Padilla, who urged the assembly to define the gospel in a comprehensive way, including the spiritual as well as the material needs of human beings (Escobar 1974; Padilla 1974, cf. Bockmühl 1974:168–73; Bockmühl 1975:7–10; Hollenweger 1995:110–13). The famous paragraph 5 of the *Lausanne Covenant* ('Christian Social Responsibility') picked up these concerns and has stirred up extensive theological reflection beyond the Congress, leading to several regional and international consultations devoted to the subject. (cf. Padilla and Sugden 1985a; 1985b; Bockmühl 1975; Bockmühl 1983). In 1980 Ronald Sider summed up these developments among evangelicals with the following words:

> An historic transformation is in process. In all parts of the world, evangelical Christians in growing number are rediscovering the biblical summons to serve the poor, minister to the needy, correct injustice and seek societal shalom. The Chicago Declaration (1973), the *Lausanne Covenant*'s section on social responsibility (1974), the Evangelical Fellowship of India's Madras Declaration on Evangelical Social Action (1979) and the Evangelical Commitment to Simple Lifestyle are symptomatic of far-reaching changes. A fundamentally new world-wide movement is emerging. It seeks justice and peace in the power of the Spirit. It consists of biblical Christians passionately committed to a new search for social justice that is thoroughly biblical, deeply immersed in prayer, and totally dependent on the presence of the Holy Spirit (1982:General Preface).

The crucial issue which has, time and again, dominated the debate is the question of the primacy of evangelisation. Despite the fact that social deeds are recognised as an equally important dimension of the Christian mission as proclamation, all evangelical statements claim the primacy of evangelisation (Bockmühl 1983:26–27; Stott 1993). Ronald Sider has provided one of the most thorough evangelical reflections on the relationship of evangelisation and social action. He advocates a clear distinction between evangelisation and social action in view of their *intentions*, which should not be confused. 'In evangelism, the central intention is to lead non-Christians to become disciples of Jesus Christ. In social action, the central intention is to improve the socio-economic or psychological well-being of people for their life here and now' (1993:163, 165). He concludes, 'Evangelism, even when it does not have a primarily social *intention*, nevertheless has a social *dimension*, while social responsibility, even when it does not have a primarily evangelistic *intention*, nevertheless has an evangelistic dimension' (1993:166).[36] Regarding the primacy-issue he raises five questions:

> (1) A logical question: Can you have Christian social responsibility without first having Christians? (2) An ontological question: Is

> anything (or indeed everything) in this world as important as a living relationship with God that leads to eternal life? (3) A vocational question: Are not different Christians gifted with different callings and do they not therefore properly allocate their time differently? (4) A temporal question: Does not the immediate circumstance (e.g., a devastating flood) influence what in particular situations one does first? (5) A resource question: How do we allocate scarce resources of time, personnel, and money (1993:167–68).

While question one supports the logical primacy of evangelism and questions three to five leave it open to the context, the 'heart of the issue' is in question two. In this case Sider decisively advocates the primacy of evangelisation (1993:168–69).

3. In *Missionarisches Handeln* by Reifler, we read in the concluding statements of 'the priority of the proclamation of the gospel without neglecting the social perspective' (Reifler:264).[37] This prioritising is based on the conviction that only faith in Jesus Christ will lead to eternal salvation, a presupposition which will ultimately lead to the priority of proclamation.[38] Helmut Burkhardt, who teaches systematic theology at *Chrischona*, affirmed this evangelical core conviction recently when he presented a paper on 'Mission from an Evangelical Perspective' at Basel University (1995). Yet there is also in Reifler's statement the phrase, 'without neglecting the social perspective.' Reifler refers to the fact that ninety per cent of the all western 'missionaries' are in reality involved in social work and not in the primary task of proclamation. He justifies this reality by pointing to the crucial task of *diakonia* which belongs to the church's expanded mission, although it is not its centre (Reifler:246–48). Based on the gospel story of Zacchaeus, Reifler points to the priority of a personal conversion, which then has definite social implications (Reifler:82–83). Following Stott, he defines the role of social action in relation to evangelism as 'a means to evangelism,' 'a manifestation of evangelism' and 'a partner of evangelism' (Reifler:88; cf. Stott 1975a:25–28). In all of this, Reifler stands in the pietistic tradition of social mission [*Diakonie*]. He moves past the *Frankfurt Declaration*,[39] and is close to the *Lausanne Covenant*. This leads him to the following definition of mission: (a) Mission is primarily God's world-wide salvific action. (b) Mission must be seen as related to God's salvation history. (c) Mission is realised by the whole church of Jesus Christ. (d) Mission takes place in our present world, which is lost, yet loved by God who wants to save it. (e) Mission comprises evangelisation, teaching and social work [*Diakonie*]. (f) Mission begins locally, where I live. (g) Mission means to move beyond one's own cultural context. (h) Mission attempts to reach all people groups with the gospel. (i) The time of mission continues until the return of Jesus Christ in power and glory (Reifler:80–81).

4. Conclusion: We realise that in this area the mission theology of *the Schools* is closer to the *Lausanne Covenant* than to the *Frankfurt Declaration*. There is definitely a strong awareness of the social component of mission. This is partially due to the discussion among evangelicals since Lausanne 1974 but is also rooted in a long-standing tradition of *Diakonie* in German pietism (cf. Bockmühl 1985). There is definitely much overlap here with Bosch's paradigm of mission. Yet German evangelicals remain sceptical about such concepts as 'holistic,' 'integrated' or 'incarnational' mission.

At this point the intra-evangelical debate on evangelisation and social responsibility deserves special attention. The development from *Lausanne 1974* to *Grand Rapids 1982*, and even to *Wheaton 1983*, was observed carefully by German evangelicals and was the subject of Berneburg's recent doctoral thesis (1997).[40]

(a) Klaus Bockmühl has taken up these issues in his review of *Lausanne* (1974:168–75). Whilst he speaks favourably of the intention of René Padilla's and Samuel Escobar's contributions at *Lausanne*, he diagnoses a lack of theological clarity. It is not the need for social responsibility as such which is criticised by Bockmühl but the foundation on which such actions are based. One of his main concerns is the mixing up of 'the order of preservation' with the 'order of salvation,' which leads to the confusion of social ethics with evangelisation. Bockmühl concludes that evangelicals, through their abstinence from social ethics for many years, lack a clear theological theory of social responsibility and he calls for serious work in this area (172–73; cf. 1982:130–45). After *Grand Rapids 1982*, the statement of the consultation was edited and introduced in German by Klaus Bockmühl (1983). In his introduction he appreciates the document as a positive step forward in the theological reflection of evangelicals on social ethics. He also holds *Grand Rapids* to be significant because it could help to avoid a possible split within the evangelical movement. On the other hand, Bockmühl identifies three areas which have not been solved and will provoke further debate: (i) the issue of equality and/or primacy; (ii) the ambiguity of the term 'social'; and (iii) the different foundations of social responsibility in the 'order of creation' or in the 'reign of Christ.' For Bockmühl, the latter point is of major significance because it mirrors the clash between two theological conceptions – on one side, the Lutheran doctrine of the two kingdoms, on the other, a Calvinistic or Anabaptist understanding of Christ's reign.[41] According to Bockmühl, this will continue to be a controversial issue among evangelicals (1983:7–8).[42]

(b) A second significant German evangelical evaluation of international evangelical views on social responsibility comes from Eckhard Schnabel. At the 1990 annual assembly of the *KBA*, he presented a paper on the theme of 'Recent Developments of the Kingdom-of-God-Idea in

Evangelical Theology,' later published in an enlarged version (Schnabel 1993). Under the heading 'Radical Evangelicals,' he reviews developments within the *Lausanne Movement* from 1974 to 1983, referring especially to the contributions of Escobar, Padilla, Sider and Sugden (Schnabel 1993:28–82). Schnabel suggests that the contemporary social-action movement among evangelicals is influenced by three currents (1993:28–30):

(i) the *social gospel movement* of the second half of the nineteenth century,

(ii) the socio-political orientation of the WCC's view of mission,

(iii) *liberation theology* and

(iv) Anabaptist views promoted by John Howard Yoder in *The Politics of Jesus*.

In his final evaluation he argues that evangelical social activists generally misuse the concept of the kingdom of God (Schnabel 1993:66–82):

(i) Evangelicals did not introduce the kingdom language supporting social responsibility on the basis of biblical research but 'functionalised' the kingdom concept for the implementation of a socio-political vision of a 'promised land.'

(ii) The concept of Jesus' message of the kingdom of God cannot provide the foundation for social ethics.

(iii) Evangelical social activists tend to be legalistic, as though our human acts could establish the kingdom of God.

(iv) There is a tendency among those evangelicals with a strong concern for social actions to move from a *premillennial* or *amillennial* view of eschatology to a *postmillennial* interpretation which overestimates the present realisation of the kingdom at the expense of its future consummation at Christ's return.

(v) Evangelical social activists also tend to diminish the centrality of Christ's death on the cross.

(vi) There are serious deficiencies in the hermeneutics of many radical evangelicals. It seems – according to Schnabel – that they are influenced by liberation theology and the ecumenical programme of contextualisation. A complete misinterpretation of the jubilee-concept is only one consequence.

(vii) In several cases, radical evangelicals use figures and statistical data about the world economic situation which cannot be objectively verified.

(viii) There is a problematic shift from individual sin to structural sin, which opens the door to the foundational misunderstanding of salvation as liberation from sinful socio-political structures. Finally, Schnabel concludes with two positive statements, suggesting

(ix) that the kingdom of God concept has something to say to the life-conduct of disciples in society and

(x) that the *Kingdom Manifesto* of the *Spirit, Kingdom, Church and Creation Consultation 1990* (*Transformation* 1990/3:6–9) presents one of most biblical and balanced definitions of the kingdom of God and can serve as a foundation for further reflections.

(c) The discussion of mission and social responsibilities among German evangelicals can also be observed in *Evangelikale Missiologie.* A revealing dialogue followed a short presentation by Peter Mayer, a founding member of the editorial board of *em* and at that time principal of *Beatenberg*, in which he edited statements in memory of Bruno Herm (Mayer 1992a). The statements express a clear rejection of any attempt to place evangelisation and social acts on an equal level. Some expressions of John Stott at *Lausanne 1974*, terms such as *Social Gospel, holistic gospel* or *mission by presence*, but also all attempts to base the social responsibility in the message of the Old Testament prophets and the ministry of Jesus, are rejected – and the primacy of proclamation is advocated (Mayer 1992). Mayer's article was countered by Martin Reppenhagen in the following issue of *em*. Reppenhagen criticises Mayer's one-sided position, advocates the contribution by Vinay Samuel, René Padilla and all the so-called *radical evangelicals* and calls for a 'constructive dialogue' among differing evangelical positions. Mayer responded in *em* 1992/4 (Mayer 1992b), explicitly rejecting the phrase in the *Lausanne Declaration*, '.... . nevertheless we affirm that evangelism and socio-political involvement are both part of our Christian duty' (# 5, cf. Hedlund:306).[43] He favourably refers to the *Wheaton Declaration* (1966) which states, 'We affirm unreservedly the primacy of preaching the gospel to every creature' (Hedlund:182). Finally, he refers again to John Stott's contribution to this issue and claims that Stott, who has 'embraced the idea of annihilation,' can no longer be a point of orientation for evangelicals (Mayer 1992b:86). This rather minor incident only underlines how deeply some of the most prominent leaders of the German evangelical mission and Bible school movement reject the view of a more holistic understanding of mission as it is expressed in the *Lausanne Declaration*.

(d) Finally in 1997, the German evangelical missiologist, Erhard Berneburg, published his doctoral thesis entitled *Das Verhältnis von Verkündigung und sozialer Aktion in der evangelikalen* Missionstheologie (The Relationship of Proclamation and Social Action in Evangelical Mission Theory). The thesis reviews developments between Lausanne 1974 and Manila 1989. Berneburg identifies *Lausanne* as the starting point of the controversial discussion among evangelicals and identifies Arthur P. Johnston on the one hand and David Bosch on the other hand as the representatives of the opposing positions. Stott's position he views as mediating (Berneburg 1997:146–48). Berneburg interprets *Grand Rapids* 1982 as a compromise, yet a step forward toward the formulation of an evangelical theology of evangelisation and social responsibility, which defines the relationship of the two more precisely and affirms the primacy of proclamation (1997:148–77). Finally, he sees *Wheaton 1983* as an additional, significant step – though in his view a problematic one, perhaps taken in the wrong direction. The *Wheaton Conference* did not concern social responsibility but the *Nature and Mission of the Church*. Nonetheless, track III was devoted to the theme *The Church in Response to Human Need* (cf. Sine). Berneburg states, 'Since precisely those participants gathered in this part of the conference, who were concerned with a far-reaching integration of evangelisation and social responsibility, *Wheaton* 1983 could move further than *Grand Rapids* 1982' (1989:145), resulting in the first international evangelical document to explicitly reject speaking of a primacy of either evangelisation or social action. (1997:196–97; referring to the statements of Padilla and Bosch).[44] He concludes that if this really represents a broadly acknowledged evangelical position, it would indicate a fundamental shift in evangelical mission theology, overcoming one of the most critical issues in the divergence between evangelicals and ecumenicals. Yet he views this result rather as an advance by a particular evangelical group which aims at introducing a holistic understanding of mission to the larger evangelical world. Whether the wider evangelical community will accept this proposal is still open – Berneburg and with him German conservative evangelicals certainly reject it (1997:197–99). He points to the remaining theological problems with this development in five statements: (a) the eschatological question of Christ's return is not taken into consideration; (b) the foundation for social responsibility does not pay attention to the salvation-historical distinction between the Old and the New Testament; (c) the clear distinction between the call to salvation and the results of salvation must be defended; (d) the concept of *social action* deserves clear definition, especially regarding the distinction between charitable deeds for the needy and socio-political actions toward the transformation of society; and (e) – following Bockmühl – a 'theology of the justice of Christ's reign' is an ambiguous grounding for a theology of social action (1997:146–47).

The conclusion is puzzling: on the hand German evangelicals represented by *the Schools* have incorporated social action into their theology of mission in a new way after *Lausanne*, although in continuity with their pietistic heritage. On the other hand they decisively reject the direction *Wheaton 1983* has taken. There is a strange divergence in the perception of the significance of *Wheaton 1983* among evangelicals. German conservative evangelicals refused – if we take Berneburg's voice as representative – to accept the results of a global evangelical consultation with a worldwide representation on the basis not only of theological disagreement but also of the claim that a small pressure-group was promoting a holistic view of mission which the mainstream of evangelicals really does not want. Evangelicals who have participated in the process at Wheaton reject this as a misrepresentation and question whether German evangelicals really understand the nature of the debate.[45]

Schnabel can be commended for his attempt to assess various contemporary understandings of the kingdom of God from a biblical-exegetical point of view. However, his discussion of the radical evangelicals cannot remain unquestioned. His historical introduction already evidences a one-sidedness in referring basically to Luther and pietism. He discusses neither a Calvinist nor an Anabaptist understanding of the kingdom of God. This lack may be one of the main causes for Schnabel's misreading of radical evangelicalism. It is an unfair imputation to blame radical evangelicals for having 'functionalised' the kingdom concept and to claim that they have given up the eschatological, futurist dimension of God's kingdom. Yoder, Padilla, Sider, Samuel and many others have demonstrated that their concern for the dawning realisation of the kingdom of God in this age does not by any means deny the fulfilment of God's kingdom in the age to come. Yoder's article 'Peace Without Eschatology?' (Yoder 1971/77:65–83), Sider's *One-Sided Christianity* (Sider 1993:49–77), as well as Sugden's chapter on Vinay Samuel's kingdom theology (Sugden 1997:346–52) are some of the statements which should be examined in this regard – unfortunately such contributions are lacking in Schnabel's bibliography.

Schnabel's, as well as in Berneburg's, argument turns once more on hermeneutics and the interpretation of the Bible. While German evangelicals claim that the Bible must be the *norma normans* for Christian theology, they often dismiss the interpretations of the Bible by theologians living in other contexts and representing other theological traditions in an arrogant manner which in a way that does not do justice to the exegetical work of those theologians. As a matter of fact, much of the theological discourse of German evangelicals takes place in the form of in-house discussions without the presence of opposing voices.[46] In the light of these dynamics, it goes without saying that the *Stuttgart 1987* consultation on evangelism, which, sponsored by WCC, brought together ecumenical and evangelical Christians and produced a statement on 'integral evangelism' (Samuel and Hauser), was not even recognised by most conservative evangelicals in Germany. The *Stuttgart Statement on Evangelism* plays virtually no role in the teaching of mission in *the Schools*. We conclude: despite a growing concern for social responsibility among the theologians of *the Schools*, they decisively reject a move in the direction of the paradigm proposed by Bosch, Samuel, Padilla, Sider and others.

e) *Salvation History and Eschatology: Focus on Salvation for Eternity*

1. Article 7 of the *Frankfurt Declaration* addresses salvation history and eschatology. Mission is defined as the 'decisive, continuous saving

activity of God among men between the time of resurrection and the second coming of Jesus Christ.' This means that for evangelicals the perspective of mission is the return of Jesus Christ to bring his kingdom to fulfilment and not an immanent historical development toward the fullness of the kingdom. The *Frankfurt Declaration* refutes

> the enthusiastic and utopian ideology that either under the influence of the Gospel or by the anonymous working of Christ in history, all of mankind is already moving toward a position of general peace and justice and will finally – before the return of Christ – be united under him in a great world community (# 7).

It also refutes 'the identification of messianic salvation with progress, development, and social change' (# 7). Beyerhaus has continually called evangelicals to hold on to their belief in the eschatological destination of world evangelisation in the light of the challenges posed by a *kingdom theology* which tends to emphasise an immanent, realised eschatology (1987:245–46). At *Lausanne 1974* he delivered a Bible study on 'World Evangelisation and the kingdom of God' (1974 vol. 1:353–84) in which he focuses on two points: (a) evangelisation is the invitation to the kingdom of grace. This finds its centre in Jesus Christ and becomes a spiritual reality for the believer already in the here and now, not lacking consequences for his life. The church is the community of the Kingdom of God. (b) Evangelisation is preparation for the coming kingdom of glory, which will be fulfilled at the return of Jesus Christ. In the meantime, the church lives in tension with the still active reign of Satan in this world and should never hope to establish the messianic kingdom already in this age.

This foundational critique of the WCC's understanding of God's acts in history (cf. Werner 1993:55–158) has been confirmed by Beyerhaus's students Gerhard Sautter and Martin Hamel in their doctoral theses (Sautter:273–74; Hamel:288–90). Both authors conclude that the WCC's view of immanent, historical progress is ultimately a deviation from the biblical understanding of salvation history.

2. The *Lausanne Covenant* speaks basically the same language:

> We believe that Jesus Christ will return personally and visibly … to consummate his salvation and his judgement… We therefore reject as a proud, self-confident dream the notion that man can ever build a utopia on earth. Our Christian confidence is that God will perfect his kingdom, and we look forward with eager anticipation to that day … (# 15).

This eschatological orientation of mission has been confirmed by the evangelical community in 1989 in the *Manila Manifesto* (Hedlund:432). Despite this general agreement, there are a variety of emphases within the larger evangelical movement. At the *Grand Rapids Consultation on Evangelism and Social Responsibility 1982*, the question of the kingdom of God and eschatology received further reflection (Bockmühl 1983:30–46). There was again unity in the view that the consummation of the kingdom of God will be ushered in by the return of Christ, which includes the rejection of all attempts to identify the historical process of humanisation with the kingdom of God as 'false dreams' (Bockmühl 1983:39–40). Yet there were also certain disagreements about the question of continuity and discontinuity between this age and the age to come. While some evangelicals believe in a higher degree of realisation of the kingdom of God in this world, others view the kingdom of God as a primarily transcendent, futuristic concept.

A differentiated analysis of the various evangelical views of the kingdom of God has been conducted by Eckhard Schnabel (1993; cf. Berneburg 1997:316–31). Based on his analysis of the biblical concept of the kingdom of God, he advocates a position between the *radical evangelicals* (Escobar, Padilla, Sider), the *restorative evangelicals* (Snyder) and the *charismatic evangelicals* (Wimber, Wagner) on the one hand and the *confessional evangelicals* (Beyerhaus) on the other. The former, he assesses, have overly high expectations regarding the realisation of the kingdom of God in this age, whereas the latter push the kingdom of God too far into the age to come.

3. In *Missionarisches Handeln*, Reifler picks up the theme of *missio Dei* briefly in the chapter on the origin of mission (Reifler:81–82). He basically follows Vicedom's definition (Vicedom 1960). Any further discussion of the *missio Dei* concept is lacking. Basically, he offers a salvation-historical and eschatological foundation for mission, in terms consonant with the German pietistic heritage. Mission is motivated by God's eternal plan for the salvation of humanity (Reifler:105–07). The concept of the kingdom of God plays a marginal role in Reifler's theology of mission (Reifler:111–12). The aim of mission is defined on the level of individual salvation and the formation of churches. There is no perspective of social transformation at all. In Reifler's presentation, mission is concerned with bringing individuals into personal relationships with Christ and into the realm of the church.

4. Conclusion: German conservative evangelicals hold decisively to a salvation-historical understanding, focusing on personal conversion in view of salvation for eternity as the main objective of mission. They claim that salvation history cannot be identified with world history; that is, God's preserving work in the world and his salvific acts in and through Jesus Christ and the church have to be distinguished from each other. From their standpoint, the future of the world should not be seen as a continuing historical process towards peace and justice; rather, the return of Christ will usher in the fulfilment of the kingdom of God. It follows from this

eschatology that they hesitate to define mission in terms of transformation towards the kingdom of God. In so doing, they not only distance themselves from the ecumenical position but also criticise those evangelicals who define mission in the language of transformation and kingdom.

There are at least two theological reasons given for the position held by conservative evangelicals in German-speaking Europe (cf. Berneburg 1997:304–16): (a) Most of them hold to a premillenial view of eschatology, which causes them to view the kingdom of God as existing mainly in the future. (b) Furthermore, many of them are rooted in the Lutheran tradition and hold to the Lutheran concept of the two kingdoms, which causes them to separate the spiritual realm from the world. This does not mean that there is no understanding of Christian involvement in society, but mission is allocated to the spiritual realm of the gospel, whereas social ethics belongs to the realm of the world. This is not outside of God's reign, but it is not to be confused with the spiritual realm.[47]

These two theological positions safeguard German evangelicals from losing sight of the eternal, transcendent and eschatological dimensions of mission. Yet the theological deficiencies of these theological concepts have been demonstrated (Moltmann 1983:34–39; 1984:133–36, Bockmühl 1982:133–34) While German evangelicals tend to be strong on the *not-yet*-side, they tend to undervalue the *already*-side. Bosch's proposal calls them to an eschatology which keeps the already and the not-yet in creative tension. Beyond this, their fundamental theological presuppositions – Lutheran theory of the two kingdoms, the separation of grace and nature, the separation of God's redeeming work in the church and his providential work in the world and the separation of general revelation and special revelation – are severely challenged by evangelical theologians from the Two Thirds World such as the two Asian theologians Mastra and Samuel, as shown by Sugden (1997:215–32).

f) The Church: Focus on Instrument and Result

1. The *Frankfurt Declaration* views the church fully in the light of its refusal of any interpretation which would view of salvation history as a process of humanisation. This leads to a twofold emphasis. (a) The church is God's instrument in carrying out his mission, as the introductory phrases reveal:

> The Church of Jesus Christ has the sacred privilege and irrevocable obligation to participate in the mission of the triune God ... Through the Church's outreach, his name shall be glorified among all people, mankind shall be saved from his future wrath and led to a new life, and the Lordship of his Son Jesus Christ shall be established in the expectation of his second coming' (Hedlund:250).

This is confirmed again in #4, which says, 'Mission is the witness and presentation of eternal salvation performed in the name of Jesus Christ by his church' (Hedlund:252). (b) The task of mission is defined as calling 'out the messianic, saved community from among all people,' and as moving 'the lost ... to a saving membership in the body of Christ' (Hedlund:253). With this, the boundaries of the church as the community of the saved are defined by the individual's personal faith in Jesus Christ. The church is simultaneously both the instrument and the result of mission. The ecclesiology of the *Frankfurt Declaration* is shaped by the Lutheran background of its writers and by the controversy with the WCC. The former emphasises the reality of the church as the community of those who are saved by faith in Jesus Christ. This is basically a spiritual and invisible reality. The church's task as a visible institution is primarily defined by the proclamation of the gospel.[48] The latter leads to statements which are directed against the ecumenical tendency to open up the boundaries of the church and to equate the church with the world. Such a new ecclesiology has been refuted by Beyerhaus and his school (cf. Sautter:158–61, 174–75, 211–13, 256–58).

2. *Lausanne* follows *Frankfurt*, but it adds several dimensions to its understanding of the church's role in relation to mission. Beyond the understanding of the church as God's 'appointed means to spread the gospel' (#6) and the affirmation that evangelism ought to lead people into the 'new community' (#4), it confesses, 'We need to break out of our ecclesiastical ghettos' and underlines in this connection that 'the church is the community of God's people rather than institutions' (#6). Furthermore, it points to the necessity of witness to Christ through the visible unity of the church (#7) and calls for an increase in partnerships between western churches and the churches of the Two Thirds World (#8, all quotations Hedlund:304–10). With this, the *Lausanne Covenant* broadens the perspective of the *Frankfurt Declaration* and includes significant ecclesiological aspects which are not only Biblically rooted but relevant to the present situation.

3. Returning to *Missionarisches Handeln*, we recognise only minimal ecclesiological references in Reifler's understanding of mission. In general he follows *Stuttgart* and *Lausanne*, emphasising the church as the instrument as well as the result of mission (:116–21, 127–28). Then, in the traces of *Lausanne II*, he affirms the recovery of the local Christian community as the agent of mission as one of the key features of the church at the turn of the century (Reifler:248–49). This is a very meagre ecclesiology in a comprehensive introduction to missiology understood to be a significant textbook. In many ways it is even behind *Lausanne* in that it lacks such important themes as ecumenical unity of the church and global partnership. Other schools rooted in the free-church tradition would correct this one-sided picture (e.g. Herm 1989).

4. There is clarity in German evangelicals' definition of the church when it is described as God's instrument in carrying out his mission and as the body of those who believe in Jesus Christ. Beyond these points, there is a great hesitation to relate ecclesiology with mission. Key aspects which belong to the powerful parts of Bosch's proposal are completely missing. In the view of this author, this is the result of a foundational lack inherited by most evangelical theology.[49] The following observation from Reifler's book will illustrate this. Towards the end of his book Reifler includes a document called the *Basler Thesen*, containing ten statements on mission formulated by theologians of *Chrischona* in 1992.[50] This document puts forward an understanding of mission in many ways in accord with what we have established as an evangelical view of mission. However – and this is the significant observation – it makes no reference to the church. Reifler comments on this statement as one of the key documents of recent years, deserving attention from both the ecumenical and the evangelical communities. Then he adds that the statement is written by theologians rooted in German Pietism and explicitly passes over ecclesiological issues,[51] because it is intended to be pragmatic and hence open for adaptation in varying ecclesiological traditions. This is a very revealing argument. Ecclesiology is disconnected from mission and reduced to denominational peculiarities. In the light of the sort of holistic, ecumenical paradigm of mission put forward by Bosch, we find ourselves forced to conclude that evangelical theology of mission, as we encounter it in some of the German textbooks, lacks a central element. One wonders how a theology of mission can be spelt out which is not intertwined with ecclesiology.

We argued earlier that this is a weakness of much of evangelical theology. Evangelicalism, as a movement which transcends confessional and denominational boundaries, is in tension with the confessional and denominational structures of the historical, established churches in Europe. The evangelical focus was and is on personal faith in Jesus Christ and mission. The issues of ecclesiology are left to the denominations. This fact is mirrored by the confession of faith of the Evangelical Alliance (Hauzenberger:455–57). Fiedler has analysed this problem in view of the faith missions and has shown the advantages as well as the deficiencies of such an approach, coining the expression 'the concept of individual unity' (Fiedler 1994:169–209).[52] However, while this concept marks significant progress beyond denominationalism, it is also represents a voyage into the open seas of individualism or toward a theology of mission without ecclesiology. The Anabaptist tradition can here make a valid contribution toward the integration of ecclesiology and the theology of mission, as demonstrated by Bender, Friedmann, Kraus, Shenk, Miller and Yoder.[53] But individualistic evangelical theology of the west has also been challenged by Christians from the Two Thirds World.[54]

There is an urgent need for most western evangelicals to grow in their understanding of community and to recover a theology of mission which integrates ecclesiology. Yoder has stated aptly the vision for such a missiological ecclesiology (1969:274): 'This new Christian community ... is not only a vehicle of the gospel or fruit of the gospel; it is the good news. It is not merely the agent of mission or the constituency of a mission agency. This is the mission.'

g) Theology of Religions: Focus on Christocentrism and Exclusivism

1. Following the quotation of Acts 4:12 – 'There is no salvation in anyone else at all, for there is no other name under heaven granted to man, by which we may receive salvation' – the *Frankfurt Declaration* states:

> *We therefore oppose* the false teaching (which is spreading in the ecumenical movement since the Third General Assembly of the World Council of Churches in New Delhi) that Christ himself is anonymously so evident in world religions, historical changes, and revolutions that man can encounter him and find salvation in him without the direct news of the Gospel (# 3).

And in # 6 the *Declaration* claims:

> The adherents to the non-Christian religions and world views can receive this salvation only through participation in faith. They must let themselves be freed from their former ties and false hopes in order to be admitted by belief and baptism into the body of Christ... *We therefore reject* the false teaching that the non-Christian religions and world views are also ways of salvation similar to belief in Christ.

In his 1984 evaluation of the Lausanne Movement, Beyerhaus concludes that a thorough evangelical theology of religions has not yet been adequately developed. His concern is that the evangelical movement has thus far dealt only with other religions on the pragmatic level of strategy and communication. He calls for a theology of religion which does not underestimate the demonic and therefore anti-Christian dimension of other religions. What is needed, according to Beyerhaus, is a theology of religion which takes seriously all dimensions of religiosity, the human, the godly and the demonic (Beyerhaus 1987:246). In a paper presented in 1994 at the University of Tübingen, Beyerhaus discusses the *exclusivist, inclusivist* and *pluralist* theories (1995). He decisively rejects the *inclusivist* as well as the *pluralist* model and identifies most closely, though not without qualification, with the *exclusivist* model.

2. The *Lausanne Covenant* has addressed the issue of the uniqueness and universality of Christ, as well as its implications for the understanding of other religions as follows:

> We affirm that there is only one Saviour and only one gospel ... We recognize that all men have some knowledge of God through his general revelation in nature. But we deny that this can save ... We also reject as derogatory to Christ and the gospel every kind of syncretism and dialogue which implies that Christ speaks equally through all religions and ideologies ... There is no other name by which we must by saved (# 3).

In general, evangelicals have confirmed this position in the years after Lausanne, though some have claimed that evangelicals have not dealt adequately with the issue of the theology of religion (Beyerhaus 1987:126–27; Samuel and Sugden 1987:142). The *pneumatological shift* in the ecumenical understanding of the trinity as a foundation of a new approach to other religions has been critically examined by evangelicals at and after the WCC's assembly at Canberra 1991 (cf. Rin Ro and Nicholls 1993, especially the open letter by evangelicals, :38–43). While many evangelicals appreciate an expanded view of the Spirit's work in creation and history, they also emphasise the unique, salvation-historical acts of God's Spirit. Together with the Orthodox Church, evangelicals argue that 'any theology ... that denies the uniqueness of Christ is unacceptable' (Padilla 1993:33). The Australian, David Parker, has criticised the WCC Assembly for not having addressed such aspects of the work of the Spirit as are central for evangelicals, such as 'evangelism, conversion, the Christian life and prayer.' But also 'that the Spirit speaks through the word and brings conviction to those outside of Christ' and 'gives new life to believers at their conversion.' (Parker:13) German-speaking evangelical theologians have held firmly to an exclusivist position (Hille and Troeger; Burkhardt 1993; Hempelmann 1997).

3. In *Missionarisches Handeln*, Reifler does not include a theology of religion. In the chapter on the theology of mission, the uniqueness of Christ is assumed but never explicitly discussed. The various traditional, theological approaches to other religions (exclusivism, inclusivism, pluralism) are not reviewed, nor are more recent proposals discussed (trinitarian approaches). Only at the end of the book, where aspects of an evangelical theology for the turn of the century are proposed, does one find an initial statement of 'the emphasis on the uniqueness of Jesus Christ and his exclusiveness for salvation' (Reifler:241), followed by a short Bible study on the subject. Reifler acknowledges a certain degree of knowledge of God in other religions based on general revelation; but this, he says, is of relevance for mission only insofar it serves as a 'methodological help' to open up

communication; salvific knowledge of God can only be received through faith in Jesus Christ (Reifler:242–43). This is in accordance with other literature used in teaching theology of religions at *the Schools* (Hille and Troeger; Burkhardt 1993; Hempelmann 1997).[55]

4. Conclusion: The uniqueness of Christ as the sole foundation of salvation remains a basic confession of evangelicals in German-speaking Europe. On the basis of this conviction, they reject an *inclusivist*, as well as a *pluralist* approach to other religions. With this, the theologians of *the Schools* are in general agreement with the *Frankfurt Declaration* and the *Lausanne Covenant* – to wit, with the majority of evangelicals. While there are differences in how the term and concept of dialogue is used and defined, evangelicals generally protest against any attempt to by-pass the personal faith-encounter with Jesus Christ as a way to salvation.

By and large, evangelicals have not engaged in the sort of search for new theologies of religions based on a rereading of the trinity which it can be observed in ecumenical circles. Only recently have some evangelicals begun to rethink their exclusivist positions (e.g., Newbigin, Pinnock, Helfenstein). For evangelicals in German-speaking Europe, Helfenstein's proposal will be most challenging because he argues a position which opens up the possibility for salvation apart from faith in Jesus Christ, while at the same time claiming to remain faithful to evangelical convictions (Helfenstein 1998:377–410). We cannot imagine that such a position would find acceptance among the evangelicals represented by *the Schools*.

However, the main challenge of Bosch, Samuel, Newbigin and others is not to engage oneself first in the formulation of the 'right' theology of religions but to engage in dialogue. The 'new methodology' proposed by Samuel and Sugden is 'praxiological'; it suggests that one 'go into a context with deep convictions shaped by the gospel. The goal is not to apply ready-made formulations of the gospel but to understand the focus, emphases and the very meaning of the biblical gospel in that context' (1983:129; cf. Sugden 1997:401).[56] This seems to be the most critical issue for evangelicals in Europe. Thus far, their approach to other religions has been carried out on a purely theoretical-theological level, formulating Bible-based truth-statements about the Christian faith and about other faiths. The educational assumption underlying this approach is that if students have acquired the 'right' theology of religions, they will be well prepared for mission work among people of other faiths. Based on experiences in the Indian context, Samuel seriously questions this approach. Sugden has summarised Samuel's challenge to western churches as follows:

> There is an important message in other parts of the world called to witness in the context of religious pluralism, that at the heart of

> mission in India are local communities from different Christian traditions who serve those in need with their meagre resources, who depend on the Spirit of God to go ahead of them into communities they serve and who discover that the Spirit uses their witness of word and deed to make Christ known and attractive. We see here the coming together of Samuel's understanding of holistic mission, the work of Christ beyond the church, the work of the Holy Spirit and his witness to the word of Jesus, and Christian witness as the witness of communities (Sugden 1997:405).

Samuel and Sugden may well have touched the central, yet sensitive, issue, pointing to the fact that many evangelicals do not engage in interreligious dialogue because of fear. They have identified several areas of fear: (a) fear of syncretism (the legacy of the Kraemerian view of religions); (b) the fear of being misunderstood by the evangelical community; (c) the fear of not having all the answers when the uniqueness of Christ is questioned; and (d) the fear of a decline in evangelism (Samuel and Sugden 1983:131–35). In the light of these experiences and the achievements of evangelicals in the Two Thirds World, it is evident how backwards German evangelical theology of mission is in the area of interreligious dialogue and the theology of religions. This definitely reduces the quality of mission studies at *the Schools*.

3. Evaluative Summary

a) Summary

1. German evangelical theology of mission, as it has developed since the 1960s, understands itself as a continuation of its pietistic heritage and the tradition of German and Dutch missiologists of the previous decades, such as Hartenstein, Freytag and Kraemer.

2. From this point of view, the development of the WCC's understanding of mission following the integration of the IMC into the WCC is perceived as a deviation from the biblical, traditional and orthodox understanding of mission; and German evangelical theology of mission understands itself as an alternative to the WCC's view of mission.

3. In the three to four decades considered in this study, German evangelical theology of mission has been strongly influenced by Peter Beyerhaus and his decisive, apologetic struggle against the course taken by the WCC. The key document of this position is the *Frankfurt Declaration* of 1970.

4. The German *Arbeitsgemeinschaft evangelikaler Missionen* has adopted the *Frankfurt Declaration* (the Swiss *AEM* the *Lausanne Covenant*) as its foundational statements. Most mission agencies and schools identify

with these two documents as well. Yet research has shown that the *Lausanne Covenant* is interpreted in the light of the *Frankfurt Declaration*, which implies that *Lausanne*'s potential of leading toward a more holistic paradigm of mission is often downplayed and neglected.

5. We also notice a significant Anglo-Saxon, predominately North American, impact on German evangelical missiology in the last three to four decades. This was experienced by German evangelicals as especially fruitful in the area of anthropological, strategic and pragmatic studies (the Church Growth Movement).

6. An actual German-speaking evangelical missiology has emerged in these decades. It centres around several newly founded institutions, such as the *Freie Hochschule für Mission*, the *Arbeitskreis für evangelikale Missiologie*, the missiological journal *Evangelikale Missiologie* and the publishing house *Verlag für Kultur und Wissenschaft*.

7. Based on the examination of literature and libraries, conferences and curricula or syllabi we have demonstrated that most of the Bible colleges and seminaries of the *Konferenz bibeltreuer Ausbildungsstätten* tend toward a more conservative theology of mission of the sort represented by Beyerhaus and the *Frankfurt Declaration*. This implies a rather decisively anti-ecumenical attitude and a strong emphasis on the primacy of evangelisation, combined with reservations about the evangelical movement toward a more integrated, ecumenical paradigm of mission.

8. We also observed that mission studies at the schools under consideration have moved from a rather simple teaching of biblical basics carried out in an affirmative and motivating style to a more complex missiological curriculum and a more academic form. This issue will be the subject of further analysis in Part Four.

9. Furthermore, we argued that *the Schools* represent an evangelical theology which distances itself from an evangelical theology of mission as it has been developing within the international evangelical community, especially among the so-called radical evangelicals and those in the Two Thirds World. The features of a holistic, contextual new paradigm of mission are ignored or rejected.

What are the consequences?

b) Evaluation: What is the Output?

In order to see the consequences of the above for mission studies in theological education, we now take the perspective of the students, asking the question: What kind of missiological training does a student receive at *the Schools*,[57] in the light of what has been identified and argued in Part Three. This will be carried out according to the agenda we outlined at the end of chapter 8 (see pp. 143–145).

(1) DOING MISSION STUDIES IN THE CONTEXT OF CRISIS AND CHANGE

An ecumenical and integral paradigm of mission calls us to teach mission in the context of crisis and change. Research has shown that students who study at *the Schools* will hardly be exposed to the tremendous shifts Christian mission has been experiencing in the post-war period. As far as curriculum, syllabi, textbooks and publications by teachers are concerned, there is hardly any critical reflection on the colonial era and its deficiencies. The IMC's struggles in the 1950s, its integration into the WCC and the development of an ecumenical theology of mission is presented mainly through the lens of Peter Beyerhaus and his successors. The students encounter a strong, apologetic approach defending a continuity with the pietistic tradition and the Kraemer-Hartenstein-Freytag school. Consequently, change is not on the agenda of the learning students acquire during their years at *the Schools*. On the contrary – the general thrust is motivation and urgency in the light of the *unreached peoples*.

Looking at this situation from the perspective of Bosch's phrase 'mission in bold humility' (cf. Saayman and Kritzinger) the strength of *the Schools* is certainly on the *bold* side. When Bosch speaks of the two dangers involved in encountering critiques, uncertainties and crises – namely *paralysis* or else moving on with *business as usual* – *the Schools* are obviously not in danger of being paralysed. This can be viewed as their strength. Students will graduate from these schools with boldness and will engage in Christian ministry, be it in Europe or abroad, with a sense of urgency and with missionary zeal. Yet the strength is at the same time a potential weakness. Graduates will lack the humility and sensitivity desperately needed for any engagement in mission in the post-colonial era, because the problematic sides of the modern western mission movement are not critically reviewed. This results in an irresponsible, 'business-as-usual' approach to mission which must be rejected.

(2) DOING MISSION STUDIES IN DIALOGUE WITH THE WIDER ECUMENICAL COMMUNITY

An ecumenical paradigm of mission demands mission studies in dialogue with the wider ecumenical and global family of God. What scope of ecumenical and global perspective do students get at *the Schools*? The answer can be given on three levels:

1. The Centre – The *Frankfurt Declaration*: the students will first of all receive a firm grounding in the conservative evangelical theology of mission represented by the *Frankfurt Declaration*. They will hardly leave the school without having read some of Beyerhaus's publications. If they have read Peters, Bockmühl and Reifler, they will have basically the same grounding, though with fewer apologetic overtones.

2. The First Circle – The wider evangelical world: beyond that, they will encounter the wider evangelical world. The documents of *Lausanne*

and *Manila* are most likely on their reading list. Following these documents, they will most probably read Patrick Johnston and John Stott and certainly literature from a North American background related to the Church Growth Movement. In many cases they will have a teacher who received missiological training in a North American evangelical school. If they follow Reifler's suggested additional reading they may also encounter René Padilla (1986), Vinay Samuel and Chris Sugden (1987a).[58] Yet, if they are brought into acquaintance with such voices as Berneburg (1997) or Schnabel (1993) – be it through reading or transmitted by a teacher – then they are warned away from that whole evangelical wing, which is portrayed as moving away from an orthodox understanding of mission. Terms such as 'holistic mission,' 'contextualisation,' 'dialogue,' 'incarnational mission' and 'mission as transformation' will have problematic connotations.

3. The Second Circle – The ecumenical world: no further evidence is needed to demonstrate that students at *the Schools* will perceive the ecumenical movement very critically. They may read some of the older publications of Jochums (1966) or Kuen (1968). Then they will encounter Beyerhaus again with his forceful condemnation of the ecumenical movement, in some schools underlined by the study of the *Berlin Declaration* of 1974 (Künneth and Beyerhaus:8–9). Presumably, students will also read some of the many publications which have transferred Beyerhaus's apologetics to a more popular level and which are on the shelves of many Bible school libraries (cf. Rhese; Grafen). In the light of this evidence, it is fair to say that students will most probably be introduced to an apologetic approach towards the ecumenical movement. In the classification of apologetics proposed by the *Evangelische Zentralstelle für Weltanschauungsfragen EZW* (Hummel and Küenzelen and Hemminger) it is an *apocalyptic* type of apologetics, which focuses on condemnation, using apocalyptic language and imagery (Anti-Christ, Babylon and the like).

Conclusion: Bosch speaks of the 'opportunities' and 'dangers' on the way through the crisis, entering new territory beyond the status quo (1991:2–3). The students graduating from *the Schools* are well prepared to grasp the possible dangers involved in being in dialogue with the wider Christian community.[59] It is a pity that they are hardly trained to see the opportunities. A statement made by Walter Hollenweger in reference to the rapidly growing proportion of Christians outside the western world, that '*Mission studies have a future only* if they see the challenge of these different Christians as an opportunity for self-critical reflection' (Hollenweger 1991:98), points to the immense ignorance of western theological education if it withdraws to the maintenance of western, conservative evangelical orthodoxy. It is therefore an even greater pity when students are not prepared to see the dangers of being captive to of their own conservative theology.

Yet the most serious issue is the effect of apocalyptic apologetics. There is apparently a tradition in conservative evangelicalism in twentieth-century Germany (more than in Switzerland) to pronounce statements of condemnation which later become insurmountable obstacles to ecumenical dialogue. The *Berlin Declaration* against the Pentecostal movement at the beginning if the century is one example (Lange:201–26, 287–90); the *Berlin Declaration 1974* against the ecumenical movement is another. A school which cultivates a climate of apocalyptic apologetics – though we are not saying that all of *the Schools* are doing this – leads its students into isolation, separatism and even sectarianism. Such a school is definitely not on the way toward an ecumenical paradigm of mission theology. *The Schools* are certainly not called to abandon uncritically their rich heritage of evangelical theology and praxis, but they are urged to engage in an open dialogue with the wider ecumenical and global Christian community. They are even obligated to do so in the light of their students' future ministry in the church and society world-wide.

(3) DOING MISSION STUDIES IN THE HORIZON OF A HOLISTIC PARADIGM OF MISSION

As we now proceed to the five theological issues of the integral, ecumenical paradigm of mission, we draw the following conclusions

1. Hermeneutics: students will get a solid foundation in terms of a conservative evangelical *bibliology*. Most schools hold to a position of biblical inerrancy and use in their teaching the *Chicago Statements* on *Biblical Inerrancy* and *Hermeneutics* (Geisler:493–502; cf. Harris:300–02). Based on the evidence of curricula, syllabi and textbooks, the introduction to contextual hermeneutics makes up the far weaker part, if such topics appear at all. Although students will learn to apply texts cross-culturally and will in most schools be introduced to mission anthropology and cross-cultural communication, they will most likely not be exposed to the key issues of contextual theologising.

The consequences are: graduates who have not learned to theologise contextually will engage in mission work by taking their – apparently unconditioned – theology to other cultures and imposing it on the people of other cultures. Doing so they will ignore one of the basic principles of missionary thinking in the new paradigm. According to Newbigin, the key issue is that the gospel be allowed to 'come alive' in a given culture to that culture's terms, not to the terms of the 'missionary' (Newbigin 1989:141–54; cf. Hollenweger 1995:116–28). The results of this research support the conclusion that *the Schools* are in danger of training students to impose a pre-defined theology on people instead of letting the gospel 'come alive' in a given situation.

2. Salvation and mission: there is no doubt that the students will learn that the proclamation of the gospel is the primary missionary task. In

most schools they will also hear that social responsibility goes with evangelism. If they read Stott and Bockmühl on these issues, they will have a fairly high degree of social awareness. In some schools they may rather have read Johnston and Peters and will hardly show much social concern. In any case, taught by teachers of a Lutheran background, they will tend rather to delegate social issues to the ethics courses than view them as an integral part of Christian mission. In some schools they may even be exposed to the intra-evangelical debate discussed in the previous section, reading Berneburg or Schnabel. Then they will be very suspicious of concepts such as 'integral mission,' 'holistic mission' and 'transformation.'

However, as long as the focus is on putting words and deeds in the right balance, we remain captives of the Enlightenment paradigm which identifies the components and then tries to put them in the right relation. Shenk (and others) have helpfully pointed beyond this to a holistic model which follows the example of Jesus and of God's *shalom* (1993b; cf. Sugden 1997:338–64) Students of *the Schools* will probably enter ministry without having caught this vision for holistic ministry. This turns out to be a serious deficiency not only in their training but in their ministry.

3. Salvation history and eschatology: given the fact that the shelves of Bible college libraries are stocked with books by authors like Beyerhaus, Bockmühl, Stott, Reifler, Sautter and Schnabel, it is fair to conclude that the students will get a strong sense of salvation history focusing on the individual's salvation and on the church. Depending on the eschatological scheme the school promotes – in most cases this will be dispensational premillenialism – Israel will also play a major role in salvation-historical thinking. Based on premillenial eschatology, students are taught to prioritise the 'not-yet' of the kingdom of God, and they will learn to exercise caution regarding the 'already' – not only in terms of social transformation but also in term of 'charismatic' expectations. If they have read Schnabel, they will certainly be very careful in their usage of the term 'kingdom of God,' and they will be warned away from such people as Ronald Sider, John Howard Yoder and Howard Snyder. Following the Lutheran pattern of social and political ethics, they will not have developed a strong sense of God's transforming individuals and society towards his kingdom and the new creation. They will tend to separate the spiritual and the social spheres and will understand mission as belonging to the spiritual realm. This will definitively determine their ministry.

In the light of a new paradigm which emphasises not only the discontinuity between God's work in the church and in the world but also the 'continuity between the work of God inside and outside the church' (Sugden 1997:279), the one-sidedness of the theological training in many of *the Schools* becomes evident. Most likely, students will enter church ministries and mission work with the perception that Christian mission is primarily concerned with the spiritual salvation of individuals in the light of their eternal destiny. This indicates a severe deviation from a biblical, holistic view which sees human beings in community and in culture, i.e., as part of God's creation and which understands salvation as God's 'shalom project,'[60] aiming at the transformation of all creation towards God's new creation (cf. Sugden 1997:318–68).

4. The church: since *the Schools* represent diverse ecclesial traditions, students will get different ecclesiological emphases. However, in most schools their reflections will be based on the ecclesiological context of European state-church Christendom and individualistic, non-denominational evangelicalism. They will certainly be taught that the church plays a vital role in mission. Based on Reifler's textbook, their view of mission will understand the church as the agent of mission and as the result of mission. Based on this evidence, they will hardly get an understanding of 'humanity-in-community' nor of the 'church as part of the gospel.' Consequently, graduates from *the Schools* will tend to see the church mainly in its functional role as a pragmatic tool for mission. Literature from a church growth background will enhance this pragmatic understanding of the church.

In the light of Bosch's proposal to see the church as sacrament, sign and instrument, the students of *the Schools* are well equipped in their understanding of the church as instrument, but they have serious gaps in their appreciation of the church as sacrament and sign. In the light of a missionary paradigm which sees the church as an incarnated authentic witness, as a messianic society, as a constitutive part of the gospel message, it is evident that the conservative evangelical missiology analysed in the study has not surmounted the deficiencies of western individualism. Consequently, students will leave many of *the Schools* with a poor ecclesiology which will lead to the perpetuation of western (evangelical) individualism through their ministry.

5. Theology of religions: students of *the Schools* will experience the theology of religion still as a step-child of conservative evangelical theology. If they read Reifler they will be introduced to an exclusivist view without any reflection on the broader scope of the discussion. In many schools students will take special courses in religion. According to the literature – Hille and Troeger, Burkhardt, Hempelmann – the exclusivist position will be predominant. Texts of ecumenical background will hardly be read. Based on the evidence of literature and syllabi it is appropriate to conclude that an exclusivist position will be claimed and defended apologetically. Graduates of *the Schools* will hardly use the term dialogue as an appropriate concept in mission, and if they do, they define it as a method of entering into communication.

In the light of Bosch's proposal this position is open to question. It is not so much the exclusivist position which provokes criticism – whether it can be defended or not depends on the quality of the defence – but the missiological approach which goes with it. Bosch calls for an approach to people of other living faiths which does not start with a theological conclusion about the validity of their faith and any possible revelation of God in that particular religion but with an open encounter with real persons of other living faiths. This means that on the level of theological methods, encounter and dialogue precedes the theology of religion in a new paradigm of mission. Students of *the Schools* are trained the other way around. They will encounter people of other faiths already possessing the answers not only regarding their own Christian faith but also regarding the theological status of the others' faith.

Thus, we are led to the conclusion that by and large *the Schools* are not moving in the direction of an new, post-anti-colonial, ecumenical and holistic model of mission as proposed not only by Bosch but also by Newbigin, Shenk, Samuel, Sugden, Padilla, Sider and many other theologians. This is not to say that there are no signs pointing in that direction in particular areas, in single schools and in the teaching and writing of individual teachers. However, the general thrust is not in that direction.

There are various reasons for this. In some cases the issue is ignorance, a lack of awareness about what is going on in the wider, world-Christian movement. In other cases it is deliberate rejection on grounds of theological disagreement. In some cases it may even be rejection based on ideological captivity of various kinds, be it ideologised anti-ecumenism or ideologised Euro-centrism. Looking at the potential of these movements of missions and Bible colleges rooted in the missionary movement of German Pietism and neo-Pietism and imagining the contribution they could make to the larger Christian community, it can only be hoped that *the Schools* will open up to the wider ecumenical and global community; otherwise, they are in danger of developing towards separatist conservatism.

c) The *Critical Issue*

This raises fundamental issues regarding orthodoxy and change. Or in other words, how do theological traditions which have created an ethos of conserving true, Biblical faith adapt to change as our world experiences the paradigm shift from modernity to post-modernity and beyond. This question is of general relevance for the Christian church. We recall Küng's thesis, affirmed by Bosch, that in the realm of the Christian church, unlike in science, 'any paradigm shift can only be carried out on the basis of the gospel and because of the gospel, never, however, against the gospel' (Küng and Tracy 1984:65; Bosch 1991:187). This touches upon such fundamental issues as hermeneutics, epistemology and truth. These are the underlying issues which emerge in all the aspects analysed in Part Three. (1) In the chapter on 'crisis and change' we encountered this issue in the question, how are the truth-claims of the tradition related to changing realities? (2) As we analysed the 'ecumenical openness' we came across this same underlying issue in the form of the question, what is the 'right' interpretation of scripture and the 'right' theology in the context of the diverse traditions and strands within Christianity? (3) In the chapter on 'hermeneutics' the underlying issue was quite obviously the tension between the normativity of the biblical text and the contextuality of biblical interpretation. (4) As we approached the theme of 'holistic gospel,' we encountered the same undercurrent. The question was, how can a theological truth-claim (that the main objective of mission is the salvation of individuals for their eternal destiny) which is well established in a given tradition (Protestant orthodoxy) be reconsidered? (5) We realised in relation to the topic 'the church' that western theology, especially in its Lutheran and interdenominational-evangelical expression, is locked into a scheme of thinking which prevents it from embracing a deeper understanding of the significance of community. Again, the issues of tradition, perceptions and change are the undercurrents. (6) We looked at the aspect 'salvation history and eschatology' and observed that the dominating undercurrent was whether God's saving work has to be seen limited to individuals and the church or whether it could also go beyond the church. On a deeper level, the resistance to acknowledge God's action outside the church is related to epistemological issues. The question can be put as follows: How do we 'know' where God is acting? (7) In the topic of 'dialogue with other living faiths,' the issue of revelation and knowledge of God is at the surface. At the centre is again the issue of epistemology.

How then do these theologians answer open questions about contextualisation, hermeneutics, epistemology and truth? While conservative German evangelicals emphatically defend the normativity of the Bible and while they critically point to the deficiencies of historical-critical methodology, liberation theology, contextualisation and the development of the ecumenical movement, they have so far not shown convincing answers about how to deal with the issues at stake. Beyerhaus, Sautter, Hamel and Berneburg have criticised the concepts of contextualisation, kingdom theology and holistic gospel. They advance a claim to biblical authority; however, none of them has proposed a hermeneutical methodology which satisfactorily answers the issues of epistemology which stand before the challenges of modernity and postmodernity.[61] This leaves us with an unsatisfactory answer. Conservative evangelical theologians are certainly right when they point to the normativity of the Bible for Christian theology, but they are not the only ones doing so. David Bosch and others discussed in this study hold to the same claim. They are certainly right in pointing to deficiencies in historical-critical exegesis, liberation theology and some of the developments of the WCC. But they are not the only ones pointing to these deficiencies. The same critique comes even from within these movements today.[62] This leads to one of the most serious critiques offered by this study: while some German conservative evangelical theologians tend to act as the conscience of world theology when it comes to the question of the authority of scripture, they do not present convincing solutions to the burning issues of contextualisation, hermeneutics, epistemology and truth. There is more work to be done.

We therefore suggest that for a deeper understanding of the developments of *the Schools* we have to look at the underlying issues of conservatism, change and epistemology, which are decisive in change processes in church and theology. It is the conviction of this author that the Kuhnian paradigm theory – in the form in which Küng has applied it to theology, updated with insights from MacIntyre – will provide a helpful tool for such an analysis. However, this must wait until the final reflections in Part Five. We must first approach *the Schools* from the angle of theological education.

Notes

1 Laubach mentions E.J. Carnell, E.F. Harrison, C.F. Henry, G.E. Ladd, J.W. Montgomery, H.J. Ockenga, C.H. Pinnock, B.L. Ramm. The same is evident in Beyerhaus 1969, and Bockmühl 1964, 1974.

2 Cf. 'Das Ziel unserer Missionarischen Arbeit' (1960/3:2–4); 'Zum evangelistischen Wort die diakonische Tat' (1962/2:2); 'Welt im Umbruch, aufgespaltene Christenheit – und wir?' (1963/4:2–4); 'Mission in einer veränderten Welt' (1968/1:2–5); 'Umfassender Dienst in Partnerschaft' (1968/6:2–4); 'Welchen Weg gehen wir in der Aussenmission in den siebziger Jahren?' (1970/1:24–5).

3 A bibliography of Beyerhaus up to 1988 in Kniffka:256–70.

4 In another study this author has analysed the missionary developments of the *Evangelische Täufergemeinde* and its mission board in Germany and Switzerland. The study demonstrates the increase of Bible school students from these churches in the late 1960s and 1970s leading to a significant growth of the missionary activities co-ordinated by the mission board (Ott 1996:174–190; 229–31). Besides other causes, such as demographics, the impact of the missionary zeal of North American evangelicals is one of the main causes for this development.

5 Unfortunately, no records of the presentations, neither written nor taped, are available. In some cases the content of the presentations can be assumed based on publications on similar issues by the authors, i.e., Schrupp's articles in *Offene Türen*.

6 Brake represents the model of schools rooted in the North American Bible school tradition.

7 Syllabi or any information on the content of the courses are not in the archives.

8 The earliest syllabi still accessible are from 1970.

9 *Bad Liebenzell* represents the mission seminary model rooted in the German neo-pietistic mission movement.

10 This is based on a list the author received by fax from the archivist of Bad Liebenzell, 8 September 1997.

11 A more comprehensive bibliography including also more than 100 articles in Beyerhaus 1987:256–70.

12 The libraries of *Brake, Wiedenest*, and *Liebenzell* have been consulted.

13 The first section of the book is based on his earlier publication, *Die neuere Missionstheologie* (1964).

14 This means that up to the present time no comprehensive evangelical theology of mission is available in the German language, written by a German or Swiss theologian. Beyerhaus is about to publish an extensive work; however, only the first volume has come to market in 1996. Hans Ulrich Reifler's *Missionarisches Handeln am Ende des 20. Jahrhunderts* was published in 1997 and, may become a major textbook, yet it is an introduction to missiology which spends only about fifty pages on the theology of mission.

15 A revised and restructured version was published in English in 1994 under the title *The Story of Faith Missions*.

16 This is a collection of articles by Padilla previously published in various journals but never published in English in one volume.

17 In the 1981 conference this is explicit, in 1982 the choice of G.W. Peters implies this emphasis.

18 Letter of 30 January 1980 by L. Pflaum of *Liebenzell* to all member schools of the *KBA* (Archive *Bienenberg*).

19 'Empfehlung' and 'Ergebnisprotokoll' of 29 March 1990 (Archive *Bienenberg*).

20 The nomenclature used in *the Schools* in relation to the EEAA standards are: A 'course' is a unit devoted to one subject-matter normally comprising 20–40 hours of lectures, plus the same amount of time for private studies.

21 The survey was conducted by Traugott Böker on behalf of the *KBA*. 24 out of 33 schools responded. A first analysis of the data was presented by Böker at the annual *KBA*-Conference in November, 1996 (Böker 1996). This author had access to the survey for further research and analysis. More results will be discussed in Part Four.

22 For level B (B.Th.) the accreditation handbook requires 'A thorough introduction to the theology and practice of missionary work.' For the C level (M.Div.) it requires 'Introduction to the main areas of missionary theology and work.' For level D (M.Th.) the requirement is 'A thorough treatment of the theology, history and practice of missions as well as non-Christian religions and cults.'

23 Syllabi of *Brake, Wiedenest*, and *Liebenzell* have been consulted. In addition, the readings suggested in Reifler, *Missionarisches Handeln am Ende des 20. Jahrhunderts*. Reifler (:48–55) refers to these three theologians as *the* evangelical mission theologians of the last third of the 20th century.

24 In his review of the first decade of the *Arbeitskreis für evangelikale Missiologie (AfeM)* (Association for Evangelical Missiology) and its journal *Evangelikale Missiologie*, Klaus Müller defines the theological frame of the *AfeM* as follows: 'The wider frame is defined by the evangelical congress at Lausanne 1974 and its "Covenant," the narrower frame by the "*Frankfurt Declaration*" of the *Konferenz bekennender Gemeinschaften* 1970' (Müller 1995:14).

25 See notice on Reifler's publication on p. 162.

26 This author has tried to find out whether a German translation of *Transforming Mission* is in preparation. In 1992 Joachim Wietzke expressed his hope for a translation of the book soon (Book review in *Jahrbuch Mission 1992*:238–40), but his hope did not come true. According to Prof. Theo Sundermeier (Heidelberg), a translation was planed, but failed because a translator was lacking (personal letter of 23 April 1996). Klaus Schäfer of the *Evangelisches Missionswerk EMW* referred to earlier projects of a translation but it seems not to be feasible to produce a German translation for the small German market (personal letter of 14 May 1996).

27 I.e., Joachim Wietzke in *ZMiss* 1992/2:122–23; Joachim Wietzke in *Jahrbuch Mission* 1992:238–40; Hans-Werner Gensichen in *Zeitschrift für Missionswissenschaft und Religionswissenschaft* 1992/3:217–18; Anton Peter in *NZM* 1993/2:142–43; Lukas Anton Mettler in *NZM* 1992/3:189–90.

28 Frankfurter Erklärung zur Grundlagenkrise der Mission (Beyerhaus 1970b:28–36). Full name in English according to Hedlund:230. It may be argued that the formulation 'crisis of the foundations' would better translate the German phrase.

29 'However it would be a mistake to take this discouragement … as a *foundational crisis* of mission, or to make these facts responsible for the *foundational crisis*' (Beyerhaus 1970:7; see also 15–17; Beyerhaus 1996:5–7).

30 Later published in an expanded version as *Christian Mission in the Modern World* (1975a).

31 See Reifler:62–63; cf. Scheffbuch 1975. The puzzling observation is that Reifler, while he is leaning towards the *Frankfurt Declaration*, has appended the *Lausanne Covenant* to his book, yet not the *Frankfurt Declaration*.

32 Beyerhaus uses the term 'ecumenical hermeneutic' (1996a:217). A thorough analysis of the development toward an ecumenical hermeneutic has been done by Martin Hamel in his doctoral dissertation (under the supervision of Peter Beyerhaus), *Bibel – Mission – Ökumene. Schriftverständnis und Schriftgebrauch in der neueren ökumenischen Missionstheologie* (1993).

33 Other textbooks used by *the Schools* not in mission but in biblical studies (Stadelmann 1985; Maier) only affirm this observation. The main focus of evangelical exegesis is to understand the biblical text linguistically and historically based on the presupposition that the God-given text has *one* clear and understandable meaning which can be discovered through grammatico-historical exegesis (cf. Stadelmann 1985:104–08). Hermeneutics only come into the picture on the level of application (Stadelmann:101–04).

34 The tendency of evangelicals to resist fundamental hermeneutical and epistemological reflections in order to protect their view of orthodoxy will be discussed again in the concluding chapter of the thesis. See also the analysis of this phenomena by Harris (:278–312) in 'Rescinding Fundamentalism? Evangelicals and Hermeneutics'.

35 The *Wheaton Declaration* includes a section on *Mission and Social Concern* which affirms the primacy of evangelisation as well as the need for social action. Yet there is a lack of theological reflection on the social dimension of salvation and the socio-political dimension of the Christian mission (Hedlund:181–82). The *Frankfurt Declaration* refers to socio-political transformation (humanisation) as a 'product of our new birth through God's saving activity in Christ within

us, or an indirect result of the Christian proclamation in its power to perform leavening activity in the course of world history' (# 2). An additional step in the development of evangelical social concerns was the *Chicago Declaration*, edited by Ronald Sider, in the context of a North American consultation on *Evangelicals and Social Concern* in 1983 (Padilla and Sugden 1985a:4–5).

36 This formulation follows closely the Grand Rapids Report on Evangelism and Social Responsibility.

37 This is one of five concluding statements on evangelical mission in the 21st century.

38 In a hypothetical way Newbigin has outlined this argument very clearly, concluding that, given the fact 'that all who do not accept Jesus as Lord and Saviour are eternally lost', 'it would be not only permissible but obligatory to use any means available, all the modern techniques of brainwashing included, to rescue others from this appalling fate' (1989:173).

39 He explicitly states that the *Frankfurt Declaration* has not sufficiently reflected on the social dimension of mission (Reifler:60).

40 Earlier, the critical assessments by Bockmühl provided the foundation for German evangelicals' position on evangelisation and social responsibility (cf. Bockmühl 1974:168–75; 1975)

41 Comparative studies of the Lutheran concept of the two kingdoms on one hand and the Calvinistic concept of God's reign on the other hand in Moltmann 1983:19–60; 1984:124–51; Webber:113–27, 144–53; and Bender:34–35. All these studies come to the conclusion that Calvinism is more open for the present realisation of God's reign and therefore hopes and strives for the transformation of society towards the kingdom of God. On the other hand, Lutherans are more pessimistic regarding the transformation of human beings as well as society. They emphasise the realisation of the kingdom of God in the future, and view the present order under the preserving rule of God carried out by the government.

42 Sautter claims that the tension between the Anglo-Saxon (Calvinistic) emphasis on the transformation of society under the Lordship of Christ and the continental (Lutheran) view of the two kingdoms is the key underlying issue in the ecumenical discussion since Edinburgh 1910 (:94, 99, 109–10, 118–21, 123–25, 163–66). This tension provides not only the explanation for rejection of the WCC's developments by German evangelicals in the post-war period, it is also a central dimension in the conflict between German (Lutheran) evangelicals and international (more Calvinist and/or Anabaptist) evangelicals (see also p. 182 of this study).

43 The German translation of the conference document reads, 'Dennoch bekräftigen wir, dass Evangelisation und soziale wie politische Betätigung gleichermassen zu unserer Pflicht als Christen gehören' (cf. Beyerhaus 1974 vol.1:12) The term 'gleichermassen' carries the meaning of 'in the same measure' or 'in like manner' which goes beyond the English '... are both part of.'

44 'Da gerade in diesem Konferenzteil die Teilnehmer der Gesamtkonferenz versammelt waren, denen an einer weitgehenden Integration von Evangelisation und sozialer Verantwortung gelegen war, konnte man in Wheaton 1983 noch weitergehen als in Grand Rapids 1982. So entsteht das erste internationale evangelikale Dokument, das ausdrücklich eine Rede vom Primat sowohl der Evangelisation als auch der sozialen Aktion verwirft.'

45 Christopher Sugden in personal discussion with the author.

46 For instance Schnabel's presentations at the *KBA* conference in 1990 was an in-house discussion about evangelical positions hardly represented among the participants of the conference.

47 For a critical analysis of the Lutheran doctrine of the two kingdoms see Moltmann 1983:419–39; 1984:124–36. Moltmann claims that an 'apocalyptic eschatology' is the determinative presupposition of the doctrine of the two kingdoms. Consequently, according to Moltmann, Christ's victory is seen mainly in apocalyptic-futuristic terms at the costs of its 'prophetic' and 'apostolic' significance in the present time (cf. Webber:113–27).

48 On the Lutheran understanding of the church see Schmidt:315–18.

49 We are referring foremost to the evangelical movement associated with the Evangelical Alliance and with the pietistic movement, i.e., with that wing of evangelicalism which did not aim at the foundation of new churches but understood itself as a fellowship of individuals within established churches (to the ecclesiology of the Evangelical Alliance see Hauzenberger:133–50; 231–40).

50 The statements were formulated by Helmut Burkhardt and Reinhard Frische and discussed in a meeting of the *Arbeitgemeinschaft für biblisch erneuerte Theologie*, 28 November 1992 at Basel (Reifler:240–41).

51 For a pietistic view of the church see Bockmühl (1985:11–14). He points to the importance of small groups and the potential of the established state church (Grosskirche, Landeskirche) as significant contributions of Pietism. Unfortunately, he does not recognise the weaknesses of this conception – namely, the reduction of the Christian faith to individual piety celebrated in small groups and the diluted visibility of the church as an alternative community in statechurch Christendom. The Anabaptist concept of the church as a new social order, most powerfully put forward by Harold Bender in his *Anabaptist Vision*, pushes beyond the pietistic-evangelical dilemma between individualism and institutionalism (cf. Kraus).

52 The analysis is even stronger in the German original of Fiedler's book, which is his doctoral thesis. It is actually a study of the ecclesiology of the faith mission movement. In the English edition, which is a reordered and expanded version, this ecclesiological approach is no longer evident. In the German version, Fiedler emphasises mainly the ecclesiological contribution of the faith missions, especially the ecumenical dimension of an interdenominational community. Furthermore, the interdenominational approach has many advantages in missionary situations over against denominational missions insofar that it is less in danger of imposing western church structures upon peoples in other cultures. However, it is this author's view that Fiedler underestimates the deep lack of ecclesiology which goes with this movement which leads to significant gaps in the theology of mission, as shown in this study. (Cf. Hauzenberger:231–41 on the ecclesiology of the Evangelical Alliance.)

53 Powerfully put forward by Bender in *The Anabaptist Vision* (:33–34): 'As we review the vision of the Anabaptists, it becomes clear that there are two foci in this vision. The first focus relates to the essential nature of Christianity. Is Christianity primarily a matter of the reception of divine grace through a sacramental-sacerdotal institution (Roman Catholicism), is it chiefly enjoyment of the inner experience of the grace of God through faith in Christ

(Lutheranism), or is it most of all the transformation of life through discipleship (Anabaptism)? The Anabaptists were neither institutionalists, mystics, nor pietists, for they laid the weight of their emphasis upon following Christ in life ... The second focus relates to the church. For the Anabaptists, the church was neither an institution (Catholicism), nor the instrument of God for the proclamation of the divine Word (Lutheranism), nor a resource group for individual piety (Pietism). It was a brotherhood of love in which the fullness of the Christian life is to be expressed' (cf. Friedmann:80–87).

54 See Vinay Samuel's integration of ecclesiology and missiology (Sugden 1997: 412–32).

55 The issues of 'Witness and Dialogue' have been addressed at the *Internationale Reichenberg-Symposium* (27 to 31 May 1998), organised by the ecumenical community '*Offensive junger Christen*', a movement which must be associated with the open wing of evangelicalism. To integrate the results of this symposium, which may break new ground into this analysis, goes beyond the time frame of this study (for a first summary see Pechmann).

56 Cf. the concept of 'convivence', introduced by Sundermeier into the ecumenical discussion, which expresses a similar concern (Sundermeier 1995; cf. Ritschl:62–63).

57 We are not saying that the critique spelled out in this section applies to all of *the Schools*, their teachers and students. Yet the evidence outlined in the previous chapters allows for the conclusion that *the Schools* have the potential for moving in this direction.

58 These are the only two titles representing evangelicals from the Two Thirds World.

59 In several schools the same attitude can be observed against the Pentecostal-charismatic movement.

60 The concept of salvation history as 'God's shalom project' has been outlined by this author in *Schalom – Das Projekt Gottes*.

61 One of the few German evangelical theologians who do reflect critically on these epistemological issues is Heinzpeter Hempelmann of *Liebenzell* (see Bibliography).

62 To the critique of some trends in critical exegesis, see Bohren 1963:65–96; Stuhlmacher:24–34; O.Betz:7–22. For an internal critical assessment of some aspects of ecumenical theology see Ritschl:16–26 (cf. Werner 1993:414–16; Raiser).

PART FOUR

THEOLOGICAL EDUCATION

EVANGELICAL THEOLOGICAL EDUCATION IN THE LIGHT OF PARADIGM SHIFTS IN THEOLOGICAL EDUCATION

In the previous chapters we have analysed *the Schools* under investigation from a historical and from a missiological angle. Now, in *Part Four* we approach *the Schools* from an educational perspective. The question is: *how* are theological education – in general – and mission studies – in particular – carried out?

Significant shifts are taking place, not only in the global scene of the post-colonial era and in the understanding of mission in the Christian church but also in theological education. What has been said regarding the theology of mission is equally true for theological education: there are many complaints about the *crisis* in theological education, and *new paradigms* are being demanded.[1] In the 1970s Ross Kinsler spoke of 'a world-wide revolution in education,' referring to challenging new models such as 'extension education' or 'open education' (1987:61). James Plueddemann claims that a 'revolutionary paradigm shift' is needed 'in the design and the methodology of theological education.' He 'urges accrediting agencies to take the lead in promoting this paradigm shift' (quoted in Ferris 1990:27).

The aim of this part is twofold:

Chapter 10 will identify what might be called *a new paradigm of theological education*. Based on this, criteria for the evaluation of mission training in theological education will be established.

Chapter 11 focuses on the analysis of *the Schools*. Based on the criteria established in chapter 10, *the School's* performance of theological education, particularly mission studies, will be assessed.[2]

Notes

1 See the proposals by Cheesman, Duraisingh, Farley, Ferris, Kinsler, Padilla, and Poerwowidagdo. The term *new paradigm* has been explicitly used in relation to theological education by Cheesman (:485); Farley (1981:108); Ferris (1990:27), and Poerwowidagdo (:47–48). As discussed in the introduction (pp. 18–20), the use of paradigm terminology is not unquestioned. We use it deliberately in this part of the study in analogy to Bosch's use of it in relation to mission.

2 Recent analytical studies on theological education in relation to the paradigm shift taking place are: (1) *Education in Mission/Mission in Education: A Critical Comparative Study of Selected Approaches* (1987) by Bongani Mazibuko. This doctoral thesis compares mission training in the context of the Project in Partnership between Black and White at Birmingham with the Alternative Theological and Staff Development Experiment of Colgate Divinity School in Rochester, New York, as well as the Black Church Experience in the context of the Research in Black Church Studies with Research Study in Oral History at Garrett-Evangelical Seminary, Evanston, Illinois. (2) *Theological Education for the Church in India: 1947–1987* (1991) by Siga Arles. This doctoral thesis focuses on the Tamilnadu Theological Seminary. It surveys and interprets the developments and struggles of theological education in India in the era following 1947. (3) In *Renewal in Theological Education* (1990) Robert Ferris has surveyed 242 evangelical institutions around the world and has analysed their performance in the light of the *Manifesto* of the ICAA.

CHAPTER 10

Theory: Towards a New Paradigm in Theological Education

This chapter argues that a new paradigm of theological education has been emerging in the last thirty to forty years. Many voices on all continents and in most Christian traditions have articulated disillusion with traditional forms of theological training and have made critiques, suggestions, proposals and experiments in recent years. Some are of a more pragmatic nature, striving after quick and measurable results. Others are thorough reflections on the philosophy of theological education. All these studies provide the raw material for what can be called a new paradigm in theological education.[1] However, an investigation which synthesises all these developments of the last three to four decades into an overall picture – similar to Bosch's synthesis of an emerging missionary paradigm – has not yet been conducted.[2] It is one of the contributions of this study to summarise and synthesise as comprehensively as possible the major strands of thinking and experimentation for a clearer glimpse of the contours of what can be called a new paradigm in theological education.

At least six strands of reflection over the past decades will be brought together in this study:[3]

1. The search for the integration of mission and mission studies into theology and theological education, mostly promoted by the community of missiologists.

2. The search for alternative models in theological education in the context of the Two Thirds World and the rise of what has now come to be known as the Theological Education by Extension Movement (TEE) (Winter 1969; Kinsler 1981; 1983; Youngblood; Padilla ed. 1988).

3. The search for the renewal of North American Seminary training carried out in the context of the ATS and its journal *Theological Education*.

4. The search for renewal of ministerial formation in the context of the Ecumenical Programme on Theological Education (PTE) of the WCC, today called Ecumenical Theological Education (ETE) (Newbigin 1978a; Kinsler 1982:137), mainly documented in *Ministerial Formation*.[4]

5. The search for renewal of evangelical theological education in the context of the International Council of Accrediting Agencies for

Evangelical Theological Education (ICAA), founded in 1980,[5] since 1996 called The International Council for Evangelical Theological Education (ICETE). The Manifesto on the Renewal of Evangelical Theological Education, first published in 1983, is a significant document. Robert W. Ferris' analysis of evangelical theological schools world-wide, based on the Manifesto, is probably the first analysis of that scope to date (Ferris 1990).

6. There is also an ongoing study process for the reform of theological education in the context of the state universities in Germany and Switzerland (Engel and Werner 1990; Werner 1995; Bittner). This too must be taken into consideration.

The following pages will propose that by synthesising the aforementioned strands of reflection and action, one can identify an emerging new paradigm of theological education which centres around the following four issues:

1. The recovery of the church in mission as the ultimate goal and purpose of theological education.
2. The implementation of insights and experiences from adult education including such concepts as self-directed learning, self-responsible learning, self-active learning and lifelong education.
3. The development of educational structures which support learning as an action-reflection process.
4. The design and implementation of integrated curricula.

In order to demonstrate clearly that a paradigmatic shift is taking place in theological education, this fourfold agenda will be addressed so as to bring out the contrasts between the *old* and the *new* paradigms. Of course, such a comparative presentation is typological in character and does not necessarily describe accurately the reality either of more traditional ways of doing theological education or of more innovative forms of theological training. However, it brings to the surface the underlying axioms which can be observed in more traditional models of theological education on the one hand and in new concepts of theological education on the other hand.

1. Mission: From the Margin to the Centre

The first aspect which can be observed in new approaches to theological education is a new emphasis on its mission-orientation. For Kinsler, 'the real challenge is to recapture for theological education the missionary passion and missionary vision it never should have lost' (Kinsler ed. xi). This already implies that there is an old paradigm which is characterised by a lack of missionary orientation.

a) The Old Paradigm: Neglect, Separation and Marginalisation of Mission Studies

The traditional paradigm of theological education is rooted in an epoch in which mission was marginal to the church's identity, mission thinking far from an integral part of theology and mission studies very far indeed from being integrated into theological education. Then, the dawn of the modern missionary movement brought on a growing need to integrate some reflection on mission into theological thought and teaching. What follows in the nineteenth and twentieth centuries is the struggle of mission to win a place in theological reflection and training – a history which has been outlined in chapter 5. In short, one may follow Bosch (1991:489–92; cf. Beaver; Kasdorf 1988) in observing three strategies for integrating mission into theology and theological education. (1) A first model, suggested by Schleiermacher, was to see missions as one of the many ministerial tasks for which the professional must be trained and therefore to add mission studies to the field of practical theology. (2) A second model, associated with names like Alexander Duff and Gustav Warneck, is the introduction of a science of mission (missiology) as a discipline in its own right, a view strongly advocated by Myklebust (1989). (3) Third, some theologians and schools have preferred an integration of mission-thinking into all the traditional disciplines without giving mission studies a separate place in the theological encyclopaedia (e.g., Zahn, according to Ustorf:103).

According to Bosch, none of these attempts are satisfactory (Bosch 1991:492). (1) The addition of mission studies to the field of practical theology limits mission to a ministerial task and tends to focus on techniques. (2) The establishment of a distinct discipline of missiology tends toward the development of a full-blown missiological curriculum, modelled by the traditional fourfold pattern, separated and parallel to the classical curriculum. (3) And finally, in the strategy of integration mission is swallowed up by the general curriculum, where specialists are preoccupied with their traditional specialisations in their respective fields and do not pay adequate attention to missiological research and reflection (Myklebust 1959:332–35; 1989:101).

Furthermore, mission studies in most cases are still limited to a rather narrow understanding of mission within the old missiological paradigm discussed in the previous part, mainly focusing on cross-cultural, overseas missions. This means that mission studies are preoccupied with the Two Thirds World, with issues of cultural anthropology and with the study of other religions. This leads to mission studies' remaining the specific interest of a minority of students who will need this specialised expertise for their future work. To satisfy the needs of these students, courses on missionary subjects are added to the curriculum; in some cases even entire departments are added. However, this is carried out at an exclusively curricular level. Hence, even if mission studies receive considerably more attention in some schools, mission remains in most cases separated and marginalised. This is far from what the new paradigm suggests.

b) The New Paradigm: Mission-Centred Theological Education

(1) FROM MISSIONARY THEOLOGY TO MISSION-CENTRED THEOLOGICAL EDUCATION

The full integration of mission into theological thinking and teaching stands at the centre of a new paradigm of theological education. However, the issue of an adequate integration of mission into theological thinking and training is not merely a problem of curriculum structure; it is a theological problem (Bosch 1991:492).

1. First, the primary issue is not the integration of missiology for the sake of missiology (to satisfy the guild of missiologists); it is the recovery of the missionary dimension of theology for the sake of theology.

2. Second, the integration of mission studies into theological education is only a counterpart to the integration of mission into the church. In other words, the integration of mission into the self-understanding of the church, as it has been implemented in the post-war period (Willingen, Achimota, New Delhi and the subsequent integration of the IMC with the WCC), ought to be brought to the level of theological education (Adamek).

Consequently, just as the recovery of the missionary nature of the church is at the heart of a new missionary paradigm (Bosch 1991:372–3), the recovery of the missionary dimension of theology is at the centre of a new paradigm of theological education. 'Just as an unmissionary church is not a church, a theology that is not missiological ... is not theology, certainly not Christian theology' (Duraisingh:42). This must be seen as an axiomatic thesis of a new paradigm of theological education.

(2) APPLYING THE DIMENSION-INTENTION-CONCEPT TO THEOLOGICAL EDUCATION

One of the most constructive contributions toward a more fruitful integration of mission into theological studies comes again from Bosch's new missiological paradigm, or more precisely, from the chapter on 'Mission as Theology' (1991:489–98) which we have not included in the discussion in chapter 8. This chapter will now provide some clues for the integration of mission into theological education. Bosch introduces the concept of dimension and intention not only to theology (1991:494–96) but also to theological education (Bosch 1982:25ff.). The concept was introduced by

Newbigin (1958:21, 43) and further developed by Vicedom (1963) and Gensichen (1971:80–95) with regard to the *missio Dei* and the church. Ecclesiologically the two terms allow one to emphasise two complementary aspects of the church:

1. On the one hand, everything the church is and does has a missionary dimension. The church is by nature *in mission* (cf. Blauw 1962). Duraisingh suggests that the first theological affirmation which needs to be made toward a new paradigm of theological education is that the 'apostolate is the singular raison d'être of the church' (1992:33). This is the missionary *dimension* of the church.

2. On the other hand, there is an intentional aspect of the church's mission. Bosch states:

> However, the church's missionary dimension evokes *intentional*, that is *direct involvement* in society; it actually moves beyond the walls of the church and engages in missionary 'points of concentration' (Newbigin) such as evangelism and work for justice and peace (Bosch 1991:373).

The dimension-intention concept ensures an integrated understanding of a missionary church, which can be summarised as follows. (1) Mission moves from the margin to the centre of the church, from particular missionary actions of a few people to the very being of the church. (2) At the same time, 'particular missionary actions' are not swallowed up into some sort of undefined 'missionary dimension' of the church but receive their important place as intentional missionary actions of the church. (3) Furthermore, the intentional missionary deeds of the church actually receive their legitimacy only from the church's missionary dimension, and (4) the missionary dimension is only credible if it leads to intentional missionary actions (cf. Bosch 1991:373; 1982a:25; Gensichen 1971:80–95).

Bosch now, as a second step, suggests applying the dimension-intention concept to theology and theological education (1982a:26ff; 1991;494–96).[6] This can only be affirmed as a helpful move toward a new paradigm of theological education.

(3) THE RESULT: MISSION-CENTRED THEOLOGICAL EDUCATION

The results of a mission-centred paradigm of theological education can be spelled out as follows:

1. On the theoretical and primary level, it gives a firm theological reason for the integration of mission into theology and theological education. The argument proceeds from theology (*missio Dei*) (cf. Gensichen 1971:85ff.) to ecclesiology and from there to the field of theological studies and to theological education.

	Dimension	Intention
Missio Dei ↓	God's missionary nature	God's act of sending his Son and his Spirit
Ecclesiology ↓	The missionary nature of the church	The church's specific missionary actions
Theology ↓	The missionary nature of all theology	Specific reflection on the church in mission
Theological education	The missionary centre of all theological education	Specific, mission-oriented training

This supports the idea that the question of the integration of mission into theology and theological education is not merely a pragmatic or structural issue but no less than the theological consequence of the *missio Dei* and the church in mission. Thus, in the new paradigm of theological education, it is mission which sets the agenda for theological education (cf. Duraisingh:33–36).[7]

2. On the practical level, the dimension intention concept calls for a missionary dimension of *all* of theology and of *all* theological education (Bosch 1982:26ff; 1991:494–96). It takes seriously that mission is the mother of theology (Kähler). There are definite signs of an emerging agreement on the missionary dimension of theology. Already in the late 1950s, a concern for a missionary orientation of all of theology was voiced (Meyer:221, 224; W.T. Thomas; E. Krüger:24–25; Adamek:106ff.). In recent years, Conn has called for a 'missiological agenda for theology' (1983:13); Cracknell and Lamb 'insist that all theological questions should be thought about from the point of view of the theology of mission' (Bosch 1991:494, referring to Cracknell and Lamb 1986:25–26); the curriculum revision committee of Andover Newton Theological School recommends relating 'each discipline specifically to a theology of mission' (Stackhouse 1988:25, cf. 49; quoted in Bosch 1991:494), and Myklebust suggests that 'concern for mission … is part of all theological disciplines. Cross-cultural issues should be incorporated throughout the whole curriculum. The Church in all its dimension is mission: theology, therefore, in all its dimensions is missiology' (1989:101).[8]

3. On the other hand, the dimension-intention concept calls for giving a distinct task to missiology. Missiologists have articulated the concern that a full integration of mission studies into the traditional disciplines would weaken the specialised academic concentration on missiological issues (Bosch 1982:19; Myklebust 1961:330–40). There is a need for distinct missiological studies, not only due to the immense task of specialised research, which cannot be conducted by people mainly committed to other fields of studies, but also because of the critical function missiology can have in the theological arena, which can only be secured by a certain

independence.[9] Bosch sees the intentional task of missiology as existing at two levels: (a) First, it

> performs a critical function by continuously challenging theology to be *theologia viatorum*... In this role, missiology acts as a gadfly in the house of theology, creating unrest and resisting complacency, opposing every ecclesiastical impulse to self-preservation, every desire to stay what we are, every inclination toward provincialism and parochialism, every fragmentation of humanity into regional and ideological blocks, every exploitation of some sectors of humanity by the powerful, every religious, ideological or cultural imperialism, and every exaltation of the self-sufficiency of the individual over other people or over other parts of creation (1991: 496).

(b) According to Bosch, the second intentional task of missiology is oriented toward missionary practice, with which it is, by obligation, in constant interaction. This second task contains the responsibility to 'critically accompany the missionary enterprise' by constant reflection on 'its aims, attitudes, message, and methods' (1991:496).

(4) SUMMARY AND CONSEQUENCES

1. It is commonly agreed that education has to be seen as a process oriented toward a goal (cf. Piper:44–51; Duraisingh:42–45). The first axiom of the new paradigm gives theological education a goal, an orientation: the church-in-mission. In the words of Duraisingh (:42), 'If theological education is truly to become a process of forming persons for mission and making them enablers of others for mission, then the very undergirding perspective of theological education must be mission'. It follows from this that in a new paradigm of theological education, a *church-in-mission perspective* is the guiding principle of the educational process.

2. Furthermore, in the new paradigm of theological education, the dichotomy of theology theological-education and mission-mission studies is surmounted. The church is understood as *missionary by its very nature,* and theology and theological education are nothing more than the reflective and educational ministry of the church in mission. The consequences are the following: (1) all of theology, and hence all of theological education as well, is *mission-centred;* (2) therefore, all disciplines and subjects of theological studies have a *missionary dimension;* (3) and are constantly challenged by the discipline of missiology, which has the *intentional task* of in-depth studies of mission subjects.

2. Andragogy: Learning from Adult Education

Initiatives in theological education which intended to break with deficiencies in the old educational paradigm have followed recent developments in education, especially adult education. In Prokop and Geissler's introduction to adult education, the key terms are 'life-long learning' [lebenslanges Lernen], 'self-active learning' [selbstaktives Lernen], 'self-responsible learning' [selbstverantwortliches Lernen] and 'self-directed learning' [selbstbestimmtes Lernen] (:7).[10] These concepts represent what Lengrand (:6) calls 'a radical transformation of the concept of education', a transformation which has been described as a shift from 'pedagogy' to 'andragogy.'[11]

Again, the characteristics of the new approach will become more obvious in comparison with the old.

a) The Old Paradigm: Institution-Oriented Theological Education

We characterise the old paradigm with the term *institution-oriented* – not to suggest that more recent trends in education do not need strong institutions but to emphasise that in traditional education, everything is oriented to educational institutions. The institutions determine the product they offer. They set the agenda in every aspect. A person who wants to get training must do so according to the conditions of the educational institution. However, these conditions were shaped more by the established traditions of the educational institution than by the needs of the persons seeking education or the society in which they live. As a matter of fact, many individuals do not participate in educational programs because suitable educational possibilities are not provided. Kidd and Titmus (:xxix) claim that 'everyone could be attracted to take part, if the content, the methods, the conditions and the time of study were right'. Such deficiencies have also been realised by theological educators.

(1) THE LEGACY OF INSTITUTION-ORIENTED THEOLOGICAL EDUCATION

The legacy of the institutionalised old paradigm of traditional theological education has been characterised by Kinsler as follows:

1. 'Traditional training patterns reinforce the dichotomy between clergy and laity; they debilitate the dynamics of ministry at the congregational level; and they make the churches dependent upon highly trained, professional pastors' (1981:8).

2. 'History teaches us that the Western academic-professional system of clergy tends to be static, incapable of responding to the needs of the masses, preoccupied with position and privilege at the expense of dynamic, corporate ministry' (1981:12)

3. 'The Western churches, whatever their concept of ministry may be, have developed an academic-professional model of ministry which is

self-defeating in terms of effective leadership. Within this system theological education serves to select young, inexperienced men and women, separate them from the normal process of leadership formation and place them artificially over the other members' (1981:14).

4. 'Traditional seminaries and Bible institutes tend to follow the elitist trends of our societies, and they perpetuate the image of education as the accumulation of information' (1981:19).

5. 'Traditional, residential theological schools are extremely expensive, especially if they attempt to reach the more mature leaders of the church. And they create a heavy financial burden for the churches, for they produce professional pastors at higher and higher support levels' (1981:21).

6. 'Traditional theological institutions are far too limited in their outreach, and they have inherent fallacies' (1981:24).

With this list Kinsler reveals some of the powerful para-messages of the traditional paradigm of theological education. There is a strong notion of domination and power which goes with this institutionalised model of western theological training.

In examining institutionalised higher education from a Christian perspective, Henri Nouwen affirms Kinsler's critique. He speaks of 'teaching as a violent process' in traditional institutionalised education characterised by three features (:5–10):

1. Institutionalised education has become a system of competition in which 'knowledge no longer is a gift that should be shared, but a property that should be defended' (:6)

2. It is 'a unilateral process' based on the still 'prevailing supposition that someone is competent and that someone else is not and that the whole game is to try to make the one just or nearly as competent as the other.' In this whole process it is obvious that the teacher is strong and the student is weak (:6–7).

3. Finally, institutionalised education is 'alienating' the students from real life because it focuses on a sort of 'indoor training' or 'dry-swim' with few connections to the future 'real life.' In so doing, claims Nouwen, institutionalised education misses the 'primary source of learning,' which is the inter-personal encounter between teachers and students in the here and now (:9–10).

Kinsler, Nouwen and others (cf. Kirk 1983:48–51) have come to the conclusion that the entire educational system has obviously reached a size which makes it resistant to any paradigmatic change. Buildings, libraries, structures of administration, university affiliations, the state and the church, as well as the guilds of academic specialisation with their respective histories, associations and publications, have grown into a sort of self-perpetuating system. Nouwen concludes that institutionalised education is no longer master of its own destiny (:3).

(2) THE FAILURE OF WESTERN INSTITUTION-ORIENTED THEOLOGICAL EDUCATION IN THE TWO THIRDS WORLD

The domination of this western model of theological education became evident when the western mission movement initiated theological education in the Two Thirds World, exporting western models of theological training to young churches. Through the efforts of the Theological Education Fund (TEF) of the WCC between 1958 and 1977, many theological institutions in non-western parts of the world have been brought 'up to the standards of the best theological faculties of Europe or North America' (Newbigin 1978b:3; cf. Kinsler 1982:137). Yet educators from the Two Thirds World, for instance J. Norberto Saracco, are critical:

> This was a time of constructing large buildings, investing in libraries, and sponsoring the preparation of professors in the United States and Europe. The various institutions followed the European or North American model without perceiving that the context of their situation was totally distinct (:26).

Saracco does not hesitate to point to the effect this had on the church in Latin America:

> The Church in Latin America was reaping its first professional theologians, for whom it paid the high price of elitism. Only those who could meet the seminaries' requirements and developed the lifestyle these demanded could attend the theological institutions. Theological education was weakened in the very area that is its reason for existing – the motivation, training, and equipping of the people of God that they might develop their ministries (:26–27).

Along the same lines, the Colombian Hugo Zorrilla complains, 'Many curricula in theological education have a limited function in the mission of the churches. In no way do they help the student develop his creativity and understandings of the historical moment in which his people live' (:374). Western models of theological education often 'lack church-centred or student-centred curricula' (:375). They provide "prepackaged' content,' and consider a programme to be 'nonbiblical, and consequently heretical, if it doesn't have sixty to seventy per cent biblical content, which consists of studies of memorized "neutral" biblical content without theological reflection or dialogue with the world to which it ministers' (:375). According to Emilio Castro's assessment, the 'difficulty with the traditional theological educational process is that it takes young people out of a given cultural milieu and makes them totally unsuitable to come back to that milieu' (1982:130).

In this context, Theological Education by Extension (TEE) and other alternative forms of theological education[12] were created in response to the need for leadership training which could not be met by traditional educational models (Kinsler 1981:8–24; Saracco:27ff.). Kinsler states: 'Theological education by extension came into existence in response to a vast, urgent need that was not being met by traditional seminaries and Bible institutes' (1981:61).

(3) DISSATISFACTION WITH INSTITUTION-ORIENTED MODELS OF THEOLOGICAL EDUCATION IN THE WESTERN WORLD

The experiences of the Two Thirds World also stirred questions regarding the effectiveness of western theological education even in its European and North American context. Michael Griffith points to the deep dissatisfaction with the current scene and urges European evangelical theological educators to implement changes, lest theological education become irrelevant (1989). Andrew Kirk claims that 'present training methods have proved inadequate to the contemporary needs of the church,' and he calls the western model of theological training 'unreal and even naive' (1983:49–50). And Tim Dearborn of the Seattle Association for Theological Education observes:

> We have entrusted to our seminaries and theological schools a daunting responsibility. They are expected to prepare wise, compassionate, theologically astute and pastorally proficient servants who can lead the church and our society through the crisis of the 21st century. However, during this century the theological schools of the Western world have adopted methods for fulfilling this responsibility which some would say, guarantee their failure (:7).

Even if some of these statements may need qualification, they bear witness to the widespread disappointment with the 'product' of traditional theological education in its outreach, as well as in the quality of the leadership it produces. Consequently, a search for reform, renewal and alternative models of ministerial training can be observed both in the evangelical (cf. Ferris 1990) and in the ecumenical world (cf. Engel and Dietrich; Dietrich 1995).

b) The New Paradigm: People- and Context-Oriented Theological Education

A growing number of theological educators are aware of the deficiencies of the old paradigm and draw from the insights of adult education in order to reshape theological education (cf. R. T. Bender, Ferris, Kinsler, Ward). Several new models of theological and pastoral training have come into existence. The concept of Clinical Pastoral Education (CPE) can be traced as far back as 1925 and must be seen as a forerunner to many more recent models of pastoral training (cf. Zehr and Egli:11–16).Today, many new structures for theological training are associated with Theological Education by Extension (TEE), a concept whose origins date back to 1962 and which incorporates a wide range of educational structures (cf. Kinsler ed.) However, other terms have been used to describe the people-orientation of new educational models including 'popular theological education' (Kinsler 1987), 'people centred theological education' (Sarraco:33), 'ministry centred theological education' (Saracco:27), 'contextual theological education' (Kinsler 1979:19) or 'open theological education' (Kinsler 1981:61ff.). They do not all refer to the same, precise form of education, but they share a common reference to what has been called 'alternative models of theological education' (Kinsler 1981:41; Padilla ed. 1988). This can be outlined in greater details as follows:

(1) GOAL-ORIENTED AND PRAGMATIC THEOLOGICAL EDUCATION

In current adult education the legacy of education 'as an end in itself' has been questioned and replaced by a clear orientation towards education 'as a means for other ends' (Kidd and Titmus:xxx–xxxi). The basic underlying assumption is that adults want to learn purposefully in view of their personal development and/or their work in professions and in society. In the new-paradigm-thinking, the question of purpose and objectives is raised with new urgency. In this view, theological education serves an aim outside and beyond *academia* and theological education itself (cf. Kirk 1983: 49–51). As shown before, there is a growing consensus that the aim of theological education is *to serve the church in its mission*. A few examples in view of the educational consequences are:

The statement of the ATS consultation with the NCC/WCC says:

> We now understand more clearly that the purpose of theological education is equipping in ministry all those who are and will be enabling their faith communities to give their lives in service and witness for the fullness of life of all people under the reign of God (ATS:3).

Duraisingh believes that 'The formation of the faithful for their participation and celebration of the life of the kingdom and for their actively partaking in the church's mission is the central purpose of all that it does through its ministries of education and nurture' (1992:34). Kinsler states, 'Theological education exists not as an end in itself, not to establish the ministry or the church as such, but to enable the church to carry out its mission' (1981:21), and, 'It is assumed that theological education, in whatever way it is conceived and practised, is necessary for the training of those who in turn are called to mobilize and equip the people of God for ministry and mission' (Kinsler 1982:133). When the objective of theological training is to educate the community of faith for its mission in the world, then the output of theological training institutions must be measured according to this objective statement. This is the argument of the new paradigm.

Consequently, it is evident that in the new paradigm, pragmatic questions receive new significance. An increasing number of individuals, churches and mission agencies are approaching theological education in this way. They are simply asking: What is the output of theological education? Do educational institutions produce the kind of leaders we need? Do theological schools serve the objectives of the church or do they have their own objectives and agenda? Does theological training reach the people in the church? Does theological education enable persons to become enablers for the church and its members to cope with the 'tide and destructive forces of this age' (Poerwowidagdo:45–46).Time and again, this pragmatic approach can be observed in the literature on alternative models of theological education.

(2) PEOPLE-ORIENTED THEOLOGICAL EDUCATION

It follows that the new paradigm is *people-oriented*. The following quotation by Kinsler summarises well the concern:

> So we must extend our seminaries and institutions to where they live, i.e., to the whole area of our church. We have to adjust our schedules to fit theirs, our thinking to communicate within the varied sub-cultures they represent, our teaching to match their different academic levels, our materials to carry a greater proportion of the cognitive input. We need to extend our concept of theological education to include besides candidates for the ministry, lay workers, elders, youth leaders, ordained pastors, i.e., those who carry the primary responsibility in our churches and congregations (:25–26).

This includes several aspects:

1. A primary level is *geographical and cultural*. It is the move from the educational centre to the people. Kinsler, occasionally called 'father of Theological Education by Extension' (Kirk 1983:46), makes the simple statement that 'extension has primarily to do with people' (Kinsler 1981:25). The key of the extension movement, he claims, is that it *extends* theological education to people; 'people who are largely beyond the reach of traditional residential seminaries and Bible institutes' (Kinsler 1981:25). *Contextual theological education* 'should take place in the geographical locations where people live and work and worship.' This means 'that the seminary classroom should be extended to the hinterland,' and 'that theological studies should be adapted to the linguistic

and cultural patterns of each sub-culture' (Kinsler 1979:19). Thus, what is called for in the new paradigm is that 'local leaders can obtain a profound, integral training while carrying on their ministry in the streets and in the life of the congregation' (Kinsler 1981:12, cf. 32–33).

2. Beyond this rather pragmatic level, contextual theological education also includes a *new pedagogy* which moves beyond 'the transferral of pre-packaged subject matter primarily through lectures, and production of graduates who will believe and perform as the institution and the churches desire' (Kinsler 1981:49; cf. 1983:22–24). People involved in ministry and everyday struggles learn differently.

> The tendency of formal school programs is to depend upon motivation within the content, have poor clarity of objectives, experience a low level of appropriate instructional technology, base validation on tradition, and offer symbolic rewards. The tendency of non-formal programs, on the other hand, is to find motivation within the learner, have a higher clarity of objectives, experience a high level of appropriate instructional technology, base validation on performance and application, and offer pragmatic rewards (Kinsler 1981:48).

This means that in contextualised theological education, students and teachers engage together in an action-reflection process which is directed toward conscientisation and liberation – to use the terminology of liberation theology – and a more effective service in the church and in the world. 'In this process no one teaches anyone; people learn together in the real world' (Kinsler 1981:49; with reference to Paulo Freire).[13] This pedagogical aspect will be further developed under the third aspect of the new paradigm below.

3. Thirdly, people-oriented, contextual theological education involves a significant shift in the orientation of the curriculum. The traditional curriculum of theological education reflects the history of theological education – the encyclopaedia of theology and the fourfold pattern – as pointed out by Farley. It is shaped by the past, thinks in the categories of the past and speaks the language of the past. Traditional theological education is based on the presupposition 'that by gaining some mastery of the past, we will inevitably be better equipped to face the complexities of the future.' Consequently, 'Greek and Hebrew, Church History and Historical Theology all have important places in the seminary curriculum' (Dearborn:9). Advocates of a new paradigm of theological education do not usually devalue the significance of historical knowledge, but they point out that 'leaders who are past, rather than future focused, are a contradiction in terms' (Dearborn:9). It is a move from 'curriculum-oriented' theological education, concerned with the transmission of the content of

the past, structured according to a pattern of the past, to (a) 'goal oriented' theological education, where the objectives determine the subject matter; (b) 'student oriented' theological education, which tries not 'to force ... all into the same shape or habit but works to develop the utmost the individual features of each species'; and (c) 'problem oriented' theological education, which focuses 'upon the urgent issues both in church and in society' (Griffith 1989:9–11)?

4. Finally, Kinsler pushes to a fourth level, toward a participatory model of education. Traditionally, 'the entire academic programme is laid out without consulting the students' (Kinsler 1981:47). Kinsler suggests, that theological education should 'actually be shaped and directed by' local people (Kinsler 1979:19). Poerwowidagdo (:48) asks:

> Do our students participate in determining their educational programme? In other words, is our educational methodology student or human centred rather then content (knowledge) centred? Do we provide for democratic participation of all those who are concerned and involved in the educational process.

This emphasis is a reaction against institutionalised education which works on a vertical model, transferring knowledge from the educated teacher down to the ignorant student. This is, in Kinsler's words, a significant pedagogical dimension of TEE theory:[14]

> Whereas the school system is hierarchical and traditional teaching tends to domesticate the students, TEE seeks to break out of both schemes, recognizing that the students are leaders whatever their academic level may be, and treating them as partners in the educational process. To achieve this change the teachers need to come down off their pedestal, and institutions need to respect the student's maturity (1987:34).

This calls for new models of learning with a strong emphasis on dialogue in an ongoing action-reflection process. It can not be achieved 'so much by curriculum design as by engaging people where they are in their historic struggle for survival, for identity, for health, for justice and dignity, for salvation, for renewed church and a new social order' (Kinsler 1987:19).

This quest for more relevant models of theological training is far from being only a Two Thirds World concern. To an increasing measure, western theological educators become aware of the deficiencies of traditional centralised and residential theological education and call for more 'context related learning' (Duraisingh 1992; Werner 1992:78–79, cf. Werner 1995:20–21; Dearborn; ATS:4–5; Zehr:17). Already in 1978,

Newbigin pointed out the challenges to the educational models of the first world by the new reflections and experiments in the Two Thirds World – and this on the levels of structure, methods, as well as content of theological training (1978:6–10). Andrew Kirk, a British theological educator with Latin American experience, advocates the contextual and people-oriented model of TEE for theological training in the west, too. He concludes, 'What I am advocating is quite simply, though not superficially, new wineskins (methods of training) for new wine (methods of doing theology)' (1983:51–54, 56).

(3) FROM 'PEDAGOGY' TOWARDS 'ANDRAGOGY'

This people-orientation in theological training must also be seen in relation to the shift from 'pedagogy' to 'andragogy' in adult education in general. According to Kidd and Titmus, a fundamental idea in the philosophy of modern adult education is 'that any adult is a free agent, responsible for his or her action, who is therefore at liberty to participate or not in any educational experience as he or she chooses and who should determine the content and nature of the experience' (Titmus: xxviii). Knowles has defined andragogy along these lines. His concept is based on four assumptions:

> ... as a person matures, (a) his self-conception moves from one of being a dependent personality toward one of being a self-directed human being; (b) he accumulates a growing reservoir of experience that becomes an increasing resource for learning; (c) his readiness to learn becomes oriented increasingly to the development tasks of his social roles; and (d) his time perspective changes from one of postponed application of knowledge to immediacy of application, and accordingly his orientation toward learning shifts from one of subject centredness to one of problem-centredness (quoted from Krajne:21).

Based on such assumptions, Knowles put forward his theory of self-directed learning, summarised in the following chart (quoted from Ferris 1984:47; based on Knowles 1975:60):

From this it follows that 'lifelong learning' is a key concept in contemporary andragogy. Lengrand calls this 'a radical transformation of education' (:6) In contrast to the traditional philosophy of education, which is built on the conception that life is 'divided into distinct parts: a period of learning and preparation, followed by a period of action,' the philosophy of lifelong education emphasises that learning is an integral part of life itself. Thus, the concept of lifelong education does not just add continuing education to traditional initial education; it alters the task of initial education. Lengrand concludes, that there is no reason to overburden the

	Teacher-directed Learning	Self-directed Learning
Concept of the learner	Dependent personality	Increasingly self-directed organism
Role of learner's experience	To be built on more than used	A rich resource for learning
Readiness to learn	Varies with levels of maturity	Develops from life tasks to problems
Orientation to learning	Subject-centred	Task- or problem-centred
Motivation	External rewards and punishment	Internal incentives, curiosity

brains of children by accumulating a capital of knowledge which ought to last a lifetime. It is much more important that in initial education people learn how to learn (Langrand:6–8).

Conceptions for theological education which can be viewed as representing a new paradigm are aware of these foundational concepts in adult education. Robert Ferris is one of the theological educators who has applied such concepts to theological education. In his definition of the process of theological education he draws from Knowles, Piaget, Carkhuff, Combs, as well as Freire (Ferris 1984:45–52). At the 1984 consultation of the International Council of Accrediting Agencies he called theological educators to a serious renewal of the *process* of theological education. He states:

> Unfortunately, traditional schooling processes teach us to be taught, but they do not teach us to learn. Residence and extension programs alike typically assign initiative to a teacher for planning, directing and evaluating learning. Whenever this occurs, our programs risk cultivating dependencies rather than the capacity for self-directed learning (Ferris 1984:45–46).

Drawing on Knowles's concept of 'self-directed' learning, he urges theological educators to facilitate 'growth from teacher-directed to self-directed learning – from dependence to maturity.'

It seems that the implementation of such conceptions of adult education would challenge traditional theological education as least as much as it challenges education in general.

(4) SUMMARY AND CRITICAL REFLECTIONS

The new paradigm is characterised by the terms *goal-oriented and pragmatic* as well as *people-oriented and andragogical*. This indicates a radical shift in perspective, in response to the question, who sets the agenda in theological training? (1) Whereas in the old paradigm the traditional, institutionalised patterns of theological studies set the agenda for theological education (fourfold pattern, academic world, curriculum and nomenclature rooted in the western history of theology), in the new paradigm *people at the grass-roots level of the church in mission* set the agenda. (2) Whereas in the old paradigm, the quality of theological training is assessed according to the standards of the academic community, in the new paradigm the quality of a programme is measured according to its service to the church in mission. (3) Whereas in the old paradigm, input matters most (academic qualification of faculty and students), in the new paradigm output matters most (are graduates prepared to give leadership to the church in mission?) (Griffith 1989; Duraisingh:33; Dearborn:7; Poerwowidagdo:45). This shift of perspective must be seen as axiomatic to the new paradigm.

Nonetheless, some aspects of this second axiom of a new paradigm of theological education deserve critical reflection and qualification (cf. Kirk 1983:54–56; Mulholland:17–23; Kinsler 1983:16–20; 1987:33–36):

1. *Institutions of theological education between the church and the academic world*. The new paradigm suggests a rather radical shift from traditional academic institutions of theological education to contextualised, people-oriented ministerial training. Traditionally, theological education takes place in institutions more or less separated from the church and even more from mission. The educational institutions are often more at home in the context of *academia* than in the context of the church. This has certainly been challenged by the new paradigm. Some would even argue that theological education should be completely integrated into the church (e.g., Simson:49–53), while others advocate the necessity of interaction with the academic world (cf. Samuel 1996:4; Harder; Jongeneel 1998). This study advocates definitions which see institutions of theological education in a creative tension between two worlds: the church and the university (R. Bender 1971:166–67; Harder). Still, in the light of the thesis stated earlier, the ultimate allegiance and obligation of theological education is to the church engaged in mission and not to the educational institution and the world of *academia*. The Associated Mennonite Biblical Seminary (Elkhart, Indiana), a denominational institution of the free church tradition has stated this conviction as follows:

> The context for theological education is therefore not first of all the university, but the community of faith. The theological school stands, to be sure, in the academic tradition as well as in the ecclesiastic tradition; however, it is the Judeo-Christian tradition (as expressed through the Free Churches in this instance) rather than the Western culture (which forms the intellectual environment of

> the university) which is the true home of theological education. In short, we look to Jerusalem rather than to Athens for our clues in shaping the form, substance, and style of our enterprise (R. Bender 1971:166).[15]

This certainly stands in contrast to the ethos of the university. Nicole (:34) notes:

> The partner of the European theologians … [is] the university, not the church. Theological educators will spend a lot of time and energy to give to the university and the world of scientists and technicians additional evidence to support the scientific character of their discipline'.

Some have argued that it is precisely part of the church's missionary presence in the world to conduct theological studies in the context of the university (Zumstein:97–98; Samuel 1996:4, Jongeneel 1998). This should not be denied; however, in the new paradigm there is a strong call for priorities.[16] The home of theological education is the church in mission and not the university. Lydia Harder, a theological educator who is involved in theological education in both a small denominational seminary (Associated Mennonite Biblical Seminary, Elkhart) and a large university (Toronto Mennonite Theological Centre at the Toronto School of Theology) reflects critically on this dual commitment of theological education. Using the language of 'centre' and 'boundary' she relates the former to the church, the latter to the university and advocates for theological education that relates to both. In so doing, theological education must keep its primary allegiance to the church in mission, and it needs to develop a bilingualism which allows it to communicate with the church as well as with the academic world. It is the conviction of this author that this provides a well-stated theory for the conduct of theological education in the tension between the church in mission and the academic world (Harder).

2. *The limitations of pragmatism.* In the new paradigm of theological education, pragmatic questions are not avoided but rather implemented as an essential tool for decision-making. One looks carefully at the output of theological education and does not hesitate to assess the educational process by assessing the effectiveness in serving the church in mission. But pragmatism is a slippery terrain, especially when it is based on superficial research and short term perspectives. Not every technique which produces immediate church growth is necessarily consistent with biblical theology nor helpful for the church in mission in the long run. The needs pronounced by people (felt needs)[17] in their local context are not necessarily what they really need (unrecognised needs) in the light of

a larger, historical and global perspective. Kirk (1983:50) rightly states that

> the most appropriate education and the best theology are not necessarily what the majority may want. Christians in local situations may need their horizons broadened and their imaginations stretched'.

The urgent call for pragmatic evaluation of theological training needs therefore to be supplemented by an insistence on careful research and responsible, long-term reflection.

3. Action-Reflection Process: Overcoming the Theory-Practice Dichotomy

There is a growing consensus among theological educators that the integration of *theory and practice* is a point of great dissatisfaction in contemporary theological training.[18] Many schools have sought ways for a deeper integration of theory and practice, often under the heading of *field education*. Again, theological educators are indebted to adult education for many new insights in this area. Concepts such as *experimental learning*, *supervised field education* or *inductive learning* have been inspiring for innovative theological educators. Furthermore, it was the pedagogy of Liberation Theology (e.g., Paulo Freire) which opened a fresh understanding of theory and praxis (cf. Ferris 1984:47–48; Kinsler 1978:41–60; Schipani:30–32).

We begin again by looking first at some contours of the old paradigm:

a) The Old Paradigm: Deductive Transmission of Knowledge and Separation of Theory and Practice

The terms *theory* and *practice* call for clarification at the beginning of this discussion. Farley, addressing the issue in his 1981 presentation to the ATS, distinguishes four ways of using theory-practice in the current discussion (1981:103–04). (1) In reference to the educational process it is common to distinguish between theoretical assignments (i.e., thinking, reading, writing) and practical assignment (i.e., 'hands-on' work in the church and in society). (2) The term practical refers also to techniques and skills over against theoretical studies of a more academic nature. (3) In the fourfold pattern, practical refers to the ministerial practice (practical theology as practical ministerial formation) as opposed to the 'theory' of Bible, theology and church history. (4) Finally, in a more general sense, practical means that studies as a whole should be relevant for life and ministry.

This can be taken as a helpful preliminary clarification but we need to tackle the problem more precisely as we look at some of the historical developments.

(1) 'PRACTICAL THEOLOGY' AS THE THEORY OF THE MINISTERIAL PRACTICE

According to Farley, the introduction of the encyclopaedic, fourfold pattern of theology has caused severe confusion regarding the understanding of theory and practice. This rather complex problem can be developed in several steps. (1) In the study-of-theology period, theory and practice were not seen as two separate elements or even disciplines but as two sides of the one *habitus* of theology. Theology was by definition theoretical *and* practical, i.e., *theologia* as *habitus* is composed both by the element of action as well as the element of reflection. (b) In Protestant dogmatics of the sixteenth and seventeenth century, *practical* still referred to that aspect of theology which has to do 'with the effect of the knowledge of God in life and action' (Farley 1981:102). In this sense, practice does not refer to the ministerial task, but to aspects of theology which affect Christian life, such as 'soteriology and prophetic theology' (Farley:102; 1983:77–78). (3) Then, in the fourfold pattern as developed in the nineteenth century, practical theology had the task of applying the theory of the three theoretical disciplines to ministerial activity; here, practical theology became a bridge-building discipline between theory and practice (cf. Farley 1981:104–9). With this, *theory* was assigned to certain disciplines which henceforward conducted theological studies on a purely theoretical level. On the other hand, practical theology was committed to practice – namely, clerical practice, as noted above. (5) In the twentieth century, practical theology developed its own curriculum, separate from the theoretical disciplines. The methodology was taken from the social sciences and each sub-discipline (homiletics, counselling, leadership, mission) developed into a professional theory of ministerial practice. Thus, even so-called *practical* theology ends up becoming theory: the theory of the ministerial function. (6) Finally, under the pressure of an increasing dissatisfaction with irrelevant academic theory and the urgent call for more relevant theological education, practical theology and the understanding of practice became more and more functional and pragmatic. Practical is that which can be *used* immediately and that which *works* within a short period of time. With this emphasis, practical theology tends to lead to a 'preoccupation with technique' (Farley 1981:105).

Thus, practical theology in the traditional paradigm is in reality theory. It is taught on the assumption that the students will be able to apply the theory when they finally get into their professional life.

(2) DEDUCTIVE LEARNING AS DOMINANT METHODOLOGY

Furthermore, the problem of application or transfer has to be seen in relation to the teaching methodology, which is predominately deductive. This means that the educational process is built upon the presupposition that *theoria* is a given truth set which can be learned beforehand, then applied to real-life situations. This implies that theory precedes practice and can be mastered on a cognitive, intellectual level without involvement and commitment to the historical situation. Consequently, most of the contemporary attempts to solve the theory-practice problem consist of some type of bridge-building (cf. Farley 1981:102–03), trying to apply theory to practical life. However, there are severe doubts as to whether they really solve the problem. All these bridge-building attempts only reinforce the aforementioned assumption that theory, as a given, abstract set of knowledge can be learned and can then be applied to every day life situations. Yet it is precisely this view of theory and practice that has been challenged (cf. Farley 1981: 101–06; Piper; Tracy 1989).

Piper, who introduced Clinical Pastoral Training to German pastoral education (1981), defines the process of *deductive learning* as follows:

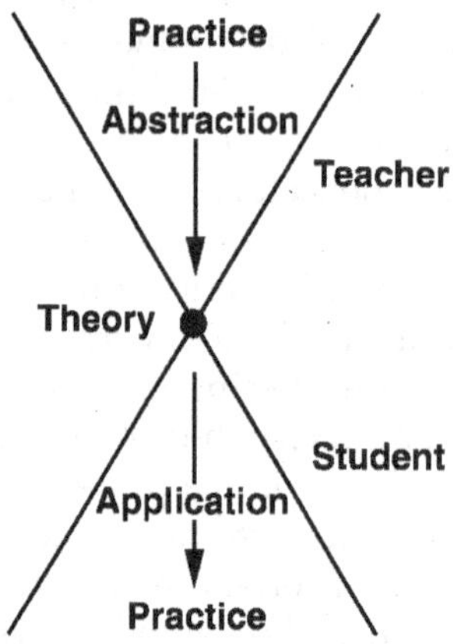

The teacher transmits to the student an abstract theory, which the student has to absorb as abstract theory. The point where teacher and student meet is abstract theory. The teacher may transmit a theory which he or she has developed inductively from personal, practical experience and may also transmit a theory already received as tradition but applied personally in practical life and now spoken 'out of experience'; and finally he or she may also transmit a theory received as tradition yet never applied to practical life. The student, on the other hand, has to absorb an abstract theory as a set of pre-packed knowledge and is left with the task of applying it to practical life.

The disadvantages of such an educational model are obvious and common knowledge:

1. Education is reduced to the transmission of theory and the appropriation of abstract knowledge.
2. It is difficult for the students to relate abstract theory to real life in a class room situation, especially when they have no previous experience in the area of the taught subject.
3. Students rapidly loose their motivation to study if they cannot connect the learned, abstract theory with real life situations.
4. There is a tendency to remain in the realm of abstraction and to conduct abstract reflection as an end in itself.
5. There is usually a large surplus of abstract theory at the end of a course taught by the traditional paradigm of learning.
6. Examinations focus on the correct reproduction of abstract theory by the student.
7. The whole system is built on the presupposition that cognitively appropriated, abstract truth can later be successfully applied to life.

It is evident that this concept of education has the potential for domination because the teacher who has the knowledge is in control of the educational process. The student depends fully on the expertise of the teacher. Paulo Freire, in his critique of the dominant paradigm of western education, speaks of the 'Bankers-Concept of Education,' (Freire 1973:57–70) because the teacher makes a deposit of knowledge in the students minds which should yield interest in the future. Freire speaks of education as 'praxis of domination' because it presupposes that people are empty vessels which ought to be filled with the pre-defined knowledge handed down by the established tradition of a given society. Kinsler has adopted Freire's pedagogy to theological education[19] and criticises traditional models of theological education for their dominant and oppressive role. Similarly, Henri Nouwen has pointed to the fact that traditional education is a unilateral process in which the teacher is strong and the student weak (:7–9). The teacher knows, the student does not know. The whole movement is from the strong to the weak. Nouwen rightly calls this 'teaching as a violent process.'

While deductive learning has value to a certain extent and for certain subjects, if it becomes the predominate method of teaching, it has the potential for domination, it tends to avoid the student's growth toward maturity, and it leads students to a tremendous degree of accumulation of abstract knowledge and alienates them from practice. Applications then becomes the almost impossible task of bridging the immense gulf between abstract theory and real life.

(3) DISTANCIATION AND DETACHMENT FROM LIFE CONTEXT

The problem caused by one-sided deductive methodology is reinforced by what Farley calls *distancing* or *distanciation*.[20] Traditional models of theological education separate students from the context of their future professional work, and this in most cases for many years. A student who follows university training in Germany or Switzerland (cf. Lange and Schmid) will study at least four to five years after the completion of the *Abitur* or *Matura*. Upon entering pastoral ministry for the first time at age twenty five or more, he/she has been learning and studying full-time in the context of educational institutions for at least eighteen years. Of course, students live as normal persons and citizens in society and church and therefore have a certain degree of life experience. However, most of their time has been spent in the distinct context of educational institutions, which is highly different from what they will experience after graduation. The educational philosophy behind this concept of theological training implies that theory precedes practice and that in initial education students can acquire most of the theory they need for life. It divides life 'into two distinct parts: a period of preparation and training, followed by a period of action' (Lengrand:6). While students learn 'the habit of critical inquiry' they do not – in the case of future pastors – learn 'the habit of ministerial practice' (Schipani:34). Consequently, despite the fact that traditional educational institutions claim to prepare people for life, graduates will enter church ministries in many ways unprepared.

Furthermore, this system reinforces the notion that the time of initial education is a time of preparation for life but not real life. Henry Nouwen has rightly pointed to the fact that in this process students are alienated from life. Although this system intends to prepare people for life, it actually prevents them – by its very structure – from living (Nouwen:9–10).

(4) EPISTEMOLOGICAL IMPLICATIONS

In view of further discussion, we should point finally to the epistemological issues involved in deductive, detached education. Ultimately, this traditional paradigm of education transmits a certain understanding of what truth is, how it can be known, articulated and learned. This is of particular significance in theological education, which claims to deal with ultimate truth. Deductive learning presupposes that truth is a defined, pre-packed set of knowledge which can be handed down from generation to generation. Therefore, the issue of theory and practice is reduced to the problem of application. The solution of the problem of theory and practice, or at least the right steps toward a solution, would then be reached through improvement in the application of the definitive theory. We will argue later in this study that the old paradigm fails exactly because of its epistemological presuppositions. This will become clear as we look at the contours of a new paradigm.

b) The New Paradigm: Integration of Theory and Practice

(1) BRIDGE BUILDING – AND BEYOND

The question of how the bridge between theory and practice can be built is not new, and educational theories have dealt with the related issues under the heading of *transfer*. Educational textbooks analyse transfer-mechanisms and suggest strategies and methodologies to enhance transfer (cf. Gage and Berliner:161–74). These are essential parts of any educational theory and remain significant in the new paradigm. However, traditional transfer methodologies are instruments for moving successfully from theory to practice – that is, they reinforce the assumption that the process of learning basically moves from the cognitive acquisition of a theory to its application into the various contexts of life.

Farley and others suggest a move beyond the bridge building model to what could be called a process-model (Farley 1981:104–05), pointing to a lifelong educational process. In this process, a 'dynamic relation between action and reflection' is necessary (Duraisingh:36). These are not just other words for theory and practice; they represent a different pedagogical understanding: (1) action, or 'praxis, is not only the goal but also the foundation of theory' (Duraisingh:36); (2) the process of learning includes 'concrete missiological involvements' and 'commitment to the struggles of people for fuller life' (Duraisingh:36); as well as (3) reflection and 'distanciation ... as a constitutive ingredient in any act of understanding' (Farley 1981:105). In the words of Siga Arles, it is a shift from 'formation through information' to 'formation through involvement' (:371).

(2) INDUCTIVE LEARNING[21]

One of the key elements of learning which moves beyond the theory-application model is *inductive learning*.[22] According to Piper (:46), the process of inductive learning can be presented with the following chart:

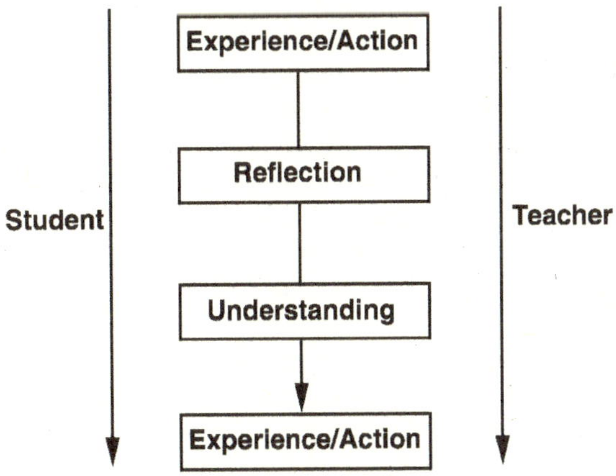

Here, learning, understood as a process moving from experience-action-practice to reflection and theory, finally leads to a deeper understanding. From here, the process moves back to experience-action-practice. It is important to take note of Piper's significant distinction between 'happening' [*Widerfahrnis*] and 'experience' [*Erfahrung*]. A happening is what happens to a person, first of all without any interpretation or understanding. A person can 'make' it into an experience by reflecting upon it. At this point, theories and teachers come into the picture. Reflecting upon what 'happened' in the light of theory, the happening can be interpreted, or understood, turning the 'happening' into an experience. In Piper's terms, the '*Aha!*-experience' [*AHA-Erlebnis*], or the moment in which students understand what has happened to them, is the most crucial moment in the learning process. Furthermore, this '*Aha!*-experience' may also occur when students get involved in action; and when certain things happen, they suddenly achieve an understanding of the happening in the light of the theory they had learned. The teacher, in this model, is the facilitator in this process. He or she, being more experienced and possessing a deeper understanding of happenings and also a wider knowledge of theory, can help in the student's attempt to understand what has happened. Of course, the teacher will transmit theory in this process, not just as a bulk of abstract knowledge, but rather as selected packages as they appear useful for the interpretation of happenings.

In practice such an educational model would have the following features:

1. The prerequisite to any larger input of theory must be a minimal exposure to practice in the area of studies (happenings) – that is, the more experience (or to use Piper's terminology, 'happenings') a person brings into the educational process, the higher the learning achievement.
2. Theoretical input ought to serve the interpretation of practice; that is, practice must occur in the teaching process.
3. A successful learning experience will lead to an '*Aha!*-Experience' and this will enhance learning motivation.
4. Reflection needs time and a certain distancing from practice; longer periods of intensive academic studies are not wrong in principle but need to be conducted as reflection and interpretation in an inductive learning process and not as the pure transmission of abstract knowledge.
5. Periods of studies will always produce a certain surplus of abstract theoretical knowledge which cannot be immediately integrated into the student's practice. This is not a problem if this time of theoretical studies is not too long and if periods of action and involvement follow.

6. Action-experience-practice and reflection-theory must be linked together and not just stand side by side in isolation.

The implementation of such a paradigm of education results in an integration of theory and practice in a way which moves far beyond all the attempts to bridge the gap within the frame of the old paradigm. Such models have been used in some TEE programs (Kinsler 1981:41–3) and in Clinical Pastoral Education (cf. Zehr and Egli).

(3) CONTEXTUAL LEARNING

It follows from the concept of inductive learning that the new paradigm emphasises learning in the context of every day life and work. Concepts such as *learning by doing, on the job training* and *experience-based learning* are frequently used in recent approaches to theological education (cf. Cochrane; Dearborn; Kinsler 1981). Adult education underlines the fact that learning occurs only in interaction with 'surrounding material and social reality,' and it therefore applies methodologies which help the learner to interact consciously and systematically with their context of living and working (Raapke and Schulenberg:46–47). This implies that learning is not possible detached and distanced from the context for which the educational process should prepare the student. Kinsler, drawing from Freire's educational concepts, identifies *conscientisation* and *liberation* as key features of a new paradigm of theological education (1981:47–57). This means that students are not distanced from their context of life and ministry and filled up with detached propositional truth to be applied later in ministry. On the contrary, through the educational process which takes place in the students' own context, the students learn to reflect upon their world and their problems, are enabled to take action to solve the problems and in so-doing are liberated to become more truly human (Kinsler 1981:48–49). For Kinsler, the paradigmatic shift towards inductive and contextual learning is put into practice in Extension Education; however, not every programme which carries the name TEE achieves this level of integration of theory and practice. TEE can be practised as a mere instrument for the purely deductive delivery of pre-packed knowledge.[23]

The notion of more context-based ministerial training has also been adopted by recent models of pastoral training in the western context. Many churches have set up alternative educational structures to train their pastors in their contexts instead of bringing them to a traditional seminary campus for several years. For example, the Mennonite Church in North America has set up a concept of *Conference-Based Pastoral Education* implementing insights from TEE and Clinical Pastoral Education (CPE) (Zehr). The significance in such models of pastoral education is the fact, 'that the congregation becomes the central context for equipping persons for ministry' (Zehr and Egli:110).

However, the context-based paradigm of education, which emphasises involvement instead of distancing, has not remained unchallenged. Despite the importance of *involvement* as a crucial element in the educational process, *distancing* must be considered as equally important. *Distancing (distanciation)*, as Farley points out, is an important aspect in the educational process. 'Without such distancing education takes on the character of underwriting the student's agenda and has little or no function in criticizing, modifying, or expanding that agenda' (1981:105). A life transforming educational process also includes critical reflection (Duraisingh:43–44), and such critical reflection requires occasional detachment and distancing. Practical involvement does not automatically lead to a learning experience; this can only be secured through critical reflection on the practical experience. Thus, in the new paradigm, the pendulum should not swing from one-sidedly detached and deductive studies toward an equally one-sided experiential learning. This would be naive. Local, church-integrated theological education is in danger of becoming narrow-minded and even sectarian. If single independent churches start their own programs of theological education, the ecumenical horizon of theological education may be at jeopardy. It should not be overlooked that there is a certain value in the educational institution's role as a centre of critical reflection in regard to the church. The external educational institution can provide room for detached critical reflection and expertise which goes beyond the church's possibilities, and it can widen students' horizons toward a global and ecumenical perspective. This is a valid and important aspect of the ministry of external educational institutions (cf. Kirk 1983:50). To use Bosch's terminology again, it may be wise to call for a *creative tension* between church-integrated theological education and educational institutions which also regard the church critically (cf. Kirk 1983:48–51). Consequently, in the new paradigm, the world and the church provide the primary context for theological education; however, it will be wise not to neglect the value of external institutions of theological studies and training. The result is an educational partnership between churches, society and educational institutions (cf. Kemper; Mitchell; Schipani:30–32).

(4) EPISTEMOLOGICAL IMPLICATIONS

At this point we have to realise that we have once again touched on issues of epistemological significance. While in the old model which has been criticised, the movement tends to flow from theory = truth to practice = application, new pedagogical models call for a hermeneutical circulation which sees the process of approaching truth as interaction between the *text* of the Bible, the *context* of the ecclesial community and the *pre-text* of the real life situation (Schipany:31).[24] This implies that truth is not a set of unchangeable propositional statements to be transmitted, but rather something which is open to the searching process of hermeneutical circulation (Schipani: 30–33; cf. Duraisingh:42–45; Mitchell). This does not necessarily imply an open process which can lead anywhere, driven only by contextual circumstances, communal group-dynamics and individual subjectivity, as many may fear. Schipani states that it must be based on the conviction that 'the Bible is viewed as the normative standard for faithfulness of life, ministry and thought' (:31). However, the key issue in inductive, contextual learning is that teacher and students are engaged in a common search for a deeper understanding of truth. Kinsler enunciates this as a challenge: 'In this process no one teaches anyone; people learn together in the real world' (1981:49). It is obvious that teachers have to learn a new role as they engage in this new educational paradigm.

(5) SUMMARY AND CONSEQUENCES

We have defined a third axiom of a new paradigm of theological education by pointing to a radical pedagogical shift articulated by a variety of educators and theologians coming from different contexts, associated with such terms as, *inductive* and *contexual learning*. All these concepts focus on the *process* of theological education, on *how* theological education is carried out; and they all emphasis the urgent need for new models of theological training which take the students' context more seriously, facilitate the student's development toward maturity and set students free to become life-long learners.

The pedagogical focus is not, as might first be imagined, that the gap between theory and practice must be successfully bridged by application. The claim is that 'praxis is *not only the goal but also the foundation of theory*' (Duraisingh:36). The new paradigm of theological education introduces a new hermeneutics which understands the task of theology as critical reflection on practice Such a hermeneutic has been advocated forcefully by theologies of liberation and signifies no less than a break with traditional epistemology (Freire 1973:71–104; Gutierrez:6–13; cf. Frostin; Bosch 1991:423–25). Beyond the justified critical assessment of contextual hermeneutics,[25] it can be claimed that contextual pedagogy is a widely acknowledged element of a new paradigm of theological education.

In this educational model (1) the process of learning includes concrete involvement and commitment (Duraisingh:36), as well as (2) distanciation and reflection (Farley 1981:105). This means that theory and practice are not understood – as in the old paradigm – as abstract truth which can be learned theoretically beforehand and then applied to various contexts but rather as the interrelationship of contextual commitment, involvement, action and experience on the one hand, with, on the other hand, reflection on and theoretical explanation of such practical experiences (cf. Duraisingh:44).

If such a learning process is successfully carried out, it will lead to a mutual influence between practice and theory. (1) Practical, contextual involvement influences theory, and critical reflection alters attitudes, behaviours and action. (2) Critical reflection and theoretical explanations lead to a deeper understanding of the experience, and practical involvement leads to a deeper understanding of theories. Given this definition of the educational process, it is also evident that neither distinct cognitive accumulation of knowledge, nor constant involvement in practice can, by themselves, be seen as effective learning experiences. Both involvement and distancing, both action and reflection are needed in contextual theological education. This means that teachers and educational institutions must say farewell to some of the pedagogical methodologies they have used in the past and grown up with and learn new ways of relating to their students.

4. Integrative Curriculum: Beyond the Legacy of Fragmentation

A fourth area needing a paradigmatic shift is curriculum design. Once more, this opens up an entire field of educational theory (for introduction to the field, see Lewy). In view of theological education, the problem of the curriculum has its specific history, most comprehensively analysed by Farley. Any attempt to move toward a new paradigm able to solve these historical problems must take Farley's analysis as a point of departure. We deliberately claim this in spite of the facts that Farley's analysis is almost twenty years old and has virtually disappeared from the current discussion on the renewal of theological education. We will argue that Farley's analysis is not only still valid, but that he also points convincingly towards possible solutions.[26]

Again, the old paradigm provides the point of departure:

a) The Old Paradigm: Fragmentation of Theology and Theological Education

The problem of the fragmentation of theological education, as Farley has traced it throughout the history of the *classical model* of theological education, has been introduced earlier (p. 45) In order to grasp the extent of the problem, the dimensions of the fragmentation need to be summarised at this point. According to Farley, the major problematic elements of contemporary (North American) theological education are: (1) 'the dominance of the fourfold pattern'; (2) 'the absence of a material unity of studies'; (3) 'a functionalist version of the clerical paradigm as that unity'; and (4) 'a theory-practice mind-set' (1983:127).

(1) THE FOURFOLD PATTERN OF THE THEOLOGICAL CURRICULUM

The widely lamented present day fragmentation of theological studies is partly the product of the encyclopaedic organisation of theology and its divisions into various – traditionally four – fields of studies. To use Farley's terminology, the shift from *study-of-theology as a single subject matter* to the study of the theological encyclopaedia as an aggregate of more or less unrelated subjects can be traced back to the Enlightenment and its effects on theological studies in the university context (Farley 1983:49–72).[27] This resulted in the 'dispersion of *theologia* into the theological sciences' in the context of the university (:57). More precisely, the fragmentation can be observed on at least four levels. (1) The subject of theology is divided into at least four distinct disciplines (Bible, history, systematics and practice), each with several sub-disciplines. In the context of the modern university, each discipline employs its own methodology, taken from other, secular disciplines of the university (thus, historical-critical methodology to inquire into ancient texts, philosophy to engage in fundamental theoretical discussion and human sciences to reflect on the various aspects of the clerical task). Furthermore, each discipline, and occasionally even sub-discipline, developed its own academic world, consisting of a distinct literature, academic journals, technical terminology and professional associations. Today this process of fragmentation has reached a very sophisticated level. No scholar can today be expected to master even all the sub-disciplines of one discipline, never mind the entire field of theology (Mildenberger:143). (2) On a deeper level, the fourfold pattern also contains a theory-practice fragmentation. Three *theoretical* disciplines (Bible, history, systematics) stand over against the field of *practical* theology, whose task is to apply the theory to the realities of the pastoral task. We have discussed this issue in the previous chapter. At this point we only affirm that the alienation between the theoretical disciplines and practical theology is critical. To take only one example: the theoretical results of the historical-critical investigation of ancient texts and the pastoral task of preaching a relevant message are often separated by an insurmountable gulf (Bohren 1963:85–117).

(2) THE ABSENCE OF A MATERIAL UNITY OF STUDIES

Yet the fragmentation goes beyond the curricular organisation. As Gerhard Ebeling states:

> The study of theology is beset by a crisis in orientation. Because our access to the unity and totality that constitutes the subject matter of theology is disrupted, the main domain of its subject matter and task has broken apart and crumbled into a bewildering conglomeration of individual items (1978:1).

Historically speaking, the shift from the *study-of-theology as a single subject matter* to the fragmentation of the curriculum discussed above also indicated a shift in the *ratio studiorum*, the rational for the study of theology. In the period of the study-of-theology, Farley says,

> the *ratio* has more the character of personal exhortation ... It says in effect: 'These are the things you must do to deepen and sustain the disposition already set in you by the Spirit, to lay hold of and understand the things made available to you in revelation.' The 'studies' therefore include prayer, learning biblical languages, reading books which set forth doctrines, and, above all, reading Scripture. The transition from the study of theology [as one subject matter] to theological encyclopedia engendered an entirely new meaning of *ratio studiorum*. The rationale for studies becomes a justification for the organization of specific 'sciences' within an overall university faculty and science (Farley 1983:53–54).

Thus, one significant result of the shift from the study-of-theology as a single subject matter to the encyclopaedic, fourfold organisation of theological disciplines is the loss of the material unity of theological studies. Today, this loss is taken as the insurmountable legacy of theological studies (Mildenberger:76, 143). Ultimately, this even means a significant change in the meaning of *theology* itself. 'In brief,' Farley states, 'this shift is from theology viewed as a *habitus*, an act of practical knowledge having the primary character of wisdom, to theology used as generic term for a cluster of disciplines.' And he concludes, 'crucial to this shift is the definition of theology by its reference and not by the subject's act' (1983:81).

(3) THE CLERICAL PARADIGM AS FUNCTIONAL UNITY OF STUDIES

Pietism, as well as Schleiermacher's *Brief Outline of Theological Studies*, have been acknowledged as the introduction of the clerical paradigm of theological studies.[28] According to Farley, the clerical paradigm was a way to find a new *ratio studiorum* for theological studies. The training of clergy became the 'teleological' rationale for theological education. The aggregate of subjects, organised according to the fourfold pattern of the curriculum, gained a teleological unity through the aim of pastoral training. Schleiermacher's thesis of the teleological, clerical rationale as the unifying centre of theology is still advocated in contemporary introductions to theological studies (Mildenberger:14–16; Dembrowski:188–90). While on the one hand the clerical paradigm has contributed to the unity of theological studies and their orientation towards the church, it has on the other hand also introduced a new set of problems. (1) It assigned the term *practical* to the clerical ministry, which is a serious limitation of the concept of Christian praxis to certain ministerial functions. Practical theology does not really deal with the praxis of Christian faith but with the theory of the clerical profession. (2) Furthermore, it contributed to the unhealthy division between theoretical and practical disciplines. By assigning the task of application to practical theology, the theoretical disciplines were left without the mandate to conduct theological studies in a holistic way. Thus, '*theoria* is the business of Bible, theology, and history; *praxis* the business of homiletics, education, and pastoral care' (Farley 1981:103). (3) Finally, the clerical focus of theological training reinforces the separation of *clergy* and *laity*. Theology and theological studies become the privilege of the professional minister, or in other words, theological studies become professional training, excluding those who do not seek a clerical career.

Conclusion: The result of the historical development of theological studies is, in the words of Farley, a 'dispersed encyclopedia' (1981:106); 'the curriculum as an aggregate of studies does not make sense as pertaining to a subject matter.' The 'student's experience of theological education tends to be that of a miscellany of courses. Since a unifying rationale is present neither in the curriculum nor in the student, there is little pattern which makes visible what is important and why.' Therefore, 'the student's education is pieced together from areas of studies solipsistically related to each other. The paradigm which would relate each one to the one thing, the study of theology, is absent' (1981:106–08). All the recent introductions to the study of theology struggle with this legacy of the encyclopaedic fourfold pattern of theological education and try to suggest some therapy to overcome the enormous and paralysing fragmentation of theological studies (e.g., Bohren 1964; Mildenberger; Ebeling 1975; Dembrowski to mention only some of the German works). There seems to be a desperate need for a new paradigm – but only little success has been made so far.

b) The New Paradigm: Holistic Theological Education

A new paradigm of theological education can only be reached once the fragmentation of theology has been surmounted. The major issue is, in Farley's terms, the recovery of *theologia* as the existential unifying centre of theological studies. Farley claims that the problem of fragmentation is not merely of a structural, but of a theological nature.[29] His thesis is, that 'the reform of theological education can be accomplished only by a theological solution to the problem of the unity and branches of theological studies' (1981:93), and later he affirms that 'the reform of theological education is not a technical problem to be solved by new pedagogical strategies and curricular constructions but a theological task' (1981:109–10). The theological task Farley demands is first of all 'the task of discerning the single subject matter of theological studies, ... a subject matter which constitutes the unity of theological education' – in other words, the recovery of 'a governing paradigm' (1981:110–11).

As mentioned above, most of the contemporary introductions to theological studies address the problem of the fragmented curriculum and suggest some solutions.

(1) MODEST PROPOSALS

In the context of the German university system, the present situation is widely acknowledged as an unavoidable fact, resulting from the development of the theological disciplines as sciences in the post-Enlightenment period. According to Mildenberger, the process of differentiation [Differenzierung] and specialisation [Spezialisierung] cannot be stopped. The extent of the field, as well as new methodologies, will rather call for further differentiation and specialisation. On the one hand, he calls for a new theory which establishes the internal unity of theology (:143–44, cf. 147–48), on the other hand, he confesses that there is no conception of theology available which would allow us to deduct a convincing division of the curriculum (:76; cf. 143–44; cf. Dembrowski).

Nonetheless, Mildenberger suggests two modest proposals: (1) he advocates Schleiermacher's teleological model, in which the ministerial task provides the unifying centre of theological studies (:14–16). (2) He calls for an increased co-operation between the various theological disciplines. Each scholar has to be concerned not only with his field of specialisation but with the unity of theology (:148). As important as these suggestions are, in the light of Farley's critique, they do not touch the centre of the problem.

Dembrowski suggests a two-part strategy to solve the problem. On the material level, he claims that God and humanity provide the unifying subject matter. Beyond this, he too suggests church ministries as a unifying centre on the functional level (:186–90) – but he sees no way to escape the problem of fragmentation on the curricular level (:191–92)

While such modest proposals intend to limit the problem, they do not really reach the centre of the issue. In order to do that an integration on four levels must be achieved: (1) on the *existential* level; (2) on the *functional* level; (3) on the *material* level; and (4) on the *structural* level.

(2) THE RECOVERY OF THEOLOGIA AS HABITUS

Farley's own proposal may be called *existential*. Reaching back to the earlier meaning of *theologia* as '*habitus* of the human soul' (1983:31), he wants to recover theology as 'a personal and existential wisdom or understanding' (1983:153). He calls for theological studies which reflect 'in some way the structure of faith itself, the structure of Christian existence and how ministry reflects such' (1981:110). For Farley, the unifying centre will not be found in theology as a theoretical subject matter or in some sort of central theme, which can serve as an organising principle of the curriculum but in 'faith's prereflective insightfulness' which he calls 'belief-full knowing.' This actually refers to faith itself as 'the way in which the human being lives in and toward God and the world under the impact of redemption' (1983:156). In a certain way, Farley advocates what Karl Barth, in his late work *Evangelical Theology: An Introduction*, summarised with the following words:

> Theology itself is a word, a human response; yet what makes it theology is not its own word or response but the Word which it hears and to which it *responds*. Theology stands and falls with the Word of God, for the Word of God precedes all theological words by creating, arousing, and challenging them. Should theology wish to be more or less or anything other than action in response to that Word, its thinking and speaking would be empty, meaningless, and futile (Barth:16–17).

Helmut Thielicke refers to the same issue with his remark that theologians too easily shift from the second person (speaking with God) to the third person (speaking about God), when talking with or about God (:32–34). What Farley, Barth and Thielicke are calling for is the existential dimension of theology as a unifying centre which renders it possible to integrate theology as subject matter.[30]

(3) TOWARD A MISSIONARY CENTRE OF THEOLOGY

In addition to this existential dimension of theological study, we need a *functional* orientation as an integrative centre. This study suggests taking the first axiom of a new paradigm – namely, the *missionary nature of the church* and consequently of theology and theological studies – as a further element which may contribute to the unity of theological studies. This is based on the understanding that 'mission is the mother of theology'; in other words, theology is the reflective task of the church as it moves on in its mission (Loewen). In a certain way this is also a teleological approach, but it moves clearly beyond the traditional clerical *telos* of theological training. The *missio Dei,* and deduced from it the people of God in its mission, provide the centre and perspective of theological studies. While this is a functional rationale for the integration of theological study, it definitely constitutes more than a merely pragmatic aim for theological education; it is, in the light of the *missio Dei*, a truly theological centre. Consequently, the church in mission provides not only the *functional* but also the *material* integrative centre.

(4) INTEGRATIVE CURRICULUM

Finally, a new paradigm of theological education will call for curriculum design which pays attention to integrative mechanisms. Several sets of such mechanisms can be identified. (1) First, on a *diachronic* level the sequence of courses ought to be ordered in such a manner that a logical development of the learning process is supported (Aebli:304–14). An advanced form of diachronic curriculum design is the 'spiral-curriculum,' which emphasises the sequence of courses as well as the repetition of subject matters (Aebli:310–12). (2) Second, a *synchronic* integration will focus on the relation of simultaneously taught subject matters – for example, by semester themes (Aebli:314–24). (3) Furthermore, integration can be enhanced by emphasising the *integral dimension* of all courses but also (4) by offering courses which *intentionally* focus on integration (Dembrowski:191). (5) Finally, integrative curriculum also pays attention to the *developmental and educational stage* of the students – that is, it engages a student in learning at a level appropriate to their capability to learn in an integrative fashion.[31]

(5) SUMMARY AND CONSEQUENCES

The transformation of theological education in the direction of the fourth axiom of a new paradigm leads to the following consequences:

1. Farley rightly foresees that if the single subject matter of theological education – in our case *the church in mission* – determines curriculum design, then 'the internal structure of that study and how that structure may be translated into a pattern of studies' need to be discerned (1981:113). What he calls for is a derivation of the internal division of sub-themes and areas of studies from the newly defined centre and not – as was the case in the old paradigm – by the traditional and unquestionable fields of studies. With this, Farley suggests nothing less than the radical rethinking of the traditional fields of studies. He concludes:

> Any significant addressing of this third task will inevitably involve certain criticism and negations, certain modifications of the present patterns of theological education. If the previously argued criticisms hold, both the fourfold and twofold patterns [i.e. theory-practice] would be transcended. If the present scholarly specialities are no longer the criteria for organizing theological study, this implies another mode of faculty existence in the school than through guild-like specialities (1981:113)

This again implies a foundational shift. The traditional fields of studies will no longer automatically define the curriculum. They have to fit in a new structure of studies which is shaped by the centre and the orientation of the church-in-mission. Some traditional areas of scholarly specialisation, or at least some parts of them, may become irrelevant. Others need to be adjusted to the new centre of theology. All areas of studies have to rethink their agenda in the light of this unifying centre. New areas of research and study will emerge. And, above all, more interaction, interdisciplinary studies and cross-disciplinary teaching is called for (cf. Farley 1981:113). Furthermore, Farley draws our attention to the nomenclature of the traditional paradigm of studies. His point is that the curriculum sends out signals 'concerning the unity, structure and perhaps sequence of theological study' (1981:114). On a very practical level, the catalogue organisation should display the 'study of theology in pattern of work which reflect in some way the structure of faith itself' (1981:110). In other words, in the new paradigm, the nomenclature of theology and theological education reflects the *church in mission* and not (only) *academia*. According to Farley, this calls for a new definition of courses in terms of content and terminology (1981:113–14). All of this belongs to the *material* and *curricular* side of the integrative process.

2. However, the new paradigm is also characterised by the *existential integration* of theological education. The goal of the educational process is not a cognitive knowledge of atomised subjects and sub-subjects but a deeper understanding of *theologia* as a single subject matter, ultimately as a *habitus* or an existential, life-transforming experience. It is appropriate to use the term *holistic* in this connection, pointing to the fact that in holism the parts are placed in an organic relationship in such a way that the whole is more than the sum of the parts. How can this be achieved in the process of theological education? (1) First of all, the time and energy devoted to the study of narrow subjects in the dispersed curriculum – a task which is to some extent unavoidable (languages, data of biblical background studies, historical investigations and the like) – must be balanced by elements (courses, reading, discussion) which contribute to the integration of the diverse subjects. In other words, integrative courses are of at least equal importance for a healthy educational process, as are in-depth studies of single disciplines. (2) Furthermore, integrative learning is promoted by process-oriented curriculum design, understood as the combination and succession of courses which support integration rather than fragmentation. (3) Finally, perhaps the most significant aspect is that integrative learning must be applied to each student's stage in the process of learning. Since integration takes place when the external input melds with the internal being of a person, it cannot be forced upon a group of people in an uniformed fashion. Each individual deserves appropriate guidance in the learning process. This calls for people-oriented, rather than content-oriented, teaching and learning.

One of the interesting proposals of an integrated, mission-oriented curriculum of theological education has been put forward recently by Andrew Kirk of Selly Oak Colleges, Birmingham (1997:53–61). Kirk writes: 'My model is based on four cardinal points of theological discipleship – pilgrimage, message, communication, and action – which, I believe, faithfully reflect a missionary theology done in Christ's way' (1997:53). Furthermore, Kirk's model contains four learning stages, leading from (a) the analysis of the students (Kirk prefers the term participants) background (understanding a persons pilgrimage), to (b) cultural and social analysis (understanding the world), to (c) message and communication (understanding the Christian faith); and finally to (d) action. This proposal incorporates many of the features of the paradigm outlined in this study.

5. Conclusion

We have thus synthesised the key elements of a reorientation in theological education, which has been developing since the early 1960s. We have structured the various strands into four key dimensions of what might be called an new paradigm of theological education. The four dimensions are closely interrelated. It became evident that in that process, many elements of the old paradigm are not completely substituted. In some sense, the new paradigm is a shift in perspective, a change of priorities, a new point of departure. We can summarise it as follows:

1. The first key element claims that the *missio Dei* and the *church participating in that mission of God* provide the orientation and the agenda of theological education. By applying the *dimension-intention* concept this vision is incorporated into the curriculum. With this, the traditional marginalisation of mission as well as the lack of orientation in theological education are surmounted.

2. The second key element emphasises *andragogical* education as it has been developing in adult education. It is basically *people-oriented* and not *institution-oriented*. This means that it calls for theological education which is *goal-oriented and pragmatic*; hence, it defines and measures the output of the educational process in view of personal and professional needs. Furthermore, it takes seriously the concepts of *self-directed, self-responsible* and *lifelong learning*. In the new paradigm, education must be made accessible to those who need and seek education. This calls for flexibility. In this way, the tradition of institution-oriented, elitist and often inaccessible theological education may be surmounted.

3. The third key element has been identified in the area of the integration of theory and practice. We claimed that the shift from *deductive transmission of theories* to a *process of inductive learning* stands at the centre of this integration. It follows that teachers must learn to play a new role as facilitators in an action-reflection process in which they are no longer the ones who know everything but become learners themselves. Consequently, the process of theological education can best be defined as an

interaction between teacher and student as they engage in action and reflection, integrating theory and practice. It also suggests shifting the centre of theological training from the academic institution to the context of the students. This implies that the church itself must be involved in the shaping of theological education and that theological education is best delivered in close relation to the context of the church engaged in mission. With this the traditional forms of education based on deductive transmission of theory in the detached context of educational institutions are surmounted.

4. The fourth key element suggests *the church in mission* as the teleological-functional and material unifying centre of theological education which must find its expression in the curriculum. This indicates a move beyond the fragmentation of the encyclopaedic fourfold pattern of the traditional paradigm.

Occasionally we have used the term *emerging new paradigm*. The question may arise as to whether – or to what degree and in which ways – the described paradigm is really emerging. Similar to the reality we observed in the case of Bosch's paradigm in mission, it is appropriate to say that at least in part, the new paradigm is emerging in the realisation of renewal in many schools around the world. Ferries has shown in his analysis of nine evangelical schools from different continents that there is a measurable development toward the implementation of the elements of the ICAA *Manifesto*. He also points to the fact that there are areas of deficiencies where more groundwork needs to be done. Of course, the *Manifesto* does not incorporate all aspects developed in this study, but Ferris's study demonstrates a certain degree of realisation. In his doctoral thesis (1987), Bongani Mazibuko compares mission training in the context of the Project in Partnership between Black and White at Birmingham, England, with the Alternative Theological and Staff Development Experiment of Colgate Divinity School in Rochester, New York; he likewise compares the Black Church Experience in the context of the Research in Black Church Studies with Research Study in Oral History at Garrett-Evangelical Seminary, Evanston, Illinois. All these experimental initiatives in theological education are clearly indicators of the paradigm we have outlined in this section. One could add, as further evidence of a new paradigm's emergence, the Seattle Association of Theological Education (Dearborn), Selly Oak Colleges in Birmingham, England, The Association for Theological Education by Extension in India (TAFTEE) (Samuel and Sugden 1983c), the educational initiatives and programmes put forward by The Oxford Centre for Mission Studies in Oxford, England, and *the Institut für Gemeindebau und Weltmission* in Zurich.

However, it goes without saying that the paradigm put forward in this study has primarily been emerging in the heads and hearts of innovative theological educators. The aforementioned list of schools which are moving in the direction of the new paradigm cannot hide the fact, that this new paradigm is still a vision, a proposal for theological education in the twenty first century. As such, the outlined paradigm provides valid criteria for the evaluation of theological education.

By analysing evangelical theological education in German-speaking Europe, this study now provides an exemplary evaluation of theological education based on the criteria outlined in this section.

Notes

1 An extensive bibliography has been compiled by Lagerwerf (:69–74).

2 One of the most significant studies moving in that direction is Max L. Stackhouse's *Apologia: Contextualisation, Globalisation and Mission in Theological Education* (1988). He addresses the major issues in the global church today and relates it to theological education.

3 This study concentrates on reflection in the realm of theological education (not including developments in Roman Catholic theological education). However, the author is aware that the recent shifts we are observing in theological education must be seen in relation to developments in secular education since the 1960s. Kinsler writes: '... we have noted that the theological education by extension movement runs parallel to or is part of a worldwide revolution in education' (1981:61). The WCC's Office of Education, established in 1968 (WCC 1970), the UNESCO's International Council for Distance Education and the rise of the Open University in the United Kingdom since 1963 (Kinsler 1981:62–63) are only a few of the strands of that broader stream of recent educational developments.

4 See also in German, Engel and Dietrich 1990. Extensive bibliography of German publications, pp. 228–31.

5 'A Brief Introduction to ICAA' by Kemp (1995, 314–15). Several texts are published in the ICAA Monograph Series. Two recent issues of *Evangelical Review of Theology* have been devoted to evangelical theological education and ICAA, 14/1 (1990) and 19/3 (1995).

6 The call for a *missionary dimension of theology* has already be formulated earlier, probably first by Meyer (1958:221, 224), cf. J.Schmidt (1973:195+96).

7 A conception of a missionary theology which meets this criteria has recently been put forward by Andrew Kirk. He suggests to focus theology and therefore theological education around the 'two tasks of theology': (1) 'To make sense of the whole of life by referring to God' (1997:31–39), and (2) 'To be an agent of transformation, so that the whole of life may reflect God's intention' (1997:39–42).

8 What this means for each of the traditional disciplines has been suggested by Bosch (1982:27–30; 1991:495–96); see also Adamek (1969:108–10). Jongeneel, who concludes that at the end of the 20th century that 'Theology of Mission' has been transformed into 'Missionary Theology' (1997:1), presents in the second volume of his *Philosophy, Science, and Theology of Mission* (1997) probably the most comprehensive attempt at a missionary theology to date.

9 Already Meyer (1958:224), 'It is my conviction that the science of mission has to play a critical role over against the other disciplines, hence it must have a certain independence.' See also Myklebust 1989:101–02.

10 All these terms have their specific history and meaning in international adult education. See definitions in *Lifelong Education for Adults. An International Handbook*, edited by Colin J. Titmus (1989).

11 The term 'andragogy' was first used by E. Rosenstock at Berlin in 1924. Since Heinrich Hanselmann's *Andragogik: Wesen, Möglichkeiten, Grenzen der Erwachsenenbildung* (1952) the term became common in German-speaking Europe and some other European countries (cf. Franz Pöggeler's *Erwachsenenbildung: Einführung in die Andragogik* (1974). M. S. Knowles (1980) has introduced the term to the English speaking world. (For a summary of the concept of 'andragogy' see Krajnc:19–21).

12 Kinsler refers to study centres, lay training centres, centres for urban mission and training, various decentralised programs, clinical pastoral education, community-based theological learning, cell groups for study and mutual care and team ministry, theological reflection in liberation movements and ad hoc educational events (workshops, conferences, short courses, etc.) (1982:133).

13 See also the educational process suggest by Duraisingh (1992:42–45).

14 The fact that these theoretical advantages of TEE are not automatically put in to practice simply by implementing a TEE structure has been demonstrated by several critical studies on TEE experiences (cf. Mulholland).

15 A more recent statement of AMBS (1992) has affirmed this philosophy (AMBS:23)

16 Samuel (1996:4) states, 'Theological education must relate to the academy and the church in mission.' This author would suggest changed priorities: to the church in mission primarily and as part of this mission also to the academy.

17 'Felt needs' are an important component of the educational process in relation to the student's motivation (Gage and Berliner:277–80).

18 Cf. Piper in the introduction to his proposal of a new models of pastoral training (1981:9): 'Since about ten years the theory-praxis-problem has been keeping on the move again academic theology as well as the church. P. Cornehl used the following words to describe the recent problem: It is not an inadmissible dramatisation if we speak of a gulf between systematic-theological science and the religious life of the church. The gulf is more then a helpful distance between theory and praxis, it indicates a severe destruction.'

19 Especially in his article 'Extension: An Alternative Model of Theological Education' (1981), where he uses the terms *contextualisation*, *conscientisation* and *liberation* to define the structure, the methodology, and the process of theological education.

20 Farley uses the two terms distancing and distanciation interchangeably (1981:105). Another common term describing the same thing is *detachement*.

21 This is not to be confused with the concept of *inductive* Bible study, a method of Bible reading which is very much appreciated by evangelicals.

22 See also the related and somewhat broader term *experiential learning* in adult education (Titmus:193–95; Raapke and Schulenberg:74–92).

23 For a critical assessment of TEE see Mulholland:17–23, and Ferries 1990a:13–15. I am also indebted to Patricia Harrison who, through her expertise in TEE, has given me an appropriate understanding of the sometimes disappointing

realities in many TEE programs. It seems that Kinsler's vision is highly idealistic and far from being put into practice in many cases.

24 Schipani refers to the Latin American sources of this view, especially to Carlos Mester.

25 The most serious critique addresses the tendency in contextual theology to let the context determine theology and minimise biblical authority (Bosch 1991:425–32; Padilla 1986:108–12).

26 Ferries, for instance, acknowledges Farley's analysis but blames him for not having put forward convincing solutions (1990:18–20).

27 Farley observes the shift between Gerhard and Nösselt (1983:56): 'When we move from John Gerhard's *Methodus studii theologici* (1620) to Johann Nösselt's *Anweisung zur Bildung angehender Theologen* (1771), we find ourselves in a different theological world. Gerhard sets forth a method of study and life pertinent to forming a disposition (*habitus*) in which God and the things of God are known for the practical purpose of edification, salvation, and glorifying God. Nösselt offers an analysis of the requirements of the "scholarly knowledge of religion" as these fall into various "sciences." '

28 Schleiermacher was not the first who proposed the clerical task as main rational of the study of theology (Farley refers to Mosheim and Bahrdt), but he helped this approach to become the dominant paradigm in theological education (Farley 1983:82–3).

29 This does not suggest that careful curriculum design based on educational theories would not make a vital contribution to a more integrated curriculum in theology. On the contrary, it is imperative that measurable objectives are formulated, that the different subject-matters are interrelated diachronically as well as synchronically and that procedures of quality assurance are incorporated (on curriculum design see Aebli:282–324).

30 In the German context this existential dimension as integrative centre of theological education has been advocated by some theologians of *the Schools* (Bockmühl 1985:38–41; Frische 1979; Riecker 1984).

31 Cf. Michael Dieterich who bases his concept of stages in professional education on Piaget's theory (:101–09). In a similar way Ross Bender applies Piaget to Christian Education (R.T.Bender 1997:92–93) However, more recent reflections on developmental stages move beyond Piaget, i.e., Kohlberg, Fowler and Oser (cf. Nipkow and Schweitzer and Fowler) and add additional insights to this issue.

CHAPTER 11

Analysis: Mission Training in Evangelical Theological Education in German-Speaking Europe[1]

This chapter investigates[2] the schools of the *KBA* between 1964 and 1996[3] based on the following data:

1. The records of the annual assemblies of the *KBA* from 1964 to 1996[4]
2. The publications and records of the EEAA[5]
3. Publications on the history of particular schools
4. Archival data of a selected number of schools[6]
5. The 1980 survey on mission training conducted by the *KBA*[7]
6. A 1996 survey conducted by the *FHM* on behalf of the *KBA* [8]
7. A 1996 survey of mission studies in German evangelical Bible Schools and seminaries conducted by Traugott Böker of WEC International[9]

The analysis follows the four criteria established in the previous section.

1. *The Schools* in the Light of Thesis 1: Mission: From the Margin to the Centre

The analysis must start with a reference to the heritage of the Bible school movement. As pointed out in the historical introduction (Part Two) the Bible school movement had world mission at its heart from its very beginnings. Bosch calls for a missionary dimension of theological education as a whole, and this was certainly the case in the Bible school movement. Almost all schools under consideration stand in this tradition. We investigate recent developments in greater detail from this standpoint.

a) The Era of the Bible School Model

In the first decade of the *KBA*, the ethos of the Bible school movement was still predominant. Life at *the Schools* was shaped by a revivalist and missionary spirit. At the same time the curricula contained only a small number of explicit mission courses. One prominent course in many schools was called *Missionskunde* (missions information) which dealt mainly with introductions to the various mission fields abroad. Missions was obviously understood as foreign missions in the traditional sense.

This spiritual and missionary ethos of the Bible school movement can also be observed in the first annual gathering of the newly founded *KBA*, as the following list of topics demonstrates:

1965 The aim of spiritual renewal in our schools and the occupation of intellectual learning (Otto Riecker)[10]
1966 The prerequisites of revival (Otto Riecker)
1967 The significance of missionary practice for Christian being and ministry and its integration into the life educational institutions (Otto Riecker)[11]
1968 Revival-oriented life at the Bible schools (Otto Riecker)
Our preparation for world mission (Ernst Schrupp)
1969 Our missionary preparation in our educational work (Ernest Klassen)
1970 The Bible school as vehicle of revival (Georg Würfel)
1972 Teaching New Testament exegesis and church history in a non-theological way (Otto Riecker)

In the first years of the *KBA* virtually every conference addressed the issues of spiritual revival and missionary dedication and how this kind of a climate can be created and maintained at the Bible schools and colleges. This self-understanding of the *KBA* schools clearly echoes the legacy of the Bible school movement.

b) The Contribution by Otto Riecker[12]

This first period of the *KBA* cannot be understood properly without recognising the significance of Otto Riecker. This Lutheran pastor and theologian, born in 1896, completed doctoral research on the evangelistic ministry of Wesley, Whitefield, Finney, Moody, Schrenk and Keller in 1935 (Riecker 1953). He was the founder of the *Bibelschule Adelshofen* and became a powerful force within the German evangelical Bible school movement in the 1960s. Riecker was a vigorous advocate of the missionary dimension of theological education. He did not call for the introduction of specialised missiological courses to the curriculum but for the missionary and spiritual permeation of theological education as a whole. He speaks of the 'air of a spiritual ministry to the world' which has to dominate every person at the school, from the director to the students, and of 'a missionary concern' which has to be in everyone's heart. 'Each one,' he emphasises, 'must have the blood group of mission, those who teach and those who learn, and no one should think in a missionary way just incidentally at certain times. A person is a missionary as a matter of life and death or is not missionary at all' (1973:42).

Though he advocated serious academic work (1974:71–77; 1984:28) he also warned of what he calls '*Theologismus*' [Theologism] (1974:78–140). His extensive study entitled *Bildung und Heiliger Geist* [*Education and Holy Spirit*] (1974) is devoted to what he sees to be the main force against authentic spirituality [*Frömmigkeitsleben*], church renewal and missionary dedication. He defines it thus:

> Theologism is a foundational approach to life ... It is the work of human thinking, starting with the human being and produced by the human being, who becomes the measure of all judgement. The theological interest is predominant; it affects the spiritual direction of the church, and dominates over spirituality (1974:129).

Theologismus, he argues, is the key enemy of spiritual life and missionary zeal. The overview of the themes dealt with at the annual gatherings of the KBA between 1965 and 1972 shows that Riecker was one of the key speakers at almost every conference. His plea – spoken and written – for the spiritual and missionary dimension of evangelical theological education must be seen as a constituting force in the early years of the *KBA*. Today, in a time of crisis, the school which he had founded is still looking back to its founder trying to recover his vision (Faix 1996).

c) From Bible Schools to Theological Colleges

In the mid 1970s changing trends within the *KBA* movement can be observed. First indicators are the assemblies of 1975 and 1976. In the context of the former there was for the first time a discussion of curricula, and the latter contained workshops on technical literature of the various fields of theological studies. This marks the beginning of a development toward more sophisticated curricula, greater academic emphasis and more advanced specialisation in the various fields of studies.

This had also affected mission studies. Several circumstances have caused mission studies to develop in new directions: (1) the need for higher theological and anthropological qualifications for missionaries in a changing missionary situation; (2) the school's pursuit of formal accreditation and recognition; and (3) a growing relationship to North American evangelical missiology.

The *Seminar für missionarische Weiterbildung*[13] of the *AEM* invited all the mission teachers of the *KBA* schools to a meeting on January 21, 1980, at *Bergstrasse*. A seminar followed the same spring, March 14 to 16 at Burbach-Holzhausen. These two meetings focused on teaching mission in Bible schools and seminaries and it issued a 'Recommendation of certain general standards for Bible believing schools.'[14] The recommendation calls for three areas of mission studies: (1) history of missions; (2) theology of mission; and (3) theology of religion. Beyond this, anthropology, methodology, indigenous churches and theologies and the missionary were suggested as possible additional courses.[15] A common nomenclature was discussed, representative syllabi designed and bibliographies put together. With this *the Schools* adopted the introduction of missiology as a subject of studies in its own right.

The implementation of curriculum and course content did not occur simultaneously in all *the Schools*. In the schools which have been investigated particularly closely, the changes have been put into practice through a new mission teacher. This adds still another dimension to the understanding of this development. The changes have to be seen in relation to a generation shift in the faculty. Many of the older mission teachers were former missionaries – to wit, practitioners and not academics; persons possessing only minimal formal theological training and certainly not advanced missiological studies. The new generation of mission teachers who have come to the various Bible Schools and seminaries since the late 1970s generally have higher degrees in formal theological education and have in most cases specialised in missiological training.

An analysis of mission courses presently taught at evangelical Bible schools and seminaries shows that all schools offer various courses in the area of mission, more or less covering the terrain recommended in 1980.[16] Nonetheless, a complete agreement regarding nomenclature and syllabi as recommended in 1980 was never reached.

All of this indicates a significant shift in mission studies in evangelical Bible schools and seminaries in Germany and Switzerland. If we may use the terms *dimension* and *intention* one more time, the thesis may be proposed that *the Schools* have improved the *intention* aspect at the cost of the *dimension* aspect. In other words they have developed a more sophisticated and specialised missiological curriculum, yet they have lost some of the missionary spirit which permeated the whole process of theological training for which Otto Riecker so desperately called. This thesis needs to be validated, and the 1996 survey provides the necessary evidence

d) 1995 and Beyond

The 1996 survey provides the following insights regarding the place and understanding of mission in the teaching at *the Schools* at the end of the period investigated in this study.

1. The questionnaires only rarely use mission terminology. For example, when the students are asked to identify what they expect from the course, none of the seventeen given options contains the terms

mission or missions (Survey 1996:68–69).[17] The few occurrences of mission terminology imply a traditional understanding of foreign missions. Thus, when students are asked what their motivation was to enter theological training, one option is 'I want to become a missionary' (Survey 1996:63–65). The question is, what do those who ask the questions mean when they use the term 'missionary'? And in fact, what do young adult persons understand when they hear the term 'missionary'?

2. The fact that such a use of mission terminology is confusing is demonstrated by students' answers. In response to the question, 'What was your motivation to enter theological training?', 76.4 per cent answered, 'To serve Jesus out of love,' 63.4 per cent chose, 'The awareness of a lost humanity.' Only at the eighth position, with 32 per cent, is the answer, 'I want to become a missionary.' While two-thirds care for lost human beings, only one third want to become missionaries. This indicates a high level of miss-communication between the leadership of *the Schools* (who formulated the questionnaire) and the students. There seems to be a need for terminological clarification.

3. Under the heading 'Desired Improvements,' any suggestion could be filled in. Of the 140 suggestions for improvement put forward by *the Schools'* faculties only four contain mission terminology:

- The expansion of missiological teaching
- Mission and Evangelisation
- Increased motivation to fulfil the mission mandate
- To show more clearly the relevance of Christian mission

If one adds the two mission-related suggestions referring to apologetics and cross-cultural practical experience, one ends up with six mission-oriented suggestions for improvement by the principals – certainly not a demonstration of a strong mission awareness, at least on the level of terminology.

The same general result can be drawn from the questionnaires filled out by students, churches and institutions: only four out of 206 suggestions mentioned by students and only seven out of 177 proposals by church-institution leaders address mission(s).

This leads to the preliminary conclusion that neither principals, nor students, nor church-institution leaders call for significant improvements in mission studies, at least not explicitly associated with the term 'mission.'

4. All questionnaires (except the one for individual faculty members) contain questions regarding the qualifications of teachers. It is astonishing to realise that none of the proposed answers refers to mission. Neither missiological studies nor mission experience are listed as possible qualifications for teachers. The questionnaire for individual faculty members asks, 'In which area do you wish further education?' In the twenty seven

different areas proposed to choose, the terms mission/missions/ missiology does not appear. Only the related term 'church planting' carries a missionary connotation. Only three out of eighty eight teachers chose 'church planting' as an area in which they desire further training. No one added an area in the field of missiology. This supports the conclusion that mission, mission studies and mission experience are neither demanded as a qualification for teachers nor desired as a field of continuing education.

The survey certainly does not reveal all aspects of mission awareness at *the Schools*. Yet in general it confirms the trend towards a marginalisation of mission in the life of evangelical Bible schools and seminaries.

e) The Traugott Böker Survey of 1996

At the same time, the call to bring mission back to the centre of evangelical theological education cannot be overlooked. At the 1996 conference of the *KBA*, Traugott Böker, Director of WEC-Germany, was asked to lead a workshop on the topic 'Mission in Evangelical Theological Education.' In preparation for that workshop, he conducted a survey among all the schools of the *KBA*.[18] This survey is a helpful addition or even amendment to the *KBA* survey. It asks specifically mission oriented questions. The results are as follows:[19]

1. The survey confirms that all schools have introduced many different missiological subjects to their curriculum. It also supports this study's earlier observation that a common nomenclature could not be introduced. Around twenty labels for mission courses are in use, making serious comparison almost impossible.

2. There are considerable differences among the number of the teaching hours devoted to mission subjects. Taking only the college level programs (at least three years of studies) the number of hours varies between fifty *(Neues Leben)* and 300 *(Liebenzell)*.[20]

3. In view of a desirable missionary dimension in the entire curriculum, it is of even greater significance to analyse in which ways and to what extent the other courses refer to mission. The survey asks this question, but the answers are difficult to interpret. Virtually all schools refer to courses which contain some references to mission. But it appears that these are not defined course objectives but rather incidental occurrences dependant on the teachers' own levels of missionary awareness (cf. Böker:5).

4. Another aspect is the quality of library holdings in the area of mission. The Böker survey shows that the average size of the mission section of the libraries is about 900 to 1000 volumes, which is around six per cent of the entire library holdings of the respective schools. In schools

with a mission specialisation, these figures are much higher (up to fourteen per cent), while some other schools have only minimal holdings in mission topics (down to 1.2 per cent). Yet this does not tell us much about the quality of the libraries, nor does it show their developments. Since several of *the Schools* have only recently (in the last two decades) started with a professional library organisation, an in-depth study of library development is virtually impossible.[21] The visitation of three selected libraries[22] by this author allows the following preliminary comments. (1) The three schools have clearly defined library sections on missiology and the study of religions. (2) They are all well documented in the area of evangelical mission history and evangelical theology of mission in the German language. (3) Some schools hold a considerable amount of English language books, especially North American evangelical missiology. (4) Critical literature, missiological publications of WCC origin and contemporary university publications can only occasionally be found. (5) The sections on ecumenical theology are weak and one-sided, containing mainly evangelical apologetic books. (6) Over all, the libraries reflect the conservative evangelical position of *the Schools* as it has been described in Part III of this study. The many publications of Peter Beyerhaus occupy a significant place in these libraries.

5. Furthermore, the Böker survey regards mission-oriented activities beyond the academic sphere. In this area *the Schools* demonstrate a high concern for mission. Practical mission work during the time at the school, mission-prayer groups, mission information, lectures by visiting missionaries, participation in the European Student Missionary Association (ESMA) and many other mission-oriented activities are mentioned by all schools. Such elements constitute a vital part of the missionary dimension of a school.

6. Nonetheless, Böker comes to the conclusion that the process of 'academisation' has been taking place in the last two decades at the cost of the missionary dimension of Bible school training.[23] His presentation at the annual assembly of the *KBA* in November 1996 was an urgent plea not to lose this heritage of the Bible school movement. He called the representatives of the Bible schools and seminaries back to the vision of Otto Riecker (Böker:2).[24]

f) Critical Remarks

1. Research shows that the German evangelical Bible school movement lost – at least to a certain extent – its mission-oriented heritage during the last two decades as it was striving for more academic excellence, driven by the aim of accreditation and academic recognition. It seems that academic rigour and a mission-oriented spirituality are in tension (cf. Riecker). Despite the fact that models of a convincing integration of

academic excellence and missionary spirituality are available in the German pietistic tradition, it appears that many of *the Schools* have not succeeded in holding the two together as they have developed from Bible schools into theological colleges.

2. The schools developed more sophisticated curricula, basically following the pattern of North American seminaries. This implies the introduction of a variety of specific missiological courses. With this the *intentional* side of mission studies was more fully developed, which certainly must be commended as an improvement. But again, this was achieved to the detriment of the *dimensional* side, which permeates the entire educational process with a mission-oriented flavour. Again, the question must be raised why it appears so difficult to keep the two aspects – *dimension* and *intention* – in creative tension.[25]

3. The study shows that these developments occur despite the fact that virtually all schools emphasise practical training in mission and cultivate mission-oriented activities around the academic work at *the Schools*. It must be proposed that all these activities can never balance the lack of a missionary dimension in the academic work. The question can even be raised whether such activities have not become an alibi, covering up the fact that a missionary dimension is actually lacking at a much deeper level.

4. The analysis suggests that the problem lies not only at the level of curriculum design but even more at the level of teacher training and qualifications. When teachers of evangelical theological schools follow an academic career and possess neither pastoral nor missionary experience when they begin teaching in a Bible college or seminary, then it is not surprising to find that a missionary dimension is lacking in their teaching. This poses serious questions to teacher training and recruitment.[26]

5. Finally, and perhaps most fundamentally, the entire discussion of mission studies among evangelical Bible schools and seminaries as documented by the surveys and consultations of the last two decades uses a language which implies a traditional western concept of mission and in no way integrates what Bosch has defined as an emerging new paradigm of mission. The term 'mission' mainly refers to the western church's activities in the non-western world. A 'missionary' is a person who departs from a so-called Christian context for a non-Christian context. What he or she is primarily doing on the 'mission field' is proclaiming the gospel so that non-Christians may by saved by faith in Jesus Christ. All the critical issues of the recent international discussion of mission – contextualisation, intercultural theology, dialogue with other religions, the deficiencies of the traditional colonial model of western missions, proclamation and social responsibility, holistic mission, mission and ecumenism – are hardly ever mentioned in the surveys, in the curricula and in the syllabi consulted for this study.

6. At this point the theological (Part Three) and the educational (Part Four) aspects merge. This leads to the tentative conclusion that the loss of the missionary dimension in evangelical theological education must also be seen in relation to developments in conservative evangelical theology. Perhaps the loss of the missionary dimension in evangelical theological education is the logical fruit of a much deeper loss – namely, the loss of the missionary dimension in conservative evangelical theology. This question does not so much regard the content of theology but the way theology is done. As long as conservative evangelical theology is mainly concerned with the transmission of evangelical orthodoxy, often with an apologetic approach,[27] it will not regain its missionary dimension. Only if conservative evangelical theologians leave the seemingly secure ivory-tower of their orthodoxy and engage in open dialogue and interaction with a post-Christian and non-Christian society – be it in their own German context or abroad – will they rediscover the missionary dimension of the Christian faith.

2. *The Schools* in the Light of Thesis 2: Andragogy: Learning from Adult Education

a) The KBA and Partnership

One way of looking at the *people-* and *context-orientation* of an educational institution is to analyse its partnership with the community which it intends to serve, i.e., to measure and evaluate how an institution or an association of institutions welcomes external input, advice and evaluation.

1. *The Schools* under consideration vary considerably in their historical church relations. Some of *the Schools* are denominational institutions and were to some degree integrated into a church body from their beginning and through their formal operational structures. Other schools are non-denominational (or inter-denominational): they were founded by individuals or (in most cases North American) mission agencies. All *the Schools* claim to serve the churches. The degree to which they achieve this aim and the character of their formal relations to churches vary.

2. A review of all the *KBA* conferences since 1964 quickly leads to a preliminary quantitative result: Only about ten to twenty per cent of all the speakers came from outside the *KBA* movement. This demonstrates a low level of external input and underscores the strong independence of the movement. External expertise was sought for the following themes:

1974 Education for service in the church (W. Sartorius)
1976 The Christian confronted by modern pedagogy (I. Lück)

1977 The scientific rebuttal of the evolution theory (W.J. Ouweneel)
Modern youth under the control of the evolution theory (W.J. Ouweneel)
1978 The contemporary situation of mission and its significant for theological education (E. Vatter)
Church and mission today (E. Vatter)
1980 Christian education and the challenges of our time (O. Schaude)
1983 The ideological framework of contemporary natural science and the facts of the history of the earth 100 years after Darwin (J. Scheven)
1988 The employment of computers in teaching at Bible Schools (E. Bertsch)
1991 Psychology in the curriculum of the Bible school (S. Pfeifer)

Besides the two major issues which deserved external input (evolution theory and anti-authoritarian pedagogy) the introduction of psychology and computers appear on the list. In only one case was a church representative (W. Sartorius, pastor of the Reformed Church in Switzerland) and in one other case a mission representative (E. Vatter) invited. It seems that the dialogue with those who send and later employ students did not have a high priority.

3. One is struck by the lack of serious interaction with the problems and grass-roots needs of the church in its mission and by the fact that the standpoints neither of church and mission representatives, nor of persons from the Two Thirds World, nor of graduates of *the Schools* were consulted. This raises serious questions regarding the effectiveness of the *KBA* as an association of theological schools. Did the council of the association really serve *the Schools* towards the development of a future-oriented, relevant theological training by reducing input and discussion at the conferences to a virtually internal matter?

b) The KBA*-Survey as an Expression of Partnership*

The fact that the *KBA* survey of 1996 also includes a questionnaire to church and mission leaders is a good sign. It implies the desire to know the viewpoints of those people who know what sort of work the graduates of the schools need to do and who experience the graduates in their professional situations. 105 individuals from 51 different institutions and churches responded, about 60 per cent of them pastors (Survey1996:98). Several items are relevant to this part of the analysis.

1. In general, church and mission leaders evaluate the level of theoretical knowledge possessed by graduates in the areas of Bible and theology as adequate (60–70 per cent). They commend *the Schools* for the quality of the theological teaching they deliver (Survey 1996:103–05).

2. They evaluate the practical dimension of the training more critically. They grade the qualification of graduates in the areas of church and mission praxis much lower than in theoretical fields (Survey 1996: 103–05). The majority of suggestions in the list of recommended improvements address aspects of praxis-oriented training (Survey 1996: 113–17).

3. Church and mission leaders also expect theological schools to do a better job in 'personality formation,' especially in the areas of 'emotional stability' and 'the ability to take stress' [Belastbarkeit] (Survey 1996: 105–06).

If the objectives of theological education are defined as (1) transmission of theoretical knowledge, (2) appropriation of practical skills and (3) personality formation, then the survey among church and mission leaders shows that evangelical colleges and seminaries are doing a good job in area (1), while they do not meet the expectations in the areas (2) and (3).

Unfortunately, the questionnaire does not ask for an evaluation of the partnership between *the Schools* and churches or missions in the educational process. In the light of the paradigms established in this thesis, this would seem to be a significant area of investigation. This omission demonstrates by implication the lack of awareness on the side of those who have set up the survey. On the list of recommendations (open, without predetermined answer-options) principals of schools (3), church or mission leaders (3), and students (2) have called for an improved partnership between schools and churches-missions. This is a low rate but at least a minimal indication of a need acknowledged by a few.

c) Other Avenues of Church-School Partnerships

Of course, the results drawn from the *KBA* survey must be complemented by the investigation of particular schools. Colleges and seminaries may perform at a higher level of partnership with churches, Christian institutions and mission agencies beyond what has been revealed by the *KBA* survey. The following relations between *the Schools* and the churches-missions are practised in most schools under consideration.

1. Many schools (especially those which relate to a particular denomination) are governed by a board of delegates from the supporting churches. This implies a certain interaction between churches and schools.

2. The schools which underwent the accreditation process with the EEAA had to show evidence of a minimal partnership with the supporting bodies and the graduates now serving in churches, Christian institutions and missions. Some (for example *Brake* and *Bienenberg*) have conducted a survey in this connection.

3. In most of *the Schools* practical courses in the areas of church ministries and mission work are taught by practitioners who serve as guest lecturers. Thus, having pastors and mission leaders on the faculty adds an outside voice to the decision processes regarding educational objectives, curriculum and other issues of the training. This seems to be another common way of partnering with the churches and missions.

All of these can be avenues of partnership, yet the quality of this partnership deserves critical evaluation, although the task goes beyond the scope of this study. In the case of a board of church delegates, the question ought to be asked whether fruitful interactions take place between church representatives and faculty on educational issues or whether board meetings are mainly overloaded with formal business matters. In the case of surveys among graduates it depends on whether the school administration will evaluate the survey and respond in an appropriate manner.[28] In the case of practitioners brought in to teach, it depends on the impact they can have at the level of educational philosophy and curriculum.

d) *Alternative Models of Theological Training*

Another aspect to be looked at is the openness toward new educational models which are more pragmatic, as well as student- and context-oriented (see p. 215). The thesis is that theological education should reach students in the context where they live and work instead of uprooting them to the foreign context of a detached academic institution. Given the fact that all schools under consideration have historically been residential schools, to develop in the direction of the new paradigm would mean putting forward new models of theological training.

In general, most of *the Schools* still see the value of residential schools where students live in a community (monastic model) as a context which promotes integrated studies emphasising academic studies, community life, spiritual disciplines and ministerial activities in groups or individually.[29]

New models of theological training moving toward a more contextual form of education and leaving students in their environment of life and work can only occasionally be observed.

1. Several institutions offer correspondence courses,[30] yet education based solely on correspondence does not really correspond to what is meant by contextual, people-oriented education.

2. Some other schools have added evening and weekend classes or extension centres.[31] Usually, these are complementary to the residential college or seminary programs. They reach non-professional lay workers in the churches and are not intended to be alternatives to the residential programs.

3. At least two schools have changed the format of the residential Bible schools, moving from a traditional campus to a building which contains only classrooms, administration rooms and libraries but no dormitories. This reduces community life to the actual time students spend at the study centre. In such cases students live in rented apartments in the city or region and are involved in the daily life of the city and local churches. This indicates a significant shift from the monastery model to a much more contextual model of theological training.[32]

4. At least one newly founded school operates according to a completely new model of education, trying to incorporate much of what is spelled out in the new paradigm of theological training. The *Institut für Gemeindebau und Weltmission (IGW)* appears to be the only school which follows a philosophy of education close to what we describe as the new paradigm. Students study part-time. At the same time they work in a church part-time. Two to three days a week students attend the local study centre to take classes or study; the rest of the time they are involved in some kind of church related ministry. They have to be supervised by local pastors. The school operates locally (regionally). The institution does not own any facilities. They rent a church building as a study centre and use local libraries. The faculty consists mainly of local pastors and theologians, and the institution itself employs only a minimum of personnel (administrator, director, academic dean). The curriculum is designed around the needs and the recourses of a particular city or region. In this model local churches, school administration, faculty and students are fully integrated.

The school started in 1991 in Zurich and opened study centres in Bern in 1994 and Stuttgart in 1995. This model looks promising, yet it is too early to conduct a sound analysis which would lead to a valid evaluation of this model. One thing can definitely be observed: the traditional colleges and seminaries are very sceptical about this experiment and *IGW* has had a hard time gaining acceptance by the older schools in the *KBA*.[33]

e) Critical Remarks

All that has been analysed in this chapter so far only touches the surface of what is actually at stake in what has been articulated as an emerging new paradigm of theological education. We have defined this aspect of the paradigm with the terms *people-* and *context-oriented*. A serious conclusion regarding the level of performance achieved by the schools under consideration can only be reached by an in-depth 'output' analysis looking critically at the long-term performance of the graduates of *the Schools* in their contexts of ministry. Since this study focuses on 'input' measurement (analysing *the Schools* themselves), it goes beyond the scope of this study to provide a final evaluation of the level of quality in this area.

Nonetheless, this study is capable of analysing the mechanisms *the Schools* have implemented to enhance a stronger people-orientation. Summarising and evaluating what has been investigated in this chapter, it can be said that research has shown the following:

1. There are some avenues of partnership established in most schools. Yet there is only minimal evidence of formal audit mechanisms which would measure the quality of that partnership.

2. At the level of the *KBA*, partnership with churches and missions has historically played only a very marginal role. The *KBA* survey of 1996 gives mixed signals regarding partnership-awareness. While church and mission leaders were surveyed with a specific questionnaire, the questions themselves do not focus on partnership.

3. Some schools have added more contextual and people-oriented tracks to their programs (evening classes, extension centres, correspondence courses), but they reach mainly non-professional lay-workers of the churches and have never become a serious alternative for vocational theological and ministerial training.

4. Some schools were forced to give up a traditional residential campus and have taken this opportunity to review their form of theological training. They now run only a study centre, having given up detached campuses and force their students to remain involved in society while studying at the school.

5. One school, *IGW*, has launched an innovative new programme which meets many of the criteria of a new educational paradigm. The programme is still too young to convincingly show its potential, but it certainly offers a challenging alternative to the traditional residential Bible schools and seminaries.

This suggests the following conclusions:

1. Many of the German-speaking evangelical colleges and seminaries would defend the residential monastic model (probably with some adjustments) as still relevant for theological and ministerial training in their context. Over against the proposal of a radical change towards a more contextual and people-oriented way of delivering theological training, they would put forward three arguments. (1) One reason for the call for more contextualised theological training comes from the Two-Thirds World and its dissatisfaction with western models of education. Where the cultural difference between the rural context of the students' origin and the city context of their place of study is so great that it up-roots the student from their original culture and makes it extremely difficult for them to return, the need for more people-oriented theological training is clear. Yet this is not the situation in western Europe. Students will not be culturally up-rooted to this extent when they live on a Bible college

campus for two, three or four years. (2) A second call for more people-oriented ministerial training comes out of the university context, where students get caught up in an ivory tower of academics with only minimal relations to their future professional context. Again, *the Schools*, which have grown out of the Bible school movement, never produced this kind of detachment from the life of the church. Living in the campus community is in itself an experience of Christian community and a learning experience which should not be underestimated. (3) Finally, it is exactly on account of our western culture, where constant involvement, amusement and action, besides a flood of media, distract persons from serious study and reflection, a certain distancing can only be of advantage for theological and ministerial training.

These objections must be taken seriously. If we are to take contextualisation seriously, then we have to pay attention to the context. Switzerland and Germany are not Guatemala, where Theological Education by Extension was born. Models which have not succeeded in India will not automatically not succeed in Germany or Switzerland. Neither are evangelical theological colleges universities. Models which have proven to be inadequate in the university context are not necessarily inadequate in the context of theological colleges and seminaries. Thus, one must recognise that the case for traditional models of residential Bible schools and colleges responds to the German and Swiss context in its own right.

2. On the other hand, the call for contextual and people-oriented theological education challenges traditional models on a much deeper level, and German and Swiss evangelical institutions are well advised to pay attention. The key issue is not just defining course objectives and curriculum in partnership with churches and missions rather than through the institution alone. Nor is the issue only the place of programme delivery – closer to people or farther. The issue is, to use Kinsler's words again, a pedagogical one, namely to move beyond 'the transferral of pre-packaged subject matter primarily through lectures and production of graduates who will believe and perform as the institution and the churches desire' (Kinsler 1981:49). Contextual, people-oriented theological education implies engagement in an action-reflection process of the teacher together with the student, a process in which both are learners, searching for a deeper understanding of truth and a deeper interaction with the cultural context and the biblical text. In this process the teacher will risk his or her pre-known theology – obviously a threatening thought for many a teacher.[34] This again brings the focus back to the way of theologising and the pedagogical process of theological training. At this level only minimal awareness of the issues at stake could be observed among German-speaking evangelical colleges and seminaries. The understanding of the task of theological education still follows the rationale of first transmitting evangelical orthodoxy, then applying it.

This leads to the following chapter, which will deal exclusively with this issue of pedagogy.

3. *The Schools* in the Light of Thesis 3: Action-Reflection Process: Overcoming the Theory-Practice Dichotomy

a) The Era of the Bible School Model

It has been pointed out in the historical part of this study (Part II) that the Bible school model has been seen in relation to the monastic model of theological training (Cheesman:487–90; cf. Farley 1983:32–34). Theory and practice are strongly integrated in this model of training. Embedded in the community life on campus, the academic, spiritual and practical dimensions of ministerial formation are interlocked in a unique way. This model of training was still predominant in German-speaking schools in the 1960s and early 1970s. We have referred to the annual assemblies of the *KBA* and the contribution of Otto Riecker earlier. It is not an overstatement to claim that the integrated training in the Bible school models was at the heart of Riecker's vision. His many contributions to the *KBA* conferences focused on this topic, which is also the subject of many of his articles and books (see some of the titles in the bibliography). Such an integrated preparation of ministers for the church would certainly include the study of scripture, church history and theology, but not with the Greek spirit which he calls 'research-spirit' [*Forschergeist*] but rather with a Christian spirit for which he uses the term 'saviour-spirit' [*Rettergeist*] (1973:10). Theological studies can only be conducted in such a manner if the student is 'embedded in a lifestyle of piety' [eingebettet in das Frömmigkeitsleben] (1974:180–97; 1980:84). More specifically, this means (1) personal spiritual life maintained and expressed through spiritual discipline (prayer, worship), (2) integration in Christian community, and (3) evangelistic practice as teams of students and teachers.[35] It was for that reason that Riecker founded not only a Bible school (*Adelshofen*) but also a community of dedicated Christians who were willing to embody this vision in a life-long commitment.[36] It is this monastic community which forms the core of the Bible school life. Students come to this community on campus for a certain period of time and receive training for ministry in church and mission through study embedded in the spiritual and practical life of the core community. In return, the community teaches the students by modelling integrated piety in common studies, spiritual disciplines and missionary practice.

Yet significantly, for Riecker the integration of academic studies in a communal life-style of practised piety is not only a matter of applying theory to practice – it is the context in which learning takes place. He comes to the conclusion that 'most useful theologians receive important spiritual thoughts and teachings for themselves and for the church not at their desks but through involvement in pietistic practice[37] and Christian community' (1974:192). In his 1984 book, *Universitätstheologie und Gemeindefrömmigkeit,* he concludes with a short chapter on epistemology [Der Erkenntnis-Vorgang] (1984:90–91). He states that he had come to certain conclusions and convictions in his life not through rational reasoning [Überlegung] nor through the teaching of others but through perception [Wahrnehmung]. Because he observed students at *Beatenberg* witnessing for Christ publicly, he says, he came to the conclusion that ministerial training must take place in the context of practised ministry.

With this Riecker is very close to what we have defined as hermeneutic circulation in the previous section (see p. 230), even though he does not use the terminology introduced in this study. For him, involvement in community and practical ministry to people has a hermeneutical dimension. He views it as an indispensable and integral part of the process of hearing what God is saying.

The model of Pastor Riecker represents the ideal of an integrated approach to ministerial training in the Bible school tradition in German-speaking Europe. The Bible school he founded at *Adelshofen* may have embodied more of that vision than any other school. Yet most of the Bible schools viewed Riecker's vision as the model they wanted to adopt. He was invited time and again to present the heart of his view at annual *KBA* conferences through the early 1970s.

b) From Bible Schools to Theological Colleges

In the 1970s the demands for higher academic qualifications increased and with it the striving for accreditation. Rising academic expectations in the context of western Europe as well as in the Two Thirds World caused *the Schools* to refocus and restructure their courses toward a more academic model of theological training. This has already been seen. At that point in time it seemed that the traditional Bible school model would no longer serve the changing needs. On-campus living lost its attractiveness for a new generation of students, spiritual disciplines could no longer be implemented by collective regulations, higher academic achievements demanded more time in the library, evangelistic action could no longer be performed in the 'old style,' a new generation of teachers with higher academic qualifications brought a new spirit of *academia* to the campuses – in short, it was difficult to maintain the sort of integrated learning once associated with the Bible school movement (c.f. Ferris and Enlow; Egelkraut 1997).

The move toward theological colleges was accompanied by the enterprise of accreditation. We must therefore look more carefully at the impact the European Evangelical Accreditation Association (EEAA) had on *the Schools*. First of all, one must note that the issue of the integration of the academic with the spiritual and the practical dimension of theological education was always a concern of EEAA.[38] The EEAA manual defines 'supervised ministry' as an integral area of the evaluation in which the schools must provide means for quality assurance (EEAA:14–17,20). The issue of integration of theory and practice is therefore dealt with under the heading 'supervised practical work' in addition to academic work. The duration of such 'practica' is defined in the manual, and schools have to give evidence that adequate supervision and evaluation is provided.

This development leads to a situation which deserves critical reflection. The reduction of the integration of theory and practice to the issue of 'practical work,' even if it is supervised, is highly problematic and does not by any means solve the problem. Field work can be added without any formal connection to the academic curriculum. Field work can be a break from academic studies, a time when students can do 'something else.' Field work can focus on 'know-how' and practical skills which are not necessarily connected with academic studies. Field work can also be seen primarily as application which does not yet reach the level of inductive learning. It has to be concluded: *The sheer addition of practical field experience is not in and of itself the solution to the theory-practice problem.*

Unfortunately, the EEAA manual does not spell out objectives which would reach that deeper level of inductive learning, nor does it provide means for the assessment of the quality of teaching at that level. Such areas would be

1. defining learning as an action-reflection process,
2. defining the teacher's role as facilitator in this process rather than transmitter of knowledge,
3. requiring students to have a minimum of prior experience in the field to be studied,
4. implementing mechanisms to integrate previous experience and field work experience into academic courses,
5. forcing teachers to introduce theories relevant to the students' experiences and expecting assignments which reflect on the experiences in the light of the theory,[39]
6. expecting teachers and students to get involved in practical field experience and action and to think critically about their experience in the light of the Bible and theories.

At this point it turns out to be a significant disadvantage that the EEAA manual is based on the North American accreditation philosophy of the 1970s and 1980s, focusing primarily on quantitative and not on qualitative analysis.[40] This leads to an overestimation of statistically measurable facts on the input level (institution, faculty, curricula, structure of course delivery) at the cost of quality management on the level of educational process and output.

c) 1995 and Beyond

The 1996 survey does not explicitly address pedagogical questions. Nonetheless, several observations implicitly shed light on the educational process at the colleges and seminaries. The theory-praxis issue certainly appears in many answers. Many of the realities discussed in the previous paragraphs of this chapter are confirmed by the survey's results.

1. The survey shows an average length of practical field work of 25 weeks during the programme (Survey1996:13). Since *the Schools'* programs vary in length this figure is of limited value. It only demonstrates that the schools under consideration are generally putting a high emphasis on practical field work. This may be interpreted as a confirmation of the thesis established earlier: moving from Bible schools to theological colleges, *the Schools* have tried to keep their heritage of practice-oriented training by putting a high emphasis on practical field work during the programme. The strengths and weaknesses of this have already been discussed.

2. Research also shows that all schools have some sort of supervision and evaluation of the field work. Asked which form of supervision or evaluation is viewed as most successful, the schools' faculties give the highest rate (80 per cent) to local supervision (Survey 1996:13). This delegates the task to local pastors and missionaries. Whether they facilitate a process of integration of theory and practice is not measured by the survey. On the other hand, the teachers cannot leave the task of integration to local personnel. If they take their role seriously as facilitators of an inductive learning process, then practical experience has to flow back to the class room, where theory will illuminate practice and where practice will affect theory (hermeneutical circulation).

3. Despite this strong emphasis on practical field work, many students suggest that the entire programme should be more practical and less theoretical. Some have expressed a wish for less teaching or studying and more practical field experience (Survey 1996:81). Given the high number of weeks generally devoted to practical field work, the call of some students for more 'practice' should probably be read as a desire to have a better integration of theory and practice. Again, to add even more practical work would probably not solve the problem.

4. Finally, the survey addresses another issue of significance for this chapter: There is a strong call for improvement in the quality of teaching and for continuing the pedagogical training of teachers (Survey 1996:19).

Asked about which teachers' qualifications should be considered when they are employed, students gave the highest rate (eighty per cent) to educational skills (Survey 1996:87). At the same time they rate teachers as high in competence in their fields (84.8 per cent) (Survey 1996:75) but wish for a greater degree of mentoring (Survey 1996:88). All of this suggests a high level of satisfaction regarding teachers' qualifications on the content-side (competence in their fields) but also significant dissatisfaction with pedagogical performance.

It seems that *the Schools* are doing their best by fitting more practical work into the curriculum; yet there still remains a rather high degree of dissatisfaction. Theory and practice are separated and the rhetoric implies that the focus is on balancing the two. Again, only a move toward inductive and contextual learning would lead towards integration. And this involves advanced and new pedagogical competencies on the side of the teachers.

d) Critical Remarks

At the conclusion of this section dealing with pedagogical issues, we realise again how strongly the shift from Bible schools to theological colleges has influenced evangelical theological education in Germany and Switzerland.

1. Beyond all the limitations the traditional Bible school model may have had, it certainly supported a deep level of integration of theory and practice. Even though contemporary educational theory and terminology was not used, it reached a level of wholeness which must be complemented. Otto Riecker's vision and the embodiment of that vision at *Adelshofen* can be viewed as an outstanding example of the Bible school concept.

2. The move from Bible schools to theological colleges has in a certain way introduced fragmentation. This fragmentation has many facets, one of them being the theory-practice division.[41] Rooted in the Bible school tradition, praxis remained a major concern in evangelical Bible college education. Required practical field work during the programme became the place where practice is located. Structures of supervision and evaluation were designed to make practical field work a fruitful learning experience. But somehow, the theory-practice issue could not be resolved by adding more practical work. Field experience as such does not yet produce integration of theory and practice. Theory and practice may remain separated matters, even when schools strive for a balance between academic courses and practical field work.

3. The key issue at stake is precisely what the paradigm change from deductive to inductive learning is focusing on. Integration of theory and practice can be reached neither by balancing academic studies and

practical field experience nor by paying more attention to the application of theory but only by a break-through toward a pedagogy of inductive learning. This implies more then a new way of doing the same thing; it is a pedagogy which changes the learning process, the content (theories and truths), the teacher and the student. Based on the research, it seems doubtful that German and Swiss evangelical theological colleges are willing and ready to take this step.[42] The concept of transmitting evangelical orthodoxy as propositional truth which then can be applied to different contexts still prevails.

4. At this point the highly critical issue of teacher training must be raised. It is obvious that the shift from traditional deductive learning (transmitting a pre-packed set of truth through classical classroom teaching) to inductive learning (entering into an action-reflection process of common, teacher and student learning in which the teacher, as the more educated, will facilitate the process) demands new forms of teaching, and this demands new areas of competence on the teachers' part. Currently, most teachers at theological colleges are seminary and university trained theologians with no, or only minimal, pedagogical training (there are exceptions). They lack not only the background of educational training; they are also shaped by the old paradigm of learning. It appears that without serious investment in pedagogical training of teachers, a paradigm shift towards a more inductive model of learning cannot be realised. Many traditionally trained theologians and college teachers do not even have the imagination to view the contours of such a paradigm shift.[43]

4. *The Schools* in the Light of Thesis 4: Integrative Curriculum: Beyond the Legacy of Fragmentation

a) The Era of the Bible School Model

The analysis of the catalogues and curricula of a selected number of schools[44] shows that in the 1960s *the Schools* had a very plain and simple curriculum. The number of subjects was low, with little diversification; a majority of Bible content courses marked the centre. Schools rooted in the North American Bible school movement (for example, *Brake*) tended to have a complete overview of the Bible at the centre of the curriculum, teaching through the biblical books from Genesis to Revelation within three years. It is obvious that in this philosophy the Bible is the material back-bone of the curriculum. Other schools, rooted in German Pietism (such as *Liebenzell*) had at that time a slightly more diversified curriculum, closer to German university curricula.

If we take these two features of the Bible school era, Bible-centredness and simplicity, together with the dimensions established above, mission-orientation and spirituality or piety, then we have an accurate picture of the integrative centre of Bible school training. It appears that fragmentation was not a major issue. What was talked about in classes and what had to be learned could be put in relation to the three-fold back-bone: Bible-centredness, mission-orientation and personal spirituality or piety. It seems that the problem of fragmentation, complained about by Gerhard Ebeling and Friedrich Mildenberger in view of German university training and sharply criticised by Edward Farley in the North American seminary context, was not really an issue at the Bible Schools. As far as the research of this study was able to analyse, this would certainly be true of German-speaking Bible schools up to the 1970s.[45]

b) From Bible Schools to Theological Colleges

The development from Bible schools to theological colleges has changed the face of evangelical theological education at the level of curriculum as well. The last twenty five years has introduced fragmentation to German-speaking evangelical theological colleges. This can be demonstrated at several levels:[46]

1. Higher academic aims have led to the introduction of new courses, especially in the area of systematic theology.
2. A new generation of teachers was trained on a higher academic level, often in the university context. With this, a higher degree of specialisation including accompanying fragmentation was introduced.
3. The upgrade of the level of training to graduate and post-graduate studies in Bible and theology called for the expansion or even introduction of courses in biblical languages.
4. Increased expectations on competencies in the area of pastoral ministries led to the introduction of social-science courses.
5. The changes in teaching missiological courses, described in previous chapters, has caused a more diversified curriculum in missiology (cf. Wolke).
6. The results of the aforementioned developments are specified in the curriculum requirements of the accreditation manual of the EEAA and become prescriptive for any school seeking accreditation (EEAA:10–22).
7. As some of *the Schools* developed into colleges and seminaries delivering courses at the undergraduate and postgraduate levels (leading to Bachelor's and Master's degrees), or when new schools at this level were founded,[47] they were in competition with the established theology departments of the state-universities. In order to demonstrate equal academic standards they introduced university curriculum and nomenclature.
8. Finally the higher academic level of course delivery demanded a

higher degree of academic training and specialisation of the faculty. While in the Bible school era teachers have often taught courses across the curriculum, they now tend to concentrate on their fields of specialisation.

From the perspective of the student this means that she/he has to study an increased number of subjects, covering a broader field of studies, on a higher academic level, with a higher degree of specialisation. This is exactly where the problem of fragmentation occurs.

As *the Schools* were moving in the described direction it appears that they had bought in to a bad habit in curriculum design, namely the habit of 'additionalism.' Whenever a certain lack in the curriculum is diagnosed, a respective course or even a department is added, and a respective specialist is hired. The need for more mission emphasis is met by adding mission courses (cf. Wolke). The need for deepening personal spirituality of the students is met by adding courses in spiritual formation. The need for an increased competency of students in pastoral counseling is met by adding courses in psychology and counseling. While such adjustments in curriculum design are mandatory in order to provide meaningful education for the changing needs in a given context, such manoeuvres also add to the fragmentation.[48]

The question is: what have *the Schools* done to counterbalance this fragmentation? Hardly any evidence of moving in the direction of the criteria spelled out earlier (pp. 237–96) could be observed. Based on the discussion of the issue with deans and teachers[49] of *the Schools* it must be concluded that there is only a low level of awareness of the problem.

c) 1995 and Beyond

Again, the survey does not address the issues developed in this study in an explicit way. The implicit insight which can be gained from the questions as well as from the answers shows the following:

1. The questionnaire lists twenty five subjects, asking students to rate the quality of course delivery (Survey1996:76–77). Yet the list of taught courses indicated by the institutions go far beyond this figure and indicate an enormous splitting of the entire material delivered in one programme. Three-year programs incorporate an average number of 37.25 subjects. Four-year programs deliver in average 57.8 courses. Programs of five years' length contain in average 42 courses (Survey 1996:26). These may be small units yet they appear as separate entities and add to the problem of fragmentation.

2. The response of the students is controversial. On the one hand they complain about the vast number of courses and call for 'fewer courses, more concentration and integration with practice' (Survey 1996:113). On the other hand they add a long list of subjects which they feel should

receive more attention (Survey 1996:113–14; 121–23). This alone reveals the problem *the Schools* are facing. Increasing and changing needs and demands in the contexts of a pluralistic, fragmented and constantly changing society put high pressure on them. 'Additionalism' is certainly the easiest answer but it only adds to the dilemma.

3. Another puzzling aspect comes to the surface when people are asked to comment on alternatives in theological education. Despite a certain conservatism among evangelical theological colleges, a considerable number of persons of all categories favour new models of training (40 per cent of the schools' directors, 45.5 per cent of the faculty members, 36.9 of the students and 42.9 per cent of the church-mission leaders). In most cases they favour models which give more flexibility, can be taken part-time, provide more practice-integration and are more modular (Survey 1996:47–48; 57–59; 95–97; 125–26).[50] Here again we have a critical indication. Moving toward a more modular credit system will certainly satisfy those who seek more flexibility, but with equal certainty it increases fragmentation. Is not this modular credit system of North American seminaries precisely the one which Farley is criticising heavily?

d) Critical Remarks

Critically reflecting on the findings in this fourth chapter of the analysis, the following can be stated:

1. In a certain way theological colleges and seminaries in Germany and Switzerland still profit from some of the advantages of the Bible school tradition. Given the highly problematic circumstances in the theological departments of universities (addressed by Ebeling, Mildenberger and others) and the dissatisfaction with North American seminary education (addressed by Farley), the colleges under consideration still experience a comparatively high degree of integration and unity. The schools are, in general, rather small. All the students run through a single programme. There is in most schools only a minimal choice of electives. Ministerial professionalism has not reached the extent of the North American scene. Many of the teachers still do some cross-disciplinary teaching. Thus, looking at these schools the heavy critique of Farley cannot have its full import.

2. On the other hand, the move from Bible schools to theological colleges has led evangelical theological education down the road of fragmentation. The details have been spelled out. Confronted with the changes of the last twenty to twenty five years and under the pressure of increasing costs and decreasing student numbers, a certain nervousness can be observed. New names of programs, new courses, changes of course titles, new emphases, even new programs and new forms of

delivery are being employed. All of this looks more flexible, more attractive, more up-to-date, yet it also witnesses to a greater degree of fragmentation.

3. In this whole development there is little evidence of serious reflection on curriculum design at a very fundamental level. The records of the *KBA* and the EEAA, the two institutional bodies which provide guidance for *the Schools*, which educate the educators, show that there was occasional discussion and instruction in certain curricular areas.[51] But never was a lecture given or a workshop conducted on curriculum development in general. It appears that in this difficult transition from Bible Schools to colleges, academic deans were left without the necessary theoretical and practical help to reflect upon and create new, integrated curricula. But this is exactly what is needed to master the deficiencies of curricular dispersion.

5. Evaluative Summary

What are the conclusions? How is the performance of evangelical theological education in Germany and Switzerland to be assessed in the light of a changing paradigm in theological education.

a) From Bible Schools to Theological Colleges: A Development with Mixed Achievements

Investigation has shown that the shifts taking place in the time frame of this study has deeply changed the face of these schools. We have labelled it a shift from *Bible schools* to *theological colleges*, using the two terms in a typological way.

1. A first significant result of this study is that the Bible school model, despite all the deficiencies it has in serving the church adequately in its contemporary context, embraces many of the features associated with 'new models' of theological education. Of course its strength is not a people/church-orientation with its closeness to the constituency. It rather follows the monastic model of personality formation in the context of a closed community, distanced from the context of life and ministry. But the other three axioms of a new paradigm of theological education are well represented in the Bible school model: (1) it models a high degree of mission-orientation; (2) it achieves a considerable level of theory-practice integration; and (3) it has kept the curriculum at an astonishingly high level of unity and integration. We have recognised that the key values of the Bible school movement, Bible-centredness, mission-orientation and personal spirituality/piety form the integrative centre and are responsible for this high performance in the analysed areas.

2. Secondly, the 1970s saw the introduction of far reaching changes.

The turning point has to be identified somewhat after 1974, if the theory holds that Lausanne 1974 and the efforts towards accreditation made a significant impact on these developments (Egelkraut 1990:33). Causes and effects of that shift have been introduced and analysed and need not to be restated (cf. Ferris and Englow; Egelkraut 1996). A simple look at the catalogues of the 1960s and the 1990s evidence the changes in professional objectives, academic level and curricular proliferation.

3. What needs to be discussed at this point is the fact that this change was not a change by decision – though many decisions were taken along the way – but rather something that happened to *the Schools*. It appears that throughout the process many of *the Schools'* leaders were rather *re*acting than acting. *The Schools* were confronted with new challenges from different sides including the following: a growing and dynamic evangelical movement on the world scene (Lausanne Movement), the rise of missiology of North American origin, the attraction of North American seminaries in general, the shift in the west European context from modernity to postmodernity bringing with it a new generation of students (Generation X) and higher demands on academic and professional quality. *The Schools* tried to respond to all of these and many other challenges. Many *KBA* and EEAA conferences document this process. Looking back, it appears that many themes came up arbitrarily or selectively. How could it have been different? As the challenges occurred, they have been dealt with. From the perspective of the historian we may have wished a more inclusive approach, looking at all parts of the picture, doing more fundamental studies in theological education, helping schools develop new curricula – and out of such a position, to act rather than to react. One reason for the lack of such fundamental and comprehensive work is certainly the very limited resources. In 1990, Egelkraut pointed to the 'lack of qualified faculty,' to the 'heavy load' of most faculty and the 'very little original research' that had been conducted by local evangelical scholars as some of the main reasons for the deficiencies in evangelical theological education in German-speaking Europe (1990:33).[52] This brings to the surface one of the major needs in evangelical theological education in Germany and Switzerland, namely research, analysis and reflection on theological education, development of concepts which embrace all aspects of theological training and education for the educators. The developments in 1995 and beyond evidence a general awareness of these deficiencies. The 1996 survey and the follow-up analysis, of which this study in a certain way is part, indicate the readiness to rethink theological training seriously. Whether there will be as much readiness for the implementation of necessary changes remains to be seen.

b) Observing Change Patterns

In all these changes which have developed in the last two to three decades it cannot be doubted that evangelical Bible colleges in German-speaking Europe are resisting very fundamental changes. Not a few of these schools look back on an impressive history. *Chrischona,* the oldest of the schools, celebrated its 150th anniversary in 1990 (E. Schmid ed.). Beyond their institutional origin they identify with theological training in the pietistic tradition (cf. Frische). Others are younger, but they are all deeply rooted in the monastic model of the Bible school movement. Despite the fact that many indicate a need for new models of ministerial training, as shown by the 1996 survey, in general *the Schools* considered by this study affirm the continuing value of the traditional residential model.[53] Only a minority of schools believe that the time for more radical shifts has come, and these are implementing new models.[54] Such new models have a hard time gaining acceptance in the community of Bible colleges. *Aarau,* a school with a longer history, has adjusted its educational model in the last decade to the changing cultural situation and seems to find more acceptance by the peer schools than *IGW,* which has started a new school with a completely alternative model.[55] The question to be answered is: why are these evangelical schools so sceptical about many aspects of what has been proposed as a new paradigm in theological education, and why are they resisting more fundamental changes? This study does certainly not provide a comprehensive answer to that question. Some factors appear evident after the investigations:

1. There is still a deep conviction that the traditional model will have a future. Despite decreasing enrolment numbers in some schools, the advantages of the residential model are still viewed as far too significant to be given up.

2. The fact that many of *the Schools* have grown into institutions of considerable size, owning large campuses with extensive infrastructures, may also be one factor that contributes to the lack of flexibility. Some schools have invested heavily in new buildings in the last decade. More radical shifts toward non-residential forms of training which would require a geographical dislocation of the institutions seems inconceivable for these schools at this time.

3. As student numbers drop, funding becomes more critical, new schools appear and the pressure rises to maintain the established institutions, there is definitely more competition. In this competitive situation schools which put new-model programs on the market are viewed as intruders, and they cannot expect to be welcomed.[56]

4. In some schools the response to the challenges of changing educational models must also be seen in relation to the generation shift in those schools. New senior leaders of a younger generation may implement

changes which are not yet possible with a leadership which has established the present structures and has a high level of ownership regarding the traditional residential model of Bible school training.

5. We must also consider Egelkraut's statement about the overload of work which is carried by the schools' leaders and faculties (1990:33). This is certainly a reality. When a struggle for sheer survival – institutional and often also personal – determines daily business, then changes are surely experienced as threats. A change resisting attitude is the logical consequence.

Furthermore, this author suggests another possible reason for the rather change-resistant attitude of the majority of schools which raise critical issues on a much deeper level.

c) The *Critical Issue*

On a superficial level one could argue that the educational issues which are the subject of this part of the study are merely on a structural and formal level. Very pragmatic solutions would be the only thing needed: which model of instruction serves best in a given situation? However, most of the elements of what we have called a new paradigm of theological education go well beyond forms and structures. They touch on such sensitive issues as hermeneutics, epistemology and truth. It appears again, as in Part III, that it is at this level that many of the evangelical theologians and educators are resisting the changes called for by the paradigm shift.

At several points we have observed that the pedagogical paradigm shift includes a hermeneutical and epistemological shift. On one side is an understanding of truth as a given set of propositional doctrinal statements, disconnected from a particular context, which can be transmitted deductively from the teacher who knows, to the student who learns. On the other side is an understanding of truth as something which has to be discovered in a particular context of every day struggle, as teacher and student engage in a process of action and reflection where both are learners. In this model it is not defined at the beginning of the educational process what truth is; it will rather be discovered in the common process of inductive learning.

Many significant questions surface in this shift: the role of the Bible as *norma normans* for the Christian faith; the role of hermeneutics in the interpretation of the Bible; the role of the interpreter's context in hermeneutics; the value of theological statements – how far do they have universal normativity? – and how far are they contextually conditioned? Already the analysis of the theology of mission of German evangelicals in Part III has evidenced their strong commitment to the Bible as the norm for Christian theology and therefore their deep scepticism about contextual hermeneutics and contextual theology. This of course is their main critique of the WWC's developments in theology and missions. Yet, even within the evangelical family they view the movement of evangelical theologians from the Two Thirds World (around INFEMIT) as going too far into contextual hermeneutics and theology. It is in this context that a resistant attitude toward more fundamental shifts in theological education must be interpreted. Any attempt to shift theological education towards more inductive contextual learning in such a way as to allow – in their view – a questioning of biblical authority will ultimately provoke resistance among German conservative evangelical theologians. This leaves us again with the issue of (evangelical) conservatism, change and the underlying question of epistemology. The final section will address these issues again (see p. 296).

Notes

1 The main aspects of the content of this chapter have been presented by the author at the annual Assembly of the *KBA*, November 21, 1997, at the Bible and Retreat Centre Hohegrete, Germany (Ott 1998a).

2 In this section social science methodologies will be applied. The author is familiar with the key issues of *quantitative and qualitative research* (Bryman), and the basic *methodological tools* of social science research (Robson). (a) The analysis of *the Schools* is primarily based on *written data*, i.e., mission statements, objectives, curricula, and course descriptions. (b) A survey was not conducted, but previously conducted surveys were analysed (see Bryman:12 on the analysis of previously collected data as a method of quantitative research). In the case of a rather extensive survey among all the member schools of the *KBA*, conducted in 1996, the author was part of the analysis team and was given firsthand access to the data for this study. (c) Furthermore, *interviews* and (d) *observation* (structured as well as unstructured) are utilised. (e) The author is also aware of the advantages and possible pitfalls of being in the role of an *practitioner-researcher.* (The role of the practitioner-researcher including the advantages and possible problems involved, are discussed in Robsen: 445–63).

3 The title of the thesis limits the time frame to the period between 1960 and 1995. The rationale for this time frame was given in the introduction. However, the *KBA* was founded in 1964 and this analysis will also include some material from 1996.

4 Archives *KBA*.

5 The author has access to the material in the archives of the Theologische Seminar Bienenberg (where he is the Director of Studies). As a member school of EEAA, *Bienenberg* holds all the data distributed to member schools.

6 The author has visited four selected schools: *Brake*, *Wiedenest*, *Adelshofen* and *Liebenzell.*

7 Archives *KBA*.

8 Research Centre of the *FHM*. The *KBA* launched a comprehensive and detailed survey on all the German-speaking Bible colleges and seminaries in

summer 1996, exactly at the time when this author wanted to conduct a survey for this thesis. Instead of launching a second survey this author sought access to the data of the *KBA* survey. He was then invited to take part in the evaluation team, which gave him the opportunity to conduct original analysis of the data and present his findings at the annual Assembly of the *KBA* November 1997. The *KBA* survey consists of four questionnaires, going to the principals of the institutions, to the faculty, to the students and to the churches and Christian agencies which employ the graduates of the schools. What first seemed to be a certain disadvantage for this study, namely the fact that the questions were not formulated by this author in view of this study, turned out to be an advantage. Now, even the way in which the questionnaires were set up and the questions asked (as well as the questions not asked) can be subjected to investigation and reveal significant aspects of the point of view of those who posed the questions.

9 Private archive of Traugott Böker, WEC International, Hof Häusel 4, 65817 Eppstein, Germany. This author has copies of all the data.

10 Later published under the title 'Intellektualität und geistliches Leben an Bibelschulen' in *B&G* 2/1968:152–59.

11 Published under the title 'Mission und missionarischer Geist an den Ausbildungsstätten' [Mission and missionary spirit at the educational institutions] in Riecker 1973:36–59.

12 The publications as well as the unpublished manuscripts of Riecker are accessible at the archive at *Adelshofen*.

13 The forerunner of the *Freie Hochschule für Mission*.

14 Letter sent by the *AEM* to the schools, March 29 1980 (Archive *Bienenberg*).

15 Minutes of the seminar March 14–16 (Archive Bienenberg).

16 This observation is based on the survey conducted by Traugott Böker in 1996 and the data gathered from the four selected schools.

17 The page numbers refer to the edition November 1997 as it was distributed at the annual assembly of the *KBA*.

18 I am indebted to Traugott Böker for making accessible the raw data of the survey (24 of the 32 schools had responded).

19 Some of the results now mentioned are drawn from Traugott Böker's own analysis, which he presented at the 1996 assembly of the *KBA* (Böker). Some additional observations and interpretations are made by this author.

20 Cf. p.164 for the definition of 'hours' in the educational system of *the Schools*.

21 Some libraries are still not on a computer data base. Others have only in the last ten years introduced a formal catalogue. At the same time *the Schools* use different catalogue systems, which makes a comparison extremely difficult. In most libraries there are no statistics about new books, which makes it impossible to trace library development.

22 *Brake, Wiedenest, Liebenzell*.

23 Personal letter to the author, July 28 1997.

24 Böker distributed copies of Riecker's speech to the *KBA* conference of 1967 (see the chapter on Riecker p. 248).

25 The fact that the faculty of the *FTA* published a volume on missiology to which faculty members of all disciplines contributed may be interpreted as a sign of a growing awareness of the need for a development towards a missionary

theology which affects all disciplines of the theological curriculum (Kasdorf and Walldorf).

26 At this point the roles of the *Staatsunabhängige Theologische Hochschule (STH)*, Basel, and the *Freie Theologische Akademie (FTA)*, Giessen, need to be considered. These two younger schools did not grow out of the Bible school movement but were established as conservative evangelical counterparts to the theological departments of state universities, which were conceived as critical (historical-critical methods) and liberal. In their attempts to compete with the university they adopted university curriculum and academic procedures. The majority of young Bible school teachers come from these schools. Many of them are highly trained in apologetics against the influences of historical-critical methods, theological liberalism, marxist pedagogy, religious pluralism and darwinistic natural sciences, but they often received little missionary spirituality and practice. Currently these two schools are trying to correct this mis-balanced situation by developing mission studies and missiological research.

27 Apologetics implies a missionary aspect in and of itself; in that sense, conservative evangelical theology necessarily contains a missionary dimension. Its primary mission appears to be the defence of evangelical orthodoxy against the attacks of biblical criticism, theological liberalism and religious pluralism. While apologetics are a vital part of the Christian mission (cf. Hummel), it ought not to become the centre of theology's missionary dimension.

28 The survey examining *Brake* was used mainly for statistical purposes. There is no evidence of an interaction on the faculty level with responses from graduates.

29 This view was expressed by several principals and deans interviewed by this author.

30 The German track of International Correspondence Institute (ICI), *Bibelstudium am Ort* (*BAO*), LOGOS International, *Theologischer Fernunterricht* (TFU), and others.

31 For example *Aarau*, *Bienenberg* and others.

32 Cf. *Bergstrasse* and *Aarau*. Whether the change was made deliberately, because of genuine reflection on models of theological training, or whether these schools were forced to that change by the buildings available on the market is another question. In both cases it would appear that external pressure was experienced first; thereafter, the schools took the chance to review their philosophies of education.

33 Information on *IGW* from the 1995 catalogue and interviews with the Director of Studies.

34 How deeply this would impact evangelical theological education was experienced by this author when he presented these theses at the 1997 assembly of the *KBA*. One participant responded in the open discussion, 'Should we follow this approach, it would be the end of evangelical theology.'

35 This entire educational concept and how it can be implemented in a Bible school context was presented by Riecker at the 1967 assembly of the *KBA* (published in Riecker 1973:36–59; see also 1974 and 1984).

36 The Bible school was founded in 1958, the community in 1962.

37 With 'pietistic practice' [erweckliche Praxis] Riecker means the combination of individual spirituality (a dedication of the heart to God), living and

ministering in community and missionary service (cf. Faix 1996:20–21). He often also uses the term *Frömmigkeitsleben* [piety] to describe the same (Riecker 1974:180–97; 1984).

38 Cf. the minutes of the biannual assemblies which give evidence of the constant struggle with this topic. It appears as no surprise that especially *Adelshofen*, the school of Otto Riecker, brought this concern to attention several times.

39 The assessment of course outlines (syllabi) of four selected schools has shown that a school rarely demands that its teachers formally incorporate the students' field experience into the teaching and the assignments of academic courses. Thus, neither teachers nor students are forced to reflect critically on their ministerial experience.

40 Quantitative research focuses on the static, the countable, the external, and the institutional (e.g., hours of instruction, hours of private study, library holdings, number of academically qualified teachers, facilities, administrative infrastructures). Qualitative research focuses on the dynamic/process, the uncountable, the internal and the individual and existential (e.g., process of learning, 'seeing through the eyes of those studied,' description of the context, experience of the individual, change processes, emotions, values). See Alan Bryman, *Quantity and Quality in Social Research*, and Colin Robsen, *Real World Research*.

41 Another area of fragmentation is at the level of curricula; this will be discussed in the next chapter.

42 There are always exceptions. One of the schools which is pioneering some aspects of inductive and contextual learning is *Aarau*. In his presentation to the biannual assembly of the EEAA, under the title 'Theological Education in a Post-Modern World,' Peter Henning, Dean of Aarau, has demonstrated how they integrate students' and teachers' experiences in their culture into academic work.

43 This author presented these theses and discussed them with colleagues of other institutions on two occasions – at the annual assembly of the *KBA*, November 1997, and at one of the meetings of Bible college teachers in Switzerland in December 1997. He was amazed at the lack of imagination many of his colleagues showed when it came to seeing what this paradigm shift would mean at the practical level of the day to day work of the schools.

44 *Brake, Liebenzell, Bienenberg, Wiedenest*, and *Adelshofen*.

45 There is also an element of 'participant observation' in this judgement, since the author himself had attended Bible school in that era.

46 These statements are based on the comparison of the curricula of the 1960s and 1970s with those of the 1980s and 1990s.

47 STH Basel, *FTA* Giessen.

48 Observance of curriculum development in *the Schools* under consideration clearly shows this trend. Currently, leadership issues are in vogue and schools have started to add courses on leadership.

49 This refers to the visitation of the four schools as well as to discussions in the context of the *KBA* assembly 1997.

50 Modular is in this case understood in terms of independent units which can be taken and added to a cumulative account of credits toward a degree.

[51] The introduction of mission studies received the most attention (see discussion and proposal 1980). The introduction of social sciences was discussed in 1991. On several occasions workshops on various disciplines were offered, at *KBA* Conferences as well as at EEAA biannual meetings.

[52] Egelkraut is referring to all west European countries with large Protestant populations, but his comments are certainly spoken out of the German context.

[53] This thesis is based on the interviews of the author with senior leaders of the following schools: *Adelshofen, Beatenberg, Brake, Chrischona, Liebenzell* and *Wiedenest*.

[54] This includes *Aarau* and *IGW*.

[55] This is based on the current discussion in the context of the *KBA* and among Bible colleges and seminaries in Switzerland, especially the meetings of December 1997 and March 1998.

[56] This is certainly the experience of *IGW*.

PART FIVE

TO CHANGE OR NOT TO CHANGE?

SUMMARY AND OUTLOOK

This concluding Part has two foci: chapter 12 will summarise the findings of this investigation and put them in context. The central question is: in what ways do the results of this investigation contribute to the wider understanding of Christian mission, theology of mission, theological education and mission studies?

In chapter 13 the underlying issues identified at the ends of Parts Three and Four, namely conservatism, change patterns and epistemology, will be reconsidered. The critical analysis will be carried one step further, looking at these issues from the perspective of Kuhn's theory of paradigm shifts and MacIntyre's theory of the rationality of traditions. This methodology will hopefully contribute to a deeper understanding of change patterns in conservative (evangelical) institutions with a significance beyond *the Schools* analysed in this study. This will also open new windows for further research.

CHAPTER 12

The Contributions of this Study

In response to the objectives stated at the outset of this study the following conclusions can be drawn:

1. A Neglected Tradition of Theological Education and Mission Studies Deserves Recognition

Part Two of this thesis focused on the history of evangelical theological education and mission studies in Germany and German-speaking Switzerland. The significance of the findings become apparent by putting the results in context. In his massive 1955–1957 study on *The Study of Missions in Theological Education* – still the most comprehensive investigation of the subject – Olav Guttorm Myklebust focuses on the theology departments of universities and theological seminaries mainly of ecumenical orientation. The contribution and the impact of the evangelical Bible school movement is neglected. In 1987–88 he conducted another survey, approaching more than 500 institutions around the world, of which 65 per cent responded (1989:87). In the resulting update article (1989), Myklebust admits that 'statistically speaking, "Lausanne" has taken a much more active interest in the Church's mission, and in the promotion of Missiology as a theological discipline, than has "Geneva" ' (1989:89). This missionary strength of the evangelical movement has to be seen in close relation to the Bible school movement, as argued by Fiedler (1994:144–48). Despite this fact, Myklebust focuses his 1989 analysis mainly on graduate institutions. He states, 'Bible Schools, strictly so-called, are left out, not because they are not important enough, but they clearly constitute a category of their own. Their number is estimated at 3000 or more' (1989:88).

This study has focused on this neglected 'category of their own' by analysing the developments of Bible schools in Germany and German-speaking Switzerland. What are the results?

1. In one area, Myklebust's assessment can only be affirmed: 'Lausanne' has taken a much more active interest in promoting mission training, than has 'Geneva.' To quote Myklebust in his 1989 analysis:

> However, a review of missiological developments in the latter half of this century also reveals less bright features. No less than 19 professorships of Missiology have ceased to exist, mostly in Europe (14). Required courses in the subject have become elective, or have disappeared from the curriculum. In not a few cases the holder of a chair of Missiology has resigned to become professor of one of the 'classical' disciplines of theology. In the majority of theological institutions the place accorded to Missiology is only a marginal one (1989:99).

This assessment is certainly true in the context of the theology departments of the universities in Germany and Switzerland. More recent studies, based on the WCC's proposal on the Renewal of Theological Education, affirm these trends (Werner 1992; Werner 1995). It is over against these facts that the results of this study gain significance. There is a tradition of evangelical Bible schools and seminaries in German-speaking Europe comprising more than thirty schools; the tradition is deeply rooted in the missionary movement of the nineteenth century. More than 10,000 students studied in these schools during the period under investigation (1960 to 1995). The vast majority of German Protestant missionaries working abroad are graduates of these schools. Any serious study on mission awareness, mission activities and mission training in German-speaking Europe has to consider the contribution of these schools.

2. This movement of Bible schools and seminaries has undergone tremendous changes in the past thirty to forty years. One of them is the significant rise of the academic level of teaching, research and writing. Today most schools have mission teachers with masters- and doctorate-level degrees in relevant fields of missiology. With the *Freie Hochschule für Mission* an interdenominational evangelical graduate school of mission was established. It includes a research centre supporting research at both masters and doctorate level. German evangelical mission theologians have joined under the umbrella of the *Arbeitsgemeinschaft für Evangelikale Missiology (AfEM)* with its journal *Evangelikale Missiologie (em)* and the AfEM edition. A growing group of German and Swiss evangelical theologians have conducted doctoral research and are engaged in academic writing. The somewhat hidden, almost sectarian Bible school movement has developed into a respectable force in academic missiological research, writing, teaching and action. Based on this evidence, this study argues that any comprehensive investigation of missiology and mission training in the context of German-speaking Europe has to incorporate the movement of evangelical missiology and mission training investigated by this thesis.

3. While the various aspects of mission studies, as expressed by what this study terms a new paradigm of theological education, will be

discussed later on, one major contribution needs to be introduced here. We have shown evidence that despite all the deficiencies of evangelical missiology and theological education, *the Schools* have incorporated some of the key features called for by the new paradigm. This refers to the mission-orientation, the integration of mission in the curriculum, the integration of theory and practice, as well as the unity and integration of the curriculum. Within this tradition of evangelical schools it was obviously possible to maintain the church and its mission at the centre of theological studies in a way called for by ecumenical educators but hardly achieved by state-university related schools.[1] This puts serious questions to theological education and mission studies in the context of state universities (at least in the German-speaking context). This study suggests that it is important to consider more carefully the contribution of these schools when issues of theological education and mission studies are discussed.

4. This leads to an additional contribution of this study. It brings to the foreground the contribution of a tradition of alternative theological training, in which 'alternative' refers to the recognised paths of the university. In the awareness of the public as well as the theological academics of the universities, the contribution of *the Schools* is often viewed at best as inferior and marginal. Such an assessment is based on the cultural values of a society which regards only those educational achievements as valuable which are conducted and reached within the system of state universities. Looking at achievements in theological and missionary training from the perspective of a new paradigm of theological education – that is, its output in view of the church in mission – this study demonstrates that high quality education can be provided in schools not formally related to the state university system. Despite possible disagreements of a theological nature, scepticism at the denominational level and the deficiencies of evangelical theological education (which will be discussed later on), one has to recognise how deeply this challenges the closed and elitist system of state universities still current in Germany and Switzerland.

2. A Movement Refuses to Go Along with the Paradigm Shift – Or David Bosch's Dream Reconsidered

In Part Three this study looked at the theology of mission represented by *the Schools* using David Bosch's proposal of 'an emerging ecumenical paradigm of mission.' This means, Bosch's paradigm serves as a grid to locate the mission theology of German evangelicals on the global and ecumenical map of mission theory. Consequently, the analysis went in two directions, first putting the German evangelical theology of mission in context, and in return, reviewing Bosch's paradigm regarding its capability to provide a global and ecumenical map.

a) German Evangelical Theology of Mission in Context

1. On the first level, research showed that German evangelical theology of mission, as represented by *the Schools*, has to be located at the *conservative*-evangelical corner of a global and ecumenical map. The heritage of Peter Beyerhaus and the impact of the *Frankfurt Declaration* play a determinative role in *the Schools'* recent history. This position centres in an emphatic commitment to the Bible as the authoritative and normative word of God. This leads to a high degree of scepticism toward all those attempts at contextualisation which have formed the core of the paradigm shift in mission. Based on this conviction, the developments in missionary thinking and action within the WCC are viewed as a severe deviation from the biblical understanding of mission, if not as heresy. Beyerhaus and people around him have attacked the WCC and its mission programme with an apocalyptic style[2] of apologetics.

2. Beyond this, conservative evangelicals in Germany have also expressed serious concerns regarding developments within the evangelical movement's understanding of mission. From the first analysis of Lausanne 1974 by Beyerhaus up to the most recent doctoral dissertation by Berneburg (1997), the so-called 'radical,' 'social-concern' or 'Two-Thirds World' evangelicals are criticised because of their high concern for contextualisation and integral mission.

3. This leads to a rather narrow scope of missiological teaching and thinking at *the Schools*. Textbooks tend to be restricted to conservative evangelical views, many of them with an apologetic flavour. Ecumenical literature plays a marginal role in most libraries, and there is a lack of German translations of literature from a broader evangelical perspective (including evangelical mission theologians from the Two Thirds World).

4. How do we evaluate this strand of evangelical theology of mission? If we follow James Barr's analysis of fundamentalism, there is nothing for which this movement must be credited and honoured (1977:344). Looking from the point of view of the research of this thesis this author suggests four areas in which German conservative evangelicals contribute to the larger discussion of the theology of mission:[3]

(a) In the struggle for contextualisation and the attempts to formulate an intercultural theology, conservative evangelicals continue to point to scripture as the norm and authority for all Christian theology.[4]

(b) In the struggle towards the articulation of a holistic and integrated understanding of mission, conservative evangelicals continue to remind us of evangelisation as an indispensable part of mission.

(c) In the struggle for an understanding of salvation in the tension between history and eternity, material and spiritual, conservative evangelicals continue to emphasise the eternal and eschatological dimension of salvation.

(d) In the struggle to solve the 'largest unresolved problem for the Christian church' (Bosch 1991:476–77), namely the articulation of a theology of religions,[5] conservative evangelicals continue to point to the fact that the biblical data on the uniqueness of Christ as the way of salvation must be included in any serious attempt to formulate how the Christian faith relates to other faiths.

Of course, German conservative evangelicals are not the only people insisting on these points, and their insistence is sometimes carried out in a very confrontational manner which terminates dialogue rather than opening it up. Furthermore, they have also so far failed to present convincing solutions for many of these difficult problems. Nonetheless, the wider ecumenical community is well advised not to stop listening to these conservative voices, as Lesslie Newbigin has stated recently, referring to the WCC's plea 'for closer links with such evangelical bodies as the World Evangelical Fellowship' as expressed in the WCC's statement, 'Toward a Common Understanding and Vision of the World Council of Churches':[6]

> But I do not think that the desire here expressed will be fulfilled unless the WCC gives much more evidence of being filled with a longing to bring the Gospel to all peoples. It is right to stress that the responsibility for mission and evangelism lies primarily with each congregation in the place where it is. But it is necessary also to remember both that there are vast areas where there are no Christian congregations, also that none of our local churches so fully reflect the glory of Christ that they do not need help from others.
> The WCC has given courageous leadership in the struggle for peace and justice in the fight against racism and in concern for peace and integrity of creation. It has been the prime mover in the search for closer Christian unity. But in so powerfully challenging the churches on these issues it does seem to have lost its missionary passion that was the vital force that created the ecumenical movement in the closing of the nineteenth and the opening years of the twentieth centuries. The demand for unity among the churches and the demand for justice and peace among the nations, if they are not rooted in what God has done for all the world in Jesus Christ, can themselves become a new form of domination. There cannot be any greater task, or any deeper joy, than to tell the world what God has done for us in Jesus Christ and to enable others to know, love, and serve him as Lord and Saviour (1997:52).

5. At the same time, we observed that this tradition of conservative evangelical schools holds mainly to a fundamentalist, anti-ecumenical position, incorporating several rather problematic elements. We have

shown evidence that the polarisation between the evangelical and the ecumenical streams of the world mission movement developed in German-speaking Europe in the time following the integration of the IMC with the WCC in 1961. This in turn has led *the Schools* into separation and isolation, resulting both in their loss of contact with the global and ecumenical developments in mission and theological education and in their resistance to changes in theological thinking. They did so not merely on biblical grounds, as they often claim, but were also influenced by ideological presuppositions. It is the thesis of this study that some of *the Schools* suffer from an ideological conservatism which causes them to resist changes which may be decisive for their future.

b) David Bosch's Proposal Reconsidered

It is the thesis of this study that in the light of the investigation of German conservative evangelical theology of mission, the 'emerging ecumenical paradigm of mission' proposed by David Bosch needs some corrections and amendments. This does not in any way limit the value of Bosch's proposal, it only expands it to a more comprehensive picture. Beyond the critiques of Bosch's thesis, discussed in the respective parts of this thesis, two final conclusions must be drawn:

1. The empirical research of this thesis identifies a strand of Christian mission (German conservative evangelical missions) that Bosch did not describe and has only marginally recognised. This strand is in many ways not developing in the direction of what Bosch describes as 'an emerging ecumenical paradigm of mission.' This calls into question the ecumenical scope of Bosch's paradigm. A paradigm which deserves the term 'ecumenical' is obligated to integrate all strands of the Christian movement, especially if a strand represents such a significant tradition as German Pietism.[7]

2. Beyond this the analysis of Bosch has shown that the core of his concern is the integration of the opposed 'evangelical' and 'ecumenical' positions. We have pointed to the fact that he intends to move 'beyond' the polarisation towards a 'creative tension.' Yet, the research of this study indicates that Bosch's 'emerging ecumenical paradigm' is highly idealistic, describing a desired convergence of opposing strands of the world Christian movement, yet not paying attention to the diverging strands of Christian mission. This does not diminish Bosch's proposal as a *vision* which deserves support. Yet the realisation of this vision seems remote, given the findings of this research.[8]

3. A New Paradigm in Theological Education Emerges – but is it Really that New?

In Part Four of the thesis, *the Schools* were analysed in the light of paradigm shifts in theological education. Unlike the preceding part on the theology of mission, a synthesis of what an *emerging new paradigm of theological education* would be is not already available. Therefore, this study has (1) first of all established such a synthesis, which is then (2) applied to *the Schools.*

a) The Synthesis of an Emerging New Paradigm of Theological Education

Research has shown that theological education has been undergoing significant changes in the Post War period, especially since the 1960s. Several streams of reflection are discussed in this study as evidence of these shifts. Using paradigm theory, this study puts forward what appears to be a *new paradigm of theological education*. The claim to be a paradigm demands synthesis, comprehensiveness and integration – that is, all observable strands must be synthesised into an integrated theory (cf. Bosch 1991:368). Based on this presupposition the thesis establishes a paradigm of theological education, synthesising seven significant strands of reflection and practice and identifying four interrelated features of this paradigm, which are mission-orientation, church/people-orientation, inductive pedagogy and integrated curriculum. The significance of this synthesis is as follows:

1. The paradigm of theological education which has been emerging in the last three to four decades has never been synthesised in such a comprehensive way. This makes the results of this study an important tool for the analysis of theological education in different contexts.

2. The synthesis of the different streams of reflection and practice has brought together ideas and experiences of various origins and context. This has shown an amazing potential of cross-fertilisation, an aspect which has not been considered thus far. This can be demonstrated on several levels:

(a) Farley's reflection on distancing and involvement inspires the discussions both of theory and practice and of extension education.

(b) Bosch's introduction of the terms 'dimension and 'intention' fertilises the entire debate on the place mission should take in the curriculum.

(c) The whole discussion on integration is inspired by several strands, each one contributing another aspect: Bosch's focus on intention and dimension, Farley's emphasis on the recovery of theology as *habitus*, the extension movement's push for contextuality and the stress placed by inductive learning theory on the action-reflection process.

(d) The sometimes euphoric experiments in the history of the extension movement are balanced by pedagogical insights both from inductive learning theory and from Farley, emphasising not only contextual involvement but also detached reflection.

Consequently the paradigm proposed by this thesis is not a mere list of items, but a holistic paradigm which reaches a quality beyond the sum of its parts (cf. Shenk 1993b).

3. In the end, a very significant result of this study is the fact that even some of the study's presuppositions require adjustment. A mission-oriented, contextual and integrated philosophy of theological education does not primarily focus on some 'mission studies' somewhere 'in theological education' – as the title of the thesis indicates. This is the Warneck-Myklebust approach,[9] seeking to secure mission a place in the curriculum. While the 'intention' aspect has its rightful place (cf. Bosch 1991:496–98), it certainly provides a much too limited scope. If put into order, the 'dimension' aspect deserves priority because it provides the foundation, a mission-oriented theology, based on which specific missiological research and teaching can alone make sense. This is what Bosch is calling for, pointing to the necessary shift 'from a theology of mission to a missionary theology' (1991:492–96). As a result of the investigation, we can therefore suggest the following subtitle for this study: 'From Mission Studies in Theological Education to Mission-oriented Theological Education.'

b) Mixed Responses and a Challenge to the Paradigm

Looking at *the Schools* in the light of such a new paradigm of theological education, the study leads to several conclusions which show potential for far-reaching contributions:

1. First of all, the schools investigated in this study are rooted in a tradition which already encompassed many features of what we have defined as a new paradigm of theological education. In this sense this study calls *the Schools* to remain faithful to the positive dimensions of their heritage. In addition to that it raises critical issues regarding the paradigm itself. This paradigm is the response to the deep dissatisfaction with western academic theological education, especially by people in the Two Thirds World. The products of the Enlightenment university model of theological education have been identifed as,

- a lack of missionary orientation,
- academic work in an ivory-tower,
- detachment from the reality of the church in mission,
- separation of theory and practice,
- fragmentation of the curriculum.

As our culture moves from modernity to post-modernity, alternative, post-modern paradigms of theological training are suggested. This study demonstrates that many of these values and features of theological education, now proposed as a 'new paradigm', are not that new and that they have been alive in certain traditions of theological education. The research in this thesis supports the view that in the context of pietism, neo-pietism and evangelicalism – or those strands of Christianity in which the Bible, personal spirituality and missionary zeal were kept alive – theological education – or better, ministerial and missionary training – were kept close to what now emerges as a 'new paradigm.'

2. Furthermore, the study shows that certain elements of that new paradigm have been stimulated by the particular problems and needs of certain contexts. These have given the impetus to create new models of theological training, theological education by extension being the key example. Yet research has shown that a significant argument in favour of the TEE structure, namely the detachment normally associated with residential schools, is not so much a problem in Germany and Switzerland as it is in Guatemala or India. Consequently, to bring the TEE type to Europe will not have the same impact as in other cultural settings. It is therefore imperative to distinguish between paradigms and types, forms or structures. A paradigm defines the way we think about theological education in terms of orientation, aims, values and pedagogical concepts. It spells out a philosophy of education, the framework in which theological training will be carried out. This can be done using different types and forms of schools and educational institutions. While the paradigm has a universal scope, the types or structures have a contextual one. Just as it did not make sense to copy western forms of training in the Two Thirds World, it does not make sense for the churches in Europe to produce carbon copies of structures successful in other parts of the world. The paradigm needs to be contextualised and this may lead to various types and structures in various cultural settings.

3. Furthermore, the investigation has revealed a disturbing tension between accreditation and the values of the new paradigm. In seeking academic accreditation through association with the EEAA, *the Schools* jeopardised some of the core values of the Bible school movement. In some ways *the Schools* can be blamed for not succeeding in integrating higher academic standards with the values of their educational tradition. However, one might also question accreditation procedures. If accreditation aims at quality assurance, then quality must be defined. If quality is according to the paradigm of theological education put forward in this study, then it certainly goes beyond the pure academic standards of the university system. Whenever theological schools seek validation through the university system, they know that the university will only measure the quality of academic work in comparison to university standards, and they may add internal values in accordance with their mission. But the case of the EEAA, where the focus is on the accreditation

of theological schools, aiming at the quality of theological education, ought to be different. Based on the research of this study, the EEAA, and other agencies supervising theological education, are urged to review their accreditation procedures in the light of the established paradigm. The task is to find means of quality measurement which include all aspects of the paradigm.

4. The research has also shown puzzling change dynamics among *the Schools*. On the one hand, *the Schools* have demonstrated great flexibility as they moved from Bible schools to theological colleges, even at the cost of some of the strengths of their heritage. On the other hand, they have obviously resisted fundamental changes at the level touching on hermeneutical and epistemological issues – or contextual, inductive learning – not to speak of the resistance to change their theology of mission. This suggests, as a tentative generalisation, that educational institutions of conservative theological orientation tend to refuse changes at the level of content and epistemology, yet they may be open for changes at the formal and structural level. Based on these observations, this author would even argue that there is a relation between conservative-fundamentalist theology and the tendency to resist a more democratic, contextual, holistic and inductive pedagogy – a thesis which certainly calls for further research.

In the light of the above, the conclusion of this study will not be complete without pointing to the critical issue of epistemology. Throughout the study – in the section dedicated to the theology of mission (Part Three), as well as in the one dedicated to theological education (Part Four) – contextualisation and hermeneutics appeared to be *the* critical issues. At the very heart of the debate, be it theological or educational, is the question of how 'true' theology can be articulated in the tension between the biblical text and the context of a particular situation. For conservative evangelicals, whose deepest concern seems to be biblical orthodoxy, epistemology appears to be an issue of central importance. The investigation leaves us with the impression – though this may be something of an overstatement – that a small group of German conservative evangelical theologians think they are the only ones who hold to true biblical orthodoxy. It is the assessment of this author that many of the conservative theologians in the context of *the Schools* do not really accept two basic realities of our time: (a) the reality that 'the traditional western concept of truth has collapsed' (Hicks:135); and (b) the reality of the diversity of the church in its ecumenical and global scope living in various cultural contexts. To withdraw from modernity and from the global and ecumenical dialogue and to retreat into an in-house conversation which only leads to the reaffirmation of the propositional claims of western conservative evangelicalism cannot be the way into the future. *The Schools* ought to engage in the global and ecumenical search for reformulating a Bible-based, contextually relevant epistemology in view of modernity, post-modernity, ecumenicity and the global church.

This final conclusion provokes a further question which can be put under the heading 'conservatism and change.' It is precisely this issue which will be considered in the concluding section.

Notes

1 See the discussion of the university model p. 49, also Engel and Werner; Werner 1992, 1995; Bittner.

2 See p. 195; also the further discussion of the apologetic style of conservative evangelical theologians p. 298.

3 The four points follow the missiological themes discussed in Part Three.

4 Cf. *Frankfurt Declaration*, # 1.

5 Cf. Gerald Anderson's recent article 'Theology of Religions: The Epitome of Mission Theology,' which he has written in response to David Bosch (1996).

6 Newbigin is not referring to *conservative* evangelicals in particular, but he points to issues which conservative evangelicals emphasise with great vigour.

7 Though not all strands within German Pietism associate with the movement of *the Schools*, these schools certainly belong to the pietistic strand of the Protestant churches in Germany and Switzerland.

8 From a Latin American point of view, René Padilla has recently affirmed that the ecumenical and the evangelical movements are diverging rather than converging (1993:192).

9 Still in his 1987/88 survey, Myklebust asked *the Schools* the following two questions: '1. Whether Missiology is recognized as a subject in its own right (separate chair/department), or whether it is combined with some other subjects (Church History, Practical Theology, Religious Studies, etc.); and 2. whether Missiology, if granted a separate status, is part of the core curriculum, or whether it is offered as an elective' (1989:87). Myklebust acknowledges the necessity of a missionary dimension of all theology but maintains his focus on the significance of departments and chairs of missiology (1989:101).

CHAPTER 13

The Critical Issue Reconsidered: Change and Epistemology

At first glance this final chapter seems to deviate from the topic of this thesis. Mission studies in theological education are no longer at the surface. Yet, as this study was proceeding, the underlying issue of *how conservative evangelicals deal with change*[1] kept emerging. Even though it is not indicated in the title, it became a main feature of the thesis and deserves some concluding reflections.

We will do this on the basis of Kuhnian paradigm theory, introduced at the beginning of the thesis. In addition to Kuhn, we will also employ MacIntyre's concept of tradition-constituted enquiry which pushes us to carry the argument beyond Kuhn.[2]

1. Understanding Change Processes

Actually, at the beginning of this study the Kuhnian theory was only introduced in order to understand David Bosch's thesis of paradigm change in mission and to define paradigm terminology which is used throughout the study. However, as this author was proceeding with research and reflection it became more and more apparent that the Kuhnian theory itself would be a very illuminating tool for the exploration of the change dynamics of *the Schools*. Such an additional analysis stands by no means in isolation from the research done in this study, as a disconnected appendix. On the contrary, it brings to the foreground what this author believes to be one of the key issues in the interpretation of the material presented here.

As a bridge from Kuhn to the analysis of *the Schools*, it is helpful to use Hans Küng's application of paradigm theory to theology. This brings us back to the Tübingen Consultation of 1984. In his paper entitled 'What does a Change of Paradigm Mean?' (Küng and Tracy 1989:212–19), Küng employs the Kuhnian theory to demonstrate how changes in theology and church develop. He sees 'clearly certain parallels, similarities and analogies' between the natural sciences and theology (1989:11) and presents them in five thesis statements. Having pointed out the areas of analogy of natural science and theology, Küng then moves on to draw our attention to the differences, which, in his view, are no less essential. He therefore complements the five analogy statements with five difference statements (1989:32ff.).[3] These five statements of Küng provide the background against which this final assessment of *the Schools'* change behaviour will be conducted. In short they are as follows:

1. The ruling paradigm is stable and any changes are resisted by its protectors.
2. Only a crisis of the ruling paradigm will open up the readiness for change.
3. Only the emergence of a valuable new paradigm candidate will enhance change readiness.
4. The decision towards a new paradigm is not only a conclusion reached by rational reasoning, it includes also an irrational step of 'faith' (conversion).
5. Change processes can take various routs: *evolutionary* transformation, *revolutionary* change, or *reactionary* repression.

Following these five steps we now proceed to an analysis of change processes among conservative evangelicals based on the research of this study.

There is one significant observation which touches on all five steps of the change process which we have noticed earlier and needs to be recalled at this point. Research has shown that there is a considerable difference in the change behaviour of *the Schools* at different levels. On the one hand, there is a high degree of stability on the level of mission theology, on the other hand, there is a fair amount of flexibility on the formal level of educational models, although the two are interrelated. Put differently, there is much change resistance on the level of theological theory and much more change readiness on the structural and formal level. This deserves special attention and interpretation as we go along.

a) Thesis 1: Stability of the Old Paradigm and Change-Resistance

One of Kuhn's observations is that 'students accept certain models of understanding, less as a result of proofs than because of the authority of the textbook they study and of the teacher to whom they listen' (Küng and Tracy 1989:11). It seems that the academic community (in all areas of academic work) is conservative and protective and does not advance fundamental changes which may challenge the existing paradigm.[4] Küng claims that this is certainly true of the theological realm and the church. 'In all times and in all places, traditional *theology* has been extremely suspicious of the category of the *novum* ... The attitude has maintained that *innovators* were heresiarchs, heretics, enemies of the church ...' (Küng and Tracy 1989:3). This leads Küng to his first thesis:

> Like natural science, the theological community has a 'normal science' with its classical authors, textbooks and teachers, which is characterised by a cumulative growth of knowledge, by a solution of remaining problems ('puzzles'), and by resistance to everything that might result in a changing or replacement of the established paradigm (1989:14).

But at least one major difference between natural science and theology must, according to Küng, be kept in mind (Küng and Tracy 1984:63). While in the natural sciences, the 'old' paradigm is constituted by the tradition of authors, publications and teachers, any theological paradigm is, by definition, rooted in the tradition of scripture, which is the *norma normans*. Thus, the tradition has, to the extent that it represents scripture, ultimate normative value.

How does this apply to the observations of this investigation?

1. On the level of the *theory of mission*, the stabilising influence of Beyerhaus's theology has been observed in this study, as well as the strong effort to legitimise the contemporary position of conservative evangelical theology of mission through an orthodox tradition. There is an implicit, and occasionally even explicit,[5] claim that the theology of mission proposed by the Beyerhaus school stands in the line of biblical orthodoxy, i.e., *is true*. We have also shown that considerable apologetic efforts have been made to defend this position. Furthermore, the analysis demonstrated that the textbooks accessible to students tend to be limited to publications advocating this position. In paradigm terminology, this indicated a very self-protecting, closed system. There are inherited change resisting patterns, such as the claim that the present paradigm *is the truth*, the discrediting of other theories and the restriction of thinking and research to the boundaries of a given doctrinal tradition.

Now, according to Küng, such conservative patterns can be rooted in mere traditionalism, or they can have biblical grounding. Yet, what Küng separates so nicely cannot so easily be separated in reality. This leads us directly to the core of the conservative-evangelical problem. Of course, they ground their theory of mission on the Bible, or should we say, on their interpretation of the Bible. With this we approach the issues of orthodoxy, hermeneutics and truth – or simply, as Peter Hicks has entitled his book, *Evangelicals and Truth* (1998).

The question of orthodoxy is without any doubt crucial to evangelicals, especially to its conservative wing, often labelled fundamentalism. Evangelicals view their beliefs as standing in line with the Christian tradition which remained faithful to the Bible. James Barr rightly states (1988:148):

> One of the beliefs of fundamentalists is that they belong to a long chain of orthodox beliefs which stretches back through older Protestantism to the Reformation itself, and beyond that to the orthodoxy of the early church.... they think, there has always been a line even if only a narrow line, in which the true faith has been maintained, and there have been periods – part of the history of the early church, and the Reformation, plus above all the evangelical revivals – which have been outcrops of brilliantly true doctrinal purity.

Barr calls this 'selective orthodoxy,' because

> it picks out from ancient orthodoxy the elements which it, in its modern situation, wishes to accentuate positively: it ignores the fact that the same orthodoxy had many elements which are quite contrary to modern evangelicalism (1988:149)

Such selective orthodoxy is not even wrong, argues Barr (1988:154). It becomes problematic only when fundamentalists use selective orthodoxy to link their view directly with the Bible and in so doing, claim ultimate truth for their positions.

One need not agree with all of Barr's assessment of fundamentalism to realise the validity of the argument we just have introduced. It reveals the circle of arguments which establish what paradigm theory would call an institutionalised tradition of knowledge. As soon as a particular theological strand claims that its interpretation of the Bible represents the tradition of *true biblical orthodoxy*, and at the same time apologetically critiques other traditions of biblical interpretation for being outside of the *truly biblical* tradition, this becomes institutionalised conservatism. In the context of theological training this may have serious effects on the educational climate and process. Some of the possible deficiencies may be the following:[6]

a) A heavy emphasis on the authority of the Bible, combined with the understanding that orthodox theology can be deduced from the Bible as propositional truth, tends to create an educational milieu in which cognitive, deductive learning is at the centre.

b) A heavy emphasis on tradition and continuity, combined with a high level of suspicion about new ideas and changes, tends to create an educational milieu in which changes will be perceived primarily as threats.

c) A heavy emphasis on the battle for truth, combined with a minority situation, tends to create a milieu of defence, prophetic vocation and martyrdom.

d) A heavy emphasis on belief in a spiritual battle in the intellectual and academic world, combined with the tendency to demonise certain theories and philosophies, tends to create a protective educational milieu which prevents broad academic research, as well as open dialogue and interaction with the other philosophical and theological strands.

e) A heavy emphasis on orthodoxy, combined with the understanding that orthodoxy is expressed by certain theological definitions (and in the right terminology), tends to create an educational milieu of mistrust, 'bounded set' thinking (cf. Hiebert 1980:92–95) based on code-words and control.

With this we have not decided whether the theology of mission defended by conservative evangelicals is wrong or right. We only point to the mechanisms of conservatism by using paradigm language. Conservative evangelical theology and its educational institutions are well advised to be aware of these mechanisms.

This is not the place to analyse other theological currents, but we may take note of the fact that all theological strands, be they called liberal, modernist, critical or feminist are in danger of functioning according to the pattern of institutionalised traditions (cf. Marsden 1997).

2. Looking at the *forms and structures* of evangelical theological education in Germany and Switzerland, we observe a much greater flexibility. Research has shown that *the Schools* have changed in the last four decades, in some areas more incidentally, in others deliberately. They have sought accreditation with certainty and decision and with it a whole range of changes. It seems that evangelicals, even their more conservative wing, are not so conservative when it comes to functional changes or, put in other words, when the successful accomplishment of their mission is at stake. This study has not focused on the universities, but from what has been gleaned, it may be fair to say that the 'conservatives' prove to be more 'liberal,' and the 'liberals' more 'conservative,' when it comes to the issue of adjusting forms and structures to new realities. The research of this study suggests several reasons for this. As regards the evangelicals, their concentration on a small core of identifiable, orthodox beliefs, combined with their strong emphasis on reaching the world with the gospel through the greatest possible measure of co-operation with other Christians who share those core convictions, as well as their relative independence from the historically established church structures and the state, allows them to exercise flexibility as long as this does not conflict with their core beliefs. On the other hand, so-called 'liberals,' while rather flexible in terms of theological thinking, are in most cases strongly related to established church traditions and – in Europe – to the state. In the case of theological departments which are part of state universities and run by state churches, the commitment to the institutional stability of church and society is obvious. This setting allows only minimal structural changes.[7]

Nonetheless we have also pointed to the limitations of the evangelicals' flexibility. The analysis has shown that the flexibility stops when critical theological issues are at stake. In praxis, contextual education and inductive learning are regarded very critically, because they touch on such sensitive issues as hermeneutics, epistemology and truth. With this we are back to the deficiencies of institutionalised conservatism discussed earlier.

Thus, paradigm theory supports the thesis we suggested earlier, namely that educational institutions claiming a conservative theory may be flexible at a formal and structural level but will resist formal and structural changes as soon as they question the status quo of their sacrosanct theory. Institutions of theological education would do well to pay attention to this pattern.

b) Thesis 2: Crisis Awareness and Change Readiness

The second thesis is based on Kuhn's observation that paradigm shifts are usually introduced by a crisis of the paradigm in function:

> As in natural science, so also in the theological community, *awareness of a growing crisis* is the starting-point for the advent of a drastic change in certain hitherto prevailing basic assumptions, and eventually causes the breakthrough of a new paradigm or model of understanding. When the available rules and methods break down, they lead to a search for new ones (Küng and Tracy 1989:20).

Again, Küng points to the fact that this thesis is also true of theology, and he gives evidence by pointing to some of the major paradigm shifts of Christian history (Küng and Tracy:15).

But again, there is also a significant difference in theology (Küng and Tracy 1981:64): whereas in the natural sciences the crisis which finally introduces a paradigm change is the result of the breakdown of the old paradigm, in theology the search for a new paradigm can be initiated by fresh encounter with the message of the Bible.[8] The search for a new paradigm is, therefore, not only caused by the crisis of the current paradigm and an innovative step *forward* but also on a serious look *back* to the very roots of Christianity.

Applied to this study this implies the following:

1. Crisis awareness and crisis response of conservative evangelical *theology of mission* have been discussed in the thesis (Part III). The emphasis is definitely on continuity, not on change. This is not to say that there is no awareness of crisis. The titles of Beyerhaus's publications alone are enough evidence of *that*. But Beyerhaus speaks not of a crisis encountered by the evangelical paradigm of mission, not of an

epistemological crisis of evangelical orthodoxy. He diagnoses an external crisis of the church as it experiences growing resistance in world mission, and he diagnoses an internal crisis in the church in general, especially in the ecumenical movement, a critical loss of biblical grounding. In Beyerhaus's view, the crisis can be identified in historical criticism, loss of biblical orthodoxy and humanism. Thus, Beyerhaus does not perceive the evangelical paradigm of mission as being in crisis. In paradigm language, since the ruling paradigm is not experienced as being in crisis, there is no need and no desire for change, in contrast to the ecumenical movement. There, the dramatic changes in the world situation and especially the heavy critique of traditional western mission in the anti-colonial period were perceived to have shaken the foundations of the western understanding of mission (Collet). The old paradigm is experienced as having collapsed. This results in a search for a new paradigm, the features of which we have discussed according to Werner's (1993) presentation (see p. 121).

2. In view of *forms and structures*, the most recent developments in *the Schools* clearly indicate a crisis-awareness. The decrease in student numbers over the last years has caused serious questions. The 1996 survey utilised in this study is only one of the expressions of the crisis-awareness. It is also evident that this crisis is perceived as caused by external factors. There are seemingly 'unidentifiable' changes in society, in the church, in the world which cause serious reflection and consideration. The traditional models of theological training are obviously called into question, be this justified or not. To use paradigm-language: the old paradigm is no longer capable of providing satisfying answers to the new realities. This has opened and will open the way for further changes. And what about Küng's scenario of biblical renewal? As far as this study shows, *the Schools* have increased their level of change readiness only under the pressure of external causes, not based on the recovery of a biblical mandate for theological training.

c) Thesis 3: Openness for New Paradigm Candidates

Furthermore, Kuhn observed that it is not merely a crisis of the existing paradigm that is needed to cause a paradigm change, but also an emerging new paradigm. 'The model to be replaced needs a worthy, a credible model to succeed it before it can retire. It needs a new "paradigm candidate" ' (Küng and Tracy 1989:20). Küng concludes:

> As in natural science, so also in the theological community, an older paradigm or model of understanding is replaced when a new one is available (1989:23).

But in natural science a paradigm shift can lead to a very radical change with great discontinuity and minimal continuity with the old paradigm; in theology, scripture, the common ground of the old and the new paradigms, always provides a major emphasis on continuity. Any paradigm change in 'theology can – if theology wants to remain biblical and Christian – only be carried out *based* on the gospel, *because* of the gospel, and never *against* the gospel' (Küng and Tracy 1984:65).

Looking at the results of this study in the light of this third thesis, we conclude:

1. The analysis of conservative evangelical *theology of mission* has shown evidence of a clear refusal of any new paradigm which has emerged in the last three to four decades. Why? What does this mean in paradigm language? One part of the answer is given with our observation in the previous sections. A tradition of institutionalised conservatism, of satisfaction with the status quo, showing no crisis awareness, will hardly look for alternatives. On the other hand, to use paradigm terminology, no other paradigm candidate has shown itself trustworthy enough to be considered as an alternative.

This is the point where we may gain a further understanding of the roads taken by other evangelicals. Some, especially those of the Two Thirds World, have developed their thinking toward a paradigm change in mission theory (e.g., Samuel 1996; Sugden 1997; Yung). Put in paradigm language, they do not have the long history of institutionalised evangelical orthodoxy, and they have, in their context, experienced a severe collapse of the traditional western understanding of mission. The old paradigm was in a crisis. This opened up changes, and as new paradigm candidates were created and emerged, some of them gained confidence and were picked up and integrated. In *Mangoes or Bananas. The Quest for an Authentic Asian Christian Theology,* Hwa Yung outlines how Asian evangelicals have overcome the westernisation of their theology and how they have moved towards an understanding of mission which is Bible based, contextual and holistic (Yung:191–242). Melba Maggey, writing in a Philippine context, searches for a theology of mission which is equally committed to the Bible and to the socio-political context. In *Transforming Society,* he comes up with a theology of mission shaped by western Constantinianism and emphasises an integrative understanding of the gospel as it is lived out by the community of believers in solidarity with the poor (Maggey:15ff.). The African evangelical theologian Kwame Bediako of Ghana has put forward a study which proposes an evangelical theology which is both true to the gospel and authentically African. Bediako is able to challenge some of the western conceptions of theology based on his observation of pre-Constantinian (African) Christianity. All these approaches witness to a paradigm change in mission – and are unknown to most evangelical theologians in Germany and Switzerland.

Beyond the language isolation in the German-speaking world it has been argued in this study that this is due to institutionalised conservatism.

2. As we look once more at *forms and structures*, the picture is different. Alternative models of theological education have been adopted as needs have changed. From the Bible school model *the Schools* moved to the college and seminary model. Even more radically alternative shifts are considered, such as extension education. Why did new models gain the necessary confidence to be accepted? For the college and seminary model, adopted in the accrediting process, the international reputation may have given them the necessary authority. New models, such as TEE, encounter much more difficulty in gaining acceptance as trustworthy paradigm candidates.

d) Thesis 4: Reason and 'Faith' in Change Processes

One of the major challenges of the Kuhnian theory is the observation that paradigm changes are not merely based on logical, rational insights but also on *subjective circumstances*. Even in the realm of natural science, the dimensions of *doubt* and *faith, non-scientific factors* and *religious convictions* play a vital role. Kuhn speaks of something like a conversion experience, which is needed if a person is to move from one paradigm to another (Küng and Tracy 1989:23–25). The similarities in theology are obvious, as Küng concludes:

> As in natural science, so in the theological community, in the acceptance or rejection of a new paradigm, not only scientific, but extra-scientific factors are involved, so that the transmission to a new model does not follow purely rational steps, but may be described as a conversion (1989:27).[9]

But Küng points to a problem which has to be considered carefully (Küng and Tracy 1984:66): paradigm theory claims that paradigm change calls for a 'conversion' of the scientist. Turning to theology, one has to distinguish between the 'non-religious' meaning of the term 'conversion' as it is used by Kuhn – as 'the turning to an embracing' of a new model of thinking – and its 'religious' content in biblical thinking – as 'turning to God.' Küng calls for a strict distinction between the two meanings, because often the conservative forces in the church will interpret this 'turning to' a new view of interpreting reality as a 'turning away' from God. Thus, paradigm-shift issues become faith-questions.

In view of this investigation, this would apply as follows:

1. Beginning with the *theology of mission*, we have to pick up the process with the statement that there appears to be neither crisis awareness nor change readiness in conservative evangelical theology of

mission represented by *the Schools*. Paradigm theory raises the question of whether the climate in which these convictions grew and in which these decisions had to be taken has contributed in any form to the development of the process. Kuhn and Küng would suggest that a state of affairs in which the issues are discussed only on an intellectual level, even in an atmosphere of threat and personal mistrust, would certainly not enhance the feasibility of the faith-step necessary for the acceptance of a new paradigm. It certainly goes beyond the scope of this study to answer this question. It is mere speculation to claim that given another constellation of persons, the story would have developed in different directions. Yet paradigm theory encourages such a speculation. These rather speculative thoughts have been articulated purposefully. If Kuhn is right, then there is much more individuality and irrationality in theological decisions and convictions than conservative evangelical theology admits. In Beyerhaus's argumentation, mission theory appears to be based purely on the reasonable interpretation of the Bible. Paradigm theory would suggest that there are more factors at the level of interpersonal dynamics, personality, biographical determination, atmosphere and irrational steps of 'faith' than conservative evangelical theology normally acknowledges.

This leads to the question of what kind of climate is created at *the Schools*. Küng's theory suggests that in institutionalised traditions of the church, the step of faith needed to embrace a new paradigm is often seen as a step outside the orthodox community of faith. This means that institutionalised conservatism does not normally create a milieu which supports changes in theological thinking. On the contrary, it creates a climate of threat, suppression and mistrust. A person ready to accept another paradigm will have to face the community's judgement that he/she has abandoned the orthodox faith. Again James Barr has identified the issue well. He concludes that the 'fear that one will lose one's evangelical identity' hinders many fundamentalists from leaving a fundamentalist position (1988:156–58). In paradigm language, it is the non-rational element of fear on the one hand or freedom on the other that hinders or supports paradigm changes as much as cognitive persuasion. A change of paradigms is very threatening when the person making the change will lose his/her acceptance within a given community of theologians. In a community showing features of institutionalised conservatism, the peer-pressure to remain orthodox can be enormous. Again, we are not saying that this is the kind of atmosphere in all *the Schools*, but conservative evangelicalism is certainly in danger of tending in this direction. *The Schools* would be wise to consider this dimension of their theological heritage.

2. If we look at changes in *forms and structures*, we first of all recognise that there is no recognisable threat which would make a shift towards new forms of theological training look like a deviation from orthodoxy.

The process by which Bible schools have developed into theological colleges has been characterised by a combination of rational pragmatism and a milieu supportive of the changes. With this we refer on the one hand to reasonable reflections on changing needs and demands, as well as available alternatives, and on the other hand to good relationships with North American seminaries, which led to the integration of many elements of North American models of theological training and mission studies, including the accreditation system.

In the area of more recent changes toward alternative models of theological education which would move more radically in the direction of the new paradigm, there is certainly more hesitation. This author has not encountered serious rational arguments against the implementation of more radical steps, such as extension education or moving away from residential schools. It just seems that the old paradigm is not (yet) in crisis, and there is no pressure which would call for changes. There may also be other irrational factors which hinder such shifts, like the fear to move too far away from the tradition.

e) Thesis 5: Evolution, Revolution or Repression?

Finally, Kuhn points to the fact, that a new paradigm will not automatically succeed. 'There are in principle three possible ways out of the crisis:' (a) the new paradigm is absorbed into the old; (b) the new paradigm replaces the old; and (c) the old paradigm resists a change, and the new paradigm is 'put into cold storage' (Küng and Tracy 1989:27). Thus,

> in the theological community, as in natural science, it can be predicted only with difficulty, in the midst of great controversies, whether a new paradigm is absorbed into the old, replaces the old or is shelved for a long period. But if it is accepted, innovation is consolidated as tradition (1989:28).

We can also speak of three models of change outcome: (1) *evolutionary* transformation; (2) *revolutionary* replacement; and (3) *reactionary* repression.

But, again, Küng draws our attention to a specific dimension in theology (Küng and Tracy 1984:66–67). If the existing paradigm of theology is identified with the gospel itself, then any new paradigm will be rejected.

Again, we apply this to the research and conclude:

1. In terms of *mission theory*, the verdict we have discovered is clear: the old paradigm has succeeded. All attempts to introduce new paradigms since the 1960s have been categorically refused. In the case of the Beyerhausian era, we should probably speak of a 'reactionary repression.' In the battle *against* the humanisation programme of the WCC and

for world evangelisation, conservative evangelical theology of mission has even gained momentum and strength. Never before have German evangelical theologians produced so many books on mission since Peter Beyerhaus's return from the mission field in the 1960s. The *Frankfurt Declaration* became a powerful milestone, which will hardly be moved in the near future. New shifts can only be introduced when a new generation of theologians experiences dissatisfaction with the current paradigm. This will lead to a crisis of this paradigm.

2. In view of *forms and structures* paradigm terminology would choose the word 'evolutionary transformation' as the most fitting description. All schools have slowly but steadily integrated the features of the Bible college and seminary model. If it comes to the acceptance of elements of a new paradigm of theological education, more reservation may be observed; however, aspects such as extension teaching, moving closer to the constituency and integration of mission have been picked up continuously. Only the *IGW* took more radical steps, presenting a completely alternative model incorporating many features of the new paradigm. Again, in the most crucial areas of contextual and inductive pedagogy, the theological emergency brake hindered deeper changes. These are the issues where the impact of institutionalised conservatism penetrates to the formal and structural level.

What are we going to do with these observations and reflections? Kuhn and Küng lead us to a number of critical conclusions:

1. They help us to understand that the change (or 'non-change') processes observed in this study are not just a matter of Bible-based rationality, as some of the evangelical protagonists want us to believe. The picture contains not only the issues of defining the 'right' theology of mission (Part III of the thesis) and/or of finding the 'right' ways of doing education (Part IV of the thesis). The *dynamics of change processes* belong in the picture too. Two examples may be helpful – one which led to a change and one which did not:

(a) When many of *the Schools* added a number of missiological courses to their curriculum in the late 1970s and early 1980s, this happened not just because, on the basis of the interpretation of scripture, they came to the conclusion that adding these courses would be theologically sound. Nor was this change purely based on the educational insight that a 'right' curriculum would contain courses in missiology. It was also, and this is the contribution of paradigm theory, the result of a process beginning with the dissatisfaction with the current curriculum, leading into a crisis, then moving on to explore possible alternatives, finding alternatives which apparently looked trustworthy. This happened in a positive relationship to North American seminaries, which created a change-supporting climate, finally leading to the change by adopting many of the features of North American mission studies.

(b) *The Schools* did not reject the integration of the concept of contextualisation into their theology of mission on the basis of purely biblical-theological reflection, but within a specific change process. In the context of institutionalised conservatism, the existing paradigm maintained its stability. There was no crisis which would have pushed them to look for alternative models. In a climate of sharp controversies with the WCC, characterised by apologetical language and atmosphere, courageous steps toward change were certainly not supported. This finally led to the rejection of any new paradigm and to the stabilisation of the old one.

2. The Kuhnian theory has also been helpful in perceiving more clearly the mechanisms of institutionalised conservatism which, to a considerable extent, characterise the evangelical movement under investigation. It is the conviction of this author that it would be helpful for *the Schools* to look more carefully at these mechanisms in order to gain a deeper understanding of their change patterns. It goes without saying that the phenomena of *institutionalised conservatism* are not limited to so-called 'conservative' traditions and institutions but that it would be meaningful for all traditions and institutions to look at their change patterns through the glasses of paradigm theory.

3. Finally Kuhn and Küng have been instrumental in helping us to see more clearly that there is a *change readiness* in some areas, while there is also *change resistance* in other areas. We have, on a preliminary level, noted a readiness for change in the area of *formal changes*, while *changes regarding content* are rather resisted. Yet, Kuhn and Küng have not helped to identify more precisely this dividing line and to explain the rationale behind it. At this point, MacIntyre can carry us further, as we will see in the following discussion.

2. *Arguments, Rationales and Epistemology*[10]

MacIntyre has carried Kuhn's theory further in that he argues that the paradigmatic shift is not as non-rational as Kuhn assumes, but that it is a 'reconstruction' of the narrative of a given tradition. There is, according to MacIntyre, a 'rationality of tradition' which allows such a reconstruction of the narrative and 'epistemological crises are occasions for such reconstruction' (1977:456, 464).

According to MacIntyre, an epistemological crisis contains potential but possible pitfalls, too. The potential is that it can lead to a reconstruction of the narrative and thus leads to an enhanced theory which not only satisfactorily answers the new set of questions in the crisis but is also capable of integrating the history in such a way that it can explain the reasons for the failure of the former paradigm and show the continuity between the old and the new paradigm (1977:456, 460, 467). In order to achieve this, 'imaginative conceptual innovation' is needed to carry the tradition beyond the limitations of the old explanations (1988:349–69). Possible pitfalls include moving toward scepticism on the one hand or toward instrumentalism (or dogmatism) on the other hand. The former refers to a person's loss of 'any means of making himself – or others – intelligible to himself, let alone to others,' i.e., becoming unintelligible. The latter refers to the perpetuation of answers which no longer satisfy, by means of contriving theories to protect the old theory (1977:462, 466, 471). As MacIntyre puts it:

> Conflict arises, of course, not only within, but between traditions and such a conflict tests the resources of each contending tradition. It is yet another mark of a degenerate tradition that it has contrived a set of epistemological defences which enable it to avoid being put in question or at least to avoid recognising that it is being put in question by rival traditions (1977:462).

From this it is possible to derive a twofold test of the tradition of conservative evangelicalism we have encountered in this study. The questions are as follows: (1) has conservative evangelical theology of mission succeeded in reconstructing its narrative in such a way that the new questions can be answered satisfactorily, that the old theory can be understood more deeply and that the continuity of the narrative can be demonstrated? If so, it is a valuable candidate for the future. (2) Has conservative evangelical theology of mission successfully avoided the two possible pitfalls? The study has shown that conservative evangelicalism did not go the route of 'capitulation to scepticism.' However, it may be in danger of 'dogmatism.' If the epistemological solutions presented by the theologians of this tradition turn out to be a contrived set of epistemological defences, then, following MacIntyre, this tradition must be deemed a degenerate tradition.

1. The fact that German evangelical theologians have reclaimed history as they encountered an *epistemological crisis* has been demonstrated at several stages of this study (see pp. 159, 169) Time and again, Beyerhaus, Bockmühl, Sautter, Hamel and Reifler have repeated that German evangelical theology of mission stands in the tradition of Pietism and in the line of Kraemer, Hartenstein and Freytag. And the point is obvious: this is the biblical tradition; the direction the ecumenical movement has taken is a deviation. In that sense, German evangelical mission theologians have successfully regained identity in the crisis of the 1960s by connecting their present situation with a history which had the potential to create identity. However, as already mentioned in connection with the Kuhnian paradigm theory, this claim of a history is not without problems (see p. 286)

a) The reconstruction of the narrative, to use MacIntyre's language, has been carried out in a selective fashion as a means of establishing a direct relation to biblical faithfulness. Following Barr, we criticised such a reconstruction of the narrative, because it is highly protective, in that it establishes a rationale for its own orthodoxy by means of a selective reconstruction of history, communicating that those who do not share the convictions of conservative evangelicals have deviated from orthodoxy.

b) Research has also shown that the criteria behind their reading of the Bible, as well as for their reconstruction of their narrative (that is, the history of the *true* evangelical faith), have been shaped by a number of contextual aspects. Sautter himself, in his thesis on the WCC's understanding of salvation history in the light of the evangelical critique, identifies them. He presupposes that German evangelicals (Beyerhaus and the *Frankfurt Declaration*) are the heirs of a biblical understanding of salvation history. He argues that five foundations enabled continental evangelicals to withstand the challenges of a redefinition of the concept of salvation history (:153–55): (1) they are rooted in Pietism and its emphasis that only conversion to Christ is the way to salvation. (2) They have recovered the premillenial eschatology of the pietistic fathers (Bengel, etc.). (3) They have been shaped by Karl Heim's reading of history under the category of the fall. (4) They have been shaped by dialectical theology, especially Oscar Cullmann's view of salvation history. (5) They live under the legacy of National Socialism and World War II, which removed any optimism about world transformation in the process of human history.

We do not have to discuss these items in detail. We only recognise that Sautter has outlined beautifully the contours of the contextual conditioning of his theology. No objection is raised here against the fact of this contextual conditionedness. We have shown that all theology is context-conditioned, thus none can be blamed because of the conditioning of his or her theology. However, on a more popular level (i.e., Reifler), these contextual factors are not mentioned, thus transmitting the message that German conservative evangelicals may objectively claim to be *the* direct and pure heirs of biblical orthodoxy. This again is a very protective argument that does not play with open cards.

c) Finally, we have to consider the apologetic structure of the reconstruction of the narrative. From Beyerhaus and Bockmühl up to Berneburg, the reconstruction of the narrative serves the affirmation of conservative evangelical identity *over against* the ecumenical movement (or in the case of Berneburg, the kingdom theology of radical evangelicals).

Again, apologetics has its right, and one cannot object to a tradition's reconstruction of its narrative, including an apologetic dimension.

However, as pointed out earlier (see p. 195), apologetics of the strongest type have been predominant in Beyerhaus's publications. Bosch concludes, in view of Beyerhaus's apologetics: 'The implications are clear: those who agree with him are on the Lord's side. But the others ...?' (1980:205). Such *apocalyptic* apologetics condemn the opponent and create an insurmountable gulf. As Hummel (:7) points out, such apocalyptic apologetics may be the only option left for the church in situations of tremendous pressure (as was faced by the Confessing Church in the context of National Socialism in Germany), yet it can also lead to 'a fundamentalist self-exclusion from the general discourse in society'.

The generation following Peter Beyerhaus (Sautter, Hamel, Berneburg, Reifler, Müller) employs a much more moderate style of apologetics. However, it is critical to notice that all three recent doctoral dissertations on mission theology, conducted under the supervision of Beyerhaus, are basically apologetic in orientation. They neither critically analyse their own theology, nor do they address one of the burning issues in the theology of mission in a way conducive to constructive solutions. They concentrate on *the other* position, be it ecumenical or radical evangelical, criticising *the other* by using the author's own 'orthodoxy' as the standard. These dissertations express hardly any self-critical awareness. In a way it is the reconstruction of the narrative of the author's own tradition by apologetically criticising *the others*. This is again a highly protective way of presenting history.

2. From this derives another deficiency which needs to be addressed. A successful reconstruction of the narrative includes satisfactory answers to the issues which are causing the epistemological crisis. What can we observe in this regard? The concentration on the apologetic reconstruction of the narrative has led to an underdevelopment as regards constructive contributions from within the evangelical tradition toward the solution of the issues at stake. Neither Beyerhaus nor any of his followers has published a significant piece which would suggest in a constructive way what evangelicals have to contribute to contextualisation, holistic mission, the interpretation of God's action outside the church or the theology of religion. As we have seen, the more recent theology of mission by Reifler is a good summary of what German evangelical theology has produced from Hartenstein to Beyerhaus, expanded with insights from North American mission anthropology. Beyond that, it does not make any contribution to the burning issues of the paradigm change discussed in this study.[11] With Helfenstein we can only confirm that evangelical theology is characterised by stagnation because it is locked into its orthodoxy in such a way that it is not capable of responding creatively to challenging new theological developments.[12] There is hardly any sign of what MacIntyre would call 'imaginative conceptual innovation' – or an innovative move

beyond the status quo, toward a new explanation which incorporates the history of the tradition as well as at least promising avenues towards the solutions of the current issues.

3. Finally, we look at the possible pitfall of dogmatism. This brings us back to the epistemological issues. We argued at the end of Part Three as well as at the end of Part Four that epistemological issues are at the heart of a certain change pattern in *the Schools*. This argument must now be carried further.

The initial observation was that *the Schools* demonstrate *change readiness* in certain areas yet show *change resistance* in other areas. According to the rationale given by some of the leading conservative evangelical theologians, the boundary which separates the area of *change readiness* from the area of *change resistance* is defined by the Bible.[13] It is the thesis of this author that this is a misperception, and that *epistemology* presents the dividing line between the two areas. In other words, this dividing line – we may call it the *epistemological barrier* – hinders *the Schools* from introducing certain changes in the theology and educational conduct. The following chart visualises this by putting examples of *change readiness* and *change resistance*, both in the theology of mission and in theological education onto two sides of the *epistemological barrier*.

Theology of Mission:

- adding new courses to the curriculum
- introducing mission anthropology
- using anthropological insights to enhance the communication of the gospel
- reflecting mission strategy
- reflecting on cross-cultural experiences
- enhancing skills of Bible translation

Education:

- seeking accreditation
- upgrading academic quality
- revising curricula
- improving course delivery
- introducing supervised field work
- introducing assessment procedures
- enhancing teachers' training

Area of change readiness

↑ ***'epistemological barrier'***

↓

Area of change resistance

- contextual theologising
- reconsidering traditional evangelical doctrine of salvation
- entering dialogue with people of other living faiths

- introducing 'inductive'/ contextual learning
- introducing dialogical learning
- introducing learning in open ecumenical dialogue

Again, the purpose of the argument is not primarily to convince *the Schools* that they should show more change readiness. The decision of whether or not a change is appropriate at a certain point in time must be based an various rationales which cannot be *pre*scribed. We are only concerned with the *de*scription of the process. And in this process, if it is conducted with a high degree of awareness of the actual state of affairs, the explicit rationale must come in accordance with the real (i.e., the determining) rationale, which may be hidden and implicit. This is the point where this study criticises conservative evangelical theological education. *While it rejects certain theological and educational concepts based on the explicit rationale of faithfulness to the Bible, we argue that the hidden rationale is a certain epistemological concept which most of the theological educators are not aware of.* Put differently, many of the conservative evangelical educators consider themselves to be following a certain *rationale*; in reality, their teaching is determined by another *rationale*, of which they are not aware, or, even worse, refuse to accept. This can be developed as follows.

The concept conservative evangelical schools claim to put into praxis can be visualised in the following way:

Epistemological Concept A:

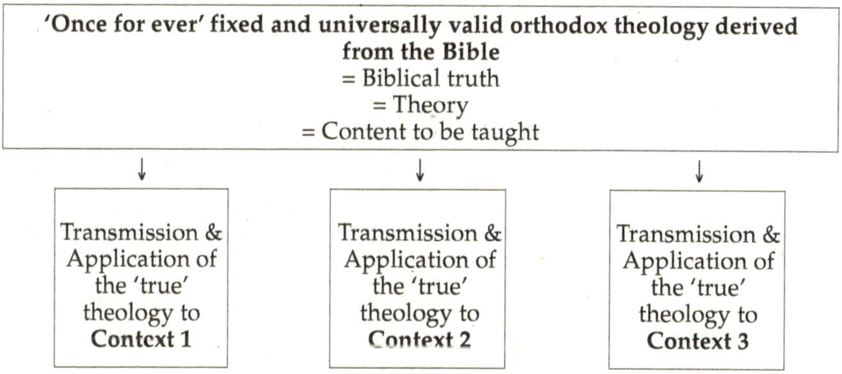

The problem with this concept is that it is based on an epistemological illusion. It assumes the existence of such a thing as a once-and-forever-defined and universally-valid-orthodox-theology – or to be more precise, the possibility that such a theology can be known and defined. However, as theologians of all shades agree, the claim to such a theology is a self-deception.

Peter Hicks demonstrates how even evangelicals follow Gadamer's theory that truth 'is not something purely objective, static, fixed, rational or propositional,' but rather shaped by us as interpreters (:111). He admits, as an evangelical, 'the truth God has given us in the Scriptures is necessarily shaped and moulded by us as interpreters' (:113). Consequentely he raises the key question: 'What implications does the admission that we at least partly shape the truth have for the traditional concept of fixed, unchanging, God-given truth?' (:113)

In his recent study *Missiological Implications of Epistemological Shifts*, the evangelical missiologist Paul Hiebert shows how theology as a 'Rational Unified System' of 'Objective Truth' is shaped by a positivist world view, a world view which, according to Hiebert, 'is flawed' (Hiebert 1999:17–22; 35). What Hiebert suggests is not a shift towards postpositivist and postmodernist relativism, which he rejects (:36–67), but a move towards critical realism. Referring to Charles Pierce, he defines:

> Ontologically it is a form of realism, for it assumes a real world that exists independently from human perception or opinions of it. It is critical, for it examines the process by which humans acquire knowledge and finds that this knowledge does not have a literal one-to-one correspondence to reality (:69).

Heinzpeter Hempelmann, a significant thinker among *the Schools*, admits in reference to postmodern pluralism that it is an accepted philosophical premise that all knowledge is conditioned by culture and language and that the search for truth needs the dialogue of differing perspectives (1996:73, 75, 79). With this Hempelmann does not accept post-modern pluralism; in fact, he refutes it decisively and convincingly.

While such insights are accessible and common knowledge for evangelicals as well as for others, the actual business of evangelical theological education appears for many to go on as usual. Hicks asks what the options are in the light of the fact that the traditional concept of truth has collapsed. One of the options he suggests is to accept it but to 'continue to live as though it had not happened' (:135). It seems that many conservative evangelical theological educators follow this path.

Hence, the underlying concept of their theological teaching is in reality different from what they assume or pretend (see concept A) and looks more like the following:

Epistemological Concept B:

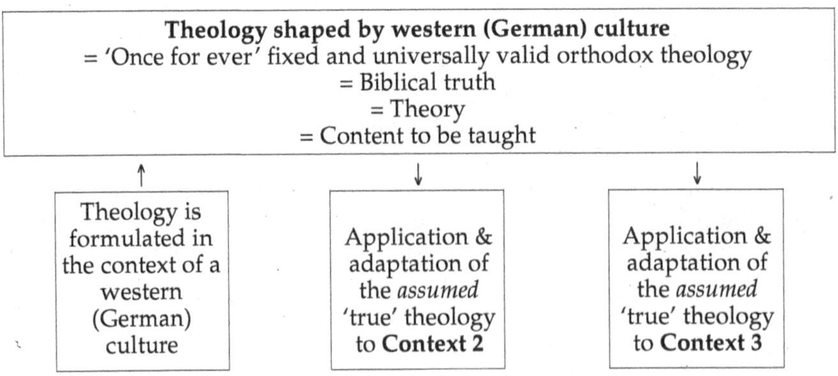

The consequences of this concept are devastating – and this on two levels. On the side of theological training it is ignorant and deceives the students. On the side of (missionary) ministry in other cultures it is paternalistic and oppressive (cf. Hiebert 1999:24–29). The primary problem we are concerned with is not the *What* (content) of conservative evangelical theology (which may be subject of critical assessment too), but our primary concern is to show *how* they build their argument – that is whether it is consistent or, in MacIntyre's terminology, an 'epistemological defence.'

A consistent hermeneutical and epistemological model has been suggested by the new paradigm in mission theology as well as in theological education. It looks as follows:

Epistemological Concept C:[14]

The Bible				
↓		↓		↓
Learning to read the Bible and to theologise in **Context 1** (Germany) in dialogue with people in other contexts	⇔	Moving into **Context 2** and probing the method of contextual Bible reading and theologising together with people in that context	⇔	Moving into **Context 3** and probing the method of contextual Bible reading and theologising together with people in that context

Yet, such a concept is rejected by most of the conservative theological educators of *the Schools*. Their rejection is based on the rationale of Concept A, which we have shown to be an illusion. Consequently, the rejection of contextualisation and inductive learning by conservative evangelical theologians is based on a void rationale. In other words, again, conservative evangelical educators *think* they have drawn an *epistemological barrier* which would safeguard them from moving from the *biblical* into the *no longer biblical* sphere. However, they have built their *epistemological barrier* on an epistemological concept which is an illusion; thus, their *epistemological barrier* is not really the boundary between the *biblical* and the *no longer biblical*.

This is not to suggest that contextualisation is not slippery terrain. There may well be good theological reasons for the definition of an *epistemological barrier*, however, these must be based on the epistemology of concept C. Such hermeneutical models have been put forward by Bosch, Samuel, Hiebert, Padilla and others, as we have outlined in this study.

From this we conclude, that the reconstruction of the narrative as we observe it among conservative evangelicals since the 1960s can hardly measure up to the criteria of MacIntyre. It instrumentalises history in an apologetic way; it is exclusive, and above all, it fails to answer the burning questions behind the epistemological crisis. We have identified mechanisms which may support the conclusion that the tradition under investigation has 'contrived a set of epistemological defences which enable it to avoid being put in question or at least to avoid recognising that it is being put in question by rival traditions' (MacIntyre 1977:462). It has not avoided the pitfall of dogmatism. As far as this applies to *the Schools* analysed in this study they are – in the light of MacIntyre's theory – in danger of becoming a 'degenerate tradition.'

3. Conclusion

Using Kuhn, Küng and MacIntyre, we have attempted to analyse at a deeper level and in relation to the underlying hermeneutical and epistemological issues the change patterns of *the Schools*. The results put serious questions to the way some conservative evangelical theologians and schools do their work of theology and education. The critique focuses not even primarily on the content of conservative evangelicals' theology of mission *per se*. The primary intention of these final reflections focuses on *the way* conservative evangelicals theologise. If conservative theological education follows this pattern of theologising and carrying out theological education, it is doomed to do theology badly and give a poor education. This is at once self-deceiving and arrogant; it deceives students and dominates people of other cultures. Harris is right when she states in view of a fundamentalist mentality among evangelicals:

> Evangelicals will draw on philosophically incompatible traditions if the different traditions provide tools for preserving biblical authority. This is a pragmatic measure. They employ phenomenological hermeneutics to enable them to deal with culturally problematic passages while retaining a level of meaning which remains constant and authoritative. Gadamer's insights are utilised only for the 'decisional' or 'applicational' level in the hermeneutical process, that is in making the text relevant for today...
>
> It would be to the benefit of many were evangelicals to develop a defensible position which succeeded in presenting and protecting these sentiments while also acknowledging the reality of cultural conditioning. As it is, evangelicals have not probed deep enough to discover and address the tensions in their composite hermeneutical theories (:311).

What is needed is serious reflection on epistemology and hermeneutics. Andrew Kirk's suggestion needs to be heard 'that all theology should begin with a "proto-theological" phase in which the theologian is prepared to reveal and discuss all hidden assumptions, and a general kind of health warning is given against all pretensions of academy to a universally valid vantage point' (1997:24). In addition to that, a high degree of intellectual virtues must be developed to overcome dogmatism and institutionalised conservativism.[15]

It can only be hoped that those conservative evangelical theologians and schools that perpetuate such institutionalised conservatism realise its underlying epistemological rationale and that they turn to a deeper awareness of the conditioning of their theology. This would by no means weaken their theology and ministry; on the contrary – it would contribute to the credibility of the Christian faith. In the light of the fact that the majority of church workers engaged in cross-cultural mission of Protestant German-speaking origin are trained in *the Schools*, the indicated changes would make a remarkable contribution to Christian mission.

Beyond this, an openness on the part of conservative evangelicals to reconsider their position would also open up new avenues for a more constructive dialogue between the two polarised parties – the ecumenical and the evangelical – which are still very much separated, certainly (but not only) in the German-speaking context. The German evangelicals Sautter and Hamel conclude their theses, which critically analyse the developments within the WCC's understanding of mission, with the suggestion that a fruitful dialogue would be important and even possible if only ecumenicals were ready to reconsider some of their positions. Based on the research of this study, this author concludes that the call to reconsider theological positions must not only be heard by ecumenicals but also by evangelicals. David Bosch – and beyond him, Two-Thirds World evangelicals – may have opened up promising avenues for a common future in mission and theological education. Unfortunately these voices have only a minimal hearing in the German-speaking context.

Notes

1 The fact that 'evangelicals and change' is the critical issue for the evangelical movement has been confirmed by Bebbington in the final chapter of *Evangelicalism in Modern Britain* (:171–76).

2 There is a considerable amount of literature which has been published in recent years dealing with issues of change dynamics. The author is aware of many of these studies. However, it goes beyond the scope of this concluding chapter to interact with this entire field of study. Being consistent with the theories already introduced in this study, it seems to be appropriate to make further use of Kuhn's theory.

3 The five difference-statements are not in the English edition, and will be translated from the German edition (Küng and Tracy 1984).

4 Marsden has demonstrated this in view of the (American) university system with regard to the exclusion of a Christian worldview from the academic discussion (1994; 1997). This indicates that we are dealing with a common phenomenon.

5 In Sautter's thesis it is very explicit.

6 This is not to suggest that *the Schools* function fully on this level, but it suggests possible dangers. Some of the schools may well show tendencies in this direction.

7 Werner comments: 'Ecumenical encouragements to reform theological education have so far made little headway where state theological faculties are concerned' (1992:78).

8 '... through a immediate, very personal spiritual experience of the original Christian message...' (1984, 64).

9 We are aware of the fact that it is at this point where MacIntyre criticises Kuhn, claiming that decisions to change are not as irrational as Kuhn thinks but that it is the 'reconstruction of the narrative' of a given tradition which provides a 'rationality of tradition' and opens up changes which stand in relation to the tradition and are not as revolutionary as Kuhn assumes (1977:464ff. 1988:349–69). However, we argue that there is much validity in Kuhn's point, especially in the way Küng applies it to the church and to theology. We will apply Kuhn's argument at this point and come back to MacIntyre's contribution in the next chapter.

10 The term epistemology is used in the sense of the German 'Erkenntnistheorie' defined by Keller as the 'philosophische Wissenschaft von der Erkenntnis' [philosophical science of knowledge] (:38). For an introduction to epistemology see Albert Keller, *Allgemeine Erkenntnistheorie*.

11 This has also to be said of Kasdorf and Walldorf, a recently published collection of twelve essays by the faculty of the *FTA*.

12 'Without rendering a general judgement on evangelicals and at the same time excluding other theological groups from it, it can be argued: The reverse of the evangelicals sharp critique is their inability to enter in to the particulars of new and differing theological conceptions. They have a hard time with theological reorientations. To a large extent, evangelicals still hold to the same objections which they had articulated already in the seventees. Stagnation rather than development determines the course of the evangelicals' (1998: 182).

13 E.g., Sautter, analysing the concept of salvation history in the ecumenical movement, comes to the conclusion that the evangelical understanding must by favoured because it is closer to the biblical understanding (:276). Hamel comes to the same conclusion in his study on the use of the Bible in the ecumenical movement (:285–293). Berneburg rejects the kingdom-theology of Two Thirds World evangelicals too, because it goes 'against the biblical foundation' (:329).

14 This chart follows to a certain extent Hiebert 1999:70, 113.

15 The relation of epistemology and intellectual virtues is outlined by W. J. Wood in *Epistemology: Becoming Intellectually Virtuous*. With regard to the issues discussed here, see especially the section on 'Intellectual Honesty and Dishonesty' where he shows how thinking in a closed and predetermined system of beliefs leads to what he calls 'epistemological Phariseeism' (61–66).

Appendix A

List of the *KBA* Schools

Name of the School	Country	Denominational Orientation & Roots	Abbreviation
Bibelausbildung am Ort	Austria	Interdenominational	*BAO*
Bibelschule Adelshofen	Germany	Lutheran, pietistic	*Adelshofen*
Bibelschule Aidlingen	Germany	Lutheran, pietistic (Gnadauer Verband)	*Aidlingen*
Bibelschule Bergstrasse	Germany	Interdenominational, American	*Bergstrasse*
Bibelschule Burgstädt	Germany	Interdenominational	*Burgstädt*
Bibelschule Brake	Germany	Interdenominational, American	*Brake*
Bibelschule Gemeinde Gottes	Germany	Denominational (Church of God)	*Fritzlar*
Bibelschule Kirchberg	Germany	Interdenominational, New Life	*Kirchberg*
Bibelschule Wallsee	Austria	Interdenominational	*Wallsee*
Bibel-Centre Breckerfeld	Germany	Interdenominational	*Breckerfeld*
Bibelseminar Bonn	Germany	Free Church, Mennonite-Baptist	*Bonn*
Bibelseminar Wuppertal	Germany	Lutheran, pietistic (Evangelische Gesellschaft)	*Wuppertal*
Bijbelinstituut Belgié	Belgium	Interdenominational, American	*Heverlee*
Brüderhaus Tabor	Germany	Lutheran, pietistic (Gnadauer Verband)	*Tabor*
Ecole Biblique de Genève	Switzerland	Interdenominational	*Genève*

Name of the School	Country	Denominational Orientation & Roots	Abbreviation
Evangelische Theologische Facultät	Belgium	Interdenominational, American	*Heverlee*
Frei Hochschule für Mission	Germany	Lutheran, pietistic, Extension Centre of Columbia University, USA	*FHM*
Frei Theologische Akademie	Germany	Interdenominational, American	*FTA*
*Gnadauer Bibelschule Fallenburg	Germany	Lutheran, pietistic (Gnadauer Verband)	*Falkenburg*
Institut Biblique Emmaus	Switzerland	Interdenominational Brethren	*Emmaus*
*Institut für Gemeindebau und Weltmission	Switzerland	Interdenominational, Study Centre of Luther Rice Seminary, USA	*IGW*
*International Correspondence Institute	Germany and Switzerland	Interdenominational, American	*ICI*
Kurzbibelschule Janz Team	Germany	Interdenominational, American	*Janz Team*
Kurzbibelschule Klostermühle	Germany	Interdenominational, Torch Bearers	*Klostermühle*
Kurzbibelschule Jugend für Christus	Germany	Interdenominational, Youth for Christ	*JfC*
*Kurzbibelschule Wort des Lebens	Germany	Interdenominational, American	*Wort des Lebens*
*Martin Bucer Seminar	Germany	Reformed	*MBucer*
Missionshaus Bibelschule Wiedenest	Germany	Free Church, Brethren & Baptists	*Wiedenest*
Neues Leben Seminar	Germany	Interdenominational	*Neues Leben*
Geistliches Rüstzentrum Krelingen	Germany	Lutheran, pietistic	*Krelingen*
Studiengemeinsch aft Wort & Wissen	Germany	Interdenominational, Study Centre on Creationism	*Wort & Wissen*

Name of the School	**Country**	**Denominational Orientation & Roots**	**Abbreviation**
Theologisch-Diakonisches Seminar Aarau	Switzerland	Reformed, pietistic	*Aarau*
Theologisches Seminar Bienenberg	Switzerland	Free Church, Mennonite	*Bienenberg*
Theologisches Seminar der Liebenzeller Mission	Germany	Lutheran, pietistic (Gnadauer Verband)	*Liebenzell*
Theologisches Seminar St. Chrischona	Switzerland	Lutheran, pietistic (Gnadauer Verband)	*Chrischona*
WEC International Missionary Training Centre	Holland	Interdenominational Mission	*MTC*

* Schools with guest membership

APPENDIX B

Ecumenical Conferences from 1910 to 1991[1]

<table>
<tr><td colspan="3">Edinburgh World Missionary Conference 1910</td></tr>
<tr><td>International Missionary Council</td><td>Faith & Order</td><td>Life & Work</td></tr>
<tr><td></td><td></td><td>Stockholm 1925</td></tr>
<tr><td></td><td>Lausanne 1927</td><td></td></tr>
<tr><td>Jerusalem 1928</td><td></td><td></td></tr>
<tr><td></td><td>Edinburgh 1937</td><td>Oxford 1937</td></tr>
<tr><td>Madras/Tambaram 1938</td><td></td><td></td></tr>
<tr><td>Whitby 1947</td><td></td><td></td></tr>
<tr><td></td><td colspan="2">First Assembly of the WCC Amsterdam 1948</td></tr>
<tr><td>Willingen 1952</td><td>Lund 1952</td><td></td></tr>
<tr><td></td><td colspan="2">Second Assembly of the WCC Evanston 1954</td></tr>
<tr><td>Achimota/Ghana 1958</td><td></td><td></td></tr>
<tr><td colspan="3">Third Assembly of the WCC III New Delhi 1961</td></tr>
<tr><td>Mexico City 1963</td><td>Montreal 1963</td><td></td></tr>
<tr><td></td><td></td><td>Genf 1966</td></tr>
<tr><td></td><td>Bristol 1967</td><td></td></tr>
<tr><td colspan="3">Fourth Assembly of the WCC Uppsala 1968</td></tr>
<tr><td></td><td>Louvain 1971</td><td></td></tr>
<tr><td>Bangkok 1973</td><td></td><td></td></tr>
<tr><td></td><td>Accra 1974</td><td></td></tr>
<tr><td colspan="3">Fifth Assembly of the WCC Nairobi 1975</td></tr>
<tr><td></td><td>Bangalore 1978</td><td></td></tr>
<tr><td>Melbourne 1980</td><td></td><td></td></tr>
<tr><td></td><td>Lima 1982</td><td></td></tr>
<tr><td colspan="3">Sixth Assembly of the WCC Vancouver 1983</td></tr>
<tr><td>San Antonio 1989</td><td></td><td></td></tr>
<tr><td colspan="3">Seventh Assembly of the WCC Canberra 1991</td></tr>
</table>

1 Cf. Van Elderen:52; Beyerhaus 1996:730–31; WCC 1978:66–67.

APPENDIX C

Consultations of the *Lausanne Movement* between 1974 and 1989

1977 Pasadena: Consultation on the Homogenous Unit Principle
1978 Willowbank: Consultation on Gospel and Culture
1978 Glen Eyrie: North American Conference on Evangelization among Muslims
1980 High Leigh/Hoddesdon: International Consultation on Simple Lifestyle
1980 Pattaya: Consultation on World Evangelisation
1982 Grand Rapids: Consultation on the Relationship between Evangelism and Social Responsibility
1983 Wheaton: WEF Consultation on the Nature and the Mission of the Church
1984 Seoul: International Prayer Assembly for World Evangelization
1985 Oslo: Consultation on the Work of the Holy Spirit in Evangelization
1985 Cambridge: Consultation on the Role of Radio in Church Planting and Evangelism
1987 Zeist: Conference on Christianity and Islam
1987 Singapore: Conference for Young Leaders
1988 Hong Kong: Consultation on Conversion
1988 Singapore: Consultation of Pastors
1988 Washington: Leadership 88
1988 Stuttgart: European Leadership Conference on World Evangelization
1989 Singapore: Global Consultation on World Evangelisation by AD 2000 and Beyond
1989 Bermuda: Consultation on the Christian Gospel and the Jewish People

APPENDIX D

The *Frankfurt Declaration* 1970[1]

The Church of Jesus Christ has the sacred privilege and irrevocable obligation to participate in the mission of the triune God, a mission which must extend into all the world. Through the Church's outreach, his name shall be glorified among all people, mankind shall be saved from his future wrath and led to a new life, and the Lordship of his Son Jesus Christ shall be established in the expectation of his second coming.

This is the way that Christianity has always understood the Great Commission of Christ, though, we must confess, not always with the same degree of fidelity and clarity. The recognition of the task and the total missionary obligation of the Church led to the endeavour to integrate missions into the German Protestant churches and the World Council of Churches, whose Commission and Division of World Mission and Evangelism was established in 1961. It is the goal of this division, by the terms of its constitution to insure 'the proclamation to the whole world of the Gospel of Jesus Christ, to the end that all men may believe in him and be saved.' It is our conviction that this definition reflects the basic apostolic concern of the New Testament and restores the understanding of mission held by the fathers of the Protestant missionary movement.

Today, however, organized Christian world missions is shaken by a fundamental crisis. Outer opposition and the weakening spiritual power of our churches and missionary societies are not solely to blame. More dangerous is the displacement of their primary tasks by means of an insidious falsification of their motives and goals.

Deeply concerned because of their inner decay, we feel called upon to make the following declaration.

We address ourselves to all Christians who know themselves through the belief in salvation through Jesus Christ to be responsible for the continuation of his saving work among non-Christian people. We address ourselves further to the leaders of churches and congregations, to whom the worldwide perspective of their spiritual commission has been revealed. We address ourselves finally to all missionary societies and their coordination agencies, which are especially called, according to their spiritual tradition, to oversee the true goals of missionary activity.

We urgently and sincerely request you to test the following theses on the basis of their biblical foundations, and to determine the accuracy of this description of the current situation with respect to the errors and modes of operation which are increasingly evident in churches, missions, and the ecumenical movement. In the event of your concurrence, we request that you declare this by your signature and join with us in your own sphere of influence both repentant and resolved to insist upon these guiding principles.

Seven Indispensable Basic Elements of Mission

1. Full authority on heaven and on earth has been committed to me. Go forth therefore and make all nations my disciples, baptize men everywhere in the name of the Father and the Son and the Holy Spirit, and teach them to observe all that I have command you. And be assured, I am with you always, to the end of time (Matt. 28:18–20; this Scripture quotation and those that follow are from the New English Bible).

We recognize and declare:

Christian mission discovers its foundation, goals, tasks, and the content of its proclamation solely in the **commission** of the resurrected Lord Jesus Christ and his saving acts as they are reported by the witness of the apostles and early Christianity in the New Testament. Mission is grounded in the nature of the Gospel.

We therefore oppose the current tendency to determine the nature and task of mission by socio-political analyses of our time and from the demands of the non-Christian world. We deny that what the Gospel has to say to people today at the deepest level is not evident before its encounter with them. Rather according to the apostolic witness, the Gospel is normative and given once for all. The situation of encounter contributes only new aspects in the application of the Gospel. The surrender of the Bible as our primary frame of reference leads to the shapelessness of mission and a confusion of the task of mission with a general idea of responsibility for the world.

2. Thus will I prove myself great and holy and make myself known to many nations; they shall know that I am the Lord (Ezek. 38:23). Therefore, Lord, I will praise thee among the nations and sing psalms to thy name (Ps. 18:49 and Rom. 15:9)

We recognize and declare:

The first and supreme goal of mission is the **glorification** of the name of the one God throughout the entire world and proclamation of the lordship of Jesus Christ, his Son.

We therefore oppose the assertion that mission today is no longer so concerned with the disclosure of God as with the manifestation of a new man and the extension of a new humanity into all social realms. **Humanization** is not the primary goal of mission. It is rather a product of our new birth through God's saving activity in Christ within us, or an indirect result of the Christian proclamation in its power to perform a leavening activity in the course of world history.

A one-sided outreach of missionary interest toward man and his society leads to atheism.

3. There is no salvation in anyone else at all, for there is no other name under heaven granted to men, by which we may receive salvation (Acts 4:12).

We recognize and declare:

Jesus Christ our Saviour, true God and true man, as the Bible proclaims him in his personal mystery and his saving work, is the basis, content, and authority of our mission. It is the goal of this mission to make known to all people in all walks of life the gift of his salvation.

We therefore oppose the false teaching (which is spreading in the ecumenical movement since the Third General Assembly of the World Council of Churches in New Delhi) that Christ himself is anonymously so evident in world religions, historical changes, and revolutions that man can encounter him and find salvation in him without the direct news of the Gospel.

We likewise reflect the unbiblical limitation of the person and work of Jesus to his humanity and ethical example. In such an idea the unbiblical limitation of the person and work of Jesus to his humanity and ethical example. In such an idea the uniqueness of Christ and the Gospel is abandoned in favour of a humanitarian principle which others might also find in other religions and ideologies.

4. God loved the world so much that he gave his only Son, that everyone who has faith in him may not die but have eternal life (John 3:16). In Christ's name, we implore you, be reconciled to God (2 Cor. 5:20).

We recognize and declare:

Mission is the witness and presentation of eternal salvation performed in the name of Jesus Christ by his church and fully authorized messengers by means of preaching, the sacraments, and service. This salvation is due to the sacrificial crucifixion of Jesus Christ, which occurred once for all and for all mankind.

The appropriation of this salvation to individuals takes place first, however, through proclamation, which calls for decision, and through baptism, which places the believer in the service of love. Just as belief leads through repentance and baptism to eternal life, so unbelief leads through its rejection of the offer of salvation to damnation.

We therefore oppose the universalistic idea that in the crucifixion and resurrection of Jesus Christ all men of all times are already born again and already have peace with him, irrespective of their knowledge of the historical saving activity of God or belief in it. Through such a misconception the evangelizing commission loses both its full, authoritative power and its urgency. Unconverted men are thereby lulled into a fatal sense of security about their eternal destiny.

5. *But you are a chosen race, a royal priesthood, a dedicated nation, and a people claimed by God for his own, to proclaim the triumphs of him who has called you out of darkness into his marvellous light (1Peter 2:9).*

Adapt yourselves no longer to the pattern of this present world (Rom 12:2).

We recognize and declare:

The primary visible task of mission is to **call out the messianic, saved community** from among all people.

Missionary proclamation should lead everywhere to the establishment of the Church of Jesus Christ, which exhibits a new, defined reality as salt and light in its social environment.

Through the Gospel and the sacraments, the Holy Spirit gives the members of the congregation a new life and an eternal spiritual fellowship with each other and with God, who is real and present with them. It is the task of the congregation through its witness to move the lost – especially those who live outside its community – to a saving membership in the body of Christ. Only by being this new kind of fellowship does the Church present the Gospel convincingly.

We therefore oppose the view that the Church as the fellowship of Jesus, is simply a part of the world. The contrast between the Church and the world is not merely a distinction in function and in knowledge of salvation; rather, it is an essential difference in nature. We deny that the Church has no advantage over the world except the knowledge of the alleged future salvation of all men.

We further oppose the one-sided emphasis on salvation which stresses only this world, according to which the Church and the world together share in a future, purely social, reconciliation of all mankind. That would lead to the self-dissolution of the Church.

6. *Remember then your former condition … you were at the time separate from Christ, strangers to the community of Israel, outside God's covenants and the promise that goes with them. Your world was a world without hope and without God (Eph. 2:11,12).*

We recognize and declare:

The offer of salvation in Christ is directed without exception to all men who are not yet bound to him in conscious faith. The adherents to the non-Christian religions and world views can receive this salvation only through participation in faith. They must let themselves be freed from their former ties and false hopes in order to be admitted by belief and baptism into the body of Christ. Israel, too, will find salvation in turning to Jesus Christ.

We therefore reject the false teaching that the non-Christian religions and world views are also ways of salvation similar to belief in Christ.

We refute the idea that 'Christian presence' among the adherents to the world religions and a give-and-take dialogue with them are substitutes for a proclamation of the Gospel which aims at conversion. Such dialogues simply establish good points of contact for missionary communication.

We also refute the claim that the borrowing of Christian ideas, hopes, and social procedures – even if they are separated from their exclusive relationship to the person of Jesus – can make the world religion and ideologies substitutes for the Church of Jesus Christ. In reality they give them a syncretistic and therefore antichristian direction.

7. And this gospel of the kingdom will be proclaimed throughout the earth as a testimony to all nations; and then the end will come (Matt.24:14).

We recognize and declare:

The Christian world mission is the decisive, continuous saving activity of God among men between the time of the resurrection and second coming of Jesus Christ. Through the proclamation of the Gospel, new nations and people will progressively be called to decision for or against Christ.

When all people have heard the witness about him and have given their answer to it, the conflict between the Church of Jesus and the world, led by the Antichrist, will reach its climax. Then Christ himself will return and break into time, disarming the demonic power of Satan and establishing his own visible, boundless messianic kingdom.

We refute the unfounded idea that the eschatological expectation of the New Testament has been falsified by Christ's delay in returning and is therefore to be given up.

We refute at the same time the enthusiastic and utopian ideology that either under the influence of the Gospel or by the anonymous working of Christ in history, all of mankind is already moving toward a position of general peace an justice and will finally–before the return of Christ–be united under him in a great world community.

We refute the identification of messianic salvation with progress, development and social change. The fatal consequence of this is that efforts to aid development and revolutionary involvement in the places of tension in society are seen as the contemporary forms of Christian mission. But such an identification would be a self-deliverance to the utopian movements of our time in the direction of their ultimate destination.

We do, however, affirm the determined advocacy of justice and peace by all churches, and we affirm that developmental aid is a timely realization of the divine demand for mercy and justice as well as of the command of Jesus 'Love thy neighbour.'

We see therein an important accompaniment and authentication of mission. We also affirm the humanizing results of conversion as signs of the coming messianic peace.

We stress, however, that unlike the eternally valid reconciliation with God through faith in the Gospel, all of our social achievements and partial successes in polities are restricted by the eschatological 'not yet' of the coming kingdom and the not yet annihilated power of sin, death, and the devil, who still is the 'prince of this world.'

This established the priorities of our missionary service and causes us to extend ourselves in the expectation of Him who promises, 'Behold! I make all things new' (Rev. 21:5, RSV).

Note

1 The following English translation is taken form Hedlund:250–55.

APPENDIX E

The *Lausanne Covenant* 1974[1]

Introduction

We, members of the Church of Jesus Christ, from more than 150 nations, participants in the International Congress on World Evangelization at Lausanne, praise God for his great salvation and rejoice in the fellowship he has given us with himself and with each other. We are deeply stirred by what God is doing in our day, moved to penitence by our failures and challenged by the unfinished task of evangelisation. We believe the gospel is God's good news for the whole world, and we are determined by his grace to obey Christ's commission to proclaim it to all mankind and to make disciples of every nation. We desire, therefore, to affirm our faith and our resolve, and to make public our covenant.

1. The Purpose of God

We affirm our belief in the one-eternal God, Creator and Lord of the world, Father, Son and Holy Spirit, who governs all things according to the purpose of his will. He has been calling out from the world a people for himself, and sending his people back into the world to be his servants and his witnesses, for the extension of his kingdom, the building up of Christ's body, and the glory of his name. We confess with shame that we have often denied our calling and failed in our mission, by becoming conformed to the world or by withdrawing from it. Yet we rejoice that even when borne by earthen vessels the gospel is still a precious treasure. To the task of making that treasure known in the power of the Holy Spirit we desire to dedicate ourselves anew. (Isa. 40:28; Matt. 28:19; Eph. 1:11; Acts 15:14; John 17:6, 18; Eph. 4:12; 1 Cor. 5:10; Rom. 12:2; II Cor. 4:7)

2. The Authority and Power of the Bible

We affirm the divine inspiration, truthfulness and authority of both Old and New Testament Scriptures in their entirety as the only written word of God, without error in all that it affirms, and the only infallible rule of faith and practice. We also affirm the power of God's word to accomplish his purpose of salvation. The message of the Bible is addressed to all men and women. For God's revelation in Christ and in Scripture is unchangeable. Through it the Holy Spirit still speaks today. He illumines the minds of God's people in every culture to perceive its truth freshly through their own eyes and thus discloses to the whole Church ever more of the many-coloured wisdom of God. (II Tim. 3:16; II Pet. 1:21; John 10:35; Isa. 55:11; 1 Cor. 1:21; Rom. 1:16, Matt. 5:17,18; Jude 3; Eph. 1:17,18; 3:10,18)

3. The Uniqueness and Universality of Christ

We affirm that there is only one Saviour and only one gospel, although there is a wide diversity of evangelistic approaches. We recognise that everyone has some knowledge of God through his general revelation in nature. But we deny that this can save, for people suppress the truth by their unrighteousness. We also reject as derogatory to Christ and the gospel every kind of syncretism and dialogue which implies that Christ speaks equally through all religions and ideologies. Jesus Christ, being himself the only God-man, who gave himself as the only ransom for sinners, is the only mediator between God and people. There is no other name by which we must be saved. All men and women are perishing because of sin, but God loves everyone, not wishing that any should perish but that all should repent. Yet those who reject Christ repudiate the joy of salvation and condemn themselves to eternal separation from God. To proclaim Jesus as 'the Saviour of the world' is not to affirm that all people are either automatically or ultimately saved, still less to affirm that all religions offer salvation in Christ. Rather it is to proclaim God's love for a world of sinners and to invite everyone to respond to him as Saviour and Lord in the wholehearted personal commitment of repentance and faith. Jesus Christ has been exalted above every other name; we long for the day when every knee shall bow to him and every tongue shall confess him Lord. (Gal. 1:6–9; Rom. 1:18–32; I Tim. 2:5,6; Acts 4:12; John 3:16–19; II Pet. 3:9; II Thess. 1:7–9; John 4:42; Matt. 11:28; Eph. 1:20,21; Phil. 2:9–11)

4. The Nature of Evangelism

To evangelise is to spread the good news that Jesus Christ died for our sins and was raised from the dead according to the Scriptures, and that as the reigning Lord he now offers the forgiveness of sins and the liberating gifts of the Spirit to all who repent and believe. Our Christian presence in the world is indispensable to evangelism, and so is that kind of dialogue whose purpose is to listen sensitively in order to understand. But evangelism itself is the proclamation of the historical, biblical Christ as Saviour and Lord, with a view to persuading people to come to him personally and so be reconciled to God. In issuing the gospel invitation we have no liberty to conceal the cost of discipleship. Jesus still calls all who would follow him to deny themselves, take up their cross, and identify themselves with his new community. The results of evangelism include obedience to Christ, incorporation into his Church and responsible service in the world. (I Cor. 15:3,4; Acts 2: 32–39; John 20:21; I Cor. 1:23; II Cor. 4:5; 5:11,20; Luke 14:25–33; Mark 8:34; Acts 2:40,47; Mark 10:43–45)

5. Christian Social Responsibility

We affirm that God is both the Creator and the Judge of all men. We therefore should share his concern for justice and reconciliation throughout human society and for the liberation of men and women from every kind of oppression. Because men and women are made in the image of God, every person, regardless of race, religion, colour, culture, class, sex or age, has an intrinsic dignity because of which he or she should be respected and served, not exploited. Here too we express penitence both for our neglect and for having sometimes regarded evangelism and social concern as mutually exclusive. Although reconciliation with other people is not reconciliation with God, nor is social action evangelism, nor is political liberation salvation, nevertheless we affirm that evangelism and sociopolitical involvement are both part of our Christian duty. For both are necessary expressions of our doctrines of God and man, our love for our neighbour and our obedience to Jesus Christ. The message of salvation implies also a message of judgment upon every form of alienation, oppression and discrimination, and we should not be afraid to denounce evil and injustice wherever they exist. When people receive Christ they are born again into his kingdom and must seek not only to exhibit but also to spread its righteousness in the midst of an unrighteous world. The salvation we claim should be transforming us in the totality of our personal and social responsibilities. Faith without works is dead. (Acts 17:26,31; Gen. 18:25; Isa. 1:17; Psa. 45:7; Gen. 1:26,27; Jas. 3:9; Lev. 19:18; Luke 6:27,35; Jas. 2:14–26; Joh. 3:3,5; Matt. 5:20; 6:33; II Cor. 3:18; Jas. 2:20)

6. The Church and Evangelism

We affirm that Christ sends his redeemed people into the world as the Father sent him, and that this calls for a similar deep and costly penetration of the world. We need to break out of our ecclesiastical ghettos and permeate non-Christian society. In the Church's mission of sacrificial service evangelism is primary. World evangelisation requires the whole Church to take the whole gospel to the whole world. The Church is at the very centre of God's cosmic purpose and is his appointed means of spreading the gospel. But a church which preaches the cross must itself be marked by the cross. It becomes a stumbling block to evangelism when it betrays the gospel or lacks a living faith in God, a genuine love for people, or scrupulous honesty in all things including promotion and finance. The Church is the community of God's people rather than an institution, and must not be identified with any particular culture, social or political system, or human ideology. (John 17:18; 20:21; Matt. 28:19,20; Acts 1:8; 20:27; Eph. 1:9,10; 3:9–11; Gal. 6:14,17; II Cor. 6:3,4; II Tim. 2:19–21; Phil. 1:27)

7. Cooperation in Evangelism

We affirm that the Church's visible unity in truth is God's purpose. Evangelism also summons us to unity, because our oneness strengthens our witness, just as our disunity undermines our gospel of reconciliation. We recognise, however, that organisational unity may take many forms and does not necessarily forward evangelism. Yet we who share the same biblical faith should be closely united in fellowship, work and witness. We confess that our testimony has sometimes been marred by a sinful individualism and needless duplication. We pledge ourselves to seek a deeper unity in truth, worship, holiness and mission. We urge the development of regional and functional cooperation for the furtherance of the Church's mission, for strategic planning, for mutual encouragement, and for the sharing of resources and experience. (John 17:21,23; Eph. 4:3,4; John 13:35; Phil. 1:27; John 17:11–23)

8. Churches in Evangelistic Partnership

We rejoice that a new missionary era has dawned. The dominant role of western missions is fast disappearing. God is raising up from the younger churches a great new resource for world evangelisation, and is thus demonstrating that the responsibility to evangelise belongs to the whole body of Christ. All churches should therefore be asking God and themselves what they should be doing both to reach their own area and to send missionaries to other parts of the world. A reevaluation of our missionary responsibility and role should be continuous. Thus a growing partnership of churches will develop and the universal character of Christ's Church will be more clearly exhibited. We also thank God for agencies which labour in Bible translation, theological education, the mass media, Christian literature, evangelism, missions, church renewal and other specialist fields. They too should engage in constant self-examination to evaluate their effectiveness as part of the Church's mission. (Rom. 1:8; Phil. 1:5; 4:15; Acts 13:1–3; I Thess. 1:6–8)

9. The Urgency of the Evangelistic Task

More than 2,700 million people, which is more than two-thirds of all humanity, have yet to be evangelised. We are ashamed that so many have been neglected; it is a standing rebuke to us and to the whole Church. There is now, however, in many parts of the world an unprecedented receptivity to the Lord Jesus Christ. We are convinced that this is the time for churches and parachurch agencies to pray earnestly for the salvation of the unreached and to launch new efforts to achieve world evangelisation. A reduction of foreign missionaries and money in an evangelised country may sometimes be necessary to facilitate the national Church's growth in self-reliance and to release resources for areas. Missionaries should flow ever more freely from and to all six continents in a spirit of humble service. The goal should be, by all available means and at the earliest possible time, that every person will have the opportunity to hear, understand, and to receive the good news. We cannot hope to attain this goal without sacrifice. All of us are shocked by the poverty of millions and disturbed by the injustices which cause it. Those of us who live in affluent circumstances accept our duty to develop a simple lifestyle in order to contribute more generously to both relief and evangelism. (John 9:4; Matt. 9:35–38; Rom. 9:1–3; I Cor. 9:19–23; Mark 16:15; Isa. 58:6,7; Jas. 1:27; 2:1–9; Matt. 25:31–46; Acts 2:44,45; 4:34,35)

10. Evangelism and Culture

The development of strategies for world evangelisation calls for imaginative pioneering methods. Under God, the result will be the rise of churches deeply rooted in Christ and closely related to their culture. Culture must always be tested and judged by Scripture. Because men and women are God's creatures, some of their culture is rich in beauty and goodness. Because they are fallen, all of it is tainted with sin and some of it is demonic. The gospel does not presuppose the superiority of any culture to another, but evaluates all cultures according to its own criteria of truth and righteousness, and insists on moral absolutes in every culture. Missions have all too frequently exported with the gospel an alien culture and churches have sometimes been in bondage to culture rather than to Scripture. Christ's evangelists must humbly seek to empty themselves of all but their personal authenticity in order to become the servants of others, and churches must seek to transform and enrich culture, all for the glory of God. (Mark 7:8,9,13; Gen. 4:21,22; I Cor. 9:19–23; Phil. 2:5–7; II Cor. 4:5)

11. Education and Leadership

We confess that we have sometimes pursued Church growth at the expense of Church depth, and divorced evangelism from Christian nurture. We also acknowledge that some of our missions have been too slow to equip and encourage national leaders to assume their rightful responsibilities. Yet we are committed to indigenous principles, and long that every church will have national leaders who manifest a Christian style of leadership in terms not of domination but of service. We recognise that there is a great need to improve theological education, especially for Church leaders. In every nation and culture there should be an effective training programme for pastors and laity in doctrine, discipleship, evangelism, nurture and service. Such training programmes should not rely on any stereotyped methodology but should be developed by creative local initiatives according to biblical standards. (Col. I:27,28; Acts 14:23; Tit. 1:5,9; Mark 10:42–45; Eph. 4:11,12)

12. Spiritual Conflict

We believe that we are engaged in constant spiritual warfare with the principalities and powers of evil, who are seeking to overthrow the Church and frustrate its task of world evangelisation. We know our need to equip ourselves with God's armour and to fight this battle with the spiritual weapons of truth and prayer. For we detect the activity of our enemy, not only in false ideologies outside the Church, but also inside it in false gospels which twist Scripture and put people in the place of God. We need both watchfulness and discernment to safeguard the biblical gospel. We acknowledge that we ourselves are not immune to worldliness of thoughts and action, that is, to a surrender to secularism. For example, although careful studies of Church growth, both numerical and spiritual, are right and valuable, we have sometimes neglected them. At other times, desirous to ensure a response to the gospel, we have compromised our message, manipulated our hearers through pressure techniques, and become unduly preoccupied with statistics or even dishonest in our use of them. All this is worldly. The Church must be in the world; the world must not be in the Church. (Eph. 6:12; II Cor. 4:3,4; Eph. 6:11,13–18; II Cor. 10:3–5; I John 2:18–26; 4:1–3; Gal. 1:6–9; II Cor. 2:17; 4:2; John 17:15)

13. Freedom and Persecution

It is the God-appointed duty of every government to secure conditions of peace, justice and liberty in which the Church may obey God, serve the Lord Jesus Christ, and preach the gospel without interference. We therefore pray for the leaders of nations and call upon them to guarantee freedom of thought and conscience, and freedom to practise and propagate religion in accordance with the will of God and as set forth in The Universal Declaration of Human Rights. We also express our deep concern for all who have been unjustly imprisoned, and especially for those who are suffering for their testimony to the Lord Jesus. We promise to pray and work for their freedom. At the same time we refuse to be intimidated by their fate. God helping us, we too will seek to stand against injustice and to remain faithful to the gospel, whatever the cost. We do not forget the warnings of Jesus that persecution is inevitable. (I Tim. 1:1–4; Acts 4:19; 5:29; Col. 3:24; Heb. 13:1–3; Luke 4:18; Gal. 5:11; 6:12; Matt. 5:10–12; John 15:18–21)

14. The Power of the Holy Spirit

We believe in the power of the Holy Spirit. The Father sent his Spirit to bear witness to his Son, without his witness ours is futile. Conviction of sin, faith in Christ, new birth and Christian growth are all his work. Further, the Holy Spirit is a missionary Spirit; thus evangelism should arise spontaneously from a Spirit-filled Church. A Church that is not a missionary Church is contradicting itself and quenching the Spirit. Worldwide evangelisation will become a realistic possibility only when the Spirit renews the Church in truth and wisdom, faith, holiness, love and power. We therefore call upon all Christians to pray for such a visitation of the sovereign Spirit of God that all his fruit may appear in all his people and that all his gifts may enrich the body of Christ. Only then will the whole world become a fit instrument in his hands, that the whole earth may hear his voice. (I Cor. 2:4; John 15:26;27; 16:8–11; I Cor. 12:3; John 3:6–8; II Cor. 3:18; John 7:37–39; I Thess. 5:19; Acts 1:8; Psa. 85:4–7; 67:1–3; Gal. 5:22,23; I Cor. 12:4–31; Rom. 12:3–8)

15. The Return of Christ

We believe that Jesus Christ will return personally and visibly, in power and glory, to consummate his salvation and his judgement. This promise of his coming is a further spur to our evangelism, for we remember his words that the gospel must first be preached to all nations. We believe that the interim period between Christ's ascension and return is to be filled with the mission of the people of God, who have no liberty to stop before the end. We also remember his warning that false Christs and false prophets will arise as precursors of the final Antichrist. We therefore reject as a proud, self-confident dream the notion that people can ever build a utopia on earth. Our Christian confidence is that God will perfect his kingdom, and we look forward with eager anticipation to that day, and to the new heaven and earth in which righteousness will dwell and God will reign forever. Meanwhile, we rededicate ourselves to the service of Christ and of people in joyful submission to his authority over the whole of our lives. (Mark 14:62; Heb. 9:28; Mark 13:10; Acts 1:8–11; Matt. 28:20; Mark 13:21–23; John 2:18; 4:1–3; Luke 12:32; Rev. 21:1–5; II Pet. 3:13; Matt. 28:18)

Conclusion

Therefore, in the light of this our faith and our resolve, we enter into a solemn covenant with God and with each other, to pray, to plan and to work together for the evangelisation of the whole world. We call upon others to join us. May God help us by his grace and for his glory to be faithful to this our covenant! Amen, Alleluia!

Note

1 The following text is taken from the internet web page: http://www.uofn.ch/lausanne/covenant.htm.

Bibliography

1. Periodicals

Allgemeine Missionsnachrichten (later *Missions-Nachrichten*)
Allgemeine Missionszeitschrift
Asia Journal of Theology
Aus dem Lebenszentrum Adelshofen
Bibel und Gemeinde
Diakisis
Direction
Christian Century
Ecumenical Review, The
EMW-Informationen
Evangelical Mission Quarterly
Evangelical Quarterly
Evangelical Review of Theology
Evangelikale Missiologie
Evangelikale Theologie
Evangelische Missionszeitschrift
Evangelisches Missionsmagazin
Exchange
Fundamentum
International Bulletin of Missionary Research
International Review of Mission
Jahrbuch Evangelische Theologie
Jahrbuch Mission
Journal for General Philosophy of Science/Zeitschrift für allgemeine Wissenschaftstheorie
Journal of Pentecostal Theology
Journal of Theology for Southren Africa
Mennonitisches Jahrbuch
Ministerial Formation
Missiology
Mission Studies
Missionalia
Monist, The
Neue Allgemeine Missionszeitschrift
Neue Zeitschrift für Missionswissenschaft
Offene Türen
OJC Freundesbrief der ökumenischen Kommunität Offensive Junger Christen
Ökumenische Rundschau
Studia Theologica
Theological Education
Theological News (Incorperating Theological Education Today)
Theologische Beiträge
Transformation

Unterwegs
Westminster Theological Journal
Zeitschrift für allgemeine Wissenschaftstheorie/Journal of General Philosophy of Science
Zeitschrift für Mission
Zeitschrift für Missionswissenschaft und Religionswissenschaft
Zeitschrift für Philosophie und Theologie

2. Encyclopedias

The Blackwell Encyclopedia of Modern Christian Thought (Oxford 1993).
Brockhaus Enzyklopädie (Mannheim 1986–1995)
Companion Encyclopedia of Theology (London 1995)
Evangelisches Lexikon für Theologie und Gemeinde (Helmut Burkhardt and Uwe Swarat, eds.). Wuppertal/Zürich (Brockhaus) 1992–1994.
Evangelisches Gemeindelexikon (Erich Geldbach, Helmut Burkhardt and Kurt Heimbucher, eds.). Wuppertal (Brockhaus) 1975.
Eurostat Jahrbuch '95 (Luxemburg 1995).
Lexikon der Philosophie (Stuttgart 1974)
Lexikon der Mission (Graz 1992).
Lexikon Missiontheologischer Grundbegriffe (Berlin 1987).
Lexikon zur Weltmission (Stephen Neill, Niels-Peter Moritzen and Ernst Schrupp, eds.). Wuppertal and Erlangen (Brockhaus and Verlag der Evang.-Luth. Mission) 1975.
The New Dictionary of Theology (Wilmington 1987)
A New Dictionary of Christian Theology (London 1984)
Religion in Geschichte und Gegenwart (Kurt Galling, ed.). Tübingen (J. C. B. Mohr) 1986.
Statistisches Jahrbuch der Schweiz 1998 (Zürich 1998)
Theologische Realenzyklopädie (Berlin 1976–)

3. Primary Sources and Archival Data

Archive *Bienenberg* Archive of *Theologische Seminar Bienenberg*
Archive *Brake* Archive of *Bibelschule Brake*
Archive EEAA Publications and records of the EEAA (The author has access to the material in the archives of the *Theologisches Seminar Bienenberg*. As a member school of EEAA TSB holds all the data distributed to member schools).
Archive *KBA* Archive of the *Konferenz Bibeltreuer Ausbildungsstätten* at *Bibelschule Wiedenest*
Archive *Liebenzell* Archive of the *Theologische Seminar Bad Liebenzell*
Archive Riecker Otto Riecker Archive at *Bibelschule Adelshofen*
Archive *Wiedenest* Archive of *Bibelschule Wiedenest*
Catalogue [+ name of school] Catalogues of *the Schools*
DEMR/DEMT Archival data of the *DEMR/DEMT* from 1968 to 1976, Archive *Liebenzell*, files *DEMR/DEMT*)
EEAA *Manual of Accreditation* (1995) of the European Evangelical Accrediting Association

Survey 1980 *KBA* 1980 survey on mission training (*KBA* Archives)
Survey 1996 *KBA* 1996 survey (edition 1997), later published in Faix and Faix and Müller and Schmidt)
BökerSurvey 1996 survey on mission studies in German evangelical Bible schools and seminaries conducted by Traugott Böker of WEC International (Private archives of Traugott Böker, WEC International, Hof Häusel 4, 65817 Eppstein)

4. Books and Articles

Adamek, Helmut, 1969 'Über die Integration der Missionswissenschaften in die Forschungs- und Lehrpraxis der evangelisch-theologischen Fakultäten,' *EMZ* 26/2:106–10.

Aebli, Hans, 1976 *Grundformen des Lehrens: Eine allgemeine Didaktik auf kognitionspsychologischer Grundlage*. Stuttgart: Klett (9th, enl. ed.).

AfeM, 1992 *Säkularismus und Mission. Referate der Jahrestagung 1992 des Arbeitskreises für Evangelikale Missiologie (AfeM) in Korntal bei Stuttgart*. Idea-Dokumentation 16/92. Luzern: Idea Schweiz.

Allen, John, 1989 *The Evangelicals: An Illustrated History*. Exeter: Paternoster.

Altbach, Philip G., 1988 *Higher Education in the Third World*. New York: Advent Books.

Amirtham, Samuel, 1982 'Learnings from P.T.E.'s Consultations,' *MForm* 20:11–16.

— 1990 'Ökumenisches Lernen: Anfragen an theologische Ausbildung im europäischen Kontext,' in Engel and Werner 1990:13–24.

Anderson, Gerald H., ed., 1961 *The Theology of the Christian Mission*. New York: McGraw-Hill.

Anderson, Gerald H., 1996 'Theology of Religions: The Epitom of Mission Theology,' in Saayman and Kritzinger:113–20.

Appiah-Kubi, Kofi and Sergio Torres, eds., 1979 *African Theology en Route. Papers from the Pan-African Conference of Third World Theologians 1977*. Maryknoll: Orbis.

Arles, Siga, 1991 *Theological Education for the Mission of the Church in India: 1947–1987*. Frankfurt: Lang.

Associated Mennonite Biblical Seminary, 1992 *Ministerial Formation and Theological Education in Mennonite Perspective*. Elkhart: AMBS.

ATS, 1995 'Toward a new vision of ministerial formation: Contextualisation, globalization and viability,' *MForm* 70:3–6.

Atullah Ramez, 1992 'Responses to "A Movement Divided" by Samuel Escobar,' in *Transformation* 1992/1:25–26.

Austad, Torleiv, 1985 'Chancen zur Erneuerung der theologischen Ausbildung,' in Cochlovius, ed:33–43.

Austin, William H., 1972 'Paradigms, Rationality and Partial Communication,' *ZaWT* 3/1:201–18.

Baillie, T. J., 1993 *Models and Methods for the Current Missionary Paradigm*. Cardiff: University of Wales (MTh thesis).

Balasuriya, Tissa, 1984 *Planetary Theology*. Maryknoll: Orbis.

Balz, Horst and Siegfried Schulz, eds., 1973 *Das Wort und die Wörter* (Festschrift Gerhard Friedrich). Stuttgart: Kohlhammer.

Barbour, Ian, 1974 *Myth, Models and Paradigms*. London: SCM.
Barr, James, 1977 *Fundamentalism*. London: SCM.
— 1988 *Escaping from Fundamentalism*. London: SCM.
Barth, Karl, 1963 *Evangelical Theology*. Grand Rapids: Eerdmans.
Basset, Jean-Claude, 1993 'Christliche Theologie im interreligiösen Gespräch,' *ZMiss* 19/2:95–106.
Bassham, Rodger C., 1979 *Mission Theology: 1948–1975: Years of Worldwide Creative Tension: Ecumenical, Evangelical and Roman Catholic*. Pasadena: William Carey Library.
Baumann, Andreas, et al., 1970 *Untersuchung zur Situation der Theologiestudenten*. Zürich: TVZ.
Bäumer, R., Peter Beyerhaus, and Fritz Grünzweig, eds., 1980 *Weg und Zeugnis: Bekennende Gemeinschaften im gegenwärtigen Kirchenkampf 1965–1980*. Bad Liebenzell: VLM.
Bayertz, Kurt, 1981 *Wissenschaftstheorie und Paradigmabegriff*. Stuttgart: Metzlersche Verlagsbuchhandlung.
Beaver, R. Pierce, 1976 'The American Protestant Theological Seminary and Missions: An Historical Survey,' *Miss* 6/1:75–87.
Bebbington, D. W., 1989 *Evangelicalism in Modern Britain: A History from the 1730's to the 1980s*. London/New York: Routledge.
Becker, Dieter, 1997 'Junger Wein und neue Schläuche: Theologische Wissenschaft heute und der Fachbereich: Religion, Mission, Ökumene,' in Becker and Feldtkeller:190– 208.
Becker, Dieter, and Andreas Feldtkeller, eds., 1997 *Es begann in Halle ...: Missionswissenschaft von Gustav Warneck bis heute*. Erlangen: Verlag der Ev. Luth. Mission.
Bender, Harold S., 1944 *The Anabaptist Vision*. Scottdale: Herold Press.
Bender, Ross T., 1971 *The People of God: Report of the study project to develop a model for theological education in the Fee Church tradition*. Scottdale: Herald Press.
— 1996 *Education for Peoplehood*. Scottdale: Herald Press.
Berneburg, Erhardt, 1989 'Zum Verhältnis von Verkündigung und sozialer Aktion in der evangelikalen Missionstheorie,' Kniffka 1989:142–48.
— 1992 'Frankfurter Erklärung zur Grundlagenkrise der Mission,' in *ELThG*: 662.
— 1993 'Das ökumenische Dialogprogramm und die Eindeutigkeit der missionarischen Verkündigung,' in Hille and Troeger:79–94.
— 1997 *Das Verhältnis von Verkündigung und sozialer Aktion in der evangelikalen Missionstheorie*. Wuppertal: Brockhaus.
Bernhardt, Reinhold, 1995 'Zwischen Relativismus und Proselitenmacherei: Zur Begründung einer Theologie der Mission,' *ZMiss* 19/3:167–84.
Bertsch, Ludwig, ed., 1990 *Herausgefordert durch die Armen*. Freiburg/Basel/ Wien: Herder.
Betz, Otto, 1981 *Wie verstehen wir das Neue Testament*. Wuppertal: Aussaat.
Betz, Ulrich, ed., 1991 *Zwischenbilanz: Evangelikale unterwegs zum Jahr 2000*. Stuttgart: Deutsche Evangelische Allianz.
Beyerhaus, Peter, 1970a *Humanisierung: Einzige Hoffnung der Welt*? Bad Salzuflen: MBK-Verlag (2nd ed.).
— 1970b *Die Grundlagenkrise der Mission*. Bad Liebenzell: VLM.
— 1970c *Die Versuchungsstunde des Ökumenischen Rates*. Bad Liebenzell: VLM.

— 1973 *Bangkok '73. Anfang oder Ende der Weltmission?* Bad Liebenzell: VLM.
— 1975 'Lausanne zwischen Berlin und Genf', in Künnerth and Beyerhaus:294–313.
— 1981 *Aufbruch der Armen: Die neue Missionsbewegung nach Melbourn.* Bad Liebenzell: VLM.
— 1986 *Theologie als Instrument der Befreiung.* Giessen/Basel: Brunnen.
— 1987 *Krise und Neuaufbruch der Weltmission.* Bad Liebenzell: VLM.
— 1995 'Das Verhältnis von Mission und Dialog im 20. Jahrhundert – Geschichte und Probleme,' *em* 1995/2:43–50.
— 1996a *Er sandte sein Wort: Theologie der christlichen Mission, Band 1.* Wuppertal: Brockhaus, and Bad Liebenzell: VLM.
— 1996b 'Der kirchlich-theologische Dienst des Albrecht-Bengel-Hauses,' *Diakrisis* 1/1996:9–21.
Beyerhaus, Peter, ed., 1974 *Alle Welt soll sein Wort hören. Lausanne-Dokumente Band 1 und 2.* Neuhausen-Stuttgart: Hänssler.
Beyerhaus, Peter/Ulrich Betz, eds., 1976 *Ökumene im Spiegel von Nairobi '75.* Bad Liebenzell: VLM.
Beyreuther, Erich, 1963 *Der geschichtliche Auftrag des Pietismus in der Gegenwart.* Stuttgart: Calwer.
— 1969 *Der Weg der Evangelischen Allianz in Deutschland.* Wuppertal: Brockhaus.
— 1977 *Die Erweckungsbewegung.* Göttingen: Vandenhoeck & Rupprecht (2nd ed.).
Bittner, Wolfgang, ed., 1993 *Studienreform – Kirchenreform.* IDEA Dokumention 141. Luzern: Idea-Schweiz.
Blaser, Klauspeter, 1987 'Should We Stop Using The Term "Mission",' *IRM* 76/1:68–71.
Blauw, Johannes, 1961 *Gottes Werk in dieser Welt: Grundzüge einer biblischen Theologie der Mission.* München: Kaiser.
— 1962 *The Missionary Nature of the Church: A Survey of the Biblical Theology of Mission.* New York: McGraw-Hill.
Bloth, Peter C., 1990 'Was fördert und behindert eine ökumenische Orientierung theologischer Ausbildung?,' in Engel and Werner 1990:35–40.
Bockmühl, Klaus, 1964 *Die neuere Missionstheologie.* Stuttgart: Calver
— 1974 *Was heisst heute Mission?* Giessen/Basel: Brunnen.
— 1975 *Evangelikale Sozialethik: Der Artikel 5 der Lausanner Verpflichtung.* Giessen/Basel: Brunnen.
— 1982 *Theologie und Lebensführung.* Giessen/Basel: Brunnen.
— 1983 *Verkündigung und soziale Verantwortung.* Giessen/Basel: Brunnen.
— 1985 *Die Aktualität des Pietismus.* Giessen/Basel: Brunnen.
— 1990 *Hören auf den Gott der redet.* Giessen/Basel: Brunnen.
Boff, Leonard, and Clodovis Boff, 1987 *Introducing Liberation Theology.* Kent: Burns & Oates.
Boff, Leonardo, Bruno Kern, and Andreas Müller, eds., 1988 *Werkbuch Theologie der Befreiung.* Düsseldorf: Patmos.
Böhler, Dietrich, 1972 'Paradigmenwechsel in analytischer Wissenschaftstheorie,' *ZaWT* 3/1:219–42.
Bohren, Rudolf, 1963 *Predigt und Gemeinde: Beiträge zur Praktischen Theologie.* Zurich/Stuttgart: Zwingli.

Bohren, Rudolf, ed., 1964 *Einführung in das Studium der evangelischen Theologie*. Munich: Kaiser.

Böker, Traugott, 1996 'Mission and bibeltreuen Ausbildungsstätten: Motivation – Prägung – Begleitung unserer Schüler.' Eppstein: unpublished manuscript.

Bonino, Jose Miguez, 1975 *Doing Theology in a Revolutionary Situation*. Philadelphia: Fortress.

Born, Heinz, 1992 'Europäische Evangelikale Akkreditierungsvereinigung EEAV,' in *ELThG*:554–55.

Börner, Fritz, 1989 'Freikirchlicher Gemeindebau in Österreich.' Korntal: Freie Hochschule für Mission (unpublished MA thesis).

Bosch, David, 1959 *Die Heidenmission in der Zukunftsschau Jesu: Eine Untersuchung zur Eschatologie der synoptischen Evangelien*. Zurich: Zwingli.

— 1978 'Hermeneutical Principles in the Biblical Foundation for Mission,' *ERTh* 17/4:437–51 (Reprinted from *Zending op weg Naorde de Toekmst*. Kampen: UJH Kok, 1978).

— 1979 *A Spirituality of the Road*. Scottdale: Herold.

— 1980 *Witness to the World*. Atlanta: John Knox.

— 1982a 'Theological Education in Missionary Perspective,' *Miss* 10/1:13–33.

— 1982b 'Mission and the Alternative Community,' *JTSA* 41:6–10.

— 1983a 'Evangelism and Social Transformation,' in Sine:273–92.

— 1983b 'The Structure of Mission: An Exposition of Matthew 28:16–20,' in Shenk , ed. 1983:218–47.

— 1986 'Towards a Hermeneutic for "Biblical Studies and Mission",' *MStud* 3/2:65–79.

— 1987 'Vision for Mission,' *IRM* 76/1:8–15.

— 1988 ' "Ecumenicals" and "Evangelicals": A Growing Relationship?,' *ER* 40: 458–67.

— 1990 'Mission in the 1990s: Three Views. A New Paradigm,' *IBMR* 14/4:149–52.

— 1991 *Transforming Mission*. Maryknoll: Orbis.

— 1992a 'The Vulnerability of Mission,' *ZMR* 76/3:201–16.

— 1992b 'A Theology of "The Signs of the Times",' *Exchange* 21/3:247–66.

— 1993a 'God's Reign and the Rulers of This World,' in Van Engen and Gilliland and , Pierson:89–95.

— 1993b 'Reflections on Biblical Models of Mission,' in Phillips and Coote:175–92.

— 1996 *An die Zukunft glauben*. Weltmission heute 24 (Studienheft). Hamburg: EMW.

Braaten, Carl E., 1977 *The Flaming Centre*. Philadelphia: Fortress.

Brandl, Bernd, 1977 'Die Neukirchner Mission als erste deutsche Glaubensmisson'. Heverlee/Leuven: Evangelisch-Theologische Fakultät (unpublished DTheol thesis).

Brereton, Virginia L., 1981 *Protestant Fundamentalist Bible Schools: 1882–1940*. Columbia University (PhD thesis).

Bright, Bill, 1971 *Wirksames Zeugnis – wie macht man das*? Neuhausen Stuttgart: Hänssler.

Brinkman, Martien E., 1994 'The Common Challenge to Ecumenicals and Evangelicals – An Ecumenical Appraisal,' *Exchange* 23/3:191–206.

Brown, Marvin, 1980 *On Time and in Place – The Work of the Evangelical Academies in West Germany*. Bad Boll: Leiterkreis der Evangelischen Akademien in Deutschland.

Bryman, Alan, 1988 *Quantity and Quality in Social Research*. London/New York: Routledge.

Bundesamt für Statistik, ed., 1998 *Statistisches Jahrbuch der Schweiz 1998*. Zürich: Verlag NZZ.

Burkhardt, Helmut, 1994 'C.F. Spittler und der Basler Theology W.M.L. de Wette,' in Frische, ed:94:35–75.

— 1993 *Ein Gott in allen Religionen: Wiederkehr der Religiosität – Chance und Gefahr*. Giessen/Basel: Brunnen (2nd ed.).

— 1995 'Mission aus evangelikaler Sicht,' *JET* 1995:81–87.

Byron, Peter, and Leslie Houlden, eds., 1995 *Companion Encyclopedia of Theology*. London: Routledge.

Cahoone, Lawrence, 1996 *From Modernism to Postmodernism. An Anthology*. Oxford: Blackwell.

Cameron, Nigel M. de S., ed., 1992 *Universalism and the Doctrine of Hell*. Carlisle: Paternoster and Grand Rapids: Baker.

Campus Crusade for Christ, ed., 1971 *Handbuch für persönliche Evangelisation*. Neuhausen-Stuttgart: Hänssler.

Carpenter, Joel A., and Wilbert R Shenk, eds, 1990 *Earthen Vessels: American Evangelicals and Foreign Missions, 1880–1980*. Grand Rapids: Eerdmans.

Castro, Emilio, 1982 'Editorial,' *IRM* 71/282, 129–32 [= 'Foreword,' in Kinsler 1983:IX-XII].

— 1990 'Mission in the 1990s: Three Views,' *IBMR* 14/4:146–49.

Cheesman, Grahame, 1993 'Competing Paradigms in Theological Education Today,' *ERTh* 17/4:484–99.

Cochlovius, Joachim, 1993 'Geistliches Rüstzentrum Krelingen,' in *ELThG*:695.

— 1996 '25 Jahre Studienarbeit im Geistlichen Rüstzentrum Krelingen,' *Diakrisis* 1/1996:26–29.

Cochlovius, Joachim, ed., 1985 *Theologie und Erweckung*. Giessen/Basel: Brunnen.

Cochlovius, Joachim, and Peter Zimmerling, eds., 1987 *Evangelische Schriftauslegung*. Wuppertal: Brockhaus.

Cochrane, J. R., 1996 'Contextualization and Globalization in Theological Education,' *MForm* 72:29–34.

Coleman, Robert E., 1979 *Des Meistes Plan der Evangelisation*. Neuhausen-Stuttgart: Hänssler.

Collet, Giancarlo, , 1984 *Das Missionsverständnis der Kirche in der gegenwärtigen Diskussion*. Mainz: Matthias Grünewald.

Collet, Giancarlo, ed., 1990 *Theologien der Dritten Welt (EAT WOT als Herausforderung westlicher Theologie und Kirche)*. Immensee: NZM.

Conn, Harvie M., 1983 'The Missionary Task of Theology: A Love/Hate Relationship?,' *WTJ* 45:1–21.

— 1984 *Eternal Word and Changing Worlds: Theology, Anthropology, and Mission in Trialogue*. Grand Rapids: Zondervan.

Conn, Harvie M. and S. F. Rowen, 1984 *Missions and Theological Education in World Perspective*. Farmington: Associates of Urbanus.

Costas, Orland E., 1982 *Christ Outside the Gate: Mission Beyond Christendom*. Maryknoll: Orbis.

Covell, Ralph, 1993 'Jesus Christ and World Religions: Current Evangelical Viewpoints,' in VanEngen and Gilliland and Pierson:162–171.

Cracknell, Kenneth, and Christopher Lamb, eds, 1986 *Theology on Full Alert*. London: British Council of Churches (rev. and enl. ed.).

Cray, Graham et al., 1997 *The Post-Evangelical Debate*. London: Triangle SPCK.

Crittin, Jean-Pierre, 1994 *Erfolgreich unterrichten*. Bern: Haupt.

Danker, W. J., and Wi Jo Kang, eds., 1971 *The Future of Christian World Mission*. Grand Rapids: Eerdmans.

Dayton, Edward R., and David A. Fraser, 1980 *Planning Strategies for World Evangelization*. Grand Rapids: Eerdmans.

Dayton, Edward R., and Samuel Wilson, ed., 1984 *The Future of World Evangelisation: The Lausanne Movement*. Monrovia: MARC.

D'Costa, Gavin, 1986 *Theology and Religious Pluralism*. Oxford: Blackwell.

— 1990 'Christ, the Trinity and Religious Plurality,' in D'Costa, ed:16–29.

D'Costa, Gavin, ed., 1990 *Christian Uniqueness Reconsidered: The Myth of a Pluralistic Theology of Religions*. Maryknoll: Orbis.

Dearborn, Tim, 1995 'Preparing New Leaders for the Church of the Future,' *Transformation* 12/4:7–12.

DeHainaut, Raymond K., 1995 'Anachronism and Adventurism: Recent mission trends,' *Christian Century* March:229–42.

Dellsperger, R., M. Nägeli, and H. Ramser, 1982 *Auf dein Wort*. Bern: Haller.

Dembrowski, Hermann, 1982 'Die Einheit der Theologie,' in Schöer:180–92.

Dempster, Murray A., Byron D. Klaus, and Douglas Petersen, 1991 *Called and Empowered: Global Mission in Pentecostal Perspective*. Peabody: Hendrickson.

Dewey, John, 1936 *Democracy and Education*. New York: Macmillan.

Dieterich, Michael, 1991 *Auf dem Weg zum Beruf: Ein pädagogisches Fachbuch für Ausbilder und Lehrer*. Hamburg: Handwerk und Technik.

Du Plessis, J. G., 1990 'For reasons of the heart: A critical appraisal of David J. Bosch's use of Scripture in the foundation of Christian mission,' *Missionalia* 18/1:75–85.

Duraisingh, Christopher, 1992 'Ministerial Formation for Mission: Implications for Theological Education,' *IRM* 81/321:33–45.

Dürr, H., 1951 'Die Reinigung der Missionsmotive,' *EMM* 95:2.

Dussel, Enrique, 1987 'The Ebb and Flow of the Gospel: When the Evangelized Poor Become Evangelizers,' *IRM* 76/1:48–56.

Ebeling, Gerhard, 1975a *Studium der Theologie: Eine enzyklopädische Orientierung*. Tübingen: J.C.B. Mohr.

— 1975b *Wort und Glaube Band 3: Beiträge zur Fundamentaltheologie,Soteriologie und Ekklesiologie*. Tübingen: J.C.B. Mohr.

— 1975c 'Zur Existenz theologischer Fakultäten an staatlichen Universitäten,' in Ebeling 1975b:164–69.

— 1978 *The Study of Theology*. Philadelphia: Fortress.

— 1995a *Wort und Glaube Band 4: Theologie in den Gegensätzen des Lebens*. Tübingen: J.C.B. Mohr.

— 1995b 'Die Bibel als ein Dokument der Universität,' in Ebeling 1995a:335–49.

Edwards, David L. and Stott, John, 1988 *Essentials. A Liberal-Evangelical Dialogue*. London.

Egelkraut, Helmuth, 1990 'Theological Education in Europe.' *ERTh* 14/1:32–36.

— 1997 'From Bible Schools to Theological Colleges.' Unpublished paper presented to the biannual assembly of the EEAA.

Egil, Jim, 1992 'Leadership Training for the Church of the Future,' in Zehr and Egli 1992:41–91.

Eicher, Peter, 1980 *Theologie: eine Einführung in das Studium*. Munich 1980.

Engel, James F., 1988 *Zeitgemässe christliche Kommunikation*. Bad Liebenzell: VLM.

Engel, Lothar, 1996 'The Study Process on Viability: Its Relevance for Theological Education in Germany,' *MForm* January:7–10.

Engel, Lothar, ed., 1983 'Theologische Ausbildung in der Dritten Welt: Erfahrungen und Herausforderungen (Einleitung),' EMW-Informationen 45:2–4.

— 1993 *Christlicher Fundamentalismus in Afrika und Amerika* (Weltmission heute 13). Hamburg: EMW.

Engel, Lothar and Dietrich Werner, eds., 1990 *Oekumenische Perspektiven theologischer Ausbildung* (Beiheft zur 'Ökumenischen Rundschau' Nr. 60). Frankfurt a.M: Otto Lembeck.

Erickson, Millard J., 1997 *The Evangelical Left: Encountering Postconservative Evangelical Theology*. Grand Rapids: Baker.

Escobar, J. Samuel, 1974 'Evangelisation und die Suche des Menschen nach Freiheit und Erfüllung,' in Beyerhaus 1974 vol 1:385–426.

— 1991 'A Movement Divided. Three Approaches to World Evangelization Stand in Tension With One Another,' *Transformation* 1991/4:7–13.

— 1996 'Mission Studies Past, Present, and Future,' *Miss* 24/1:3–29.

Escobar, J. Samuel/John Driver, 1978 *Christian Mission and Social Justice*. Scottdale: Herald.

Evangelische Arbeitsstelle Ökumene Schweiz, 1987 *Was bekennen die evangelischen Kirchen in der Schweiz*. Bern: Evangelische Arbeitsstelle Ökumene Schweiz.

Faix, Tobias, Wilhelm Faix, Klaus W. Müller, and Klaus Schmidt, eds., 1998 *Theologische Ausbildung zu Beginn des 21. Jahrhunderts*. Bonn: Verlag für Kultur und Wissenschaft.

Faix, Wilhelm, 1996 'Akzente richtig setzen: Gedanken zur Situation der Bibelschulausbildung,' *Aus dem Lebenszentrum Adelshofen* 2:19–23.

— 1998 'Theologische Ausbildung im Umbruch,' *em* 2:42–45.

Farley, Edward, 1981 'The Reform of Theological Education as a Theological Task,' *Theological Education* 1:93–117.

— 1983 *Theologia – The Fragmentation and Unity of Theological Education*. Philadelphia: Fortress.

Ferris, R. W., 1984 'The Future of Theological Education,' in Youngbood:41–64.

— 1990a *Renewal in Theological Education – Strategies for Changes*. Wheaton: Wheaton College.

— 1990b 'Renewal of Theological Education: Commitments, Models, and the ICAA *Manifesto*,' *ERTh* 14/1:64–77.

Ferris, R. W. and Ralph E. Enlow, 1995 'Reassessing Bible College Distinctives.' AABC: unpublished manuscript.

Fiedler, Klaus, 1992 *Ganz auf Vertrauen. Geschichte und Kirchenverständnis der Glaubensmissionen*. Giessen/Basel: Brunnen.

— 1994 *The Story of Faith Missions from Hudson Taylor to Present Day Africa*. Oxford: Regnum.

— 1999 'It is Time to Write the History of German-Speaking Evangelical Missions,' *Direction* 28/1:28–45.

Fife, Eric S. and Glasser, Arthur F., 1961 *Mission in Crisis*. Chicago: Moody.

Ford, Leighton, 1987 'A Vision for the Future.' *IRM* 76/1:105–16.

Franz, Andreas, 1993 *Mission ohne Grenzen. Hudson Taylor und die deutschsprachigen Glaubensmissionen*. Giessen/Basel: Brunnen.

Freytag, Walter, 1961 *Reden und Aufsätze (Teil 1)*. Munich: Kaiser.

Freytag, Walter, ed., 1952 *Mission zwischen Gestern und Morgen*. Stuttgart: Evangelischer Missionsverlag.

Freire, Paulo, 1973 *Pädagogik der Unterdrückten*. Stuttgart: Kreuz Verlag.

— 1974 *Erziehung als Praxis der Freiheit*. Stuttgart: Kreuz Verlag.

Freire, Paulo, ed., 1997 *Mentoring the Mentor. A Critical Dialogue with Paulo Freire*. New York: Peter Lang.

Friedmann, Robert, 1973 *The Theology of Anabaptism*. Schottdale: Herald Press.

Frieling, Reinhard, ed., 1984 *Die Kirchen und ihre Konservativen*. Göttingen: Vandenhoeck & Rupprecht.

Frische, Reinhard, 1979 *Theologie unter der Herrschaft Gottes*. Giessen/Basel: Brunnen.

Frische, Reinhard, ed., 1994 *Zur Initiative befreit. C.F. Spittler und unser Auftag heute*. Giessen: Brunnen.

Frostin, Per, 1985 'The Hermeneutics of the Poor – The Epistemological "Break" in Third World Theologies,' *StuT* 49:127–50.

Gadamer, Hans-Georg, 1986a *Hermeneutik I: Wahrheit und Methode. Grundzüge einer philosophischen Hermeneutik (Gesammelte Werke Vol. 1)*. Tübingen: J.C.B. Mohr.

— 1986b *Hermeneutik II: Wahrheit und Methode. Ergänzungen, Register (Gesammelte Werke Vol. 2)*. Tübingen: J.C.B. Mohr.

Gage, Nathaniel L. and David C. Berliner (trans. and ed. by Gerhard Bach), 1983 *Pädagogische Psychologie (Vol. 1)*. Weinheim/Basel: Beltz (3rd ed.).

Garrett, James Leo Jr., ed., 1969 *The Concept of the Believers' Church*. Scottdale: Herald Press.

Geiger, Max, ed., 1969 *Gottesreich und Menschenreich: Ernst Staehelin zum 80. Geburtstag*. Basel/Stuttgart: Helbling & Lichtenhahn.

Geiser, Daniel, ed., 1986 *Das Leben wagen – die Zukunft gewinnen. Festschrift Samuel Gerber*. Weisenheim/Berg: Agape.

Geisler, Norman L., ed., 1979 *Inerrancy*. Grand Rapids: Zondervan.

Geldbach, Erich, 1984 'Evangelikalismus: Versuch einer historischen Typologie,' in Frieling:52–83.

— 1989 *Freikirchen – Erbe, Gestalt und Wirkung*. Göttingen: Vandenhoeck & Rupprecht.

— 1992 'Freikirchen,' in *ELThG*:637–39.

— 1993 'Der protestantische Fundamentalismus in den USA – Grundzüge seiner Entwicklung und Ausgestaltung,' in Engel 1993:9–62.

Gensichen, Hans-Werner, 1969 *Missionsgeschichte der neueren Zeit*. Göttingen: Vandenhoeck & Rupprecht (2nd ed.).

— 1971 *Glaube für die Welt*. Gütersloh: Gütersloher Verlagshaus.

— 1985 *Mission und Kultur: Gesammelte Aufsätze*. Munich: Kaiser.

Gerber, Vergil, 1979 *Handbuch für Evangelisation und Gemeindeaufbau*, Bad Liebenzell: VLM.

Gerber, Vergil, ed., 1980 *Discipling through Theological Education by Extension*. Chicago: Moody.
Gilmore, Alec, ed., 1996 *An International Directory of Theological Colleges 1997*. Geneva: WCC Publications.
Giroux, Henry A., 1996 'Towards a Postmodern Pedagogy,' in Cahoone:687–97.
Glasser, Arthur F., 1985 'The Evolution of Evangelical Mission Theology since World War II,' in *IBMR* 1:9–13.
Glasser, Arthur and Donald McGavran, 1983 *Contemporary Theologies of Mission*. Grand Rapids: Baker.
Gleiss, Dagmar, 1994 'Geschichte der Arbeitsgemeinschaft Evangelikaler Missionen, AEM.' Korntal: Freie Hochschule für Mission (unpublished MA thesis)
Gnanakan, Ken, 1992 *The Pluralistic Predicament*. Bangalore: Theological Book Trust.
Goodall, Norman, 1968 *Uppsala spricht*. Genf: ÖRK.
Grafen, Heinrich, 1987 *Gemeinde Jesu – ökumenisch-katholisch vereinnahmt*. Wuppertal: Verlag und Schriftenmission der Evangelischen Gesellschaft für Deutschland.
Green, Michael, 1975 'Die Urgemeinde und ihre Methoden und Strategien in der Evangelisation,' in Beyerhaus 1975:215–38.
Griffiths, Michael, 1972 *Es gibt Grösseres*. Giessen/Basel: Brunnen.
— 1989 'Theological Education Need not Be Irrelevant.' Unpublished paper presented to the biannual assembly of the EEAA.
Grüber, Hans L.E., Elisabeth Meier, and Emory A. Griffin, 1989 *Kommunikation – Kultur – Kontakte*. Bad Liebenzell: VLM.
Guinness, Os, 1994 'Mission and Modernity: Seven Checkpoints on Mission in the Modern World,' in Sampson/Samuel/Sugden:322–52.
Guttierrez, Gustavo, 1973 *A Theology of Liberation*. Maryknoll: Orbis.
Hafner, Herman, 1978 'Ausbildung, theologische (Theologisches Hochschulstudium),' in *EGL*:36–38.
Hafner, Thomas, 1993 'Versuche zur Reform des Theologiestudiums,' in Bittner: 11–13.
Hamel, Martin, 1993 *Bibel – Mission – Ökumene*. Giessen/Basel: Brunnen.
Hanselmann, Heinrich, 1951 *Andragogik: Wesen, Möglichkeiten, Grenzen der Erwachsenenbildung*. Zurich: Rotapfel.
Harder, Lydia, 1997 'Formal Theological Education: The Centre and the Boundaries,' in Heisey and Schipani:103–12.
Harley, David, 1995 *Preparing to Serve: Training for Cross-Cultural Mission*. Pasadena: William Carey Library.
Harris, Harriet A., 1998 *Fundamentalism and Evangelicalism*. Oxford: Clarendon.
Harrison, Pat, 1983 'A Rural Australian Experiment in Training Church Leaders,' in Kinsler 1983:273–83.
— 1991 'Issues in Evaluating Theological Education by Extension,' *ERTh* 15/1:84–94.
Hauzenberger, Hans, 1985 *Einheit auf evangelischer Grundlage:Das Werden und Wesen der Evangelischen Allianz*. Giessen: Brunnen.
— 1992 'Allianz, Evangelische,' in *ELThG*:39–40.

Hauzenberger, Hans, ed., 1981 *Im Ringen um biblisch erneuerte Theologie*. Giessen/Basel: Brunnen.

Hedlund, Roger E., 1993 *Roots of the Great Debate in Mission: Mission in Historical and Theological Perspective*. Bangalore: Theological Book Trust (2nd ed.).

Heisey, Nancy R. and Daniel S. Schipany, eds., *Theological Education on Five Continents: Anabaptist Perspectives*. Strasbourg: Mennonite World Conference.

Helfenstein, Pius F., 1991 *Evangelikale Theologie der Befreiung: Das Reich Gottes in der Theologie der 'Fraternidad Teológica Latinoamericana' und der gängigen Befreiungstheologie im Vergleich*. Zurich: TVZ.

— 1998 *Grundlagen des interreligiösen Dialogs. Theologische Rechtfertigungsversuche in der ökumenischen Bewegung und die Verbindung des trinitarischen Denkens mit dem pluralistischen Ansatz*. Frankfurt: Lembeck.

Hemminger, Hansjörg, 1994 'Glauben verantworten: Methoden und praktische Fragen,' in Hummel and Küenzlen and Hemminger:24–36.

— 1995 'Unsere pluralistische Gesellschaft und die Herausforderung des Evangeliums,' EMW-Informationen 107:30–37.

Hempelmann, Heinzpeter, 1987a *Kritischer Rationalismus und Theologie als Wissenschaft: Zur Frage nach dem Wirklichkeitsbezug des christlichen Glaubens*. Wuppertal: Brockhaus (2nd ed.).

— 1987b 'Der wissenschaftstheoretische Ansatz Th. S. Kuhns und seine Konsequenzen für die theologische Wissenschaft heute,' in Cochlovius and Zimmerling: 353–57.

— 1995 ''Wir haben den Horizont weggewischt' (F. Nietzsche). Das Evangelium verkündigen unter den Bedingungen der Postmoderne,' EMW-Informationen 107:19–29.

— 1996 'Dialog unter Ausschluss der Wahrheit,' in *OJC* 2/1996:65–80.

— 1997 *Glauben wir alle an denselben Gott?. Christlicher Glaube in einer nachchristlichen Gesellschaft*. Wuppertal: Brockhaus/Bad Liebenzell: VLM.

Henning, Peter, 1997 'Theological Education in a Post-Modern World.' Unpublished paper presented to the biannual assembly of the EEAA.

Henkel, Willi, 1997 'German Centres of Mission Research,' *IBMR* 21/2:103–10.

Hering, Wolfgang, 1980 *Das Missionsverständnis in der ökumenisch-evangelikalen Auseinandersetzung – ein innerprotestantisches Problem*. Sankt Augustin: Steyler.

Herm, Daniel, 1989 *Gemeinde und Mission*. Wuppertal/Zürich: Brockhaus.

Herm, Bruno and Daniel Herm, eds., 1985 *Werkbuch Mission*. Wuppertal: Brockhaus.

Hermelink, Jan and Jochen Margull, eds., 1959 *Basileia (Walter Freitag zum 60. Geburtstag)*. Stuttgart: Evangelischer Missionsverlag.

Herrmann, Wolfgang and Gerd Lautner, 1965 *Theologiestudium: Entwurf einer Reform*. Munich: Kaiser.

Hess, Hans-Erich and Heinz Eduard Tödt, eds., 1967 *Reform der theologischen Ausbildung*. Munich: Kaiser.

Hesselgrave J. David and Edward Rommen , 1989 *Contextualization: Meanings, Methods, and Models*. Grand Rapids: Baker.

Heubach, J. and H.-J. Ulrich, eds., 1958 *Sammlung und Sendung (FS Heinrich Rendtorff)*. Berlin: Christlicher Zeitschriftenverlag.

Hicks, Peter, 1998 *Evangelicals and Truth: A Creative Proposal for a Postmodern Age*. Leicester: Apollos.

Hiebert, Paul G., no date 'Contextualization's Challenge to Theological Education.' Unpublished paper.
— 1988 'Metatheology: The Step Beyond Contextualization,' in Kasdorf and Müller 1988:382–95.
— 1991 'Beyond Anti-Colonialism to Globalism,' *Miss* 19/3:263–81
— 1993a 'Popular Religions,' in Phillips and Coote:253–65.
— 1993b 'Evangelism, Church, and Kingdom,' in VanEngen:152–61.
— 1999 *Missiological Implications of Epistemological Shifts: Affirming Truth in a Modern/Postmodern World*. Valley Forge: Trinity Press International.
Hille, Rolf, 1992 'Evangelikal,' in *ELThG*:560–562.
— 1993 'A Spirit and Soil Theology,' in Rin Ro and Nicholls:64–68.
— 1995 'Evangelikale Theologie – als missionarische Herausforderung und missiologisches Programm,' *em* 11:3–12.
Hille, Rolf and Eberhard Troeger, eds., 1993 *Die Einzigartigkeit Jesu*. Wuppertal/ Zurich: Brockhaus and Giessen/Basel: Brunnen.
Hoekendijk, Johannes Christian, 1967 *The Church Inside Out*. London: SCM.
Hogg, William Riches, 1996 'The Teaching of Missiology: Some Reflections on the History and Current Scene,' *Miss* 15/4:487–506.
Holland, Martin, 1992 'Albrecht-Bengel-Haus,' in *ELThG*:34.
Hollenweger, Walter J., 1973 *Evangelisation gestern und heute*. Stuttgart: Steinkopf.
— 1979 *Erfahrungen der Leibhaftigkeit (Interkulturelle Theologie I)*. Munich: Kaiser.
— 1982 *Umgang mit Mythen (Interkulturelle Theologie II)*. Munich: Kaiser.
— 1988 *Geist und Materie (Interkulturelle Theologie III)*. Munich: Kaiser.
— 1989 *The Future of Mission and the Mission of the Future*. Birmingham: Selly Oak Colleges (Occasional Papers No. 2).
— 1991 'Mission Perspectives for the Nineties,' *IRM* 80/317:91–104.
— 1995a 'Evangelism: A Non-Colonial Model,' in *JPT* 7/1995:107–28.
— 1995b 'Theology and the Church of the Future,' in Byron and Houlden:1017–35.
— 1997 *Charismatisch-pfingstliches Christentum. Herkunft. Situation. Ökumenische Chancen*. Göttingen: Vandenhoeck & Rupprecht.
Holthaus, Stephan, 1992 *Fundamentalismus in Deutschland: Der Kampf um die Bibel im Protestantismus des 19. und 20. Jahrhunderts*. Bonn: Verlag für Kultur und Wissenschaft.
— 1995 *Gott ist treu: Die Geschichte der Bibelschule Brake*. Bielefeld: Christliche Literatur- Verbreitung.
— 1997 *Wir brauchen Fundamente*. IDEA-Dokumentation 3/97.
Holthaus, Stephan and Müller, Klaus W. (eds.), 1998 *Die Mission der Theologie (Festschrift für Hans Kasdorf zum 70. Geburtstag)*. Bonn: Verlag für kultur und Wissenschaft.
Holzhaus, Andreas, ed., 1996 *Mission unter Beschuss: Missionspraktiker antworten auf kritische Fragen*. Neuhausen-Stuttgart: Hänssler.
Hough, Jr., Joseph C., 1981 'Reform in Theological Education as Political Task.' *TEd* 1:152–66.
Howard, David M., 1986 *The Dream That Would Not Die. The Birth and Growth of the World Evangelical Fellowship 1846–1986*. Exeter: Paternoster.
Huber, Friederich, 1988 'Überlegungen zum Thema "Ganzheitlich und Ganzheitlichkeit",' in Huber and von Tucher:198–225.

Huber, Friederich and Paul Freiherr von Tucher, eds., 1988 *Mission: erfahren – gepredigt – reflektiert (FS N.-P. Moritzen)*. Erlangen: Evang. Luth. Mission.

Hummel, Reinhardt, Gottfried Küenzlen, and Hansjörg Heminger, 1994 *Begegnung und Auseinandersetzung: Apologetik in der Arbeit der EZW*. Stuttgart: Evangelische Zentralstelle für Weltanschauungsfragen.

Hummel, Reinhardt, 1994 'Apologetische Modelle,' in Hummel and Küenzlen and Hemminger:4–13.

IDEA-Schweiz, 1996 *Symposium 'Kirche 2000' Davos. Referate und Zusammenfassungen der Workshops der idea-Veranstaltung vom 13.–16. November 1996 in Davos*. Luzern: Idea-Schweiz.

International Missionary Council, 1952 *The Missionary Obligation of the Church (Willingen Germany July 5–17 1952)*. Edinburgh: IMC.

Jacobs, Donald R., 1983 *Pilgrimage in Mission*. Scottdale: Herald.

— 1993 'Contextualization in Mission,' in Phillips and Coote:235–44.

Jaspers, Karl, 1959 *The Idea of the University*. London: Peter Owen.

Jensen, Bonnie L., 1992 'Process in Education for Mission,' *IRM* 81/321:91–96.

Jensen, Evelyn, 1993 'Women's Issues in Context,' in Van Engen and Gilliland and Pierson:213–18.

Jochums, Heinrich, 1966 *Gemeinde Jesu – Allianz – Oekumene*. Wuppertal-Elberfeld: Verlag und Schriftenmission der Evangelischen Gesellschaft für Deutschland.

— 1973 *Das Ende des Protestantismus*. Wuppertal-Elberfeld: Verlag und Schriftenmission der Evangelischen Gesellschaft für Deutschland.

Johns, Cherly Bridges, 1994 'Pentecostals and the Praxis of Liberation: A Proposal for Subversive Theological Education,' *Transformation* 11/1:11–15.

Johnston, Arthur, 1984 *Umkämpfte Weltmission*. Neuhausen-Stuttgart: Hänssler.

Jongeneel, Jan A. B., 1995 *Philosophy, Science, and Theology of Mission in the 19th and 20th Centuries: A Missiological Encyclopedia (Part I): The Philosophy and Science of Mission*. Frankfurt: Peter Lang.

— 1997 *Philosophy, Science, and Theology of Mission in the 19th and 20th Centuries: A Missiological Encyclopedia (Part II): Missionary Theology*. Frankfurt: Peter Lang.

— 1998 'Is Missiology an Academic Discipline?' in *Transformation* 15/3:27–32.

Jongeneel, Jan A. B., ed., 1992 *Pentecost, Mission and Ecumenism: Essays on Intercultural Theology (Festschrift Walter J. Hollenweger)*. Frankfurt: Peter Lang.

Jung, Friedhelm, 1992 *Die deutsche evangelikale Bewegung – Grundlinien ihrer Geschichte und Theologie*. Frankfurt: Peter Lang.

Kamlah, Andreas, 1980 'Wie arbeitet die analytische Wissenschaftstheorie,' *ZaWT* 21/1:23–44.

Kane, J. Herbert, 1978 *A Concise History of the Christian World Mission*. Grand Rapids: Baker.

Kane, J. Herbert, 1990 *Weltenbürger in Christus. Lokal oder Global*. Marburg: Francke.

Kasdorf, Hans, 1976 *Gemeindewachstum als missionarisches Ziel*. Bad Liebenzell: VLM.

— 1988 'Missiology as a discipline in historical perspective,' in Kasdorf and Müller:219–38.

— 1990 *Gustav Warnecks missiologisches Erbe*. Giessen/Basel: Brunnen.

— 1992 'David Jacobus Bosch: In Memoriam,' *em* 3:49–53.

— 1994 'Der gegenwärtige Stand der Missiologie: Gedanken zu den letzten 25 Jahren (1968–1993),' *em* 4:99–111.

— 1995 *Missiologie und Theologische Ausbildung*. Giessen: FTA.

— 1996 'Gedanken zum Verständnis der Weltmission,' in Kasdorf and Walldorf:15–32.

Kasdorf, Hans and Klaus W. Müller, eds., 1988 *Bilanz und Plan: Mission an der Schwelle zum Dritten Jahrtausend (Festschrift George W. Peters)*. Bad Liebenzell: VLM.

Kasdorf, Hans and Friedemann Walldorf, eds., 1996 *Werdet meine Zeugen. Weltmission im Horizont von Theologie und Geschichte*. Neuhausen-Stuttgart: Hänssler.

Keller, Albert, 1982 *Allgemeine Erkenntnistheorie*. Stuttgart: Kohlhammer.

Kemp, Roger, 1995 'A Brief Introduction to ICAA,' *ERTh* 19/3:314–15.

Kemp, Roger, ed., 1994 *Text and Kontext in Theological Education*. Springwood: ICAA.

Kemper, John C., 1996 'The Educational Community as a Paradigm for Field Education.' *MForm* 73:24–27.

Keyes, Larry E. and Larry D Pate, 1993 'Two Thirds World Missions: The Next 100 Years,' *Miss* 21/2:187–206.

Kinnamon, Michael and Cope, Brian E., eds., 1997 *The Ecumenical Movement: An Anthology of Key Texts and Voices*. Grand Rapids: Eerdmans.

Kindi, Vasso P., 1995 'Kuhn's *The Structure of Scientific Revolutions* Revisited,' *ZaWT* 26/1:75–92.

Kinsler, F. Ross, 1979 'New Approaches to Leadership Development in North America,' *MForm* 6, 16–20.

— 1981 *The Extension Movement in Theological Education*. Pasadena: William Carey Library.

— 1982 'Equipping God's People for Mission,' *IRM* 71/282:133–44 [= 'Theological Education by Extension: Equipping God's People for Mission,' in Kinsler 1983:1–29].

— 1983 'Ökumenische Perspektiven und theologische Aus- und Fortbildung für kirchliche Mitarbeiter,' EMW-Informationen 45:5–17.

— 1987 'Popular Theological Education – An Historical Perspective,' *MForm* 37:31–35.

— 1995 'Incarnation and Viability: The Evolution of a Model,' *MForm* 68:36–37.

Kinsler, F. Ross, ed., 1983 *Ministry by the People: Theological Education by Extension*. Geneva: WCC/Maryknoll: Orbis.

Kirk, J. Andrew, 1983 *Theology and the Third World Church*. Downers Grove: InterVarsity and Exeter: Paternoster.

— 1992 *Loosing the Chains: Religion as Opium and Liberation*. Sevenoaks: Hodder & Stoughton

— 1997 *The Mission of Theology and Theology of Mission*. Valley Forge: Trinity Press International.

Kniffka, Jörg, ed., 1989 *Martyria (Festschrift Peter Beyerhaus)*. Wuppertal: Brockhaus.

Knitter, Paul F., 1985 *No Other Name. A Critical Survey of Christian Attitudes Toward the World Religions*. London: SCM Press

Knowles, M. S., 1975 *Self-Directed Learning: A Guide for Learners and Teachers*. Chicago: Follett Publishing Company.

— 1980 *The Modern Practice of Adult Education: From Pedagogy to Andragogy*. Chicago: Follett Publishing Company (Revised and updated edition).

Kornfield, David, 1984 'Seminary Education: Toward Adult Education Alternatives,' in Conn and Rowen.

Kraemer, Hendrik, 1940 *Die christliche Botschaft in einer nichtchristlichen Welt*. Zollikon-Zürich: Evangelischer Verlag.

Krajnc, A., 1989 'Andragogy,' in Titmus:19–22.

Kramm, Thomas, 1979 *Analyse und Bewährung theologischer Modelle zur Begründung der Mission*. Aachen: Missio Aktuell.

Kraus, C. Norman, 1979 *The Authentic Witness*. Grand Rapids: Eerdmans

Kraus, C. Norman, ed., 1979 *Evangelicalism and Anabaptism*. Scottdale: Herald.

— 1980 *Missions, Evangelism, and Church Growth*. Scottdale: Herald.

Kritzinger, J.N.J. and W.A. Saayman, eds., 1990 *Mission in Creative Tension. A Dialogue with David Bosch*. Pretoria: SAMS [=*Missionalia* 18/1 1990].

Krüger, E., 1960 *Wesen und Aufgabe der Missionstheologie*. Wuppertal: Rheinische Missionsgesellschaft.

Krüger, Hanfried, 1975 *Ergebnisse aus Nairobi 75*. Frankfurt: Lembeck.

Kuen, Alfred, 1968 *Auf dass sie alle eins seien: Eine biblische Studie über die Einheit der Kirche Jesu*. Giessen: Brunnen.

Küenzler, Gottfried, 1994 'Kirche und die geistigen Strömungen der Zeit: Grundaufgaben heutiger Apologetik,' in Hummel and Küenzlen and Hemminger:14–23.

Kuhn, Thomas S., 1970 *The Structure of Scientific Revolution*. Chicago: The University of Chicago Press (2nd enl. ed.).

— 1979 *Die Struktur wissenschaftlicher Revolutionen*. Frankfurt/M: (2nd ed.).

Külling, Samuel, 1966 'Das Übel an der Wurzel erfassen,' *B&G* 4:258–74.

Kulosa, Christfried, 1993 *Die Funtamentalismus-Debatte und die Evangelikalen*. Idea-Dokumentation 25/93. Luzern: Idea-Schweiz.

Küng, Hans, 1989a 'Paradigm Change in Theology: A Proposal for Discussion,' in Küng and Tracy 1989:3–33.

— 1989b 'What Does a Change of Paradigm Mean,' in Küng and Tracy 1989:212–19.

— 1989c 'A New Basic Model for Theology: Divergencies and Convergencies,' in Küng and Tracy 1989:439–52.

Küng, Hans and David Tracy, eds., 1984 *Theologie – wohin?* Zurich: Benziger and Gütersloh: Gerd Mohn.

Küng, Hans and David Tracy, eds., 1989 *Paradigm Change in Theology*. Edinburgh: T. & T. Clark.

Künneth, Walter and Peter Beyerhaus, eds., 1975 *Reich Gottes oder Weltgemeinschaft: Die Berliner Ökumene-Erklärung zur utopischen Vision des Weltkienrates*. Bad Liebenzell: VLM.

Lagerwerf, L., 1985 'Rethinking Theological Education (1978–1985): A Bibliography,' in *Exchange* 40:69–74.

Lang, August, 1972 *Puritanismus und Pietismus: Studien zu ihrer Entwicklung von M. Butzer bis zum Methodismus*. Darmstadt: Wissenschaftliche Buchgesellschaft (reprint of the 1st ed. of 1941).

Lange, Dieter, 1990 *Eine Bewegung bricht sich Bahn: Die deutschen Gemeinschaften im ausgehenden 19. und beginnenden 20. Jahrhundert und ihre Stellung zu Kirche, Theologie und Pfingsbewegung*. Giessen/Basel: Brunnen (3rd ed.).

Lange, Markus and Karin Schmid, 1997 'The Council of Students of Protestant Theology (SETh) on Theological Education in Germany,' in *MForm* 76:36–40.

Latourette, Kenneth Scott, 1956 *Geschichte der Ausbreitung des Christentums*. Göttingen: Vandenhoeck & Rupprecht.

Laubach, Fritz, 1972 *Aufbruch der Evangelikalen*. Wuppertal: Brockhaus.

Laubach, Fritz and Helge Stadelmann, eds., 1989 *Was Evangelikale glauben: Die Glaubensbasis der Evangelischen Allianz erklärt*. Wuppertal: Brockhaus.

Lausanne Committee for World Evangelization, 1987 *The Lausanne Story*. n. p: LCWM

Lengrand, P., 1989 'Lifelong Education: Growth of the Concept,' in Titmus:6–9.

Lewy, Arieh, ed., 1991 *The International Encyclopedia of Curriculum*. Oxford: Pergamon.

Liedholz, Martin, 1993 'Konferenz bibeltreuer Ausbildungsstätten,' in *ELThG*: 1145–46.

Lindt, A., 1969 'C.F. Spittler und W.M.K. de Wette. Zur Begegnung von Erweckungsfrömmigkeit und Universitätstheologie im Basel des 19. Jahrhunderts,' in Geiger:361–84.

Linn, Gerhard, 1992 *Ökumene: Hoffnung für eine gespaltene Menschheit?* Leipzig: Evangelische Verlagsanstalt.

Linz, Manfred, 1984 *Anwalt der Welt: Zur Theologie der Mission*. Stuttgart: Kreuz.

Little, Paul, 1973 *Weitersagen. Zeugnis geben – wie macht man das?* Wuppertal: Aussaat.

Livingston, Kevin, 1989 *A Missiology of the Road: The Theology of Mission and Evangelism in the Writings of David J. Bosch*. Aberdeen: University of Aberdeen (PhD thesis)

— 1990 'David Bosch: An Interpretation of Some Main Themes in His Missiological Thought,' *Missionalia* 18/1:3–19.

Loewen, Howard J., 1983 'The Mission of Theology.' Fresno: Mennonite Brethren Biblical Seminary (unpublished manuscript).

Löwen, Heinrich and Kasdorf, Hans (eds.), 1999 *Gemeinsam im Auftrag des Herrn (Festschrift John N. Klassen)*. Bornheim/Bonn: Puls Verlag.

Lyall, Leslie, 1973 *Die Welt gewinnen*. Giessen/Basel: Brunnen.

Lynn, Rober Wood, 1981 'Notes Toward a History: Theological Encyclopedia and the Evolution of Protestant Seminary Curriculum.' *TEd* 1:118–44.

MacIntyre, Alasdair, 1977 'Epistemological Crises, Dramatic Narrative and the Philosophy of Science,' *The Monist* 60:453–72.

— 1984 *After Virtue*. Notre Dame: University of Notre Dame.

— 1988 *Whose Justice? Which Rationality?* Notre Dame: University of Notre Dame.

Maggay, Melba, 1994 *Transforming Society*. Oxford: Regnum.

Maier, Gerhard, 1990 *Biblische Hermeneutik*. Wuppertal: Brockhaus.

Mann, Wilfried, 1992 'Arbeitsgemeinschaft evangelikaler Missionen (AEM),' in *ELThG*:113–14.

Margull, Hans Jochen, ed., 1968 *Mission als Strukturprinzip*. Genf: WCC.

— 1980 'Das Fach "Religionen, Mission, Ökumene" an der Universität Hamburg,' in Sundermeier ed: 312–21.

Marquardt, Manfred, 1984 'Strukturen evangelikal-fundamentalistischer und traditionalistischer Theorie und Frömmigkeit,' in Frieling:84–103.

Marsden, George M., 1994 *The Soul of the American University. From Protestant Establishment to Established Nonbelief*. New York/Oxford: Oxford University Press.

— 1997 *The Outrageous Idea of Christian Scholarship*. New York/Oxford: Oxford University Press.

Mauerhofer, Armin, 1987 *Eine Erweckungsbewegung im 19. Jahrhundert: Karl von Rodt und die Entstehung der Freien Evangelischen Gemeinden in der Schweiz*. Giessen/Basel: Brunnen.

Mayer, Peter, 1992a 'Bruno Herm zum Gedenken: Gedanken zum Thema Heilsgeschichte und Missiologie,' *em* 2:24–26.

— 1992b 'Ganzheitliche Mission: Eine Replik zu Martin Reppenhagens Stellungnahme in em 3/1992, 45–46,' *em* 4:85–86.

Mazibuko, Bongani, *Education in Mission – Mission in Education: A Critical Comparative Study of Selected Approaches*. Frankfurt: Lang.

Mennonite Brethren Biblical Seminary, 1980 'Call To Theological Education in Mission(s) Perspective.' Fresno: Mennonite Brethren Biblical Seminary (unpublished manuscript).

McGrath, Alister E., ed., 1993 *The Blackwell Encyclopedia of Modern Christian Thought*. Oxford: Blackwell.

Mester, Carlos, 1981 'The Use of the Bible in Christian Communities of the Common People,' in Torres and Eagleson:197–210.

Meyer, Heinrich, 1958 'Die Existenz junger Kirchen als kritische Frage an die abendländische Theologie,' in Heubach and Ulrich:218–24.

Mildenberger, Friedrich, 1972 *Theorie der Theologie: Enzyklopädie als Methodenlehre*. Stuttgart: Calwer.

Miller, Larry, 1993 'The Church as Messianic Society: Creation and Instrument of Transfigured Mission', in Shenk ed. 1993:106–29.

Mitchell, Sarah, 1996 'Ministerial Formation: A Model,' *MForm* 72:11–14.

Moderow, Hans-Martin and Matthias Sens, eds., 1987 *Orientierung Ökumene*. Berlin: Evangelische Verlagsanstalt (2nd rev. ed.).

Moltmann, Jürgen, 1975a *Gott kommt und der Mensch wird frei: Reden und Thesen*. Munich: Kaiser.

— 1975b *Kirche in der Kraft des Heiligen Geistes: Ein Beitrag zu einer messianischen Ekklesiologie*. Munich: Kaiser.

— 1983 *Following Jesus Christ in the World Today*. Elkhart: Institute of Mennonite Studies (Occasional Papers No. 4).

— 1984 *Politische Theologie-Politische Ethik*. Munich: Kaiser.

Montgomery, Jim, 1990 *Eine ganze Nation gewinnen. Die DAWN-Strategie: Entstehung-Praxis- Perspektiven*. Lörrach: Simson.

Mouat, Carol, 1996 'Theological Education by Extension: A Survey of TEE Philosophy,' *MForm* 73:28–34.

Mueller, Karl, 1987 *Mission Theology: An Introduction*. Nettetal: Steyler.

Mulholland, Kenneth B., 1984 'TEE Come of Age: A Candid Assessment after Two Decades,' in Youngblood:9–25.

Müller, Klaus W., 1994 'Vicedom, Georg Friederich (1903–1947),' in *ELMThG*: 2099.

— 1995 'Bilanz und Plan: Auftrag, Weg und Ziel des AfeM,' *em* 1&2:12–42.

Müller, Klaus W. and Schirrmacher, Thomas (eds.), 2000 *Ausbildung als missionarischer Auftrag*. Bonn: Verlag für Kultur und Wissenschaft.

Murphy, Nancey, 1990 *Theology in the Age of Scientific Reasoning*. New York: Cornell University.
Myers, Bryant L., 1992 'A Funny Thing Happened on the Way to Evangelical-Ecumenical Cooperation' *IRM* 81/323:397–407.
— 1993 'The Changing Shape of World Mission,' in Siewert and Kenyon:1–2.
Myklebust, Olav Guttorm, 1955/1957 *The Study of Missions in Theological Education*. Oslo: Egede Institute.
— 1961 'Integration or Independence? Some Reflections on the Status of the Study of Missions in the Theological Curriculum,' in Hermelink and Margull:330–40.
— 1989 'Mission in Contemporary Theological Education: A Factual Survey,' *MStud* 7/2:87–107.
Netland, Harold A., 1994 'Truth, Authority and Modernity: Shopping For Truth in a Supermarket of Worldviews,' in Sampson and Samuel and Sugden:89–115.
Neufeld, Alfred, 1994 'Wege und Irrwege in der Frage der Kontextualisation,' *Fundamentum* 3:44–56.
Newbigin, Lesslie, 1958 *One Body, One Gospel, One World*. London/New York: IMC.
— 1969 *The Finality of Christ*. London: SCM.
— 1978a *The Open Secret*. Grand Rapids: Eerdmans.
— 1978b 'Theological Education in World Perspective,' *MForm* 4:3–10.
— 1980 *Sign of the Kingdom*. Grand Rapids: Eerdmans.
— 1983 *The Other Side of 1984 – Questions for the Church*. Geneva: WCC.
— 1988 *Christliches Zeugnis in einer pluralistischen Gesellschaft*. Bern: Evangelische Arbeitsstelle Ökumene Schweiz.
— 1989 *The Gospel in a Pluralist Society*. London: SPCK.
— 1990 'Religion for the Marketplace,' in D'Costa, ed:135–48.
— 1995 'Das Evangelium und Wahrheit,' EMW-Informationen 107:55–60.
— 1997 'The Dialogue of Gospel and Culture: Reflections on the Conference on World Mission and Evangelization, Salvador, Bahia, Brazil,' *IBMR* 2:50–52.
Nicholls, Bruce, ed., 1985 *In Word and Deed: Evangelism and Social Responsibility*. Exeter: Paternoster.
Nicole, Jacques, 1994 'Brief History of the So-Called "Classical Model" for Theological Education,' *MForm* 67:33–34.
Niebuhr, Richard H., 1951 *Christ and Culture*. New York: Harper & Row.
Nipkow, Karl E., Friederich Schweitzer, and James W. Fowler, eds., 1988 *Glaubensentwicklung und Erziehung*. Gütersloh: Gerd Mohn.
Nouwen, Henri J. M., 1971 *Creative Ministry*. Garden City/New York: Doubleday.
OCMS, 1996 'Vision-Statement'. Oxford: OCMS (Unpublished handout).
Ohlemacher, Jörg, 1992 'Gemeinschaftsbewegung,' in *ELThG*:727–30.
Osthatios, Geevarghese Mar, 1987 'Divine Sharing: Shape of Mission for the Future,' *IRM* 76/1:16–20.
Ott, Bernhard, 1984 'Toward a Holistic Theological Education,' Fresno: Mennonite Brethren Biblical Seminary (unpublished paper).
— 1995 'MBM/S Germany-Austria Evaluation 1995,' Fresno: Mennonite Brethren Mission/Services (unpublished manuscript).
— 1996a *Schalom: Das Projekt Gottes*. Weisenheim: Agape.

— 1996b *Missionarische Gemeinde werden. Der Weg der Evangelischen Täufergemeinden*. Uster: Verlag ETG.
— 1998a 'Die *KBA*-Schulen im Lichte globaler Veränderungen in theologischer Ausbildung', in Faix and Faix and Müller and Schmidt: 38–76.
— 1998b 'Kreative Spannung jenseits der Polarisierung. Die Spannungen zwischen "Evangelikalen" und "Ökumenikern" als friedenskirchliche Herausforderung,' *Mennonitisches Jahrbuch 1998*:35–44.
— 1999 'Denken und handeln im Kontext einer nachchristlichen Gesellschaft: Eine Tagesordnung für Theologie und theologische Ausbildung in Westeuropa an der Schwelle zum 21. Jahrhundert,' in *Gemeinde mit Zukunft: Herausforderungen und Perspektiven an der Schwelle zum 21. Jahrhundert* (Bienenberg Studienheft 3). Liestal: Theologisches Seminar Bienenberg: 8–30.
— 2000 'Missionstheologie in evangelikaler theologischer Ausbildung,' in Löwen and Kasdorf:123–139.
Padilla, C. René, 1974 'Evangelisation und die Welt,' in Beyerhaus 1974 vol.1: 146–94)
— 1985 *Mission Between the Times: Essays on the Kingdom*. Grand Rapids: Eerdmans.
— 1986 *Anstiftung: Evangelium für die Armen Reichen*. Moers: Brendow.
— 1991 'Come, Holy Spirit–Renew the Whole Creation,' *Transformation* 4:1–6.
— 1993a 'Gestaltwandel der Mission' *OJC* 5:189–93.
— 1993b 'Come, Holy Spirit, Renew the Whole Creation,' in Rin Ro and Nicholls: 22–37.
— 1995, 'Glaubwürdiges Christsein in Europa – Anstösse von den wachsenden Kirchen in Lateinamerika.' Aarau: Theologisch-Diakonisches Seminar (unpublished lecture).
Padilla, C. René, ed., 1977 *Zukunftsperspektiven. Evangelikale nehmen Stellung*. Wuppertal: Brockhaus.
— 1988 *New Alternatives in Theological Education*. Oxford: Regnum.
Padilla, C. René and Chris Sugden, eds., 1985a *Texts on Evangelical Social Ethics 1974–1983*. Nottingham: Grove Books.
— 1985b *How Evangelicals Endorsed Social Responsibility*. Nottingham: Grove Books.
Parker, David, 1993 'Biblical Reflections on the Holy Spirit,' in Rin Ro and Nicholls:12–21.
Paulsen, Friedrich, 1919 *Geschichte des Gelehrten Unterrichts auf den deutschen Schulen und Universitäten vom Ausgang des Mittelalters bis zur Gegenwart Vol. 1*. Leipzig: Verlag von Veit & Comp (3rd, enl. ed.).
— 1921/1960 *Geschichte des Gelehrten Unterrichts auf den deutschen Schulen und Universitäten vom Ausgang des Mittelalters bis zur Gegenwart Vol. 2*. U Berlin/ Leipzig: de Gruyter (reprint of the 3rd, enl. ed.).
Pechmann, Ralph, 1998 'Zeugnis im Dialog: Zukunftsfähiges Christsein in der Jahrtausendwende', in *OJC* 3:113–27.
Peters, George W., 1972 *A Biblical Theology of Missions*. Chicago: Moody Press
— 1977a *Missionarisches Handeln und biblischer Auftrag*. Bad Liebenzell: VLM.
— 1977b *Evangelisation: total-durchdringend-umfassend*. Bad Liebenzell: VLM.
— 1982 *Gemeindewachstum. Ein theologischer Grundriss*. Bad Liebenzell: VLM.
— 1985 'Evangelische Missionswissenschaft,' *em* 1:3–8.
Plueddemann, James E., 1990 'The Future of Evangelical Theological Education,' *ERTh* 14/1:14–24.

Pfister, Rudolph, 1984 *Kirchengeschichte der Schweiz (Vol. 3)*. Zurich: Theologischer Verlag.

Phillips, James M. and Robert T. Coote, eds., 1993 *Toward the 21st Century in Christian Mission*. Grand Rapids: Eerdmans.

Piepel, Klaus, 1993 *Lerngemeinschaft Weltkirche: Lernprozesse in Partnerschaft zwischen Christen der Ersten und der Dritten Welt*. Aachen: Misereor-Dialog.

— 1995 'Lerngemeinschaft Weltkirche,' *ZMR* 79/1:3–26

Pierard, Richard V., 1990 ''Pax Americana' and the Evangelical Missionary Advance,' in Carpenter and Shenk:155–79.

Piper, Hans-Christoph, 1981 *Kommunizieren lernen in Seelsoerg und Predigt*. Göttingen: Vandenhoeck & Rupprecht.

Pobee, John, 1992 'Equipping People of God for God's Mission Today,' *IRM* 81/321:21–31.

Pobee, John, ed., 1997 *Towards Viable Theological Education: Ecumenical Imperative, Catalyst of Renewal*. Geneva: WCC.

Poerwowidagdo, Judo, 1995 'Remembering the Future: The Task of Ministerial Formation Today,' *MForm* 69:45–49.

Pöggeler, Franz, 1974 *Erwachsenenbildung: Einführung in die Andragogik* (Handbuch für Erwachsenenbildung Vol. 1). Stuttgart: Kohlhammer.

Pöggeler, Franz and Bernt Wolterhoff, eds., 1981 *Neue Theorien der Erwachsenenbildung*. (Handbuch der Erwachsenenbildung Vol. 8). Stuttgart: Kohlhammer.

Potter, Philip A., ed., 1973 *Das Heil der Welt heute: Ende oder Beginn der Weltmission (Dokumente der Weltmissionskonferenz Bangkok 1973)*. Stuttgart/Berlin: Kreuz Verlag.

Power, John, 1970 *Mission Theology Today*. Dublin: Gill & Macmillan.

Preiswerk, Matías, 1987 'Popular Education and Popular Theological Education: Towards a Definition of their Spheres,' *MForm* 37:5–23.

Prokop, Ernst and Karlheinz A. Geissler, 1974 *Erwachsenenbildung. Modelle und Methoden*. Munich/Basel: Reinhardt.

PTE (Program on Theological Education of WCC)

— 1980 'Theologische Ausbildung im europäischen Kontext. Schlussdokument der PTE-Tagung über "Theologische Ausbildung in Europa" in Herrnhut/DDR 1980,' in Engel and Werner:123–29.

— 1982 'Mandat der Unterabteilung "Theologische Ausbildung" des Ökumenischen Rates der Kirchen. Revidierte Fassung 1982,' in Engel and Werner:85–87.

— 1982 'Programm on Theological Education 1977–1982,' *MForm* 20:6–10.

— 1986 'Theologie von unten – Theologie durch das Volk: Impulse zu einer theologischen Praxis in der Gemeinschaft des Volkes Gottes. Auszug aus einer PTE-Studie von 1986,' in Engel and Werner:99–112.

— 1987a 'Pia desideria oecumenica: Ökumenische Perspektiven theologischer Ausbildung im westdeutschen Kontext. Stellungnahme für eine PTE-Tagung in Iserloh 1987,' in Engel and Werner:130–41.

— 1987b 'Die geistliche Dimension der theologischen Ausbildung. Studiendokument einer PTE-Tagung in Iona, Schottland, 1987,' in Engel and Werner:113–18.

— 1989 'Theologische Ausbildung für den missionarischen Dienst der Kirche heute. Bericht einer PTE-Konsultation in Limuru, 1989,' in Engel and Werner:119–22.

Raapke, Hans-Dietrich and Wolfgang Schulenberg, eds., 1985 *Didaktik der Erwachsenenbildung*. (Handbuch der Erwachsenenbildung Vol. 7). Stuttgart: Kohlhammer.

Rahner, Karl, 1969 *Zur Reform des Theologiestudiums*. Freiburg/Basel/Wien: Herder.

Raiser, Konrad, 1991 *Ecumenism in Transition: A Paradigm Shift in the Ecumenical Movement*. Geneva: WCC.

Ramachandra, Vinoth, 1996 *The Recovery of Mission*. Carlisle: Paternoster.

Ramm, Bernard, 1983 *After Fundamentalism: The Future of Evangelical Theology*. San Francisco: Harper & Row.

Ramser, Hansueli, 1982 'Die Evangelische Gesellschaft des Kantons Bern im Dienst der Ausbreitung des Reiches Gottes,' in Dellsperger and Nägeli and Ramser:15–151.

Ramseyer, Robert L., ed., 1979 *Mission and the Peace Witness: The Gospel and Christian Discipleship*. Scottdale: Herald.

Rathmair, Franz, 1987 'Die Mennonitische Brüdergemeinde in Österreich,' Fresno: Mennonite Brethren Biblical Seminary (unpublished research paper).

Rehse, Theophil, 1970 *Ökumene – auf dem Weg zur Weltkirche?* Wetzlar: Schulte.

Reifler, Hans Ulrich, 1997 *Missionarisches Handen am Ende des 20. Jahrhunderts*. Basel/Giessen: Brunnen.

Reimer, Ingrid, 1991 *Evangelistisch-missionarische Werke und Einrichtungen im deutschsprachugen Raum*. Stuttgart: Christliches Verlagshaus.

Rennstich, Karl, 1992 'Evangelisches Missionswerk (EMW),' in *ELThG*:577–78.

Reppenhagen, Martin, 1992 'Ganzheitliche Mission,' *em* 8/3:45–46.

Riecker, Otto, 1953 *Das Evangelisische Wort*. Neuhausen-Stuttgart: Hänssler (2nd ed.).

— 1968 'Intellektualität und geistliches Leben an Bibelschulen,' in *B&G* 2:152–59.

— 1972 *Herausforderungen an die Gemeinde*. Neuhausen-Stuttgart: Hänssler.

— 1973 *Mission oder Tod*. Wuppertal-Elberfeld: Verlag und Schriftenmission der Evangelischen Gesellschaft für Deutschland.

— 1974 *Bildung und Heiliger Geist*. Neuhausen-Stuttgart: Hänssler.

— 1984 *Universitäts-Theologie und Gemeinde-Frommigkeit*. Neuhausen-Stuttgart: Hänssler.

Riesman, David and Verne A. Stadtman, eds., 1973 *Academic Transformation: Seventeen Institutions under Pressure. A volume of essays sponsored by the Carnegie Commission on Higher Education*. New York: McGraw-Hill Book Company.

Rin Ro, Bong, 1993 'Die Verkündigung Jesu Christi im Kontext des asiatischen Synkretismus,' in Hille and Troeger:45–57.

Rin Ro, Bong and Bruce J. Nicholls, eds., 1993 *Beyond Canberra. Evangelical Responses to Contemporary Ecumenical Issues*. Oxford: Regnum.

Rivera, Juan Marcos, 1987 'The Future of Mission: Sowing the Seeds of Shalom,' *IRM* 76/1:98–104.

Ritschl, Dietrich, 1994 'Ökumenische Theologie', in Ritschl and Ustorf:7–97.

Ritschl, Dietrich and Werner Ustorf, eds., 1994 *Ökumenische Theologie/Missionswissenschaft*. Stuttgart/Berlin/Köln: Kohlhammer.

Robert, Dana L., 1990 ''The Crisis of Mission': Premillennial Mission Theory and the Origin of Independent Evangelical Missions,' in Carpenter and Shenk 1990:29–46.

Robson, Colin, 1993 *Real World Research: A Resource for Social Scientists and Practitioner- Researchers*. Oxford/Cambridge: Blackwell.

Rommen, Edward, 1985 *Namenchristentum: Theologisch-soziologische Erwägungen*. Bad Liebenzell: VLM.

— 1987 *Die Notwendigkeit der Umkehr: Missionsstrategie und Gemeindeaufbau in der Sicht evangelikaler Missionswissenschaftler Nordamerikas*. Giessen/Basel: Brunnen.

Rott, Ludwig, 1968 *Die Englischen Beziehungen der Erweckungsbewegung und die Anfänge des wesleyanischen Methodismus in Deutschland*. Frankfurt/M: Studiengemeinschaft für Geschichte des Methodismus.

Ruhbach, Gerhard, 1992a 'Erweckungsbewegung,' in *ELThG*:531–36.

— 1992b 'Pietismus,' in *ELThG*:1571–73.

Rupp, George Erik, 1981 'Theological Education as Historical-Critical Appropriation of Traditions,' *TEd* 1:145–51.

Russell, Bertrand, 1950 *Philosophie des Abendlandes*. Zürich: Europa Verlag.

Rüttgard, Jan O., 1992 'Francke, August Herrmann (1663–1727),' in *ELThG*:619–21.

Saayman, Willem, 1990 'Bridging The Gulf: David Bosch and the Ecumenical/Evangelical Polarisation,' *Missionalia* 1:99–108.

Saayman, Willem and Kritzinger, Klippies, eds., 1996 *Mission in Bold Humility: David Bosch's Work Considered*. Maryknoll: Orbis.

Sampson, Philip, Vinay Samuel, and Chris Sugden, eds., 1994 *Faith and Modernity*. Oxford: Regnum.

Sampson, Philip, 1994 'The Rise of Postmodernity,' in Sampson and Samuel and Sugden:29–57.

Samuel, Vinay, 1986 'Gottes Mission – Unsere Aufgabe: Ein evangelikaler Beitrag aus Indien.' *JM*:126–44.

— 1996a 'Models and Directions of Theological Education in the Two Thirds World.' Oxford: OCMS (unpublished manuscript).

— 1996b 'Mission in Context,' in Resources for Research Students at OCMS. Oxford: OCMS.

Samuel, Vinay and Albrecht Hauser, eds., 1989 *Proclaiming Christ in Christ's Way*. Oxford: Regnum.

Samuel, Vinay and Chris Sugden, 1983a 'God's Intention for the World: Tension between Eschatology and History,' in Sine:179–230.

— 1983b 'Gegenwärtige Entwicklung in der Theologie: Eine Dritte-Welt-Perspektive.' EMW-Informationen 32.

— 1983c 'An Indian Approach to Theological Education by Extension,' in Kinsler ed.

— 1985 'Evangelism and Social Responsibility: A Biblical Study on Priorities,' in Nicholls ed.

— 1987 'Dialog mit anderen Religionen – eine evangelikale Sicht,' in Samuel and Sugden 1987:134–60.

Samuel, Vinay and Chris Sugden, eds., 1982 *Evangelism and the Poor*. Oxford: Regnum.

— 1987a *Der ganze Christus für eine geteilte Welt: Evangelikale Christologie in der Zwei-Drittel-Welt*. Erlangen: Evangelisch-Lutherische Mission.

— 1991 *A.D. 2000 and Beyond. A Mission Agenda (Festschrift for John Stott)*. Oxford: Regnum.

Sanneh, Lamin, 1995 'Religion und Kultur: Eine schwierige Ehe? Theologische Überlegungen zur Frage von Mission und westlicher Kultur,' EMW-Informationen 107:8–18.

— 1996 'Partnership, Mission and Cross-Cultural Sensitivity.' Oxford: OCMS (unpublished manuscript of a lecture delivered on July 5 1996).

Saracco, J. Norberto, 1988 'Search for New Model of Theological Education,' in Padilla ed. 1988:25–35.

Sautter, Gerhard, 1985 *Heilsgeschichte und Mission*. Giessen/Basel: Brunnen.

Schäfer, Klaus, ed., 1995 *Das Evangelium in unserer pluralistischen Gesellschaft* (Dokumentation einer internationalen theologischen Konsultation in Bad Urach vom 4–8. Juli 1994). Hamburg: Evangelisches Missionswerk (EMW-Informationen 107).

Scheffbuch, Rolf, 1974 *FRAG-würdige Oekumene*. Neuhaussen-Stuttgart: Hänssler.

— 1975 'Die Abgrenzungen von Lausanne,' in Künnerth and Beyerhaus:314–20.

— 1987 'Die Evangelikalen und ihr Verhältnis zum Pietismus.' IDEA Dokumentation 28/1987.

Scherer, James A. and Stephen B. Bevans, eds., 1992 *New Directions in Mission and Evangelization 1: Basic Statements 1974–1991*. Maryknoll: Orbis.

— 1994 *New Directions in Mission and Evangelization 2: Theological Foundations*. Maryknoll: Orbis.

Scherer, James A., 1971 'Missions in Theological Education,' in Danker and Kang.

— 1987a 'Missiology as a Discipline and What It Includes,' *Miss* 15/4:507–22.

— 1987b 'On Learnings From the Past to be Open to God's Future,' *IRM* 76/1:86–89.

— 1993 'Mission Theology,' in Phillips and Coote 1993:193–202.

Schindler, Alfred, ed., 1994 *Kirche und Staat*. Zürich: TVZ.

Schipani, Daniel S., 1997 'The Church and its Theological Education: A Vision,' in Heisey and Schipany:5–35.

Schirrmacher, Thomas, 1994 'Biblische Grundlagen evangelikaler Missiologie: 30 Thesen,' *em* 10/4:112–20

Schlatter, Wilhelm, 1916 *Geschichte der Basel Mission (Vol. 1)*. Basel: Basler Missionsbuchhandlung.

Schleiermacher, Friedrich, 1987 [1831–32] *Theologische Enzyklopädie (1831/32)*. Nachschrift von David Friederich Strauss. Herausgegeben von Walter Sachs. Berlin/New York: de Gruyter.

Schmid, Edgar, 1978 'Ausbildung, theologische (Bibelschulen und Seminare),' in *EGL*:38–39.

Schmid, Edgar, ed., 1990 *Wenn Gottes Liebe Kreise zieht: 150 Jahre Pilgermission St. Chrischona 1840–1990*. Giessen/Basel: Brunnen.

Schmid, Johannes H., ed., 1984 *Unterwegs zu biblisch erneuerter Theologie*. Giessen/Basel: Brunnen.

Schmidt, Johann, 1973 'Die missionarische Dimension der Theologie,' in Balz and Schulz:193–201.

Schmidt, Norbert, 1991 *Von der Evangelisation zur Kirchengründung: Die Geschichte der Marburger Brasilienmission*. Marburg: Francke.

Schnabel, Eckhard J., 1993 *Das Reich Gottes als Wirklichkeit und Hoffnung*. Wuppertal/Zürich: Brockhaus.
— 1995 *Sind Evangelikale Fundamentalisten?* Wuppertal/Zurich: Brockhaus.
Schreiner, Lothar, 1990 'Beobachtungen an theologischer Ausbildung in Nordamerika,' in Engel and Werner:41–44.
Schröder, Hartwig, 1996 *Lernen und lehren im Unterricht*. Munich: Michael Arndt
Schröer, Henning, ed., 1982 *Einführung in das Studium der evangelischen Theologie*. Gütersloh: Gerd Mohn.
Schrupp, Ernst, 1977 'Wesen und Wollen der Evangelikalen und ihrer Allianz,' *ThBeitr* 8/6:275–79.
— 1978 'Ausbildung, theologische (Missionsausbildung),' in *EGL*:39–40.
— 1980 *Im Dienst von Gemeinde und Mission: 75 Jahre Bibelschule und Mission*. Wiedenest: Missionshaus Bibelschule Wiedenest.
— 1995 *Gott macht Geschichte: Die Bibelschule und das Missionshaus Wiedenest*. Wuppertal/Zurich: Brockhaus.
Schulz, Wolfgang, 1996 *Anstiftung zum didaktischen Denken*. Weinheim/Basel: Beltz
Schwöbel, Christoph, 1990 'Particularity, Universality, and the Religions,' in D'Costa, ed:30–46.
Scott, Waldron, 1980 *Bring Forth Justice*. London: Marshall, Morgan & Scott.
Shenk, Wilbert R., ed., 1980 *Mission Focus – Current Issues*. Scottdale: Herald.
— 1983 *Exploring Church Growth*. Grand Rapids: Eerdmans.
— 1984 *Anabaptism and Mission*. Scottdale: Herald.
— 1993 *The Transfiguration of Mission*. Scottdale: Herald.
Shenk, Wilbert R., 1980 'Which Paradigm of Mission?' in Shenk 1980.
— 1987 'The Future of Mission,' *IRM* 76/1:59–63.
— 1992 'Reflections on the Modern Missionary Movement 1792–1992,' *MStud* 9-1/17:62–78.
— 1993 'The Whole is Greater than the Sum of the Parts: Moving Beyond Word and Deed,' *Miss* 20/1:65–75.
— 1994 'The Role of Theory in Anglo-American Mission Thought,' *MStud* 11/2:155–72.
— 1995 'Eine Missionslehre für den Westen,' EMW-Informationen 107:76–85.
— 1996 'The Role of Theory in Mission Studies,' *Miss* 24/1:31–45.
Sider, Ronald J., ed., 1981 *Evangelicals and Development: Toward a Theology of Social Change*. Philadelphia: Westminster.
— 1982 *Lifestyle in the Eighties: An Evangelical Commitment to Simple Lifestyle*. Philadelphia: Westminster.
Sider, Ronald J., 1993 *One-Sided Christianity*. Grand Rapids/San Francisco: Harper and Row.
— 1994 *Bread of Life: Stories of Radical Mission*. London: SPCK.
Siewert, John A. and John A. Kenyon, eds., 1993 *Mission Handbook*. Monrovia: MARC.
Simson, Wolfgang, 1995 *Gottes Megatrends: Sechs Wege aus dem christichen Ghetto*. Emmelsbühl: C & P.
Sine, Tom, ed., 1983 *The Church in Response to Human Need*. Monrovia: MARC.
Smith, Oswald J, 1952 *Glühende Retterliebe*. Frankfurt: Jugend für Christus.
Snyder, Graydon F., 1981 'Theological Education from a Free Church Perspective,' *TEd* 1:175–81.

Spener, Philipp Jakob [Erich Beyreuther ed.], 1975 *Umkehr in die Zunkunft: Reformprogramm des Pietismus. Pia Desideria*. Giessen/Basel: Brunnen (2nd rev. ed.).

Spindler, M. R., 1991a 'A New Typology of Protestant Missions,' *Exchange* 20/1:56–68.

— 1991b 'Mission Reaffirmed: Recent Authoritative Statements of Churches Around the World (1982–1991),' *Exchange* 20/3:161–257.

Sprunger, W. Frederic, 1981 *TEE in Japan*. Pasadene: William Carey Library.

Stachowiak, Herbert, 1973 *Allgemeine Modelltheorie*. Wien/New York: Springer.

— 1980 'Der Modellbegriff in der Erkenntnistheorie,' *ZaET* 21/1:53–68.

Stackhouse, Max L., 1988 *Apologia: Contextualisation, Globalization and Mission in Theological Education*. Grand Rapids: Eerdmans.

Stadelmann, Helge, 1985 *Grundlinien eines bibeltreuen Schriftverständnisses*. Wuppertal: Brockhaus.

— 1996 'Die Freie Theologische Akademie in Giessen: Viele Gründe sprechen für ein alternatives Konzept,' in *Diakrisis* 17/1:29–35.

Stadelmann, Helge, ed., 1998 *Bausteine zur Erneuerung der Kirche: Gemeindeaufbau auf der Basis einer biblisch erneuerten Ekklesiologie*. Giessen/Basel: Brunnen.

Staub, Hans, ed., 1965 *Wir sind sein Werk: 125 Jahre Pilgermission St. Chrischona*. Giessen/Basel: Brunnen.

Steuernagel, Valdir R., 1988 *The Theology of Mission in its Relation to Social Responsibility within the Lausanne Movement*. Chicago (doctoral thesis).

— 1990 'Social Concern and Evangelization: Our Journey since Lausanne I', in *Transformation* 7/1:12–16.

Stevens, R. Paul and Brian Stelck, 1993 'Equipping Equippers Cross-Culturally: An Experiment in Appropriate Globalization of Theological Education,' *Miss* 11/1:31–40.

Stewart, Bruce C., 1990 'Tensions in North American Theological Education,' *ERTh* 14/1:42–49.

Stirnimann, H., ed., 1970 *Ökumenische Erneuerung der Mission*. Freiburg: Paulus Verlag (Ökumenische Beihefte zur Freiburger Zeitschrift für Philosophie und Theologie, 4).

Stockwell, Eugene L., 1987 'Editorial: 1912–1987,' *IRM* 76/301:1–7.

— 1991 'Tension or Irreconcilability?–A Response to "A Movement Divided" ', *Transformation* 8/4:14–15.

Stott, John R. W., 1975a *Christian Mission in the Modern World*. London: Falcon Books.

— 1975b *Einheit der Evangelikalen. Gegen die falsche Polarisierung*. Giessen/Basel: Brunnen.

— 1989a 'Christus und Mission – die Herausforderung der Gegenwart,' *JET* 3:19–28.

— 1989b 'A note about the Stuttgart Statement on Evangelism,' in Samuel and Hauser:208–11.

— 1993 'Die ganzheitliche Mission,' *OJC* 5:194–204

— 1995 'Twenty Years After Lausanne: Some Personal Reflection,' *IBMR* 19/2:50–55.

Stott, John R. W. and Robert Coote, 1980 *Down to Earth: Studies in Christianity and Culture*. Grand Rapids: Eerdmans.

Stuhlmacher, Peter, 1986 *Vom Verstehen des neuen Testaments: Eine Hermeneutik.* Göttingen: Vandenhoeck & Rupprecht (2nd rev. and enl. ed.).

Sugden, Christopher, 1996 'Placing Critical Issues in Relief: A Response to David Bosch,' in Saayman and Kritzinger:139–50.

— 1997 *Seeking the Asian Face of Jesus: The Practice and Theology of Christian Social Witness in Indonesia and India 1974–1996.* Oxford: Regnum.

Sundermeier, Theo (Ed. Volker Küster), 1995 *Konvivenz und Differenz. Studien zu einer verstehenden Missionswissenschaft.* Erlangen: Verlag der Ev.-Luth. Mission.

Sundermeier, Theo, ed., 1980 *Fides pro mundi vita: Missionstheologie heute (Festschrift H.W. Gensichen).* Gütersloh: Gerd Mohn.

Sundermeier, Theo and Werner Ustorf, eds., 1991 *Die Begegnung mit dem Anderen. Plädoyers für eine interkulturelle Hermeneutik.* Gütersloh: Gerd Mohn.

Sundermeier, Theo, 1990 'Missiology Yesterday and Tomorrow,' in Kritzinger and Saayman:259–69.

Taber, Charles R., 1981 'Some Evangelical Questions,' in *Miss* 1:87–91.

Taylor, Charles, 1995 *Philosophical Arguments.* Cambridge, Mass./London: Harvard University Press.

TEF (Theological Education Fund of WCC), 1972 'Kontextualisierung theologischer Ausbildung: Aus den Richtlinien der dritten Mandatsperiode des Theologischen Aufbildungsfonds (TEF) 1972,' in Engel and Werner: 88–91.

Thampu, Valson, 1995 *Rediscovering Mission: Toward A Non-Western Missiological Paradigm.* New Delhi: TRACI.

Thielicke, Helmut, 1983 *Auf dem Weg zur Kanzel.* Stuttgart: Quell.

Thomas, M. M., 1996 'The Future of Ecumenical Theology.' Oxford: OCMS (unpublished manuscript of a lecture delivered on 4 July 1996).

Thomas, Winburn T., 1959 'Notes on Mission in the Curriculum,' in Hermelink and Margull:326–29.

Tiénou, Tite, 1993 'Forming Indigenous Theologies,' in Phillips and Coote:245–52.

Titmus, Colin J., ed., 1989 *Lifelong Education for Adults: An International Handbook.* Oxford: Pergamon.

Tomlinson, Dave, 1995 *The Post-Evangelical.* London SPCK.

Torres, Sergio and John Eagleson, eds., 1981 *The Challenge of Basic Christian Communities.* Maryknoll: Orbis.

Tracy, David, 1981 'Theoria and Praxis: A Partial response,' *TEd* 1:167–74.

Troeger, Eberhard, 1987 'Theologie als missionarische Aufgabe,' in *em* 3/4:51–55.

— 1992 'Arbeitskreis für evangelikale Missiologie,' in *ELThG*:115–16.

Tucker, Ruth A., 1988 *Guardians of the Great Commission: The Story of Women in Modern Missions.* Grand Rapids.

— 1993 'Women in Mission,' in Phillips and Coote:284–94.

Uda, Susumu, 1974 'Biblische Autorität und Evangelisation,' in Beyerhaus 1974:85–98.

Ustorf, Werner, 1989 'Anti-Americanism in German Missiology,' in *MStud* 6/1:23–34.

— 1991a *Mission to Mission? – Rethinking the Agenda.* Birmingham: Selly Oak Colleges.

— 1991b 'Der Begriff der "missionarischen Kompetenz" im Rahmen der kulturellen Mehrsprachigkeit Europas,' in Sundermeier and Ustorf: 182–96

— 1994 'Missionswissenschaft,' in Ritschl and Ustorf:99–144.

Utuk, Efiong S., 1994 'From Wheaton to Lausanne,' in Scherer and Bevans 1994:99–112.

VanElderen, Marlin, 1991 *Zeugnis-Dienst-Einheit-Erneuerung: Der Ökumenische Rat der Kirchen stellt sich vor.* Frankfurt: Lembeck.

Van Engen, Charles, Dean S. Gilliland, and Paul Pierson, eds., 1993 *The Good News of the Kingdom: Mission Theology for the Third Millennium (Essays in Honour of Arthur F. Glasser).* Maryknoll: Orbis.

Vatter, Ernst, 1987 'Der umstrittene Auftrag – das Ringen um das biblische Ziel der Mission heute,' in *em* 3/1: 2–9.

Veiel-Rappard, Friederich, 1940 *Die Pilgermission von St. Chrischona 1840–1940.* Basel: Brunnen.

Verkuyl, J., 1978 *Contemporary Missiology: An Introduction.* Grand Rapids: Eerdmans.

Verstraelen, Frans J., 1987 'The Future of Mission: A Western Perspective,' *IRM* 76/1:42–47.

Verwer, George F., 1964 *Konfrontiere Menschen mit Jesus.* Zaventem: Operation Mobilisation.

Vicedom, Georg F., 1958 *Missio Dei.* Munich: Kaiser.

— 1967 *Die Mission am Scheideweg.* Berlin/Munich: Lutherisches Verlagshaus.

— 1975 *Actio Dei.* Munich: Kaiser.

1963 *Die missionarische Dimension der Gemeinde.* Berlin/Hamburg: Lutherisches Verlagshaus.

Volf, Miroslav, 1990 'On Loving With Hope: Eschatology and Social Responsibility,' in *Transformation* 7/3:28–31.

Vorländer, Wolfgang, 1989 'Zwei Lausanne-Bewegungen unter einem Dach?' in IDEA-Dokumentation 22:28–30.

Wagner, William L., 1993 *North American Protestant Missionaries in Western Europe: A Critical Appraisal.* Bonn: Culture and Science Publ.

— no date 'Structuring Higher Education for Church Growth.' (EEAA: unpublished manuscript).

Walker, Andrew, 1996 *Telling the Story: Gospel, Mission and Culture.* London: SPCK.

Wallmann, Johannes, 1970 *Philipp Jakob Spener und die Anfänge des Pietismus.* Tübingen: J.C.B. Mohr.

— 1990 *Der Pietismus.* Göttingen: Vandenhoeck & Rupprecht.

Walls, Andrew F., 1987 'The Old Age of the Missionary Movement,' *IRM* 76/1:26–33

— 1990 'The American Dimension in the History of the Missionary Movement,' in Carpenter and Shenk:1–25.

Ward, Pete, 1996 'The Tribes of Evangelicalism,' in Cray *et al*:19–34.

Warneck, Gustav, 1877 *Das Studium der Mission auf der Universität.* Gütersloh.

— 1913 *Abriss einer Geschichte der protestantischen Missionen von der Reformation bis auf die Gegenwart.* Berlin: Martin Warneck.

WCC, 1967 *Die Kirche für andere.* Geneva: WCC

— 1970 *Seeing Education Whole.* Geneva: WCC.

— 1978 *What in the World is the World Counsel of Churches*. Geneva: WCC.
— 1981 'Europäische Konsultation über theologische Ausbildung,' EMW-Informationen 20.
— 1982 'Program on Theological Education 1977–1982,' *MForm* 20:6–10.
Webber, Robert E., 1979 *The Secular Saint: The Role of the Christian in the Secular World*. Grand Rapids: Zondervan.
Welter, Rüdiger, 1979 'Bibliographie zur Selbstthematisierung der Wissenschaft,' Burrichter:213–66.
Werner, Dietrich, 1990 'Theologische Ausbildung für eine ökumenische Zukunft der Kirche,' in Engel and Werner:45–72.
— 1992 'Ecumenical Renewal of Congregations,' *IRM* 81/321:57–79.
— 1993 *Mission für das Leben – Mission im Kontext*. Rothenburg: Ernst Lange.
— 1995 'Theologie zum Leben bringen. Anforderungen an eine zukunftsorientierte Ausbildung,' EMW-Informationen 105.
Wietzke, Joachim, ed., 1993 *Mission erklärt: Ökumenische Dokumente von 1972–1992*. Leipzig: Evangelische Verlagsanstalt.
Williams, Stephen,, 1990 'The Partition of Love and Hope: Eschatology and Social Responsibility,' in *Transformation* 7/3:24–27.
Winter, Ralph D., 1982 'The Two Structures of God's Redemptive Mission,' in Winter and Hawthorn:178–90.
— 1992 'Responses to "A Movement Divided" by Samuel Escobar,' *Transformation* 1992/1:26–29.
Winter, Ralph D., ed., 1969 *Theological Education by Extension*. South Pasadena: William Carey Library.
— 1973 *The Evangelical Response to Bangkok*. Pasadena: William Carey Library.
Winter, Ralph D. and Steven C. Hawthorn, eds., 1982 *Perspectives on the World Christian Movement*. Pasadena: William Carey Library (2nd ed.).
Witmer, S.A., 1962 *The Bible College Story: Education with Dimension*. New York: Channel Press.
Wolke, Günter, 1982 'Die Ausbildung von Missionaren in Deutschland: Untersuchung der gegenwärtigen Situation und Vorschläge für ein neues Curriculum.' Deerfield: Trinity Evangelical Divinity School (unpublished MA Thesis).
Wood, W. Jay, 1998 *Epistemology: Becoming Intellectually Virtuous*. Leicester: Apollos.
Yates, Timothy, 1994 *Christian Mission in the Twentieth Century*. Cambridge: .
Yoder, John H.
— 1964 *The Christian Witness to the State*. Newton: Faith and Life Press.
— 1969 'A People in the World: Theological Interpretation,' in Garrett:250–83.
— 1971/77 *The Original Revolution. Essays on Christian Pacifism*. Scottdale: Herald Press.
— 1979 'The Contemporary Evangelical Revival and the Peace Churches,' in Ramseier:68–103.
— 1981 *The Politik Jesu – der Weg des Kreuzes*. Maxdorf: Agape Verlag
Youngblood, Robert L., ed., 1984 *Cyprus: TEE come of age*. Exeter: Paternoster.
Zehr, Paul M. and Jim Egli, 1992 *Alternative Models of Mennonite Pastoral Formation*. Elkhart: Institute of Mennonite Studies (Occasional Papers No. 15).
Zehr, Paul M. , 1992 'A Curriculum Guide for Mennonite Conference-Based Pastoral Education,' in Zehr and Egli:1–39.

Zimmerling, Peter, 1985 *Pioniere der Mission im älteren Pietismus*. Giessen/Basel: Brunnen.

Zimmermann, Jakob, 1965 'Das Werk und die Schulen der Pilgermission auf St. Chrischona,' in Staub:24–72.

Zorrilla, Hugo, 1980 'Crucial Issues in Theological Education in Latin America,' in Shenk 1980a:367–78.

Zumstein, Jean, 1994 'Theologische Fakultäten an staatlichen Hochschulen,' in Schindler:82–100.

Index